THE LABOR-MANAGED FIRM

In previous work, Gregory K. Dow created a broad and accessible overview of worker-controlled firms. In his new book, *The Labor-Managed Firm: Theoretical Foundations*, Dow provides the formal models that underpinned his earlier work, while developing promising new directions for economic research. Emphasizing that capital is alienable while labor is inalienable, Dow shows how this distinction, together with market imperfections, explains the rarity of labor managed firms. This book uses modern microeconomics, exploits up-to-date empirical research, and constructs a unified theory that accounts for many facts about the behavior, performance, and design of labor-managed firms. With a large number of entirely new chapters, comprehensive updating of earlier material, a critique of the literature, and policy recommendations, here Dow presents the capstone work of his career, encompassing more than three decades of theoretical research.

Gregory K. Dow has been Professor of Economics at Simon Fraser University since 1995 and chaired the economics department during 2001–2006. He has held previous academic positions at the University of Alberta and Yale University. His articles have appeared in the leading journals of the profession, including the *American Economic Review* and the *Journal of Political Economy*. His previous book *Governing the Firm: Workers' Control in Theory and Practice* was published by Cambridge University Press in 2003.

The Labor-Managed Firm

Theoretical Foundations

GREGORY K. DOW

Simon Fraser University, British Columbia

CAMBRIDGE
UNIVERSITY PRESS

CAMBRIDGE
UNIVERSITY PRESS

University Printing House, Cambridge CB2 8BS, United Kingdom

One Liberty Plaza, 20th Floor, New York, NY 10006, USA

477 Williamstown Road, Port Melbourne, VIC 3207, Australia

314–321, 3rd Floor, Plot 3, Splendor Forum, Jasola District Centre,
New Delhi – 110025, India

79 Anson Road, #06–04/06, Singapore 079906

Cambridge University Press is part of the University of Cambridge.

It furthers the University's mission by disseminating knowledge in the pursuit of
education, learning, and research at the highest international levels of excellence.

www.cambridge.org
Information on this title: www.cambridge.org/9781107132979
DOI: 10.1017/9781316459423

First published 2018

Printed in the United States of America by Sheridan Books, Inc.

A catalogue record for this publication is available from the British Library.

Library of Congress Cataloging-in-Publication Data
Names: Dow, Gregory K., 1954– author.
Title: The labor-managed firm : theoretical foundations / Gregory K. Dow, Department
of Economics, Simon Fraser University, Burnaby, British Columbia.
Description: Cambridge ; New York : Cambridge University Press, [2017] | Includes
bibliographical references and index.
Identifiers: LCCN 2017009674 | ISBN 9781107132979 (alk. paper)
Subjects: LCSH: Industrial management – Employee participation. | Industrial
organization (Economic theory)
Classification: LCC HD5650 .D643 2017 | DDC 338.6/9–dc23
LC record available at https://lccn.loc.gov/2017009674

ISBN 978-1-107-13297-9 Hardback

For Margaret

"*This model will be a simplification and an idealization, and consequently a falsification. It is to be hoped that the features retained for discussion are those of greatest importance in the present state of knowledge.*"

– *Alan Turing, 1952 (quoted in Andrew Hodges,* Alan Turing: The Enigma, *Vintage, 2014, p. 546)*

Contents

Figures

Preface

In every generation, social critics raise questions about the prevailing economic order. One recurring set of questions involves the organization of production. Why are there bosses? Why are the rewards from firms distributed so unequally? Can work be made more humane? If democracy is good for political systems, why is it not good for economic systems? Why are corporations designed to encourage the pursuit of profit, when this often conflicts with the interests of workers, consumers, and communities?

Why are firms usually controlled by capital suppliers rather than labor suppliers? I have been intrigued by this question for more than forty years. It is an easy question to ask but a hard one to answer. I will sketch my answer in Chapter 1 and elaborate on it throughout the book. Here I want to say how this book arose and thank some of the people who made it possible.

Over the past several decades I have published numerous journal articles and book chapters on labor-managed firms (LMFs). Some of these writings appeared in high-profile venues, while others did not. A reader would have trouble tracking them all down and piecing together the connections among them. My publication trail also left some major theoretical gaps that needed to be filled.

My 2003 book *Governing the Firm* (GTF) surveyed some of this territory. GTF started out as a long introduction to a planned book that was intended to focus mainly on formal models. The introduction gradually evolved into a 300-page manuscript and had to stand on its own. At the time, some friends said things like "Nice book, but where's the math?" Eventually I decided to write a book containing the kind of formal theory a professional economist would want to see. The present book is organized around the economic logic of the subject as I understand it. This has allowed me to build from the ground up while exploiting earlier publications when they became relevant to the story. Those who read GTF either before or after reading this book will benefit from seeing both, but they are two different animals, and the present volume is self-contained.

A few remarks on math and economic theory may be useful for potential readers. I have not made any compromises with regard to theoretical content—nothing has been watered down. But any professional economist comfortable with applied microeconomic theory will be able to follow the reasoning, as will graduate students who have taken the usual required courses in micro theory, game theory, and the economics of information. Advanced undergraduates should understand much of what is going on. Several chapters have no math at all, and the introductory and concluding sections of the technical chapters explain the economic arguments in words. Readers who prefer to skim through the math should be able to grasp the overall logic of the book by focusing on these verbal sections.

In a narrow sense, this book took eighteen months to write. In a broader sense, it took about fifteen years, the period since the completion of *Governing the Firm*. But in the largest sense, it took about thirty-five years, the length of my career as an economist. Over such periods one accumulates countless intellectual debts, and I cannot possibly thank everyone who has influenced this book. The people mentioned here are not responsible for the uses I have made of their ideas, which may differ considerably from what they had in mind. These acknowledgments are roughly in chronological order, although some important early individuals will not be thanked until near the end.

Murat Sertel shaped my thinking about membership markets for labor-managed firms in the 1980s and early 1990s. Sadly, we never met, so Sertel's influence occurred through his books and journal articles. I often felt that we were brothers in arms, battling an array of misguided theoretical notions about LMFs. Sertel's ideas feature prominently in Chapters 3–5.

Louis Putterman and I met in the early 1980s when I was at Yale and Louis was at Brown University, where he remains today. We shared interests in labor-managed firms and the theory of the firm more generally. In the 1990s we coauthored several working papers, journal articles, and book chapters surveying explanations for the rarity of LMFs. Echoes of this joint work can be heard in Chapter 8 of the present volume.

Gil Skillman and I received PhDs in economics from the University of Michigan a few years apart, but we did not meet until the mid-1980s when Gil was at Brown and I was at Yale. We found that we shared a critical view of the capitalist firm, among other things. We began to work together on the theory of the labor-managed firm in 1992, and this collaboration eventually led to the material presented in Chapter 12.

Oliver Williamson's work on transaction cost economics also shaped my thinking. Ollie might be surprised that I would say this, because we had pointed debates in print in the 1980s and 1990s. However, although I was unable to accept Ollie's overall intellectual program, I plundered his trove of economic concepts (incomplete contracts, opportunism, asset specificity, and so on). The results can be found in Chapters 14 and 15.

My first encounter with an economist who cared about the lack of democracy in capitalist firms occurred in my undergraduate years, at a public lecture given by Samuel Bowles in the early 1970s. I came to know Sam and his coauthor Herb Gintis in the late 1980s and early 1990s. Their joint research on contested exchange helped stimulate my interest in how firms could function without legally binding contracts. This notion plays a large role in Chapters 16–18. I also found their arguments about the financial problems facing labor-managed firms important and enlightening.

A less obvious influence came from Uskali Mäki, a philosopher of science I met in the early 1990s. Uskali was well read on the subject of transaction cost economics and had taken an interest in my debates with Williamson. His work, and in particular his whole-hearted commitment to philosophical realism, was a breath of fresh air in a period when realism was under heavy fire. This perspective colors my methodological approach throughout the book.

I supervised Xiao-yuan Dong's PhD work at the University of Alberta in the early 1990s. We coauthored two journal articles at that time; one appeared in the *Journal of Political Economy* and the other in the *Journal of Comparative Economics*. Both were on Chinese collective farming, and the key ideas for both papers came from Xiao-yuan. These projects helped me think about mutual monitoring among workers and the role of repeated games in firm organization.

Another friend who guided me along the path to this book was Bo Gustafsson. With Sam Bowles and Herb Gintis, Bo put together a conference on firm organization at the Swedish Collegium for Advanced Study in the Social Sciences (SCASSS) in June 1991. This led to an invitation for Gil Skillman and me to visit SCASSS in the fall of 1992. During that visit, Bo asked me to give a talk on labor-managed firms. I decided to discuss economic explanations for the rarity of LMFs. This led directly to my work with Louis Putterman in the late 1990s, my explanatory efforts in *Governing the Firm* in 2003, and eventually to the present book.

I have benefitted considerably from the work of a number of other authors. Avner Ben-Ner stands out for his empirical research, along with his theoretical insights into the dilemmas facing labor-managed firms. Bentley MacLeod influenced my thinking about LMFs and the application of game theory to labor markets. John Bonin provided advice on several of my papers, and I have learned a great deal from his writing. Other people who have influenced my views on labor-managed firms include Saul Estrin, Derek Jones, John Pencavel, Virginie Pérotin, Stephen Smith, and Jan Svejnar. I also want to mention the work of several people on "shared capitalism" and other hybrid forms of organization; these include Margaret Blair, Doug Kruse, Joseph Blasi, and Richard Freeman.

Over the past fifteen years, I have often taught a seminar course on labor-managed firms for fourth-year economics majors at Simon Fraser University. I am grateful to all of the students who took this course for their participation in the class discussions, which sharpened my thinking on many of the issues addressed in the book.

In my own student days I was fortunate to have some exceptional teachers, and I want to thank two of them. As an undergraduate, my exposure to economics was limited to a principles course and a few courses in economic history and the history of thought. These were interesting, but I did not see them as having special relevance for my career path. My initial contact with intermediate microeconomic theory came during my first semester in the Master of Public Policy program at the University of Michigan in 1975.

The instructor for this course was William J. (Jim) Adams. Through Jim's course I saw that economics provided a theoretically coherent way of thinking about interesting questions. Jim's teaching style was friendly, enthusiastic, and inspiring (this is not hype—he has university-wide teaching awards to prove it). A year later, I took Jim's course in industrial organization, which featured a long reading list of journal articles and showed me how economists think, write, and argue. More than any other person, Jim led me to pursue a PhD in economics. Thanks, Jim.

The person who bears the greatest responsibility for turning me into an economic theorist is Ted Bergstrom. I first met Ted in a graduate course that was nominally about government expenditure but really was a course on microeconomic theory where public goods and free rider problems were sometimes mentioned. My second course from Ted was called something like "Advanced Micro Theory II." Here I heard about game theory and learned that equilibria are not always Pareto efficient. Through Ted's courses, I also found that I enjoyed playing with formal models. Thanks, Ted.

My years as a graduate student in Ann Arbor were literally life changing, and not just because I discovered my career path and occasionally thought about labor-managed firms. In the fall of 1977, I met Margaret Duncan. Since then, we have shared life, the universe, and everything. Margaret strongly encouraged me to write this book. Thanks to Margaret for that, and for all the love along the way.

No author produces a book alone. I am grateful to Karen Maloney of Cambridge University Press for supporting this project at an early stage when its goals were modest and its structure was murky. I also want to extend thanks to Stephen Acerra, Kris Deusch, Sathish Rajendran, Lois Tardío, and Kaye Tengco for their assistance during the production process. Haiyun Kevin Chen, a PhD student in economics at Simon Fraser University, created the graphs.

Several people provided feedback on one or more chapters, including Ran Abramitzky, Gabriel Burdín, John Pencavel, Virginie Pérotin, Louis Putterman, Clyde Reed, and Gil Skillman. The prize goes to Gil, who read every chapter in draft and commented extensively. I deeply appreciate Gil's heroic efforts to improve my logic and exposition. I tried to respond conscientiously to the comments I received, although the limits of time and space made it impossible to do this in every case. Needless to say, I bear sole responsibility for all errors, omissions, and opinions.

At an institutional level, I want to thank the Department of Economics at Simon Fraser University, which has been my academic home since 1995, and the chairs, deans, and other administrators who provided study leaves that enabled me to think and write. The Social Sciences and Humanities Research Council of Canada has supported my research for many years. Other funders will be acknowledged in the relevant chapters.

Although much of the material in this book is published here for the first time, I am grateful for permission to use previous journal articles and book chapters. Elsevier gave permission to use "Control Rights, Competitive Markets, and the Labor Management Debate," *Journal of Comparative Economics* 10(1), March 1986, 48–61; "The Function of Authority in Transaction Cost Economics," *Journal of Economic Behavior and Organization* 8(1), March 1987, 13–38; and "On the Neutrality of Asset Ownership for Work Incentives," *Journal of Comparative Economics* 28(3), September 2000, 581–605. The American Economic Review gave permission to use "Why Capital Hires Labor: A Bargaining Perspective," *American Economic Review* 83(1), March 1993, 118–134. Springer gave permission to use "Replicating Walrasian Equilibria Using Markets for Membership in Labor-Managed Firms," *Economic Design* 2(2), November 1996, 147–162; and "Partnership Markets with Adverse Selection," *Review of Economic Design* 18(2), June 2014, 105–126. John Wiley and Sons gave permission to use "Collective Choice and Control Rights in Firms" (coauthored with Gilbert L. Skillman), *Journal of Public Economic Theory* 9(1), February 2007, 107–125. The University of Toronto Press gave permission to use "Worker Participation and Adverse Selection," chapter 10 in Gregory K. Dow, Andrew Eckert, and Douglas West, eds., *Industrial Organization, Trade, and Social Interaction: Essays in Honour of B. Curtis Eaton*, University of Toronto Press, Toronto, 2010, 203–222.

No author would accomplish much without readers, so my final thanks go out to all those who take the time to read this book. I hope you will find something of value here.

PART I

SETTING THE STAGE

1

The Puzzling Asymmetry

1.1 Introduction

A firm can be defined as an organized set of individual agents who participate in a common production process and sell the resulting output on a market. These agents may supply labor, capital, or other inputs. Because the contracts among the agents are usually incomplete, production activities require coordination. For firms of significant size, this involves a hierarchical authority structure in which managers decide what goods will be produced and how.

A fundamental question is who chooses the top management of the firm. In most large firms, capital suppliers (or a subset of them) have the power to hire and fire top managers, and thus have ultimate control over the firm. Indeed, capitalism can be defined as an economic system in which most firms are ultimately controlled by capital suppliers. Such a system is not written in the stars. One could instead imagine systems in which firms are controlled by labor suppliers, raw material suppliers, or consumers.

Of course, one can define capitalism in other ways. In casual conversation, the term "capitalism" is often used as a blanket label for any system in which resources are allocated through markets. This is much too broad, because firms controlled by workers or consumers can also allocate resources through markets. According to another popular definition, capitalism is a system in which productive assets are privately owned. Again, this is too broad, because groups of workers could manage the firms in which they work while privately owning any required machinery, buildings, and so on. Groups of workers could also manage firms while leasing assets from private nonworker owners.

In this book, I take for granted the existence of markets and the private ownership of productive assets. I largely ignore control over firms by consumers or suppliers of raw materials. Instead, I assume that capital and labor suppliers are the main candidates for the possession of control rights within firms.

I define a capital-managed firm (KMF) to be a firm where ultimate control is held by capital suppliers and a labor-managed firm (LMF) to be a firm where ultimate control is held by labor suppliers. The use of the letter K stems from the usual algebraic notation for "capital." At an abstract level, "control" refers to whatever collective choice procedure is used to make decisions when legally enforceable contracts are silent about what needs to be done. In practice, this generally involves voting or bargaining among the individual members of the ultimate control group, where in the KMF votes or bargaining power are proportional to the capital supplied by individuals, and in the LMF votes or bargaining power are proportional to the labor supplied by individuals. The qualifier "ultimate" is meant to emphasize that we are not primarily concerned with the behavior of managers hired by the controllers. When such managers exist, the ultimate control group is the set of individual agents who can collectively hire and fire top managers, should they choose to do so (see Dow, 2002, for a formalization of this idea).

I focus on firms with enough formal structure that it is reasonably clear whether ultimate control rests with capital or labor. Small firms are often managed by individual entrepreneurs who contribute both inputs. Attempts to classify such firms as KMFs or LMFs are unlikely to be useful. However, in larger firms this classification system is generally easy to apply. Another complication arises from the fact that control rights may be held by a subset of capital suppliers (e.g., those who supply equity rather than debt) or a subset of labor suppliers (e.g., senior but not junior personnel). I consider a firm to be a KMF when control rights are held by a subset of its capital suppliers, and similarly for LMFs.

Suppose that we accept the premise that capitalism is an economic system in which most large firms are KMFs. One strategy for explaining why KMFs dominate modern economies is to investigate the historical process through which such firms arose during the Industrial Revolution or earlier. This is an interesting agenda. However, in this book I take a different approach and ask why LMFs are rare in modern economies.

Those who are skeptical about the merits of LMFs have a ready answer. They usually argue that under conditions of market competition, only the efficient will survive. Because KMFs are common and LMFs are rare, one can infer that LMFs are inefficient. Now that the market has spoken, we can move on to more important matters.

However, the skeptics have some explaining to do. First, it would be interesting to know exactly how or why LMFs are inefficient relative to KMFs. What is it about the DNA of the labor-managed firm that makes it poorly adapted to a market environment? Even if one is convinced that a genetic defect of this kind must exist, one could harbor some curiosity about the nature of the defect.

Second, LMFs can be found in the real world. They are rare, but not in the sense that unicorns are rare. In some developed economies, LMFs number in the thousands. A skeptic therefore needs to explain how LMFs overcome their genetic defects at certain times and places, or in certain industries. The skeptic might try to argue that when LMFs do exist, it is only because they receive support from sympathetic governments that tilt the field of market competition in their favor. However, some LMFs thrive without any obvious governmental support, or at least no more support than their KMF rivals receive.

Finally, we will see later that in a world of complete and competitive markets, a properly designed LMF behaves in ways that make it indistinguishable from a KMF. This pushes the skeptic into a corner. In order to explain why LMFs are rare, the skeptic must grant that market imperfections exist. But if markets are imperfect, can we really be sure that market competition guarantees efficient organizational outcomes?

Those who support LMFs also have some explaining to do. It is easy to see why having workers manage their own firms might be appealing for reasons of democracy, equality, dignity, or community (Dow, 2003, ch. 2). But LMF advocates also frequently claim that such firms have efficiency or productivity advantages. At this point a skeptic usually asks, "If LMFs are so great, why are they so rare?" Assuming that the LMF advocate does not want to abandon economic arguments entirely, some answer is required.

As noted previously, it is necessary to depart from complete and competitive markets simply in order to explain why LMFs are rare in the first place. Perhaps the same market failures that account for the rarity of LMFs can be remedied through public policy. And perhaps sensible policies to promote the creation of LMFs will yield efficiency gains for the economy as a whole. If this is true, then there is no trade-off between democracy and efficiency—one can pursue both goals simultaneously.

In order to make this case, the LMF advocate must do quite a bit of work. First, it is necessary to explain how LMFs could have economic advantages. What can LMFs do that KMFs cannot do, and why? Second, it is necessary to identify market failures that keep LMFs from competing effectively with KMFs despite their efficiency advantages. Do LMFs face obstacles that KMFs do not? If so, what are they? Third, it is necessary to devise policy interventions that enable LMFs to compete more effectively against their KMF rivals, and do so without imposing economic costs that outweigh the benefits from having more LMFs. This is a tall order.

I will put my own cards on the table at the outset. I believe that LMFs are likely to have productivity advantages over similar KMFs in a range of industries; that there are obstacles to the creation and expansion of LMFs that similar KMFs do not confront; and that well-designed policies could help LMFs overcome these obstacles, while enhancing economic efficiency. However, I readily concede that such arguments require persuasive theory and strong evidence. In particular, we need a clear explanation of why LMFs are rare before we can make convincing arguments on their behalf.

1.2 Some Facts

The asymmetry between the abundance of capital-managed firms and the rarity of labor-managed firms poses a fundamental economic puzzle. Both for policy reasons and those of simple intellectual curiosity, we need to understand why LMFs are so rare. But this is not the only interesting fact about LMFs.

Empirical researchers have discovered many ways in which LMFs differ from KMFs. A good theory about the rarity of LMFs should account for some or all of these additional regularities. If a theory cannot do so, its credibility as an explanation for the rarity of LMFs is suspect. All other things being equal, a theory accounting for more facts is preferable to a theory accounting for fewer facts.

Several generalizations about LMFs are listed here. These are intended only as statistical assertions, not ironclad laws of nature. Chapters 6 and 7 discuss these claims in detail and provide references to the literature.

(a) LMFs have less-elastic quantity responses to price shocks than similar KMFs. Such shocks tend to be absorbed through fluctuations in the incomes of LMF members rather than fluctuations in inputs and outputs.

(b) LMFs have substantially more compressed wage distributions than similar KMFs.

(c) LMFs are less likely than KMFs to enter industries with high capital requirements and high levels of risk.

(d) In industries where both LMFs and KMFs exist, LMF productivity appears to be at least as high as KMF productivity, and sometimes higher.

(e) In industries where both LMFs and KMFs exist, LMF survival rates appear to be at least as high as KMF survival rates, and sometimes higher.

These generalizations are supported by careful econometric research. Some have been replicated using data from multiple countries, time periods, or industries. A number of additional patterns will be discussed in later chapters. The well-documented empirical asymmetries between KMFs and LMFs demand some theoretical explanation.

1.3 Some Principles

Throughout the book, I use the term "perfect markets" as shorthand for "complete and competitive markets." Chapters 3–5 will show that in a world of perfect markets, LMFs can be designed so that they behave identically to KMFs. Both types of firms maximize profit, and for the same reason: the members of the firm's control group are also consumers, and in this role they want their budget sets to be as large as possible.

One implication follows immediately:

The imperfection principle. Any theory claiming to explain the empirical asymmetries between KMFs and LMFs must specify one or more departures from the framework of complete and competitive markets.

Candidate types of market imperfections could include monopoly or monopsony power, informational asymmetries, or an inability to make binding commitments. A full theory must identify imperfections in both the capital and labor markets, because if either market is perfect, there is no reason why the corresponding input suppliers need control rights, any more than the suppliers of paper clips or office furniture need control rights.

Although they are necessary, market imperfections are not sufficient to explain patterns like those in Section 1.2, because such imperfections may have symmetric effects on KMFs and LMFs. One must therefore find some difference between capital and labor that, when combined with a source of market imperfection, can account for the empirical differences between KMFs and LMFs. I summarize this point as follows:

The asymmetry principle. Any theory claiming to explain the empirical asymmetries between KMFs and LMFs must identify a causally relevant asymmetry between capital and labor.

The asymmetry principle could be irrelevant if noneconomic factors dominate. For example, KMFs (or LMFs) could be favored by political movements that have the power to regulate and subsidize, local culture could be biased toward one governance structure at the expense of the other, historical events could have given KMFs a head start from which LMFs have been unable to recover, and so on. However, when one is doing economic theory, the asymmetry principle imposes useful intellectual discipline.

I believe that the most important asymmetry between capital and labor is the fact that capital is alienable whereas labor is not. Simply put, ownership of nonhuman productive assets can be transferred from one person or group to another, while this is not true for endowments of time, skill, and experience. This fundamental asymmetry has several implications that will be important in later chapters. I sketch four of them briefly here.

(a) *Control transactions:* In a KMF, there can be turnover in the membership of the firm's control group while the firm's physical inputs remain unchanged, because ownership of the firm's capital stock can be transferred from one person or group to another. In an LMF, turnover in the membership of the control group changes the firm's physical inputs by changing the identities of the firm's labor suppliers.

(b) *Composition of control groups:* Firms of significant size require a worker team of significant size, but a few investors may be able to finance the firm's capital stock. For this reason, LMF control groups are often larger than KMF control groups. I will also argue that the inalienability of labor tends to make LMF control groups more heterogeneous with respect to preferences over firm decisions.

(c) *Stocks and flows:* Capital can be owned by a firm as a stock, whereas labor is only available as a flow. When collective asset ownership by firms is important, LMFs must finance such assets. For workers with limited wealth, this implies a need for transactions with outside investors.

(d) *Role in the production process:* Workers participate directly in production, while investors do not. This can give workers valuable knowledge about technology, organization, market conditions, and the performance of coworkers. As a result, LMFs sometimes enjoy a productivity advantage over similar KMFs.

These four aspects of the alienability distinction will receive varying degrees of emphasis as the book proceeds. I will combine them to construct an overall causal framework for the LMF in Chapter 19.

A third principle is intended to avoid arbitrariness in how KMFs and LMFs are defined. It can be viewed as a corollary of the asymmetry principle and requires that asymmetries between KMFs and LMFs be essential rather than superficial.

The replication principle. No economic advantage should be regarded as intrinsic to the KMF if the factors responsible for it can be easily replicated by an LMF, and conversely.

The point of the replication principle is that KMFs and LMFs are defined by the identity of the input suppliers who have ultimate control over the firm, not other optional features. For example, supposing that KMFs are more productive than similar LMFs, it would not be satisfactory to explain this by asserting that KMFs have managerial hierarchies but LMFs do not. There is nothing about the principle of ultimate control by labor suppliers that rules out the use of a managerial hierarchy. To make the argument convincing, one would have to show that control by labor suppliers makes a managerial hierarchy more costly or less effective than it would be in an otherwise identical KMF.

Conversely, supposing that LMFs are more productive than similar KMFs, it would not be satisfactory to explain this by asserting that LMFs have worker committee meetings while KMFs do not. Again, there is nothing about ultimate control by capital suppliers that rules out employee meetings. For this argument to get off the ground, one would have to show that control by capital suppliers makes such meetings less productive than they would be in an otherwise identical LMF.

A broader methodological point is that no single formal model can capture every distinction between KMFs and LMFs. Alienability operates through too many different causal channels, and interacts with too many market imperfections, for this to be possible. The only feasible strategy is to create a family of related models stitched together through words. Fortunately, no rule of scientific method requires a theory to be described in one mathematical model, and no rule prohibits the use of words. I will use math where I can and rely on ordinary language elsewhere, but it is all one theory.

1.4 The Structure of the Book

A highly abbreviated summary of the theoretical argument in the book runs as follows. One can demonstrate that with complete and competitive markets, there is an isomorphism between KMFs and LMFs. In this environment, the two kinds of firms are behaviorally indistinguishable, and economies with each institutional arrangement can support identical resource allocations.

Nevertheless, in the real world there are systematic differences between KMFs and LMFs. To account for these differences, we need to consider market imperfections. However, this is only a necessary condition. We also need to identify some asymmetry between capital and labor. The main candidate for this role is the alienability of capital and inalienability of labor.

The combination of market imperfections with this difference in alienability has causal effects through four main channels. First, there are appropriation problems that arise when control rights in firms are treated as commodities that can be bought and sold on markets. For various reasons it is important to have markets of this kind. However, I argue that this is more readily accomplished for KMFs than for LMFs, because it is easy to transfer title to a firm's capital stock from one person to another, but it is impossible to transfer ownership of human capital from one person to another.

Second, there are public good problems that are associated with collective choice and free riding within firms. I argue that the alienability of capital tends to induce unanimity among investors with respect to the policies pursued by the firm. On the other hand, the inalienability of labor tends to yield heterogeneous preferences among workers. This difference typically makes KMFs more stable than LMFs. A related problem is that employees face free rider problems in deciding whether to buy out a KMF, but investors need not face parallel problems in deciding whether to buy out an LMF.

Third, there are problems of opportunism. Firms arise due to the incompleteness of contracts and give controllers authority over noncontrollers. However, authority can be abused in opportunistic ways. Furthermore, alienability of capital allows firms to acquire capital as a stock, but inalienability of labor means that they acquire labor as a flow. This difference in the intertemporal features of the two inputs can lead to situations where the temptation for opportunism by LMFs against capital suppliers exceeds the temptation for opportunism by KMFs against labor suppliers. If so, LMFs will have greater difficulty in attracting capital than KMFs have in attracting labor.

Fourth, there are managerial benefits from LMFs that arise because workers are directly involved in production while investors are not. As a result, workers can acquire knowledge that is valuable for decision-making. This can give LMFs advantages with respect to productivity and survival that are hard for KMFs to replicate.

Chapters 2–5 begin the analysis by considering a world of perfect competition. Chapter 2 develops basic ideas about Walrasian equilibrium, profit maximization, and control rights in firms. The next three chapters present isomorphism results. Chapter 3 addresses short run decisions about the use of variable inputs, Chapter 4 studies long run decisions about investment, and Chapter 5 presents a general equilibrium model.

Chapters 6 and 7 survey empirical asymmetries between KMFs and LMFs, along with other stylized facts about LMFs. I focus primarily on recent econometric research involving large representative samples. These chapters are meant to constrain the later theoretical analysis by developing a set of empirical regularities that a satisfactory theory should accommodate. Chapter 8 reviews several popular hypotheses about the rarity of LMFs and evaluates their plausibility in light of the evidence.

The subsequent chapters consider the causal channels through which alienability can affect firm behavior. Chapters 9–11 address appropriation problems. In Chapter 9, I present a series of models where insiders cannot fully appropriate the surplus generated by the firm. This yields comparative static behavior that differs from profit maximization and can potentially explain why LMFs tend to avoid quantity adjustments in response to economic shocks. Other sections of this chapter show that with imperfect appropriation, LMFs can be tempted to hire nonmember employees and to underinvest. I argue at the end of the chapter that alienability (or, more precisely, its absence in the case of labor) is an important source of imperfect appropriation.

Chapters 10 and 11 investigate additional appropriation problems associated with adverse selection. In Chapter 10, I show that when there is incomplete information about the value of entrepreneurial projects, workers may not be willing to pay much to join an LMF, and therefore entrepreneurs may prefer to establish KMFs. Chapter 11 argues that for LMFs, buying and selling membership rights usually requires approval by other firm members because of adverse selection in the labor market.

The same is not generally true for KMFs, because the alienability of capital makes it possible to buy and sell control rights without altering the physical inputs of the firm.

Chapters 12 and 13 address public good problems. In Chapter 12 (based on joint work with Gil Skillman), I use results from the shareholder unanimity literature to argue that alienable (and therefore more-mobile) capital tends to imply unanimous preferences among investors in a KMF. However, inalienable (and therefore less-mobile) labor tends to imply heterogeneous preferences among workers in an LMF. One implication is that it is relatively easy for profit-maximizing investors to take over an LMF but more difficult for heterogeneous employees to take over a KMF. In Chapter 13, I follow up on this idea by arguing that information about the productivity gains from conversion of a KMF to an LMF is a public good from the standpoint of the KMF employees, and that free riding with respect to such information tends to limit the number of employee buyouts.

Chapters 14 and 15 begin the study of opportunism, with a focus on firm-specific investments. Chapter 14 reviews basic concepts in transaction cost economics (TCE) and criticizes previous applications of TCE to labor-managed firms. Chapter 15 develops a model where capital and labor suppliers invest in specialized physical and human assets and the resulting quasi-rent is distributed differently in KMFs and LMFs. In equilibrium, control rights over the firm typically go to capital suppliers when physical assets are more specialized, and labor suppliers when human assets are more specialized. Efficiency can be enhanced through collective ownership of nonhuman assets by LMFs, but this raises the question of how such assets are to be financed.

Chapters 16–18 take a more radical approach to the opportunism problem by assuming that legally binding contracts do not exist. Accordingly, input contributions and side payments must be self-enforced through repeated game mechanisms. The model in Chapter 16 shows that incentives for work effort are the same regardless of whether the firm's capital stock is owned by outside investors or the workforce of the firm itself. Any resource allocation that can be supported in an economy with outside ownership can also be supported when workers own the capital stocks of their firms.

Chapter 17 returns to the alienability distinction between capital and labor, and uses a repeated game model to establish that asymmetries between KMFs and LMFs do arise when this distinction is taken into account. In particular, KMFs prevail when the temptation for LMFs to depreciate capital quickly and withhold payments to investors is greater than the temptation for KMFs to cheat on wage payments to employees. Chapter 18 uses a similar repeated game framework to study adverse selection with respect to entrepreneurial projects. I argue that the greater financial liquidity of investors, which enables them to pay wages prior to production, alters the strategic interaction between capital and labor suppliers in ways that tend to favor KMFs.

Chapter 19 summarizes the results from Chapters 9–18, weaves them together into a unified theoretical framework based on the alienability difference between capital and labor, discusses the consistency of this framework with the evidence from Chapters 6 and 7, and proposes an agenda for further research. Chapter 20 uses the theory from Chapter 19 to devise policy remedies for the market failures that currently limit LMF formation.

1.5 Related Literature

My previous book *Governing the Firm* (Dow, 2003) gives references to the LMF literature through approximately December 2001, when the manuscript for that book was completed. In a search of the EconLit database for January 2002 through August 2016, the term "labor-managed firm" led to 502 hits, including a wide range of working papers, journal articles, book chapters, and books. Clearly this research topic is not going away. If anything, scholarly activity in the field has accelerated over the past decade and a half.

Many of the items returned by the EconLit search were case studies of individual firms, regions, or countries; adopted a psychological, sociological, political, or historical perspective; or were in languages other than English. This speaks to the level of interest labor-managed firms have sparked across many countries and academic disciplines. At the same time, the scale of the literature makes a comprehensive survey impossible, and in any event this is not my goal. My citations are strongly skewed toward sources I have found particularly useful in developing my preferred theoretical framework. But almost certainly I have missed some contributions that are both relevant and of high quality, and I extend my apologies to the authors of these works.

Broadly speaking, there are three theoretical traditions in the study of LMFs. The earliest derives from comparative economics and assumes that LMFs maximize income per worker. I will frequently criticize this approach, which I believe is misguided and has had unfortunate effects on the evolution of the field. A second theoretical tradition arises out of transaction cost economics, or more generally the new institutional economics. I have some discomfort with this approach as well and therefore criticize it in Chapter 14. However, I also borrow important concepts from it, including ideas about incomplete contracts and asset specificity. The third theoretical approach is based on the economics of information and game theory. This approach is often used in the second half of the book, and it is the one I find most congenial.

Early books on labor-managed firms include Vanek (1970), Bonin and Putterman (1987), and Drèze (1989). The Vanek book was a formative work within the comparative economics tradition. Bonin and Putterman survey developments during the fifteen years or so following the publication of Vanek (1970). The Drèze book likewise belongs to the comparative economics stream, but with some differences in emphasis relative to Vanek.

Two recent books will be mentioned in order to convey the current state of the literature. Mikami (2011) attempts to explain why capitalist firms, worker cooperatives, consumer cooperatives, and government enterprises emerge in particular market niches. The equilibrium type of firm is the one maximizing the sum of the utilities of all agents. The author considers three principal sources of market failure: monopoly or monopsony, asymmetric information, and externalities. In equilibrium, a firm assigns ownership to the agents located in the market where the most severe problems of market failure would otherwise occur. Labor-managed firms are discussed in two chapters, and other chapters investigate consumer cooperatives and government enterprises. Mikami argues that LMFs may emerge in response to monopsony in the labor market or to protect the value of firm-specific human capital.

Jossa (2014) is exclusively concerned with labor-managed firms. Roughly half of the book is devoted to the issue of whether LMFs constitute a new mode of production in the Marxian sense and whether a system consisting of such firms would be compatible with the Marxian concept of socialism. Other chapters discuss the mainstream economic literature on LMFs but make little use of contemporary microeconomic theory and do not address recent empirical research. Jossa is clearly a supporter of LMFs but does not attempt to answer the skeptic's question "If LMFs are so great, why are they so rare?"

Interested readers may want to explore a series of books entitled *Advances in the Economic Analysis of Participatory and Labor-Managed Firms* published by Emerald in Bingley, U.K. Volumes numbered 11–16 have appeared during 2010–2015. Each volume has a separate editor, and individual chapters run the gamut from case studies to empirical research, theoretical modeling, and policy discussion.

Readers who want anthologies of classic articles on labor-managed firms have two sources available. One is a two-volume set edited by Prychitko and Vanek (1996), and the other is a single-volume anthology edited by Pencavel (2013a). Of these two the Pencavel collection is more up to date and more consistently focused on theoretical and empirical issues relevant for the present book. However, Prychitko and Vanek cover a wide range of topics and include some early work omitted by Pencavel. Readers looking for a compact intellectual history of the subject may be interested in Dow (2018).

Newcomers to the LMF literature can easily become confused by terminology, so a comment on this topic may be useful. I use "labor-managed firm" (LMF) to mean a firm in which ultimate control rests with the firm's labor suppliers—nothing more and nothing less. The same term is sometimes used in narrower ways. For example, various authors define an LMF to be a firm that maximizes income per worker rather than treating this as one (possibly false) behavioral hypothesis about what an LMF might do. Other authors reserve the term "labor-managed firm" for a firm controlled by workers where investment is financed through debt and use "worker-managed firm" for a firm controlled by workers where investment is financed from retained earnings. Moreover, "workers' enterprise" has sometimes been used to denote an LMF with an exogenously given number of members. I do not use these terminological conventions here. In this book, the term "LMF" implies nothing about the way in which a firm is financed or how its membership is determined. These are questions for theoretical and empirical investigation, not issues to be resolved through definitional fiat.

Many chapters of the present book are newly written, but some have been adapted from earlier publications. For the latter chapters, I include a short postscript that provides information about the source material for the chapter, describes the context in which that material was originally written, and acknowledges advice or financial support.

1.6 Hybrid Firms

Another body of related literature, on hybrid firms, deserves separate discussion. I use the expression "hybrid firm" to mean a firm that is ultimately controlled by its capital suppliers, in the usual sense that shareholders choose the board of directors and the board chooses top managers, but where the employees have a substantial amount of financial participation, decision-making participation, or both. Common examples of financial participation include employee stock ownership, employee stock options, profit sharing, and bonuses for team performance. Examples of decision-making participation include informal shop floor consultation, joint labor-management committees on innovation, quality, or safety, as well as employee representation on boards of directors (codetermination). Employee stock ownership plans (ESOPs) are common in the U.S., and codetermination is common in Europe. Descriptions and histories of these institutional arrangements are provided in Dow (2003, ch. 4).

There is an extensive literature on hybrid firms, perhaps more extensive than the literature on LMFs per se. Much of this addresses empirical questions similar to those raised about LMFs. For example, researchers have explored whether ESOPs or profit sharing increase productivity, and whether employee financial participation yields productivity gains only when employees are also involved in decision-making. Because hybrids are becoming more common in most developed economies, such questions are of substantial policy interest.

Although hybrid firms are more widespread, this book remains focused on LMFs in the pure sense. This is partly for practical reasons. There is already much to say about LMFs, and it is impossible to do justice to a second large literature in the available space. Hybrid firms are highly varied, and one could easily write an entire book on a particular subset of this topic, such as ESOPs or profit sharing. Furthermore, much of the literature on hybrids has an empirical or policy emphasis, and my expertise lies elsewhere. In any event, such firms have already received considerable attention in other books (see Kruse et al., 2010, and Carberry, 2011).

There are also theoretical reasons to focus on pure LMFs. Maintaining a sharp conceptual contrast between KMFs and LMFs forces one to think carefully about how capital and labor differ, and how these differences might affect firm behavior. The more complex organizational landscape of the hybrid world tends to obscure these qualitative differences. In particular, I want to build a theoretical framework around the qualitative distinction between alienable capital and inalienable labor. This would be difficult to do while simultaneously considering institutional structures through which capital and labor suppliers share control rights or financial returns.

Another reason for concentrating on LMFs is that this subject has distinctive theoretical traditions that I want to address in a systematic way. These include deeply entrenched assumptions such as the notion that LMFs maximize income per worker or that they have shorter time horizons than KMFs for investment decisions. Because these traditions have diverted the literature into channels I believe are unproductive, a thorough housecleaning is needed. Accordingly, I focus attention tightly on the theory of the LMF.

Nevertheless, there is a close connection between the study of LMFs in the pure sense and the study of hybrid firms with a strong component of employee participation. Many authors have made important contributions to both areas, and each literature helps illuminate the other. For example, if one wants to know whether expanding worker participation within otherwise conventional firms will increase productivity, it might be useful to treat the LMF as an extreme case with maximal workers' control and examine the productivity of LMFs. Conversely, if one wants to interpret empirical findings about LMFs, it might be useful to think about these findings in light of what is known about the behavior of conventional firms where workers share in control rights or financial results.

These complementarities extend further. For example, models of distributional conflict between capital and labor suppliers in pure KMFs and LMFs may shed light on parallel conflicts arising in hybrid firms and suggest institutional solutions to protect one set of input suppliers from strategic behavior by the other. Similarly, policies to facilitate hybrid arrangements, such as employee stock ownership, might also facilitate conversion of KMFs into LMFs. I hope the theoretical framework in this book contributes to a better understanding of the large and complex world of hybrid firms.

PART II

PERFECTION AND SYMMETRY

2

Profit Maximization and Control Rights

2.1 Introduction

Few assumptions are more deeply entrenched in modern economic theory than the idea that firms maximize profit. Almost every economist, apart from a few specialists in the theory of the firm, routinely assumes profit maximization whenever something needs to be said about firm behavior. Academic economists in North America teach this idea to their students at all levels, from introductory courses to PhD programs.

Here I review the underpinnings of this hypothesis, because economists interested in labor-managed firms have often assumed that LMFs maximize something else. I will sketch some preliminary arguments for the view that LMFs do indeed maximize profit, or at least that there should be a presumption to this effect in the absence of any argument to the contrary. Sections 2.1 and 2.2 discuss the usual Walrasian model and its institutional setting. Sections 2.3, 2.4, and 2.5 introduce the notion of control groups and develop the theoretical connections between input supply and firm behavior. Section 2.6 concludes with a preview of Chapters 3–5. I focus on the objectives of the ultimate control groups in firms rather than implementation problems involving such matters as transaction costs or principal-agent problems.

In Walrasian general equilibrium theory (Debreu, 1959; Arrow and Hahn, 1971), the firm maximizes profit because it is owned and controlled by individual consumers, and consumers are better off when they have more income. I introduce some notation to show how the model works. Consumers are indexed by $i = 1.. I$, and firms are indexed by $j = 1.. J$. Goods and services are indexed by $g = 1.. G$. Each good or service has a separate market price p_g, and the vector of market prices for all goods is $p = (p_1.. p_G) > 0$. Individual consumers or firms have no influence over prices. Each consumer i chooses a consumption bundle $x_i = (x_{i1} .. x_{iG})$ subject to a budget constraint, and each firm j chooses a production plan $y_j = (y_{j1} .. y_{jG})$ subject to a technology constraint.

Consumers must have nonnegative consumption levels, so $x_i \geq 0$ for all i. The same is not true for firms. In the usual notational convention, a positive element of the vector y_j indicates an output for firm j, and a negative element of this vector indicates an input for firm j. Multiplying the price vector by the firm's production plan gives $py_j = \Sigma_g p_g y_{jg}$. This is profit for firm j, where the negative sign of each input means that costs are automatically subtracted from revenues.

Consumers have initial ownership rights or endowments of two kinds. First, they may be endowed with goods. For consumer i, this endowment vector is indicated by $\underline{x}_i = (\underline{x}_{i1} .. \underline{x}_{iG}) \geq 0$ and reflects the ownership rights consumer i has over goods and services before the market opens. I adopt the convention that underscored variables indicate an endowed quantity before market transactions occur, while the same variable without an underscore is a quantity arising after market transactions are complete. Consumers do not choose their endowment vectors, which are exogenous to the model. The value of consumer i's endowment of goods is the scalar product $p\underline{x}_i$, because this is the income the consumer can obtain by selling his or her endowment at prevailing prices.

In addition to their endowments of goods, consumers are endowed with shares in firms. Share endowments are denoted by $\underline{\theta}_{ij}$ where this is the fraction of firm j's profit paid to consumer i. Share endowments are nonnegative so $\underline{\theta}_{ij} \geq 0$ for all (i, j), and sum to unity for a given firm so $\Sigma_i \underline{\theta}_{ij} = 1$ for all j. The latter equality says that all of firm j's profit must go to someone. As with the goods endowments $\underline{x}_i$, the share endowments $\underline{\theta}_{ij}$ are not chosen by consumers but instead reflect ownership claims on firms before the market opens. In the simplest version of the model, there are no markets for the shares of firms; the only markets are those for goods and services. Share markets are discussed in Section 2.5 and Chapters 3–5.

Consumer i's budget constraint is typically written in the form $px_i \leq p\underline{x}_i + \Sigma_j \underline{\theta}_{ij} py_j$—where px_i is expenditure on the consumption bundle x_i, $p\underline{x}_i$ is income obtained by selling the goods endowment $\underline{x}_i$, and py_j is the profit of firm j. Consumer i receives the fraction $\underline{\theta}_{ij}$ of py_j, and the sum $\Sigma_j \underline{\theta}_{ij} py_j$ is consumer i's total profit income from all of the firms in the economy. The $\underline{\theta}_{ij}$ could be zero for some or all firms, so consumer i may receive zero profit income from some or all firms.

Consumer i's *budget set* is the set of bundles that satisfy the budget constraint. In Walrasian theory, i's preferences over consumption bundles x_i are summarized by a utility function. Consumer i chooses the bundle within her budget set that maximizes utility.

Now return to the issue of profit maximization. If consumer i were asked to give an opinion about what firm j should do, it is clear what that opinion would be. Consumer i achieves a higher utility level when the right-hand side of the budget constraint is larger, because then the consumer has more income. Any consumer with $\underline{\theta}_{ij} > 0$ therefore wants py_j to be as large as possible subject to technological constraints on feasible choices of y_j, because this makes the consumer's own income as large as possible. A consumer with $\underline{\theta}_{ij} = 0$ is indifferent toward the production plan used by firm j. Because consumer-owners are unanimous, there is no need for any voting or bargaining process to resolve conflicts among them. I call this rationale for profit maximization *budget set dominance*.

Starting from these foundations, standard methods can be used to derive demand and supply functions for consumers and firms. A Walrasian equilibrium exists if there is a price vector p at which supply and demand are equated for all goods simultaneously. It is unnecessary to pursue questions of this kind here. Textbook treatments at the graduate level can be found in Varian (1993) and Mas-Colell, Whinston, and Green (1995).

2.2 The Institutional Setting of Walrasian Theory

Various institutional requirements must be satisfied for the Walrasian defense of profit maximization to hold together. These fall into two categories—assumptions about market structure and assumptions about firm organization:

Market structure. Walrasian theory assumes two key things about markets. First, there is a complete set of markets for all goods and services. Each good or service must be traded on a separate market and must have its own price. In particular, there must be separate prices for otherwise identical goods or services that differ by quality, by the time at which they are delivered, by the place at which they are delivered, and by the state of the world in which they are delivered. Second, no individual consumer or firm can alter the price of any good or service. In short, markets are perfectly competitive.

Firm organization. Individual consumers are endowed with claims on the profits of firms. There is no attempt to explain how these claims arise.

There is also no explicit mechanism for aggregating the desires of individual consumers into a production plan for the firm. Given the prices a firm faces, its consumer-owners unanimously favor profit maximization, and the firm behaves accordingly.

I will begin by indicating why the assumptions about market structure are needed. Consider the following possible objection to the idea of profit maximization. Suppose that a consumer receives 100% of a firm's profit but must exert effort in order to make good managerial decisions. Because effort is unpleasant, the consumer could be concerned about the trade-off between higher income and higher effort, and therefore could decide not to maximize profit, because this would require too much effort. From a Walrasian standpoint, the problem is that there is no market for managerial effort and the solution is to have a price for such effort, so the consumer maximizes profit inclusive of effort costs.

A more subtle form of market incompleteness involves externalities. Suppose that firm j generates pollution. If consumer i is harmed by this pollution, it may make sense for consumer i to favor pollution abatement by firm j even if consumer i owns part of firm j (i.e., $\underline{\theta}_{ij} > 0$) and even if pollution abatement reduces j's profit. The Walrasian solution is to introduce a new market, in this case to create a price for pollution. This leads all consumer-owners to support profit maximization inclusive of pollution costs.

Aside from the completeness of markets for all goods (or bads), the Walrasian defense of profit maximization requires that prices be determined in competitive markets. Suppose that firm j has a monopoly on the output of good g and can drive up price p_g by reducing its output of this good. If consumer i wants to buy this good but has a claim on the profit generated by firm j, this consumer faces a dilemma: is it better to have a high price p_g in order to have high profit from firm j and therefore a high income, or is it better to have a low price p_g in order to buy the good more cheaply? The Walrasian assumption of price-taking behavior for all firms and consumers rules out dilemmas of this kind.

Putting aside possible deviations from complete and competitive markets, the idea of profit maximization has also faced some challenges based on arguments regarding firm organization. In the 1960s, there was a flurry of interest in firm objectives involving the alleged goals of firm managers, such as sales maximization, growth maximization, or managerial utility maximization. None of the resulting suggestions led to a sustained research program. However, there is a huge modern literature on principal-agent models in which a firm owner (the principal) wants to create incentives for a manager (the agent) to act in ways that are profitable to the owner. For a textbook version, see Mas-Colell, Whinston, and Green (1995, ch. 14).

Another challenge dating back to the 1960s came from authors who questioned the entire framework of constrained optimization and replaced it with a theory based on satisficing behavior and the evolution of organizational routines (see Nelson and Winter, 1982). This heterodox school failed to dethrone the hypothesis of profit maximization in mainstream economics but had an early influence on the field of behavioral economics.

Starting in the 1970s, a literature from financial economics studied the conditions under which shareholders unanimously support maximization of profit or present value when firm shares can be traded on a stock market and there is uncertainty about the state of the world. It turned out that the required conditions are far from trivial (see Hart, 1979a). This literature will be discussed in detail in Chapter 12.

Another school of thought that diverged from the Walrasian framework in the 1970s is transaction cost economics (Williamson, 1975). In TCE, the firm's production plan is determined through incomplete contracts among market participants, along with authority structures that fill contractual gaps when necessary. I will return to this vision of the firm in Chapter 14.

2.3 Control Groups and Walrasian Theory

The Walrasian approach makes no connection between control over a firm and the supply of inputs. The agents who choose the firm's production plan need not be the same people who supply capital or labor to it. The idea that firms are controlled by consumers may suggest that the Walrasian firm is a peculiar kind of consumer cooperative, but this is not the case either. The consumer-owners of a Walrasian firm producing Frisbees need not buy their products from this particular firm. They could just as well buy their Frisbees from some other firm or buy none at all.

As discussed in Chapter 1, in a capitalist firm the agents who supply capital to the firm choose its production plan. By this definition, Walrasian theory is not a theory about capitalist firms. Of course, one can claim that capitalist firms maximize profit and hence behave precisely like Walrasian firms. However, this claim requires an argument. One must describe the preferences, beliefs, and constraints of the individual agents who supply capital to the firm, say how the preferences of the individual capital suppliers are aggregated, and show that such a firm indeed adopts a production plan identical to the one a Walrasian firm would adopt. Arguments of this kind are rarely made. The typical practice of the economics profession instead involves sleight of hand: (a) the Walrasian firm maximizes profit; (b) it is convenient to assume that capitalist firms also maximize profit, because then the Walrasian model can be applied to the real world; so (c) for most purposes, the distinction between these two kinds of firm will be ignored.

As we will see in Chapters 3–5, the profession was not willing to engage in the same sleight of hand when it came to labor-managed firms. Such firms were assumed to maximize something other than profit (generally income per worker), and their behavior was thus assumed to differ from that of the Walrasian firm. Later I will trace the history of this intellectual deviation from the postulate of profit maximization and explain what the consequences have been for the theory of the LMF.

For now, it suffices to make the following point. If one wants to explain why KMFs are common and LMFs are rare, assuming that both kinds of firms maximize profit is not very helpful. On the other hand, assuming that KMFs maximize profit while LMFs do not merely begs the question "What accounts for this alleged asymmetry?" The only fruitful way forward is to study how groups of input suppliers reach collective decisions about a firm's production plan and to show why the decisions made by capital suppliers would differ systematically from those made by labor suppliers.

2.4 Control Groups with Fixed Membership

I will use the term "insiders" for agents who both supply an input to a firm and also exercise control rights over it. In the rest of this chapter, I consider how insiders make decisions about the firm's production activities, including the use of inputs supplied by the insiders themselves. I start with a fixed group of insiders who supply capital. The implications for insiders who supply labor will be discussed afterward.

I modify the Walrasian model from Section 2.1 as follows. Choose a particular firm and drop the earlier j subscript used to index individual firms. Let there be one physical input called capital that is continuously variable. Output is given by the strictly concave production function $f(K)$, where K is the total capital contributed to the firm by all agents. The firm sells its output at the competitive price $p > 0$, and individual agents who are endowed with capital can sell it on a market at the competitive price $r > 0$.

Let $\underline{\theta}_i{}^K \geq 0$ be consumer i's endowment of *capital shares* in the firm, where $\Sigma\underline{\theta}_i{}^K = 1$. These capital shares differ from the Walrasian shares $\underline{\theta}_{ij}$ from Section 2.1 in two ways. First, they convey both a claim on the net income of the firm *and* an obligation to supply capital to the firm. This reflects common practice in capitalist firms. An investor who supplies the fraction $\underline{\theta}_i{}^K$ of the firm's total capital K generally appropriates the same fraction $\theta_i{}^K$ of the firm's profit.

Second, the capital share $\underline{\theta}_i{}^K$ gives individual i the right to participate in decisions about the firm's production plan. For concreteness, imagine that these control rights are voting rights, so the investor i has the fraction $\theta_i{}^K$ of total votes. Here only one issue can arise: what total amount of capital K should the firm use? I define the *control group* $\underline{C}$ for the firm to be the set of agents with positive capital shares in the firm, so $\underline{C} = \{\text{i such that } \theta_i{}^K > 0\}$. Other agents have no voting rights, no obligation to supply capital to the firm, and no claim on profit.

For the rest of this section, the capital shares $\theta_i{}^K$ are exogenous to the model, just as the Walrasian shares $\underline{\theta}_{ij}$ were exogenous. Endowments of physical capital are likewise exogenous, where $\underline{K}_i \geq 0$ is agent i's endowment of physical capital. Keeping in mind that capital shares entail an obligation to supply an input, there is a constraint on the firm's choice of K, because each member of the control group $\underline{C}$ must be able to meet the resulting input supply obligation. The total input K is consistent with the endowed distribution of capital shares $\{\theta_i{}^K\}$ if and only if $\underline{\theta}_i{}^K K \leq \underline{K}_i$ for all $i \in \underline{C}$.

We do not know yet what preferences an individual member of the control group will have over the firm's total input K, because we do not know how profit is calculated, or how insiders are compensated for their capital contributions. However, the following institutional arrangements provide one natural approach. Suppose that when agent $i \in \underline{C}$ contributes the capital $K_i = \theta_i{}^K K$, agent i receives rK_i from the firm's bank account. This makes agent i indifferent between selling K_i on the open market at the price r or instead supplying it to the firm. Thus the firm exactly covers the opportunity cost of capital for each insider. I also assume that the firm's profit is computed as

$$\pi(K) = pf(K) - r\sum K_i$$
$$= pf(K) - rK\sum \theta_i^K \qquad (1)$$
$$= pf(K) - rK$$

Ignoring other firms, these rules imply that agent i receives the following overall income from his or her capital endowment:

$$m_i = \underline{\theta}_i^K \pi(K) + rK_i + r(\underline{K}_i - K_i) \qquad (2)$$

The first term on the right-hand side is agent i's share of firm profit, the second reflects the payment made by the firm to cover the opportunity cost of agent i's capital supply, and the third indicates the income agent i derives by selling off any remaining capital endowment after his or her obligation to the firm has been met.

This income expression reduces to $m_i = \underline{\theta}_i^K \pi(K) + r\underline{K}_i$. Agent i has no control over $\underline{\theta}_i^K$ (a share endowment), r (a market price), or $\underline{K}_i$ (a physical endowment). The only item over which agent i may have influence is the firm's total input K, and this influence is exercised through the voting rights attached to the capital share $\underline{\theta}_i^K$. Agent i's preferred input level is the value of K that solves the following problem:

choose $K \geq 0$ to maximize $\pi(K)$ subject to $\underline{\theta}_i^K K \leq \underline{K}_i$ for all $i \in \underline{C}$ $\quad$ (3)

As discussed earlier, the constraint arises because it must be possible for all members of the control group to contribute their required capital inputs simultaneously. The reason for profit maximization here is the same as in Section 2.1: budget set dominance. Agent i wants to have the maximum possible income to spend on goods and services. Because all members of $\underline{C}$ have the same objective, all vote for the same level of K. Accordingly, the firm maximizes profit, subject to the constraints involving personal capital endowments.

The constraints in (3) could be eliminated in the following way. Suppose that agent i cannot comply with her obligation to supply capital to the firm because $\underline{\theta}_i^K K > \underline{K}_i$. This does not pose a problem if agent i can make the following transactions: (a) go to the capital market and purchase an additional amount of capital $\underline{\theta}_i^K K - \underline{K}_i > 0$ at the price r per unit and then (b) hand over this amount of capital to the firm in exchange for a payment from the firm equal to $r(\underline{\theta}_i^K K - \underline{K}_i)$. The net cost of these transactions to agent i is zero, so there is no effect on the agent's budget constraint, and the agent can now comply with the entire input supply obligation $K_i = \underline{\theta}_i^K K$. If all insiders $i \in \underline{C}$ can make such transactions, the constraints in (3) can be dropped, and the firm chooses $K \geq 0$ to maximize $\pi(K)$. This restores the profit maximization hypothesis of Walrasian theory.

Nevertheless, there are important differences from the Walrasian frame-work of Section 2.1. First, we have tied control rights to the supply of an input. Second, we have tied the role of profit recipient to the role of input supplier. Third, we have spelled out accounting rules that determine how individuals are compensated by the firm for their input contributions and how the profit generated by the firm is calculated. Fourth, we have derived preferences of input suppliers over production plans and spelled out a way of aggregating these preferences (through voting) to determine how the firm behaves.

The logic of this section extends easily to other situations. If the firm uses more than one input and these other inputs can be acquired on competitive markets, then the members of the control group will choose the other inputs in a profit-maximizing way. In the case of a capitalist firm, this includes labor inputs. Assuming that the production function is differenti-able, the standard first order conditions apply. If the firm produces more than one output, we will need to describe its production technology in a more general way, but again the firm maximizes profit.

The same logic applies if the members of the control group $\underline{C}$ are labor suppliers rather than capital suppliers. In this case we would replace the input K by an input L, the price of capital r by a price of labor w, the capital share θ_i^K by a labor share $\underline{\theta}_i^L$, and the capital endowment $\underline{K}_i$ by a labor endowment $\underline{L}_i$. These notational changes are irrelevant to the structure of the argument.

The only possible exception to the symmetry of capital and labor involves the role of the constraint from (3). Such constraints can be dropped in the case of a capitalist firm if the insiders can augment their own capital endowments by buying capital on the market and handing it over to the firm in exchange for financial compensation. This is plausible for physical capital. However, it is not obvious that parallel transactions can be carried out in a firm where the insiders are labor suppliers.

In the latter case, an agent i in the firm's control group might have $\theta_i^L L > \underline{L}_i$, so the agent would be unable to meet the corresponding input supply obligation out of her own endowment of labor time. Suppose that this agent went to the labor market, hired labor $\underline{\theta}_i^L L - \underline{L}_i > 0$ at the wage rate w, and "handed this labor over to the firm" in exchange for financial compensation from the firm to cover the costs involved. It is not clear whether such a firm should count as labor-managed, because some agents are contributing labor to the firm without having had anything to say about the input level L, which by assumption is the only decision made by the firm.

The underlying issue is that capital is alienable while labor is not. Because capital is alienable, it makes sense to say that a member of the firm's control group can purchase capital on the market and then supply it to the firm. All of the capital contributed by the agent in question is actually owned by that agent when it is supplied to the firm. Because labor is inalienable, it does not make equal sense to say that an agent can buy labor on the market and give it to the firm. Such transactions imply that some people contribute labor through employment contracts without being members of the control group. However, if we ignore the alienability issue, there is no other asymmetry between capital and labor in the model developed here.

In particular, suppose that (a) the firm's only input is labor, (b) the members of the control group are a fixed set of labor suppliers, (c) each of these agents receives hourly compensation from the firm equal to the external wage, and (d) firm profit is calculated as revenue minus the sum of these wage payments. Then provided that each member of the control group is endowed with enough personal labor time so that the constraints on input supply are nonbinding, the insiders in this LMF unanimously want the total labor input L to maximize profit $\pi(L)$. This conclusion generalizes to an LMF that requires both labor and capital. In this case, the LMF chooses both labor and capital in a profit-maximizing way, where capital is purchased on the external market at a competitive price. The same reasoning applies to LMFs using additional inputs or producing multiple outputs.

2.5 Transactions between Insiders and Outsiders

Section 2.4 treated the distribution of capital shares (or labor shares) across individual agents as fixed. Here I allow transactions in which the initial insiders for a firm can sell their share endowments to outsiders. This provides a way to remove the constraints on firm production plans associated with individual input endowments, while preserving support for the objective of profit maximization.

Return to the case of a firm in which the only input is capital and output is f(K). As before, let the initial endowment of capital shares for agent i be denoted by $\underline{\theta}_i^K \geq 0$, where $\Sigma \theta_i^K = 1$. In this section I refer to the exogenously given share endowments $\underline{\theta}_i^K$ as *ex ante capital shares*. The *ex ante control group* is the set of agents with positive initial share endowments: $\underline{C} = \{i$ such that $\underline{\theta}_i^K > 0\}$. As before, voting rights are proportional to ex ante capital shares. Agent i is initially obligated to contribute the capital $K_i = \underline{\theta}_i^K K$, where K is the firm's total capital input. In return, agent i receives the payment rK_i from the firm, which covers the agent's opportunity cost. Agent i also receives profit income $\underline{\theta}_i^K \pi(K) = \underline{\theta}_i^K [pf(K) - rK]$.

Now suppose that individual members of the ex ante control group are allowed to transfer their capital shares to outsiders. The capital share positions prevailing after these transactions are called *ex post capital shares* and are denoted by θ_i^K (with no underscore). Transactions of this kind are subject to an institutional rule: outsiders must be indifferent toward the purchase of capital shares in the firm. I am not concerned for the moment with the reasons for this rule, only with its effects. Finally, suppose that the members of the ex ante control group choose the firm's capital input K and buyers of capital shares take this input level as given.

Let v be the price for 100% of the firm's capital shares. An outsider who buys the ex post share $\theta_i^K > 0$ acquires both the obligation to contribute the capital input $K_i = \theta_i^K K$ and the right to receive the profit $\theta_i^K \pi(K)$. Ex post capital suppliers are automatically compensated for their opportunity costs rK_i under the accounting rules of the firm. An outsider is indifferent toward buying the capital share θ_i^K if and only if $v(K) = \pi(K)$, because then the expenditure on shares $\theta_i^K v(K)$ is equal to the resulting profit claim $\theta_i^K \pi(K)$, and the transaction has no net effect on the budget constraint of the outsider.

How do such transactions affect the members of the ex ante control group? If $i \in \underline{C}$ fully disposes of the ex ante share $\underline{\theta}_i^K$, then agent i is no longer personally responsible for the capital contribution $K_i = \underline{\theta}_i^K K$ and no longer receives compensation from the firm to cover the opportunity cost of this contribution. These effects wash out. The only other effect is that the insider would have received the profit share $\theta_i^K \pi(K)$ but instead receives the payment $\underline{\theta}_i^K v(K) = \underline{\theta}_i^K \pi(K)$ from one or more outsiders. All of the insiders still want to make $\pi(K)$ as large as possible, because this also makes the price $v(K)$ as large as possible. Thus, whether an insider intends to sell all, some, or none of the ex ante shares $\underline{\theta}_i^K$, the insider continues to support profit maximization.

This conclusion may seem trivial. By assumption, outsiders derive no net benefit from their transactions with insiders, so if the insiders want to maximize profit when they will keep their shares, they should also maximize profit when their shares will be sold to outsiders at a price reflecting the profitability of the shares. However, two points require emphasis.

First, the possibility of selling ex ante shares to outsiders eliminates the earlier problem in Section 2.4 where insiders might not be able to meet their input obligations out of their own resource endowments. As long as there are outsiders with sufficiently large capital endowments, it is always possible to shift input obligations to these agents. The constraint from (3) can then be ignored, and all members of the ex ante control group support whatever level of K maximizes the profit $\pi(K)$.

We have already seen that the constraint in (3) is irrelevant if individual members of the control group can go to the capital market, buy the capital they need, and hand it over to the firm in exchange for financial compensation. The point here is that a system in which insiders sell capital shares to outsiders is an alternative institutional mechanism that achieves the same thing. Of course, one might still wonder whether there are enough outsiders with enough capital to satisfy the firm's demand. Later chapters will show that this reduces to a conventional supply and demand problem where supply is brought into equality with demand through the market price of capital (r).

Second, one might ask whether it makes sense to call a firm "capital-managed" when the firm's production plan (here, just the input level K) is chosen by the ex ante owners of capital shares while some or all capital is actually supplied by the ex post owners of capital shares. To see why this is not a problem, imagine that the ex post capital suppliers can make similar share transactions with further outsiders. Replace the ex ante share distribution by the ex post share distribution and the ex ante control group $\underline{C}$ by an ex post control group C. If the ex post owners of capital shares were asked what level of K the firm should choose, again there would be unanimous support for the level of K that maximizes profit. Thus it is legitimate to call this type of firm a KMF, because all of the (ex post) capital suppliers support the firm's production plan and prefer not to revise it, given an opportunity to do so.

It should be evident that all of the preceding arguments continue to apply when we replace the word "capital" by "labor." In an LMF, the ex ante control group is made up of agents with ex ante labor supply obligations, and these agents are free to transfer their labor shares to outsiders who would take over both the duty to supply labor and the right to claim a corresponding share of profit. Assuming (importantly) that the outsiders derive no net benefit from their transactions with the insiders, it is still true that the insiders want to choose the firm's labor input (as well as other inputs or outputs) in a profit-maximizing way. It is also true that the members of the ex post control group, who actually supply labor to the firm, prefer not to alter the firm's production plan once it has been chosen. Thus it is legitimate to call this type of firm an LMF.

This mechanism gets around the problem in Section 2.4 where the ex ante owners of labor shares might not be endowed with enough labor time to satisfy their obligations to a firm. A question remains about the size of the firm's demand for labor in relation to the capacity of outsiders to supply it, but this is a standard question about supply and demand for labor. As I show in later chapters, these are equalized through the market wage (w).

2.6 A Preview

Chapter 3 studies the LMF in the short run. A highly influential premise from the comparative economics tradition holds that LMFs maximize income per worker-member. Such "Ward-Domar-Vanek" firms have strange comparative static behavior and typically misallocate labor across firms. Chapter 3 shows that these problems vanish if the LMF has a competitive market for membership rights, because such a market induces worker-members to maximize profit. This is established first for a single firm in the short run. The results are then extended to an economy with many firms.

Chapter 4 shifts to a long run setting in which firms make investment decisions. Critics of the LMF have often asserted that LMFs have defective investment incentives. These critics usually rule out LMF membership markets by definitional fiat. However, when such markets exist, the alleged investment issues disappear, for the same reason that stock markets induce present value maximization in capitalist firms. Despite the fact that individual workers come and go in the LMF, there is no problem of time inconsistency.

Chapter 5 utilizes a general equilibrium framework to compare an LMF economy with other systems. Similar analyses by Vanek (1970) and Drèze (1989) have assumed that LMFs maximize income per unit of labor, although Drèze considers corrective taxes or subsidies that induce profit maximization. I assume competitive membership markets and show that any Walrasian equilibrium allocation can be supported in an economy with LMFs, KMFs, or consumer cooperatives. The upshot is that KMFs and LMFs are isomorphic when markets are complete and competitive.

If one wants to explain the empirical asymmetries between KMFs and LMFs, one must identify relevant deviations from these conditions. The literature often embraces these conditions when discussing KMFs while abandoning them when discussing LMFs. This approach is incoherent. Theoretical discipline requires a comparison of KMFs and LMFs under parallel assumptions about market structure, where LMFs are allowed to replicate the institutional arrangements of KMFs (or vice versa) unless some explicit difference between capital and labor prevents replication.

Chapters 3–5 emphasize the symmetries that emerge when markets are perfect and there are no qualitative differences between capital and labor. This provides a theoretical benchmark. Chapters 6–8 discuss empirical asymmetries between KMFs and LMFs, and the rest of the book develops theoretical explanations for these asymmetries.

3

The Labor-Managed Firm in the Short Run

3.1 Introduction

This chapter begins the study of LMF membership markets using a short run framework where capital is fixed. I show that in this setting, LMFs with competitive membership markets maximize profit, for the same reason that Walrasian firms or KMFs with competitive stock markets maximize profit: the members of an LMF have more income to spend on consumption goods if they pursue this goal. I will refer to any profit-maximizing firm (whether it is a Walrasian firm, a KMF with a stock market, or an LMF with a membership market) as a PMF.

The theoretical literature on labor-managed firms has been strongly influenced by the early work of Ward (1958), Domar (1966), and Vanek (1970), who assumed that LMFs maximize income per worker. It will be convenient in what follows to call any firm that maximizes income per worker a WDV firm. Elsewhere (Dow, 2003, ch. 7), I have called these "Illyrian" firms, borrowing from the title of Ward's 1958 article.

One should not treat the WDV firm as definitionally equivalent to the LMF. Many writers do so, but this can only cause conceptual grief. As was discussed in Section 1.5, I use the term "LMF" to mean any firm controlled by its labor suppliers. How such a firm behaves, or what it maximizes, is a separate question. The WDV assumption is one hypothesis about how LMFs behave, and this hypothesis could be incorrect. The phrase "WDV firm" refers only to a theoretical model, not necessarily to any real LMF.

The WDV firm is notorious for its perverse comparative static behavior in the short run, relative to the benchmark behavior of a PMF. This can include a negatively sloped output supply curve, so the firm decreases output when the price of its output rises. By contrast, a PMF increases its output when the output price rises. The WDV firm also tends to increase output when fixed cost rises. By contrast, the level of fixed cost has no effect on PMF behavior. Bonin and Putterman (1987) provide formal derivations of these results, and I explore related ideas in Section 9.2.

The reason for these strange results is that the WDV firm maximizes a ratio (income per worker). There are two ways to increase a ratio: one can either increase the numerator or decrease the denominator. The latter motivation causes the WDV firm to restrict the number of workers allowed to share in firm income, so when profit is positive, the WDV firm hires fewer workers than an otherwise identical PMF. When output price rises, the WDV firm has a stronger incentive to shrink the denominator, leading to the possibility of a negatively sloped supply curve. The WDV firm expands its workforce when fixed cost rises, in order to spread this cost over more workers.

In simple models of the WDV variety, there is no labor market, so the firm ignores the outside wage that its workers could get by quitting. This is superficially reasonable when income per worker within the firm exceeds the outside wage. But because there is no labor market, there is no mechanism to equalize the value of labor's marginal product across firms, and labor is generally misallocated across firms in the short run. This contrasts with PMFs in a competitive labor market, where firms adjust their labor inputs until the value of labor's marginal product is equal to the market wage, which is identical for all firms.

Another consequence of the missing labor market in the WDV model is that there are unexploited gains from trade between insiders and outsiders. Suppose that the WDV firm generates an income per worker above the wage available to outsiders, so the outsiders would like to join. Mathematically, it must be true that the maximized level of income per worker is equal to the marginal value product of labor. Thus, the marginal value product exceeds the external wage. This implies that both insiders and outsiders can be made better off by having an outsider join the firm in exchange for a payment from the insiders above the external wage but below the marginal value product of labor. The WDV model rules out such Pareto-improving transactions.

More-specific managerial procedures for the WDV firm were proposed by Steinherr and Thisse (1979), Brewer and Browning (1982), and Miyazaki and Neary (1983), among others. These authors all posited an initial membership, determined through long run processes of entry and exit or coalition formation, that holds collective authority over short run production decisions. In these models, the firm's short run labor input can be reduced below the potential labor supply from current members by randomly assigning layoffs to redundant members. If workers are risk averse, ex ante insurance to equalize incomes between the employed and laid-off members is attractive. When these compensation payments correctly reflect the external opportunity cost of labor, the firm's short run labor input is identical to the labor input chosen under profit maximization, as long as the size of the firm's membership is large enough to permit this. However, this institutional fix does not work when profit maximization requires the firm to expand its short run labor input beyond what existing members can supply.

A WDV economy does allocate resources efficiently in the long run if there is free entry and exit of firms in all industries (see Section 4.1). However, the free entry requirement is frequently unrealistic. Even if one grants free entry, Pareto efficiency can only be guaranteed for a WDV economy in the long run, while a Walrasian economy also achieves Pareto efficiency in the short run.

The most fundamental problem with the WDV model is that it does not anchor the objective function of the firm in the interests of an identifiable set of individual agents. It is unclear what group of labor suppliers has authority over the firm's labor input or why this group wants to maximize income per worker. This is not an issue when the current membership is fixed and equal to the current workforce, because then maximizing total income and income per worker are the same thing, but such issues are immediate when the number of workers is variable. For example, the maximization of income per worker may require that some workers be expelled. This creates obvious conflict between those who expect to remain and those who expect to leave. The WDV model does not specify any collective choice procedure to resolve such conflicts, or any system of individual property rights with respect to firm membership.

Meade (1972) was the first to study LMFs in which any change in membership was constrained to be fully voluntary, though he did not describe a market mechanism to implement this principle. One way to respect Meade's principle is through the use of membership markets, where LMFs sell new memberships when they expand and buy back existing memberships when they contract. Sertel (1982) provided the first static analysis of membership markets. Dow (1986, 1993a) extended membership markets to a dynamic setting where workers collectively invest in physical assets. I refer to an LMF in which membership rights are traded on competitive markets as a Sertel-Dow (SD) firm, in contrast to the WDV firm.

In the SD model, ex ante control rights are held by a well-defined group of worker-owners who expand or contract the firm when it is in their interest to do so. I show in this chapter that such LMFs maximize profit rather than income per capita. The membership market induces unanimous support for profit maximization among the ex ante worker-owners, even if the size of the workforce is decreased as a result. This occurs because the SD firm must buy back the membership rights of departing workers, which compensates these workers for the loss of their claims on firm profit. Such an economy supports the same resource allocations as a Walrasian economy.

I begin in Section 3.2 by discussing a single firm and the differences between the WDV and SD models. After this elementary treatment, Section 3.3 describes the SD model for an economy with a single consumption good. Section 3.4 constructs an equilibrium for the SD economy, while Section 3.5 establishes that SD equilibria are isomorphic to Walrasian equilibria.

Section 3.6 returns to the comparison between the WDV and SD models. I will show that both the WDV and SD models satisfy an ex post optimality condition: starting from the equilibrium labor input of the firm, no ex post member can gain from a deviation to a different membership size. But unlike the WDV firm, the SD firm satisfies the further condition that no ex ante member can gain from a deviation to a different membership size. Section 3.7 concludes with reflections on the recent literature in this area.

3.2 From the WDV Firm to the SD Firm

Consider a firm with two inputs, labor and capital, and one output. Profit is

$$\pi(L, K) \equiv pf(L, K) - wL - rK \qquad (1)$$

The prices (p, w, r) are positive and determined on competitive markets. I will limit attention to short run situations where capital is fixed and positive $(K > 0)$, so the only choice variable is L. The production function has $f'(L, K) > 0$ and $f''(L, K) < 0$ for all (L, K) where primes indicate differentiation with respect to labor. I assume that $f'(0, K) = \infty$ and $f'(\infty, K) = 0$.

For a profit-maximizing firm, textbook analysis gives the first order condition

$$pf'(L, K) = w \qquad (2)$$

The (sufficient) second order condition holds by assumption. This yields a unique solution for L and leads to the standard comparative static results: labor demand and output supply are increasing functions of the output price p, variations in fixed cost do not affect the firm's short run supply decision, and so on. Under the assumptions of this section, the firm produces positive output at any positive price.

A WDV firm instead maximizes net income per worker, where I assume that each worker supplies one unit of labor time. This objective function will be called the (labor) dividend and will be written as

$$d(L, K) \equiv [pf(L, K) - rK]/L \tag{3}$$

The wage w plays no role in the WDV objective function. In order for maximization of d(L, K) to make sense, we require rK > 0. Otherwise, the firm would maximize the average product of labor, which gives an arbitrarily small labor input. With a positive fixed cost, the first order condition for a maximum is

$$pf'(L, K) = d(L, K) \tag{4}$$

I ignore the second order condition for the WDV problem here, but (4) has a unique solution, and this solution is a global maximizer (see Chapter 9).

Superficially, Equation (4) is similar to Equation (2), with the wage replaced by the dividend. However, the comparative static implications are quite different because in (2) the wage w is exogenous, while in (4) the dividend d(L, K) depends on L. For this version of the WDV model, it can be shown that labor demand and output supply are decreasing functions of the output price p.

In the Sertel-Dow firm, an initial group of L^0 worker-members is entitled to choose the labor input L. If $L > L^0$, then the firm recruits $L - L^0$ new members, and if $L < L^0$, then $L^0 - L$ existing members leave. I will show that under the rules of the SD firm these departures are voluntary. Each worker who is a member of the firm at the production stage receives d(L, K) as in (3).

The maximum price any outsider would be willing to pay for membership is

$$v(L, K) \equiv d(L, K) - w \tag{5}$$

because this is the net benefit from working in the LMF and receiving the dividend d(L, K) rather than working in the external labor market and receiving the wage w. At a lower price there would be a queue of applicants, and at a higher price no one would want to join the LMF. The expression in (5) is therefore the competitive market price for an individual membership position.

The total income an initial member derives from the firm is

$$x(L, K) \equiv d(L, K) + v(L, K)(L - L^0)/L^0 \qquad (6)$$

The second term on the right-hand side reflects the fact that each new member pays $v(L, K)$ to join the firm; there are $L - L^0$ new members; and revenue from sales of new membership positions is distributed equally among the L^0 initial members. If instead some existing members leave, $L - L^0$ is negative and each departing member receives the compensation $v(L, K)$ for accepting the wage w instead of the dividend $d(L, K)$.

Some algebra shows that (6) reduces to

$$\begin{aligned} x(L, K) &= w + [pf(L, K) - wL - rK]/L^0 \\ &= w + \pi(L, K)/L^0 \end{aligned} \qquad (7)$$

Capital is fixed in the short run, the prices (p, w, r) are parametric, and L^0 reflects an exogenous initial assignment of membership rights. The only choice variable in (7) is the labor input L. Therefore the maximization of income $x(L, K)$ in (7) is equivalent to the maximization of profit $\pi(L, K)$ in (1). The first order condition in (2) applies, and as a result the comparative static behavior of the SD firm is identical to that of a profit-maximizing firm.

The total market value of membership shares is $V(L, K) \equiv v(L, K)L = \pi(L, K)$ from (5). Thus, maximizing the firm's profit is equivalent to maximizing the value of its membership shares. When I say that the membership market is "competitive," I do not mean that the firm's share value is fixed regardless of its production plan. Rather, I mean that its share value is determined using the equilibrium condition (5). It is true that individual workers regard the price of shares as parametric when they buy or sell them. However, from the standpoint of the firm as a whole, the share value adjusts in response to the firm's production plan, just as profit does.

The logic of the argument is the same as in Chapter 2. The membership market for the SD firm ensures that outsiders do not gain any surplus when they join the firm. All surplus from the firm goes to the insiders, with each appropriating an exogenously given fraction of the total. Accordingly, each insider wants to maximize total surplus. The same logic applies when some members leave the firm. All insiders support profit maximization whether or not they themselves will leave, because members who depart are fully compensated through the repurchase of their membership rights by the firm.

The rest of the chapter extends this idea to an economy with many firms and many workers but just one consumption good. The resulting equilibria not only yield profit maximization by every firm, but also resource allocations identical to those of a Walrasian economy. I suppress the capital stock K and the fixed cost rK, which play no substantive role in Sections 3.3–3.5.

3.3 The Labor-Managed Economy: Description

Workers are indexed by $i = 1.. I$, and firms are indexed by $j = 1.. J$. There is a single consumption good whose price is normalized at unity, and all firms produce this good. Because there is only one good, there is no need for utility functions; each agent simply maximizes consumption.

I adopt the following notation:

Endowments
- $\underline{L}_i \equiv$ worker i's endowment of labor time
- $L_j^0 \equiv$ total ex ante stock of membership deeds for firm j
- $L_{ij}^0 \equiv$ worker i's ex ante stock of membership deeds for firm j
  where $\sum_{i=1}^{I} L_{ij}^0 = L_j^0$ for all $j = 1.. J$
- $\theta_{ij} \equiv L_{ij}^0 / L_j^0 \equiv$ worker i's endowed share of firm j's ex ante membership deeds

Resource allocation
- $L_{ij} \equiv$ labor supplied by worker i to firm j
  $\equiv$ worker i's ex post stock of membership deeds for firm j
- $L_j \equiv$ total labor input for firm j
- $f_j(L_j) \equiv$ total output from firm j
- $x_i \equiv$ worker i's consumption level

Prices
- $v_j \equiv$ price of an individual membership deed in firm j
- $w \equiv$ implicit wage per hour of labor

The $\underline{L}_i$ and L_j^0 are positive. All other variables are nonnegative. The production functions satisfy $f_j' > 0$ and $f_j'' < 0$, with $f_j'(0) = +\infty$ and $f_j'(\infty) = 0$ for all j. The individual workers treat the prices v_j as parametric when buying or selling membership deeds. The nature of the implicit wage w will be discussed later in this chapter.

Transactions proceed in three stages:

Stage 1. The manager of each firm j chooses a labor demand L_j (I will provide an interpretation of the manager's role later in this section). This determines the number of membership deeds offered for sale to individual workers. Deeds of firm j are supplied to the market from two sources. First, workers sell off their endowments L_{ij}^0, yielding the supply L_j^0. Second, if $L_j > L_j^0$, then firm j sells new deeds in the amount of $L_j - L_j^0$. If $L_j < L_j^0$, then the firm repurchases existing deeds in the amount of $L_j^0 - L_j$. Either way, the net supply of membership deeds on the market equals the firm's labor demand L_j.

Stage 2. After each firm manager has chosen L_j and the net supply of membership deeds for each firm has been determined, each worker i buys a portfolio of deeds $(L_{i1}.. L_{iJ})$. In purchasing L_{ij} deeds of firm j, worker i promises to provide this number of labor hours to firm j. Worker i's portfolio must satisfy the constraint $\sum_{j=1}^{J} L_{ij} \leq L_i$ so that these promises can be carried out. Transactions in the membership market take place at prices $(v_1.. v_J)$ such that the total demand by workers for each firm's deeds equals the available supply L_j.

Stage 3. Each worker supplies labor to firms according to his or her membership portfolio. After production occurs, worker i gets the fraction $\theta_{ij} \equiv L_{ij}/L_j$ of firm j's output.

Next, consider the consumption level of worker i. This is given by

$$x_i \equiv \sum_{j=1}^{J} \underline{\theta}_{ij}(L_j - L_j^0)v_j + \sum_{j=1}^{J}(L_{ij}^0 - L_{ij})v_j$$
$$+ \sum_{j=1}^{J} L_{ij}f_j(L_j)/L_j \quad \text{where} \tag{8}$$

(a) The first summation in (8) is worker i's share in the revenue from each firm's sale of new membership deeds. This revenue is distributed in proportion to the ex ante deed endowments $\underline{\theta}_{ij}$. If $L_j < L_j^0$, then firm j repurchases existing deeds and worker i must contribute a share $\underline{\theta}_{ij}$ of the expenditure for this purpose.

(b) The second summation in (8) is worker i's net revenue from portfolio adjustments involving the sale of the L_{ij}^0 and the purchase of the L_{ij}.

(c) The third summation in (8) is the stream of dividends flowing to worker i from the ex post portfolio $(L_{i1}.. L_{iJ})$.

Using the identity $\underline{\theta}_{ij} \equiv L_{ij}^0/L_j^0$ in (8), worker i's consumption level simplifies to

$$x_i = \sum_{j=1}^{J} v_j(\underline{\theta}_{ij}L_j - L_{ij}) + \sum_{j=1}^{J} L_{ij}f_j(L_j)/L_j \qquad (9)$$

Note that x_i is linear in L_{ij}. I will provide a formal definition of equilibrium later, but in any reasonable definition the membership prices v_j must equalize the net return $f_j(L_j)/L_j - v_j$ per hour of labor in each firm. Otherwise, all workers would demand deeds in firms where the net return is highest and supply zero labor to firms having lower net returns.

Equalization of net returns yields a uniform implicit wage w. Writing the share prices as a function of labor demands and this implicit economy-wide wage, we have

$$v_j(L_j, w) = f_j(L_j)/L_j - w \quad j = 1 .. J \qquad (10)$$

The definition of equilibrium will include a requirement that the aggregate demand and supply of labor be equal, and this condition will determine the wage level in (10).

Substituting (10) into (9) gives

$$\begin{aligned} x_i &= \sum_{j=1}^{J} \underline{\theta}_{ij}[f_j(L_j) - wL_j] + w\sum_{j=1}^{J} L_{ij} \\ &= \sum_{j=1}^{J} \underline{\theta}_{ij}V_j(L_j, w) + w\sum_{j=1}^{J} L_{ij} \end{aligned} \qquad (11)$$

The first expression in the first line is worker i's ex ante claim on firm profits, computed using the implicit wage w, and the second expression is worker i's imputed labor income, again using the implicit wage w. The second line follows from the fact that firm j's profit is identical to the aggregate value of its membership shares $V_j(L_j, w) = v_j(L_j, w)L_j$.

We can now define a Sertel-Dow equilibrium.

Definition

An SD equilibrium consists of a *labor allocation* $(L_1^* .. L_J^*)$; a collection of *worker portfolios* $(L_{i1}^* .. L_{iJ}^*)$, i = 1.. I; a vector of *membership prices* $(v_1^* .. v_J^*)$; and an *implicit wage* w^* satisfying the following five conditions.

(a) *Feasibility of total labor demand*

$$\sum_{j=1}^{J} L_j^* \leq \sum_{i=1}^{I} \underline{L}_i.$$

(b) *Equality of labor supply and demand for each firm*

$$\sum_{i=1}^{I} L_{ij}^{*} = L_{j}^{*} \qquad \text{for all } j = 1..\,J.$$

(c) *Equilibrium membership prices*

$$v_j* = v_j(L_j*, \, w*) \qquad \text{for all } j = 1..\,J.$$

(d) *Optimal membership portfolios*
Fix $L_j = L_j^*$ and $v_j = v_j^*$ in Equation (9) for all $j = 1..\,J$. For each $i = 1..\,I$, the portfolio $(L_{i1}^*..\,L_{iJ}^*)$ maximizes worker i's consumption x_i in (9) subject to the labor endowment constraint $\sum_{j=1}^{J} L_{ij} \le \underline{L}_i$.

(e) *Optimal labor demands*
Fix $w = w^*$ in (11). Let L_{-j} be the vector of labor inputs for the $J-1$ firms other than firm j. For each (i, j), any fixed L_{-j}, and any fixed $(L_{i1}..\,L_{iJ})$, the input L_j^* maximizes worker i's consumption x_i in (11).

The rationale for conditions (a)–(d) in the Sertel-Dow equilibrium definition should be clear. The unusual condition is (e), which imposes a strong form of unanimity with respect to each firm's production plan. In equilibrium, it must be true for each firm j that no worker can gain from any deviation $L_j \ne L_j^*$, regardless of the production plans that may be adopted by the other firms and the portfolio of membership deeds the individual worker may hold. Whether such equilibria exist will be taken up in Section 3.4.

Condition (e) has the following interpretation. The manager of firm j reports to the ex ante members of firm j. Assume that these ex ante firm members have voting rights in proportion to their endowments L_{ij}^0, so worker i has the vote share $\underline{\theta}_{ij}$. When (e) holds, the plan L_j^* receives unanimous support from the ex ante members of firm j, no matter what the managers of other firms may do and no matter how the individual agents plan to allocate their labor endowments across firms. The manager of firm j therefore adopts the equilibrium plan L_j^*.

There is an important distinction between the optimization problem facing an individual worker in (d) and the problem of the manager in (e). When choosing their portfolios, individual workers treat the production plans L_j^* and the membership prices v_j^* as parametric. Thus, an individual worker i calculates the consumption level x_i by substituting the equilibrium values L_j^* and v_j^* into (9) and treating the portfolio $(L_{i1}..\,L_{iJ})$ as a choice variable.

Firm managers regard the wage w^* as parametric because they believe they have no influence on the net return available to workers elsewhere in the economy. However, the managers understand that they determine the membership prices for their own firms, because they control the supply of deeds for their own firms. In particular, the manager of firm j knows that for any choice of L_j, the price v_j will settle at a level where the net return to a worker in firm j is equal to the implicit wage w^* available elsewhere. This relationship is given by (10). Thus, the manager of firm j calculates the consumption level x_i by substituting the equilibrium value w^* into (11) and treating the labor input L_j as a choice variable. When the manager of firm j maximizes profit, she automatically maximizes the aggregate market value of firm j's labor shares.

The present model is competitive in the usual sense that decision-makers within a firm ignore any effect of their own actions on the (implicit) prices of inputs. This point can be clarified by an analogy with capitalist stock market economies. Managers in capitalist firms regard the opportunity cost of capital as given but recognize that the stock market value of their own firm depends on the production plan they choose. Without this recognition, the idea that a manager maximizes the stock market value of the firm would be meaningless. Individual shareholders want the manager of a capitalist firm to maximize its market value because this enhances their own consumption opportunities. At the same time, individual investors regard the share prices of firms as parametric when choosing their personal financial portfolios.

3.4 The Labor-Managed Economy: Equilibrium

We next construct an equilibrium of the SD variety, thereby proving existence. The proof also shows the reason for unanimity with respect to production plans: a profit-maximizing input choice by firm j maximizes the consumption opportunities of every ex ante member of firm j simultaneously.

Proposition 1
An SD equilibrium satisfying requirements (a)–(e) in Section 3.3 exists.

Proof
Each requirement will be considered in sequence.

(a) First we derive the economy-wide implicit wage w^* by equating the aggregate demand and supply of labor. Define the labor demand functions $L_j(w)$ using the identities $f_j'[L_j(w)] \equiv w$ for all $j = 1..\ J$. Let $w^* > 0$ be the unique implicit wage satisfying $\sum_{j=1}^{J} L_j(w) = \sum_{i=1}^{I} \underline{L}_i$.

Such a w^* exists due to the assumption that $f_j'(0) = \infty$ and $f_j'(\infty) = 0$ for all $j = 1.. J$. Next choose the labor allocation $(L_1^* .. L_J^*)$ so that $L_j^* = L_j(w^*)$ for all $j = 1.. J$. This ensures that condition (a) holds.

(b) To satisfy condition (b), set $L_{ij}^* = (\underline{L}_i /\Sigma_{i=1}^I \underline{L}_i)L_j^*$ for all (i, j). The vector $(L_{i1}^* .. L_{iJ}^*)$ is worker i's portfolio. This gives $\Sigma_{i=1}^I L_{ij}^* = L_j^*$ for all $j = 1.. J$.

(c) Choose the membership prices $v_j^* = v_j(L_j^*, w^*)$ for all $j = 1 .. J$ using (10). The v_j^* are strictly positive because $v_j(L_j^*, w^*) = f_j(L_j^*)/L_j^* - f_j'(L_j^*) > 0$.

(d) Upon substituting the L_j^* from (a) and the v_j^* from (c) into (9), we obtain

$$x_i = \sum_{j=1}^J \underline{\theta}_{ij} v_j^* L_j^* + \sum_{j=1}^J L_{ij}[f_j(L_j^*)/L_j^* - v_j^*]$$
$$= \sum_{j=1}^J \underline{\theta}_{ij} v_j^* L_j^* + w^* \sum_{j=1}^J L_{ij}$$

Worker i has no control over any term in the first summation and thus wants a portfolio $(L_{i1} .. L_{iJ})$ that maximizes $\Sigma_{j=1}^J L_{ij}$ subject to $\Sigma_{j=1}^J L_{ij} \leq \underline{L}_i$. Any portfolio such that the constraint holds with equality solves this problem. This includes the portfolio $(L_{i1}^* .. L_{iJ}^*)$ from (b), using the fact that $\Sigma_{j=1}^J L_j^* = \Sigma_{i=1}^I \underline{L}_i$ from (a).

(e) Consider any $i = 1 .. I$ and any $j = 1 .. J$. Fix L_{-j} and $(L_{i1} .. L_{iJ})$ in (11). Set $w = w^*$ as in (a). If $\underline{\theta}_{ij} > 0$, maximization of x_i with respect to L_j in (11) gives the first order condition $f_j'(L_j) = w^*$, which is both necessary and sufficient for a solution. From (a), L_j^* satisfies this first order condition so L_j^* maximizes x_i. If $\underline{\theta}_{ij} = 0$, then worker i is indifferent toward L_j, and hence L_j^* weakly maximizes x_i.

This completes the proof.

3.5 Comparison with the Walrasian Economy

The Pareto efficiency of the equilibrium labor and output allocation $(L_1^* .. L_J^*; x_1^* .. x_I^*)$ from Section 3.4 is easily verified. All firms equate the marginal product of labor to a common implicit wage rate, so marginal products are equalized across firms and aggregate output is maximized. Because there is a single consumption good, any distribution of this maximum output is efficient.

Proposition 2
An SD equilibrium is Pareto efficient.

Proof
As above

From (11), the equilibrium consumption level for worker i is

$$x_i* = w*\underline{L}_i + \sum_{j=1}^{J} \underline{\theta}_{ij}[f_j(L_j*) - w * L_j*]$$

The first term is the equilibrium value of i's labor endowment. The second is i's share in economy-wide profits. The profit of a particular firm j is paid out in proportion to the ex ante share endowments of individual workers. Any desired distribution of this profit can be achieved through a corresponding distribution of the membership endowments.

The isomorphism between the SD economy and a twin Walrasian economy is transparent. The implicit wage w* corresponds to the Walrasian wage that clears the labor market. At this wage, firms hire identical amounts of labor in the two economies, so outputs and the allocation of labor across firms are the same. The two economies can also support identical distributions of the consumption good. The labor endowments $\underline{L}_i$ play parallel roles in distributing output. In the Walrasian case, the distribution of profit across consumers is determined by ordinary share endowments, while in the SD case it is determined by membership share endowments.

Proposition 3
The allocations supportable in the SD economy and its Walrasian twin are identical.

Proof
As above

Chapters 4 and 5 will show that this equivalence result extends to models with investment decisions, many consumption goods, many productive inputs in each firm, heterogeneous labor, and a labor-leisure trade-off. Moreover, SD firms can coexist with capitalist firms. The implicit wage rate for LMFs is then just the explicit wage paid in the capitalist sector. In this case, membership prices for LMFs settle at levels such that the net return to labor in each LMF is equal to the wage paid to employees in KMFs.

3.6 Ex Ante and Ex Post Workers' Control

To decide whether a particular formal model corresponds to a firm that is "labor-managed," we need some criteria. It is helpful to distinguish between ex ante and ex post workers' control, depending on whether the firm's membership has already been determined through market transactions. Ex post, we want to know whether the members of firm j would seek revisions to the firm's labor demand L_j. Ex ante, we want to know whether the choice of L_j is in the interest of any definite set of agents. I compare the Ward-Domar-Vanek firm to the Sertel-Dow firm on each of these criteria.

Ex post. Consider the WDV model where firms adopt a level of labor input that maximizes per capita income. First, note that if we interpret this objective as the average product of labor and make the same technological assumptions as in Sections 3.3–3.5, the WDV firm has an arbitrarily small membership because the average product of labor goes to infinity as labor input goes to zero. Such problems can be avoided by adding a fixed cost to the model, which does not alter the previous results for the SD economy.

Let the WDV labor input be L_j'. Suppose that the firm considers a deviation to some other membership size $L_j \neq L_j'$. If $L_j > L_j'$, then all existing workers remain in the firm and some new workers enter. This reduces income per worker and is opposed by the existing members (the interests of the prospective entrants to the firm are ignored). On the other hand, if $L_j < L_j'$, then some current members must be expelled. Income per worker falls for those who remain in the firm, so the deviation is opposed by anyone who expects to continue as a member. The WDV model is silent on the fate of the expelled workers and the procedure by which they are selected, but it is reasonable to assume that they are no better off (otherwise they would already have left the firm voluntarily). It follows that no ex post member of the WDV firm wants to revise L_j' once it has been achieved.

Now consider the SD firm in an equilibrium state. It is convenient to define the ex post membership shares $\theta_{ij}{}^* \equiv L_{ij}{}^*/L_j{}^*$. Suppose that firm j considers a deviation to some $L_j \neq L_j{}^*$. Would this move ever be endorsed by those workers for whom $\theta_{ij}{}^* > 0$ (i.e., the ex post members of firm j)?

The answer is no. Section 3.4 showed that profit maximization by firm j is unanimously supported by the ex ante deedholders—those workers for whom $\underline{\theta}_{ij} > 0$. This is true for an arbitrary initial stock of deeds $L_j{}^0$ and an arbitrary distribution $(\underline{\theta}_{1j} .. \underline{\theta}_{Ij})$ of these deeds among individual agents. By the same reasoning, profit maximization is still unanimously supported when we replace $L_j{}^0$ by $L_j{}^*$ and $(\underline{\theta}_{1j} .. \underline{\theta}_{Ij})$ by $(\theta_{1j}{}^* .. \theta_{Ij}{}^*)$. Because the ex post members of firm j cannot gain by deviating from L_j^* to some other labor input, the SD firm also passes the ex post test for workers' control.

The SD firm maximizes profit rather than the labor dividend defined in (3), so it is generally true that firm members can increase the dividend by deviating to some $L_j \neq L_j^*$. But the incumbent workers in the SD firm are not interested only in the dividend. They are also concerned with the revenues or costs to the firm in the membership market when it deviates to $L_j \neq L_j^*$. This concern is captured by the first summation in (8). A worker who understands the pricing mechanism for membership deeds—that is, one who knows that the revised deed price will be $v_j = v_j(L_j, w^*)$ from (10)—will oppose deviations from L_j^* that raise income per worker, because deviations of this sort reduce consumption after transactions in the membership market are taken into account.

Ex ante. The key weakness of the WDV model is its failure to specify whose ex ante interests are served by the maximization of income per worker. Before the number or identity of the firm members has been determined, in what sense is the labor input L_j' selected by workers? To put the question another way, if a firm is run by a dictator who is accountable to no one, should we call the firm "labor-managed" merely because workers recruited by the dictator cannot gain from ex post revisions in the firm's membership?

In the SD model, the profit-maximizing choice of L_j serves the interest of a well-defined constituency—namely the ex ante membership of firm j (those workers for whom $\theta_{ij} > 0$). In an ongoing labor-managed economy, the θ_{ij} are determined by past decisions to supply labor to firm j, so yesterday's ex post members are today's ex ante members. I will return to this point in Chapter 4.

Every worker wants firm managers to choose profit-maximizing production plans due to condition (e) in the definition of SD equilibrium. It is hard to imagine a stronger sense in which firms could be worker-controlled. Specifically, ex ante members always benefit from profit-maximizing decisions with respect to expansion or contraction of the firm. When the SD firm contracts, those who depart do so voluntarily by selling their membership rights to the firm at the prevailing market price. This contrasts sharply with the WDV model, where workers can be expelled against their will in order to raise the incomes of those who remain.

The analysis of Sections 3.3 and 3.4 shows that an economy consisting of labor-managed firms can replicate Walrasian equilibria in the short run without relying on free entry or corrective taxes. This is not true for WDV firms, so one should not identify the LMF in general with the Ward-Domar-Vanek firm in particular. The results also reveal that when markets are complete and competitive, a capitalist economy has no efficiency advantage over its labor-managed counterpart.

3.7 Postscript

Sections 3.1 and 3.2 are newly written. Sections 3.3–3.6 are based on the article "Replicating Walrasian Equilibria Using Markets for Membership in Labor-Managed Firms," published in *Economic Design* (Dow, 1996a). This journal has subsequently been retitled *Review of Economic Design*. I have done extensive rewriting for brevity, clarity, and style, as well as to maintain consistency with notation used in other chapters. The conclusion of the original article, which discussed why labor-managed firms are rare, has been dropped here because this topic is addressed at length later.

The 1996 article arose out of conversations with John Roemer, Leonid Hurwicz, Ernst Fehr, and Louis Putterman at a conference hosted by the Swedish Collegium for Advanced Study in the Social Sciences (SCASSS) at Uppsala University in June 1991. The "dictator question" in Section 3.6 was suggested by Ernst Fehr. Papers presented at the conference can be found in Bowles, Gintis, and Gustafsson (1993). I am grateful to Bo Gustafsson for inviting me to spend the fall of 1992 at SCASSS, where my thinking on this subject took shape. Financial support was also provided by the Social Sciences and Humanities Research Council of Canada.

Given that the Ward-Domar-Vanek model took shape in the 1950s and 1960s and had its heyday in the 1970s and 1980s, some readers may think I am beating a dead horse by continuing to criticize it today. Actually, like the legendary Monty Python parrot, this horse is only stunned. The notion that LMFs maximize income per worker still pops up from time to time in journal articles. I omit a review of these articles here, but interested readers can search the EconLit database using the term "labor-managed firm" and look for theoretically oriented titles or abstracts. I offer some further remarks on the intellectual history of the WDV model in Section 5.7.

4

The Labor-Managed Firm in the Long Run

4.1 Introduction

As discussed in Chapter 3, the Ward-Domar-Vanek firm that maximizes income per worker exhibits odd comparative static behavior. There is one important exception, however. Early theorists of the WDV firm recognized that when an otherwise identical Walrasian firm had zero profit, the behavior of the WDV firm and the Walrasian firm would coincide (Vanek, 1970; Drèze, 1976).

The reason is not hard to see. Let net income per worker in the WDV firm be $d = (pQ - rK)/L$ where Q is output, K is capital, L is labor, p is output price, and r is the price of capital. Let w be the wage paid by a Walrasian firm. Imagine that new WDV firms enter the market whenever $d > w$ (so workers receive a dividend in the WDV firm above the wage paid by the Walrasian firm) and existing WDV firms exit the market whenever $d < w$ (so workers prefer to take jobs in Walrasian firms). Long run equilibrium requires $d = w$. This implies that the profit of a Walrasian firm is zero because $pQ - rK - wL = 0$.

The WDV firm maximizes income per worker by hypothesis. A bit of calculus shows that when income per worker is maximized, the value of labor's marginal product must equal income per worker (d). In the long run, d is equal to w. Thus the value of labor's marginal product is also equal to w. This is the first order condition for profit maximization. Assuming that the second order condition is satisfied, the WDV firm must in fact be maximizing profit. As long as free entry and exit maintain zero profit, the behavior of the WDV firm and a profit-maximizing firm are identical, and the odd comparative static features of the WDV firm disappear. Labor is allocated efficiently across firms, because in every WDV firm labor's marginal value product is equal to the same external wage.

While this conclusion was somewhat reassuring for proponents of labor-managed firms, two problems remained. First, in the short run the WDV firm still had perversities of the kind discussed in Chapter 3. Second, the requirement of zero profit in the long run was clearly not reasonable in all cases. For industries with significant entry barriers, the persistence of positive profit meant that the WDV firm was not out of the woods.

In the meantime, writers skeptical of the entire concept of the labor-managed firm (not just its WDV incarnation) opened another line of attack by arguing that LMFs have defective investment incentives (Pejovich, 1969; Furubotn and Pejovich, 1970; Furubotn, 1971). The premise of the argument was entirely reasonable. As Furubotn (1976, 104) remarked, "An adequate theory of the self-managed firm must consider the preferences and wealth-increasing opportunities of those individuals *actually making economic decisions.* At any moment of time, particular individuals are members of the working collective, and it is this constituency that must decide the firm's actions in the next time frame" (emphasis in original).

It is quite true that in any coherent theory of the labor-managed firm, there must be some specific group of labor suppliers who are empowered to make decisions in each time period. It is also true that in any coherent theory, the behavior of the firm must be related to the preferences and opportunities of current individual members. A corollary is that if today's members change the labor inputs of the firm, they change the set of agents who will be collectively empowered to make decisions tomorrow.

Furubotn (1976) and Jensen and Meckling (1979), among others, used this point to argue that an LMF cannot make efficient investment decisions. The idea was that each individual member would expect to spend a finite amount of time in the firm and would put no weight on investment returns arriving after his or her departure date. For example, a worker who planned to retire in two years would not want to sacrifice wages today in exchange for investment returns that would arrive three years from now. Accordingly, LMF members would systematically undervalue investment opportunities compared to a firm that maximized present value in the usual way. This line of criticism came to be known as "the horizon problem" in the LMF literature.

The criticisms went further. LMF members with different time horizons could be expected to disagree over the investment policies of the firm, creating internal conflict. A majority of current workers might hesitate to expand the firm's membership, because the new workers might have different preferences with regard to investment decisions. And in any case, current workers would usually be unwilling to admit new members because existing members would then have to share the returns from previous investments with the newcomers. The latter issue came to be known as "the common property problem."

These arguments only make sense if one imposes certain constraints on the LMF. For example, Furubotn assumed that the LMF could not borrow against future income or liquidate its capital stock. Jensen and Meckling assumed that LMF members would be legally prohibited from selling their membership rights. Such assumptions immediately run up against the replication principle from Section 1.3. The critics provided no reason why an LMF would face constraints of this kind while a KMF would not. I will show in this chapter that when LMF members can buy and sell membership rights on a competitive market, the members unanimously support the same investment decisions as would be made by a conventional firm interested in the maximization of present value.

The saga of the horizon problem resembles the saga of the WDV model in several ways. In both cases, theorists imposed behavioral assumptions or institutional constraints on the LMF that were not imposed on the KMF. Unsurprisingly, the LMF suffered in the resulting comparison. Moreover, in both cases the theorists failed to justify the assumed asymmetries by citing any deeper differences between capital and labor. As I will argue later in the book, such differences do exist, but for the most part the LMF literature failed to identify them. Finally, in both cases assumptions that lacked a convincing theoretical foundation nevertheless had a long half-life and retain some influence today.

Sections 4.2 and 4.3 present a dynamic generalization of the static Sertel-Dow model from Chapter 3. This model includes the KMF and LMF as special cases. I will show that under suitable institutional rules, in a competitive environment, both types of firms evaluate production plans using the criterion of present value maximization.

Section 4.4 considers the distinction between capital assets owned by the firm and capital assets rented from external owners. In a competitive environment, this distinction is unimportant: the KMF can own some assets while renting others, and the same is true for the LMF. Section 4.5 discusses rent appropriation by the firm's founders. Section 4.6 is a postscript.

4.2 The Share-Goods Firm: Description

Consider a firm that comes into existence at time $t = 0$ and engages in production activities at discrete dates indexed by $t \in \{0, 1 ..\}$. The firm's activities on date t are described by the production vector (x_t, y_t), where $x_t =$ $(x_{1t} .. x_{Mt})$ is a vector of M ordinary commodities having no managerial significance and $y_t = (y_{1t} .. y_{Nt})$ is a vector of N *share goods* to which managerial prerogatives are attached. The entries in x_t and y_t are negative for inputs and positive for outputs.

For an LMF, the entries in y_t are (negatively signed) quantities of labor. If there is only one type of labor, there is only one entry in the y_t vector. However, if labor inputs differ according to skill or experience or involve different kinds of activities, each type of labor corresponds to a distinct element in the y_t vector. For an LMF, capital goods are included in the x_t vector. For a KMF, on the other hand, the entries in y_t are (negatively signed) quantities of capital, or service flows from capital goods, while labor inputs are included in x_t. The treatment of capital inputs as stocks or flows is discussed in Section 4.5. For a consumer cooperative, y_t is a vector of output quantities with positive signs. I assume that share goods are inputs of either capital or labor, but the conclusions apply to consumer cooperatives with an appropriate change in algebraic signs.

In period t, the firm's control group chooses a plan for production activities in that period as well as all future periods. A *collective plan* is a sequence of production vectors beginning with the present date and extending into the future:

$$(x^t, y^t) \equiv [x_t, \ y_t, \ x_{t+1}, \ y_{t+1}, ..].$$

The set of feasible collective plans at time t is $F[x(t), y(t)]$, where

$$x(t) \equiv [x_0, .., \ x_{t-1}]$$
$$y(t) \equiv [y_0, .., \ y_{t-1}].$$

Feasible plans in period t may thus depend on the history of past actions by the firm, including the acquisition of capital assets, maintenance activities, or learning by doing. The feasible set $F[x(t), y(t)]$ is nonempty and compact for all possible $x(t)$ and $y(t)$. Although the feasible plans in period t could depend upon the calendar date t as well as the history $x(t)$ and $y(t)$, I ignore this complication.

Let $F[x(0), y(0)] \equiv F_0$ be given. For $s > t \geq 0$, let (x^s, y^s) be the subvector of (x^t, y^t) starting with date s; let x(s) be the vector $[x(t); x_t .. x_{s-1}]$ that has the history x(t) prior to date t and follows the plan x^t through date s–1; and let y(s) be the vector $[y(t), y_t .. y_{s-1}]$ that has the history y(t) and follows the plan y^t through date s–1. To ensure intertemporal consistency of value maximization, the following technical requirements are imposed for all $s > t \geq 0$.

A1   If $(x^t, y^t) \in F[x(t), y(t)]$, then $(x^s, y^s) \in F[x(s), y(s)]$.

A2   If $(x^t, y^t) \in F[x(t), y(t)]$ and there is a plan $(x^s, y^s)' \in F[x(s), y(s)]$ where $(x^s, y^s)'$ is not necessarily identical to (x^s, y^s), then $[x_t, y_t .. x_{s-1}, y_{s-1}, (x^s, y^s)'] \in F[x(t), y(t)]$.

A1 says that if a collective plan is feasible on date t, it can be carried out at future dates, given that the intervening steps of the plan have been taken. A2 says that if the initial steps of a feasible collective plan have been taken and it becomes possible to adopt a new continuation of the original plan later, the original constraint set $F[x(t), y(t)]$ must have allowed this sequence of actions. Under this assumption, the set F_0 and the history $x(t), y(t)$ suffice to identify $F[x(t), y(t)]$. Consistency axioms for intertemporal choice models are discussed in Dow (1984).

For control rights to have any significance in the periods s > t, decision-makers in period t must have a limited capacity to bind the firm's actions at later dates. Although the decision-makers in period t may care about the firm's subsequent actions, I assume that they only control the firm's period t production vector. Any production vector that is the first step of a feasible collective plan at date t can be adopted on that date.

For each t, there is a vector of spot prices for ordinary goods, $p_t = (p_{1t} .. p_{Mt})$, and a vector of shadow prices for share goods, $w_t = (w_{1t} .. w_{Nt})$. In an LMF for which labor is differentiated, w_t will be the vector of (shadow) wages for the various labor inputs. The shadow price of an input is the opportunity cost incurred by its owner in supplying it to the firm—that is, the best return available by deploying the same resource elsewhere in the economy. Price-taking behavior requires that spot and shadow prices be perceived as unaffected by a firm's collective plan and also by the decisions of individual agents about participation in the firm. In the event that a share-goods firm competes with other firms that hire share goods directly as ordinary inputs, the relevant shadow prices are simply the explicit prices at which these inputs are hired by the latter firms. All future spot and shadow prices are assumed to be known by the current decision-makers. This certainty assumption is adopted mainly to prevent a proliferation of subscripts. The arguments in this chapter can be readily extended to a model with state-contingent claims.

Individuals supply share goods to the firm by purchasing the corresponding shares or memberships. The share of the firm's input requirement y_{nt} supplied by agent i on date t will be denoted by θ_{int}. Contributing a share good to the firm entitles an individual to a dividend payment that will be specified later. A single person may supply more than one type of share good (e.g., both labor and capital) in the same period by purchasing separate shares of each type, provided that multiple share goods exist. I assume that labor, capital, and other goods are infinitely divisible and that individuals can diversify their contributions of labor, capital, or other goods across firms.

The sequence of events runs as follows:

Production decisions. At the beginning of period t, the suppliers of share goods from period t–1 collectively choose the production vector (x_t, y_t) for period t. I use the notation $\underline{\theta}_{int} \equiv \theta_{in,t-1}$ to indicate the ex ante share positions in period t. I will show in Section 4.4 that ex ante shareholders are unanimous, so the specific collective choice procedure used by the firm is unimportant. However, for concreteness one can imagine that suppliers of share good n have aggregate voting power equal to $\beta_n > 0$ where $\Sigma\beta_n = 1$ and that individual suppliers of share good n have voting rights proportional to $\underline{\theta}_{int}$.

Participation decisions. After (x_t, y_t) has been chosen in period t, both members and nonmembers of the firm (the latter having $\underline{\theta}_{int} = 0$ for all n) can buy or sell shares in light of the announced production vector. Because the share θ_{int} obliges individual i to supply a physical quantity of share good n in period t, the constraint $0 \leq \theta_{int} \leq 1$ applies (no short positions). An individual is also constrained to buy a share θ_{int} compatible with her endowment of share good n in period t. Trading occurs at share prices determined by the equilibrium conditions

$$\sum_i \theta_{int} = 1 \qquad \text{for all } n = 1.. N.$$

The aggregate value of type n-shares at date t will be denoted by V_{nt}.

Dividend payments. After trading ceases, production occurs, and the firm obtains the inner product $p_t x_t$ as net revenue from the purchase and sale of ordinary goods. This revenue is distributed as dividends to the suppliers of share goods in period t. The total dividend paid on participation with respect to share good n is

$$\beta_n(p_t x_t + w_t y_t) - w_{nt} y_{nt}$$

This is distributed across individuals in proportion to their ex post shares θ_{int}. The β_n are positive and sum to unity. These are fixed weights allocating imputed firm profit across suppliers of different share goods. The last term in the dividend expression is an imputed value assigned to contributions of type n, which is a bonus when good n is an input (so $y_{nt} < 0$). The sum of all dividend payments is $p_t x_t$, as required for budget balancing.

4.3 The Share-Goods Firm: Value Maximization

In an environment of certainty, all individuals and firms can borrow and lend at a common interest rate in each period. To avoid intertemporally inconsistent planning in a regime of period-by-period decisions, I assume that this interest rate is constant through time. For familiar reasons, these conditions induce all individuals to evaluate personal investment opportunities in present value terms.

This section shows that under the institutional rules described earlier, the ex ante shareholders of each type, in each period, unanimously support the goal of present value maximization by the firm. As a result, the behavior of a share-goods firm is identical to that of a Walrasian firm. The argument parallels DeAngelo's (1981) proof of unanimity for shareholders in an environment of uncertainty.

For individual i, the net benefit from participation in the firm in period t is

$$\sum\nolimits_n \{\theta_{int}[\beta_n(p_t x_t + w_t y_t) - w_{nt} y_{nt}] - V_{nt}(\theta_{int} - \underline{\theta}_{int}) + \theta_{int} w_{nt} y_{nt}\} \quad (1)$$

The first term in this expression is the dividend received from share-good participation. The second is the cost of i's net change in share holdings during period t, and the third is the opportunity cost of share-good contributions. By the sign convention, the third term is negative if share good n is an input and positive if it is an output.

In (1), the spot prices p_t and shadow prices w_t are parametric for the firm and for all individuals. The firm's production vector (x_t, y_t) is announced before decisions about share participation and is taken as given by individuals when they choose the shares θ_{int}. These shares are chosen in light of the market share prices V_{nt}, which are parametric for individuals but vary with the firm's collective plan as described in Equation (4).

On date t, the present value to individual i from participation in the firm is

$$PV_{it} = \sum\nolimits_{s=t}^{\infty} \delta^s \sum\nolimits_n [\theta_{ins} \beta_n (p_s x_s + w_s y_s) - V_{ns}(\theta_{ins} - \underline{\theta}_{ins})] \quad (2)$$

where the discount factor δ is common to all parties. Recalling that $\underline{\theta}_{ins} = \theta_{in,s-1}$, some manipulation of the summation over s yields

$$PV_{it} = \sum_n \delta^t \underline{\theta}_{int} V_{nt} + \sum_{s=t}^{\infty} \delta^s \sum_n \theta_{ins}[\beta_n(p_s x_s + w_s y_s)$$
$$+ \delta V_{n,s+1} - V_{ns}] \tag{3}$$

The maximand PV_{it} is the component of individual i's wealth on date t that is attributable to planned investments in the supply of inputs to the firm. An increase in PV_{it} implies an expansion of agent i's budget set and thus is to be favored.

Now consider the determination of the share prices V_{nt}. For any collective plan involving the production vector (x_t, y_t), individual participation decisions in period t will ensure that V_{nt} satisfies

$$V_{nt} = \beta_n(p_t x_t + w_t y_t) + \delta V_{n,t+1} \qquad \text{for all } n = 1 .. N \text{ and all } t \geq 0 \tag{4}$$

This follows from the fact that in share market equilibrium, the coefficient of θ_{int} in (3) must be zero. If V_{nt} is greater than the right-hand side of (4), the coefficient of θ_{int} in (3) is negative, so all agents set $\theta_{int} = 0$. This violates the equilibrium condition $\Sigma_i \theta_{int} = 1$ and means that the corresponding shares are in excess supply. If V_{nt} is less than the right-hand side of (4), the coefficient of θ_{int} in (3) is positive and all agents choose the highest-possible level of θ_{int} permitted by their physical endowments of share good n in period t. Assuming that the economy-wide endowment of this good exceeds the firm's demand, as will be true in a competitive setting, the corresponding shares are in excess demand. The equilibrium condition (4) in effect says that a competitive firm must offer input suppliers a return equal to what they can get elsewhere in the economy.

If agents in period t anticipate (correctly) that (4) will hold for all periods $s \geq t$, the resulting difference equation can be solved to obtain current share prices as a function of the firm's collective plan:

$$V_{nt} = \beta_n \sum_{s=t}^{\infty} \delta^{(s-t)}(p_s x_s + w_s y_s) = \beta_n V_t \quad \text{for all } n = 1 .. N \text{ and } t \geq 0 \tag{5}$$

where V_t is the present value of the firm's profit stream in period t and V_{nt} is the part of this present value assigned to suppliers of share good n. Using the equilibrium condition (4), the present value for individual i in (3) reduces to

$$PV_{it} = \delta^t \alpha_{it} V_t \qquad \text{where } \alpha_{it} \equiv \sum_n \underline{\theta}_{int} \beta_n \geq 0 \qquad (6)$$

Each individual with a positive ex ante share position $\underline{\theta}_{int} > 0$ for one or more share goods has $\alpha_{it} > 0$. These agents are the control group for the firm in period t and are responsible for choosing (x_t, y_t). All such agents favor a collective plan that maximizes V_t. This goal is independent of the inputs supplied by an individual agent, the agent's preferences about consumption goods, and the agent's intentions regarding future participation in the firm.

The unanimous preference for value maximization among each period's control group motivates the following definition:

A collective plan (x^0, y^0) is an *equilibrium plan* if (x^t, y^t) maximizes V_t over $F[x(t), y(t)]$ for all $t \geq 0$.

Using the intertemporal consistency of the F sets and the present value criterion, it is easy to show that (x^0, y^0) is an equilibrium plan if and only if it maximizes V_0 over F_0. Given that an equilibrium plan has been implemented thus far and the control group in period t expects value-maximizing decisions by the control group in period t+1, it can be shown that the period t controllers have no incentive to deviate from the equilibrium plan. When the value-maximizing collective plan is unique, the controllers in period t strictly prefer to follow the equilibrium plan, given that value maximization is expected in period t+1.

These conclusions are unaffected by whether labor and capital is the input with share-good status. Moreover, a Walrasian firm using the same technology as the share-goods firm, and facing explicit prices for share goods equal to the opportunity costs w_t, also adopts a production plan that maximizes V_t in each period. Because the Walrasian and share-goods firms adopt identical production plans at given prices, their comparative static properties are identical. In particular, an LMF that adheres to the rules of the share-goods firm inherits the behavioral and efficiency properties of the Walrasian firm.

4.4 Collective Ownership and Rental of Capital

Capital inputs can be represented in the technology of the share-goods firm in two ways. First, producer durables such as structures or machinery could appear as negative entries in the firm's production vector on some date t. The services of these inputs would then be registered implicitly by their effect on the set of feasible collective plans at dates s ≥ t. Alternatively, the service flows from capital goods could be treated as inputs. The firm would then purchase service flows of each type in each period, leaving acquisition and maintenance of the assets themselves to the external parties who own them.

Which representation is used depends on the contractual status of capital assets rather than technological factors. I refer to the first as *collective ownership* of capital, and the second as capital *rental*. In the collective ownership mode, the firm must make investment decisions: that is, decisions about the purchase of producer durables whose benefits are implicit in the production vectors available on future dates. In the rental mode, there are no "investment" decisions per se, because the firm purchases capital services in the period when they yield their return.

The KMF can use either mode of capital supply, and the same is true for the LMF. A modern corporation is a KMF in which physical assets are "contributed" by shareholders when they are purchased by the firm. These assets are owned and managed collectively, and the stock market value of the firm reflects the present value of the future services to be derived from them. In an LMF using the collective ownership mode, the firm acquires physical assets directly, these assets are managed by the members, and the market value of labor shares reflects the present value of future services to be derived from the assets.

In a KMF using the rental mode, individuals retain ownership of capital assets and exercise voting rights in proportion to the flow of capital services supplied by each agent. An LMF using the rental mode is similar but does not grant any voting rights to the asset owners. Either the KMF or LMF can own some physical assets while renting others. In this case, the market value of a capital or labor share includes the value of future services for assets owned by the firm, but not for assets rented from external owners.

4.5 Rent Appropriation

Ex ante share positions in period $t = 0$ are interpreted as follows. From (6), the maximized rent V_0 is shared among initial claimants in proportion to $\alpha_{i0} \equiv \Sigma_n \underline{\theta}_{in0}\beta_n$. Because persons who lack shares at the founding stage obtain no rents from their later participation in the firm, it is a matter of indifference to outsiders how the weights β_n are fixed at the outset, and the founding insiders will be concerned with the $\underline{\theta}_{in0}$ and β_n only insofar as these determine the α_{i0}.

These initial shares do not reflect the contribution of inputs to the firm, but rather the value to the founders of controlling access to the production technology represented by the feasible set F_0. If the same technology is available to others, "long run" forces of entry and exit will drive this rent to zero in the initial period. However, if technological knowledge is proprietary or there are nonmarketed inputs specific to the firm, positive rents may arise.

The founders of an LMF can appropriate the present value of their production technology by selling initial-period labor shares. This is analogous to a firm in which a capitalist entrepreneur sells equity shares through an initial public offering. One might think that legal rules requiring firms to be organized as LMFs (or KMFs) would lead to inefficiencies by limiting the set of feasible contractual arrangements, but in a world of complete and competitive markets, this intuition is not correct. Because each successive control group pursues value maximization, no inefficiency arises, and a constraint that the founding members must organize the firm as an LMF does not bind. The entrepreneurial rent appropriated by the firm founders will be identical under LMF, KMF, and Walrasian institutional arrangements.

4.6 What Does the Model Show?

This chapter shows that in an environment of complete and competitive markets, control rights can be assigned to any set of input suppliers (or output demanders) without endangering allocative efficiency. In particular, the share-goods model establishes that the following results hold regardless of the input suppliers who have control rights.

(a) At each point in time, members of the current control group adopt production plans unanimously, although the consumption preferences of individual agents and their intended dates of departure from the firm may vary.

(b) The firm's production decisions are identical to those of a Walrasian firm having the same technology and operating in the same economic environment.

(c) Production plans are intertemporally consistent, so if current controllers cannot bind the future actions of the firm, the production plan preferred by these agents will still be carried out on subsequent dates.

(d) It does not matter whether capital assets are collectively owned by the firm or rented from external owners.

Because the share-goods model includes the LMF as a special case, the LMF exhibits the behavioral and efficiency properties of the Walrasian firm.

This conclusion runs counter to many adverse judgments that have been rendered on the efficiency of workers' control, even by its proponents. These negative judgments have generally resulted from the imposition of dysfunctional behavioral or institutional rules on LMFs without any imposition of parallel dysfunctions on KMFs. In the Ward-Domar-Vanek model, the absence of a membership market causes the LMF to ignore labor's opportunity cost. In the criticisms of Furubotn (1976) and Jensen and Meckling (1979), the absence of a membership market causes the LMF to underinvest. Both of these analyses violate the replication principle from Section 1.3, by constraining LMFs not to use specific organizational arrangements (a labor share market), while simultaneously assuming that KMFs can use parallel organization arrangements (a capital share market).

A corollary to be pursued in later chapters is that interesting comparisons between KMFs and LMFs require the consideration of market imperfections. The task facing both advocates and skeptics of workers' control is to identify market failures that differentially affect labor-managed and capital-managed firms, even when each is given the benefit of the doubt through the replication principle.

4.7 Postscript

Section 4.1 is new for this book. Sections 4.2–4.6 are derived from the article "Control Rights, Competitive Markets, and the Labor Management Debate," published in the *Journal of Comparative Economics* (Dow, 1986). This material has been edited for style, clarity, and notation. The 1986 article was based on a 1983 working paper (see Section 5.7 for details). Related topics are discussed in Dow (2001; 2003, ch. 7).

The horizon problem has had a major impact on the LMF literature. Partly due to concerns with this issue, a number of influential LMF advocates (Vanek, 1971a,b; Jossa and Cuomo, 1997, ch. 10) have argued that LMFs should finance their investments using debt rather than retained earnings. For a critique of Jossa and Cuomo (1997), see Dow (1998). For a recent discussion of these issues, see Jossa (2014, ch. 4). For recent discussions of LMF membership markets and related topics, see Mikami (2013, 2016).

In my view, the emphasis given to the horizon problem and to the desirability of debt financing for LMFs is misplaced for several reasons. First, at a theoretical level the horizon problem disappears when LMFs have competitive membership markets. More generally, this problem vanishes if LMF members receive compensation payments from the firm at the time of their departure that accurately reflect their share of the net present value of the firm at that point in time, because then future investment returns and debts accumulated by the firm in the past are capitalized in the payment to the member who is leaving. Second, as I discuss in Section 7.5, there is little evidence that underinvestment has been a problem in European worker cooperatives—probably due to institutional rules requiring a high level of retained earnings. Third, as I will argue in Chapters 19 and 20, LMFs have trouble financing investments from external sources of capital, so it would be counterproductive to insist that external sources be used. LMFs should be encouraged to finance investment out of retained earnings whenever possible.

5

The Labor-Managed Firm in General Equilibrium

5.1 Introduction

This chapter provides a general equilibrium framework for comparing labor management with other economic systems under competitive conditions. The analysis builds on the partial equilibrium "share goods" model from Chapter 4. In the share-goods economy, several classes of residual claim can exist for each firm, corresponding to the various input suppliers and output demanders who are assigned a role in the collective choice procedure governing the firm. When perfect competition prevails in all markets, claimants of each type unanimously support value maximization as a decision criterion, and the resulting production choices are identical to those in a Walrasian economy.

5.2 The Share-Goods Economy: Description

I consider two types of goods: ordinary and share. Ordinary goods are traded on conventional markets and are bought or sold by firms at explicit prices without any transfer of control rights. Share goods represent a generalization of the usual stock market economy to a setting with multiple kinds of residual claim.

Each firm issues as many types of residual claims as there are share goods, and these claims carry the right to participate in a collective choice procedure that determines the firm's production plan. A given type of share in a firm obligates the agent who holds it to supply (or consume) a fraction of the corresponding total input (or output) specified by the firm's production plan. In exchange, the agent receives a dividend equal to part of the firm's net income from transactions involving ordinary goods.

I will show that a model with this structure has the following features.

(a) Whether control rights are assigned to a single class of shareholders (e.g., capital suppliers, labor suppliers, or output consumers) or to some combination of input suppliers and/or output consumers, there is an imputation scheme for valuing the contributions of each group that guarantees unanimity with respect to the firm's production plan. The resulting plan is independent of the specific group(s) that have control rights, and it maximizes the total market value of the firm's shares.

(b) Regardless of the imputation scheme, if costless side payments among the initial shareholders are feasible, the production plan chosen in each firm will be identical to that chosen under the imputation scheme in (a) and unanimity will be preserved.

(c) Any allocation that can be supported by an equilibrium of a Walrasian economy with given preferences, technology, and resource endowments can be supported by an equilibrium in a parallel economy where one, several, or all goods are share goods to which control rights are assigned.

These assertions will be made more precise as the model is developed. The basic elements of a share-goods economy are as follows:

- Consumers indexed by $i = 1 .. I$
- Firms indexed by $j = 1 .. J$
- Ordinary goods traded by both consumers and firms on conventional markets, indexed by $m = 1 .. M$
- Share goods traded by consumers on conventional markets but traded by firms only through shares, indexed by $n = 1 .. N$

The following notation will be used:

- $y_j = (y_{j1} .. y_{jM}; y_{j1} .. y_{jN})$ = production plan for firm j
- $x_i = (x_{i1} .. x_{iM}; x_{i1} .. x_{iN})$ = consumption bundle for consumer i
- $b_i = (b_{i1} .. b_{iN})$ = vector of net share good purchases by consumer i from other consumers
- $\underline{x}_{im}$ = consumer i's endowment of ordinary good m
- $\underline{x}_{in}$ = consumer i's endowment of share good n
- $p = (p_1 .. p_M)$ = price vector for ordinary goods
- $w = (w_1 .. w_N)$ = price vector for share goods
- r_{jn} = imputed value assigned by firm j to share good n

- β_{jn} = fraction of firm j's imputed value paid out in dividends to n-claimants
- V_{jn} = total value of firm j's shares for share good n
- V_j = imputed value of firm j
- θ_{ijn} = consumer i's chosen fraction of claims on firm j with respect to good n
- $\underline{\theta}_{ijn}$ = consumer i's endowment of claims on firm j with respect to good n

Inputs are indicated by negative entries in production vectors, while outputs are indicated by positive entries. Goods are infinitely divisible, as are shares in firms. The goods may be delivered at various dates or in various states of nature, with the price being that of a contingent claim in the present.

A share θ_{ijn} obligates agent i to supply the quantity $\theta_{ijn}y_{jn}$ of share good n to firm j if $y_{jn} < 0$, or to consume this quantity if $y_{jn} > 0$. Firm j's imputed value is defined to be

$$V_j = \sum_m P_m Y_{jm} + \sum_n r_{jn} Y_{jn} \qquad \text{for all } j = 1 .. J \qquad (1)$$

The shares θ_{ijn} of type n held by consumer i on firm j pay out the dividend

$$\theta_{ijn}(\beta_{jn}V_j - r_{jn}Y_{jn}) \qquad (2)$$

The $\beta_{jn} > 0$ are fractions such that $\sum_n \beta_{jn} = 1$ for all $j = 1 .. J$, where β_{jn} is the exogenously determined share of firm j's imputed value paid to claimants of type n. The second term in (2) compensates n-claimants for the imputed value of their contributions. If n is an input, then this term is a bonus to the n-claimants for the input supplied, while if n is an output, then this term is a deduction for the value of the output delivered. When $\sum_i \theta_{ijn} = 1$, the sum of firm j's dividends over i and n is equal to firm j's net income from transactions in the markets for ordinary goods. This will be treated as an equilibrium condition in Section 5.3.

Some comments on the role of the imputed values r_{jn} may be useful. One way to interpret these values is that they form part of the exogenous institutional architecture of the economy, along with the income shares β_{jn} and the classification of goods as "share" or "ordinary" goods. In this interpretation, there is no requirement that the r_{jn} be equal to the equilibrium prices w_j at which consumers trade share goods. I will show that an arbitrary imputation is consistent with unanimity if costless side payments can be made within the control group. This will lead to result (b) stated earlier.

One can secure unanimity even without side payments if the imputed values r_{jn} are equal to the equilibrium prices w_j. In this interpretation, the r_{jn} are regarded as part of the market equilibrium. When firms are required to value the contributions of input suppliers (and output demanders) at their equilibrium opportunity costs, then the stronger result (a) goes through. I refer to the case $r_{jn} = w_n$ for all (j, n) as the "normal" imputation scheme.

The consumption levels x_{im} for ordinary goods are chosen directly by consumer i in the usual way. Consumption of a share good is equal to an agent's endowment of that good net of transactions with other consumers and firms:

$$x_{in} = \underline{x}_{in} + b_{in} + \sum_j \theta_{ijn} y_{jn} \qquad \text{for all } i = 1 .. \text{ I and } n - 1 .. \text{ N} \quad (3)$$

Consumer i's budget constraint is

$$0 \le \sum_n \sum_j \left[\underline{\theta}_{ijn} V_{jn} - \theta_{ijn} (V_{jn} + r_{jn} y_{jn} - \beta_{jn} V_j) \right]$$
$$- \sum_n w_n b_{in} + \sum_m P_m (\underline{x}_{im} - x_{im}) \quad (4)$$

The term involving $\underline{\theta}_{ijn}$ is the value of the share endowments of consumer i, and the term involving θ_{ijn} is the cost of shares purchased by consumer i net of the dividends paid as in (2). The term involving b_{in} is the cost of share goods acquired from other consumers, or the value of goods sold to them if $b_{in} < 0$. The term involving $\underline{x}_{im}$ and x_{im} is the value of i's physical endowment of ordinary goods minus the value of the goods purchased.

Consumer i's choice variables are the x_{im}, b_{in}, and θ_{ijn}. The prices p_m, w_n, and V_{jn} are determined in equilibrium and parametric for consumers. The endowments $\underline{\theta}_{ijn}$ and $\underline{x}_{im}$ are exogenous, as are the distributional coefficients β_{jn}. Unless the contrary is stated, I treat the imputations r_{jn} as exogenous institutional features of the firms. However, I will also be interested in situations where these imputations correspond to equilibrium prices. The determination of the production plans y_j is discussed in the next section.

5.3 The Share-Goods Economy: Equilibrium

Let U^i be consumer i's utility function, and let Y^j be firm j's technology set. I use the following assumptions:

A1 U^i is defined over a subset of the nonnegative orthant of Euclidean M+N space.

A2 U^i displays nonsatiation.

A3   Each consumer's endowment of ordinary and share goods is a feasible consumption bundle.

A4   The technology set Y^j is a subset of Euclidean M+N space containing the origin.

A5   The inner product $y_j z$ has a finite maximum over Y^j for any nonnegative vector z.

A6   The ex ante shares satisfy $\underline{\theta}_{ijn} \geq 0$ and $\Sigma_i\, \underline{\theta}_{ijn} = 1$ for all (j, n).

A7   The ex post shares satisfy $\theta_{ijn} \geq 0$.

A1–A5 are standard, but A6 and A7 require elaboration. The ex ante shares $\underline{\theta}_{ijn}$ in A6 serve two purposes simultaneously. First, they play a distributional role in the budget constraint (4) by dividing the good-n share values V_{jn} across individual agents. Second, the relative voting powers of the various claimant groups (j, n) in firm j with respect to production plans are taken to be given by the parameters β_{jn}, and within each of the (j, n) groups, the voting powers of individual agents are proportional to $\underline{\theta}_{ijn}$.

The nonnegativity of the ex post shares θ_{ijn} in A7 reflects the fact that such shares entail obligations to supply physical inputs or consume physical outputs. Similar nonnegativity constraints were used in Chapters 3 and 4. In principle, one could allow short positions ($\theta_{ijn} < 0$) by having the firm obtain excess inputs from some type n shareholders and distribute the inputs not used in production to other type n shareholders. None of the results would differ in an alternative model of this kind. However, it may be reassuring that the isomorphism with a Walrasian model discussed in Section 5.4 holds even under the more restrictive assumption in A7, so I adopt this assumption here.

It may also be helpful to discuss the way in which a firm j's shares of type n are valued. To fix ideas, suppose we are considering an LMF. In partial equilibrium models like those of Section 3.2 and Chapter 4, the value of a labor share is simply the difference between the dividend paid to a worker within the LMF and the worker's opportunity cost. The latter is the wage or net return available on the external labor market.

In a general equilibrium model, the worker's opportunity cost is endogenous. For the model developed in Sections 3.3–3.6, I argued that in equilibrium all firms must offer the same net return to workers, treated this economy-wide net return as the implicit wage, and computed the implicit wage level that cleared the labor market. This approach was straightforward in Chapter 3, because labor was the only input for each firm. However, matters become more complicated with many inputs and outputs.

I solve this problem here by allowing consumers to trade all goods, including the ones used as inputs by firms, at explicit market prices, just as they would in a Walrasian world. The price at which a consumer can trade a good with other consumers serves as the opportunity cost when a consumer supplies the same good as an input to a firm. The only difference from the Walrasian setting is that firms are constrained to acquire certain inputs through shares that have control rights attached, rather than purchasing the inputs directly at a competitive market price.

No quantity restrictions are imposed on the transactions between consumers and firms, because individual consumers believe they can buy or sell unlimited quantities of each good at the going price. A consumer who wants to supply a firm with a quantity of an input greater than his or her personal endowment can always make up the difference by purchasing additional amounts of the input from other consumers and then supplying it to the firm. I will ignore difficulties associated with the inalienability of labor in this context (see Section 2.4). The point of the exercise is to show that if the inalienability of labor can be neglected, then there is an isomorphism among Walrasian, capital-managed, and labor-managed economies. The question of how this isomorphism might break down in practice due to the inalienability of labor will be left for later chapters.

Fixing the production plans y_j defines an exchange economy in which resource endowments and the net outputs of the firms are to be allocated among the consumers. An equilibrium for such an economy is defined as follows.

An *exchange equilibrium* for the share-goods economy (relative to fixed production plans y_j for $j = 1 .. J$) is a nonnegative price vector (p, w); an array of share values V_{jn} for $j = 1 .. J$ and $n = 1 .. N$; and choice variables $(x_{i1} .. x_{iM})$, $(b_{i1} .. b_{iN})$, and $(\theta_{i11} .. \theta_{ijN})$ for $i = 1 .. I$ such that

(a) U^i is maximized with respect to consumer i's choice variables subject to (4), for each $i = 1 .. I$; and

(b) The equilibrium conditions (5), (6), and (7) are satisfied:

$$\sum_i x_{im} = \sum_i \underline{x}_{im} + \sum_j y_{jm} \qquad \text{for all } m = 1 \dots M \qquad (5)$$

$$\sum_i \theta_{ijn} = 1 \qquad \text{for all } j = 1 \dots J \text{ and } n = 1 \dots N \qquad (6)$$

$$\sum_i b_{in} = 0 \qquad \text{for all } n = 1 \dots N \qquad (7)$$

Using (3) and (6), the equilibrium condition (7) is equivalent to the more conventional market-clearing requirement

$$\sum_i x_{in} = \sum_i \underline{x}_{in} + \sum_j y_{jn} \qquad \text{for all } n = 1 \dots N \qquad (7')$$

The existence of equilibrium will be taken up in Section 5.4. For the moment it is convenient to assume that an equilibrium exists and to investigate the pricing of firm shares. In any exchange equilibrium, it must be true that

$$V_{jn} = \beta_{jn} V_j + (w_n - r_{jn}) y_{jn} \qquad \text{for all } j = 1 \dots J \text{ and } n = 1 \dots N \qquad (8)$$

The proof runs as follows: Suppose $y_{jn} > 0$, so good n is an output of firm j. The implicit price of a unit of good n from firm j is $(V_{jn} + r_{jn}y_{jn} - \beta_{jn}V_j)/y_{jn}$—that is, the total net cost of firm j's shares of type n divided by firm j's total output of good n. A consumer can also buy or sell the share good n at the explicit price w_n. If $(V_{jn} + r_{jn}y_{jn} - \beta_{jn}V_j)/y_{jn} < w_n$, then a consumer i can obtain any amount of good n from the firm by acquiring correspondingly large shares θ_{ijn} and sell good n to other consumers at the higher price w_n. This relaxes the budget constraint in (4). But then the nonsatiation assumption A2 implies that U^i was not maximized at the original levels of consumer i's choice variables, contradicting the definition of an exchange equilibrium. This gives $(V_{jn} + r_{jn}y_{jn} - \beta_{jn}V_j)/y_{jn} \geq w_n$.

Now suppose that the strict inequality holds: $(V_{jn} + r_{jn}y_{jn} - \beta_{jn}V_j)/y_{jn} > w_n$. I will show that in equilibrium no consumer can have $\theta_{ijn} > 0$. A consumer with $\theta_{ijn} > 0$ could switch to a new portfolio with $\theta_{ijn}' = 0$, choose a new net trade b_{in}' with the other consumers such that the consumption level x_{in} remains the same as in the original situation, and relax the budget constraint in (4). Due to nonsatiation, this implies that U^i was not maximized at the original levels of consumer i's choice variables, which contradicts the definition of equilibrium. But if every consumer i has $\theta_{ijn} = 0$, then the equilibrium condition (6) is violated. Together with the results in the preceding paragraph, this shows that $(V_{jn} + r_{jn}y_{jn} - \beta_{jn}V_j)/y_{jn} = w_n$ holds in any exchange equilibrium. A parallel argument applies when $y_{jn} < 0$, so good n is an input to firm j rather than an output. Thus (8) holds for these cases.

When $y_{jn} = 0$, the share θ_{ijn} does not involve any physical transaction between consumer i and firm j with regard to good n and has no effect on agent i's consumption bundle. If $\beta_{jn}V_j > V_{jn}$, then a consumer can obtain unlimited income in (4) by increasing θ_{ijn}. By nonsatiation, this is inconsistent with utility maximization. If $\beta_{jn}V_j < V_{jn}$, then no consumer can have $\theta_{ijn} > 0$ because this implies that reducing θ_{ijn} would relax the budget constraint in (4). This is also inconsistent with utility maximization. Thus all consumers must have $\theta_{ijn} = 0$, but this violates (6). Therefore $\beta_{jn}V_j = V_{jn}$, which again gives (8).

Equation (8) states the equilibrium relationship among the prices of n-shares for firm j, the production plan of the firm, and its imputation scheme. If firm j's imputation scheme $\{r_{jn}\}$ is exogenously determined, it will not generally assign good n the price w_n at which consumers trade this good directly in equilibrium. The resulting gap between the opportunity cost of the good and the value placed on it by the firm is capitalized in the value of the firm-specific claim to that good. However, if the firms value share goods at their equilibrium opportunity costs, then we obtain the *normal imputation* $r_{jn} = w_n$ for all $n = 1 .. N$. In this case, (8) indicates that the individual share values V_{jn} add up to the total market value V_j, which is firm j's profit in the usual sense.

From the standpoint of an individual consumer, the NJ assets θ_{ijn} are redundant. Their availability does not expand the budget set, because each share good could equally well be bought or sold at the explicit price w_n. The role of shares is not to allocate goods or risks among consumers, but rather to distinguish the parties responsible for managing firms and to ensure unanimity among these parties.

Assertions (a) and (b) from Section 5.2 on unanimity in the share-goods economy can now be established. In exchange equilibrium, the share prices V_{jn} can be eliminated from the budget constraint (4) by using (8), and the ex post shares θ_{ijn} can be eliminated from (4) by using (3). This gives the new budget constraint

$$\sum_m p_m x_{im} + \sum_n w_n x_{in} \le \sum_m p_m \underline{x}_{im} + \sum_n w_n \underline{x}_{in}$$
$$+ \sum_j \alpha_{ij} V_j + \sum_n \sum_j \underline{\theta}_{ijn}(w_n - r_{jn})y_{jn} \tag{9}$$

where

$$\alpha_{ij} = \sum_n \underline{\theta}_{ijn}\beta_{jn} \ge 0 \tag{10}$$

From A4, the origin is in each firm's technology set. Combining this with
(1), it is always possible to choose production plans y_j for $j = 1 .. J$ such that
the last two sums on the right-hand side of (9) are nonnegative. From A3,
each consumer's endowment of physical goods is a feasible consumption
bundle. Therefore it is possible to choose a set of production plans and
consumption bundles such that (9) is satisfied for all $i = 1 .. I$, whatever the
prices may be.

Now assume *competitivity*: each consumer believes that the prices of all
ordinary and share goods, the imputations and distributional coefficients
within all firms, and the production plans of all other firms are unaffected
by firm j's choice of y_j. Due to nonsatiation, consumer i supports
a production plan y_j that maximizes the sum of the last two terms on the
right-hand side of (9) at prevailing prices. These maximization problems
are independent across firms.

For the normal imputation, the last term in (9) vanishes, and every
consumer with $\alpha_{ij} > 0$ favors the maximization of

$$V_j = \sum_m P_m y_{jm} + \sum_n w_n y_{jn} \qquad (11)$$

by firm j. For nonnegative prices, A5 ensures that the maximum is well
defined. If $\alpha_{ij} = 0$, consumer i is indifferent toward the production plan
y_j. From A6, no consumer has $\alpha_{ij} < 0$. Recalling that a consumer i has
voting rights within firm j if and only if $\alpha_{ij} > 0$, this confirms assertion
(a) in Section 5.2, which says that there is an imputation such that the
agents with control rights in a firm unanimously support value
maximization.

Now suppose that imputation schemes are exogenous and need not
reflect equilibrium prices for share goods. If costless transfers among
consumers interested in the policies of firm j are possible, this group
will unanimously support maximization of the total income generated by
firm j, which from (9) is

$$\sum_i \alpha_{ij} V_j + \sum_i \sum_n \underline{\theta}_{ijn} (w_n - r_{jn}) y_{jn} = \sum_m P_m y_{jm} + \sum_n w_n y_{jn} \qquad (12)$$

The equality follows from A6, (1), and (10). Regardless of the imputation
formally in effect, this is the same criterion as under the normal imputation
in (11), which confirms assertion (b) from Section 5.2. Note that when
imputations are assigned arbitrarily, $\alpha_{ij} = 0$ is not a sufficient condition for
consumer i to be indifferent toward the production plan y_j. In general such
consumers must be included in the group among whom side payments are
exchanged. Also note that assertion (b) holds even when the ex ante shares

$\underline{\theta}_{ijn}$ can be negative so $\alpha_{ij} < 0$ can hold for some agents, as long as $\Sigma_i\,\underline{\theta}_{ijn} = 1$ still holds in A6.

The results in the past two paragraphs show that controllers unanimously support value maximization at arbitrary prices for ordinary and share goods (not just equilibrium prices) as long as the relevant budget constraint is given by (9). However, recall that (9) was obtained by substituting (8) into (4). It is therefore necessary that controllers grasp the valuation mechanism in (8) and believe that share values will respond to production decisions as described there. The key point is the same as the one discussed at the end of Section 3.3. When choosing the personal portfolio $\{\theta_{ijn}\}$, an individual consumer i treats the share values V_{jn} as parametric. Equilibrium in the market for firm shares yields (8) for arbitrary goods prices p_m and w_n, and arbitrary imputations r_{jn}. But when a control group makes collective decisions about a firm's production plan, its members know that *share values* for that firm are affected by their decisions as in (8), although *goods prices* are parametric for the control group. With this understanding, unanimity follows from budget set dominance. We can then determine the goods prices (for both ordinary and share goods) through the usual market-clearing conditions.

5.4 Comparison with the Walrasian Economy

In this section I show that a share-goods equilibrium exists whenever a Walrasian equilibrium exists. This section also establishes assertion (c) in Section 5.2 by showing that for any Walrasian equilibrium, the same allocation can be supported in a share-goods equilibrium as long as the preferences, technology, and goods endowments are identical.

To define a Walrasian equilibrium, consider the budget constraint

$$\sum_m p_m x_{im} + \sum_n w_n x_{in} \leq \sum_m p_m \underline{x}_{im} + \sum_n w_n \underline{x}_{in} + \sum_j \alpha_{ij} V_j \quad (13)$$

where $\alpha_{ij} \geq 0$ is consumer i's ownership share in firm j and

$$V_j = \sum_m p_m y_{jm} + \sum_n w_n y_{jn} \quad (14)$$

is the value (profit) of firm j. Because only normal imputations are used, the role of V_j as firm j's value in both the Walrasian and share-goods economies should cause no confusion.

A *Walrasian equilibrium* is a nonnegative price vector (p^*, w^*), a list of consumption bundles x_i^* for $i = 1 .. I$, and a list of production plans y_j^* for $j = 1 .. J$ such that

(a) For each $i = 1 .. I$, the bundle x_i^* maximizes U^i over the budget set from (13) and (14) at the prices (p^*, w^*) when the production plans in (14) are the y_j^*;

(b) For each $j = 1 .. J$, the plan y_j^* maximizes V_j over Y^j at the prices (p^*, w^*);

(c) The following market-clearing conditions hold:

$$\sum_i x_{im}^* = \sum_i \underline{x}_{im} + \sum_j y_{j_m}^* \quad \text{for all } m = 1 .. M \quad \text{and}$$

$$\sum_i x_{in}^* = \sum_i \underline{x}_{in} + \sum_j y_{jn}^* \quad \text{for all } n = 1 .. N$$

Assumptions A1–A5 in Section 5.3 apply to the Walrasian economy as well. Thus, the maximized value of each firm is nonnegative, and each consumer's goods endowment is a feasible consumption bundle. Use any additional set of restrictions on the U^i and Y^j sufficient to guarantee the existence of a Walrasian equilibrium. Then select a specific equilibrium for the given preferences, technology, and endowments.

Now return to the share-goods economy. In what follows, I assume a normal imputation and nonnegative ex ante shares. Recall that the definition of an exchange economy from Section 5.3 included requirements for (a) consumer optimality and (b) market clearing. For a production equilibrium, I maintain (a) and (b) and add a new condition (c) that control groups unanimously support the existing production plans.

A *production equilibrium* for the share-goods economy is an exchange equilibrium for the share-goods economy such that

(c) For each firm $j = 1 .. J$, no consumer i with $\underline{\theta}_{ijn} > 0$ for some n prefers to replace the production plan y_j by some alternative plan in Y^j.

Starting from a Walrasian equilibrium, I will construct a production equilibrium for the share-goods economy with the same consumption bundles and production plans. Retain the prices p^* for the ordinary goods, and let w^* be the prices at which consumers directly trade the share goods among themselves. Set $\beta_{jn} = 1/N$ for all j and n, and assign $\underline{\theta}_{ijn} = \alpha_{ij}$ for all i, j, and n, where the α_{ij} are the firm shares from the Walrasian economy. This ensures that (10) is satisfied for the share-goods economy. Use a normal imputation $(r_{jn} = w_n^*$ for all j, $n)$, and use the share prices $V_{jn} = \beta_{jn} V_j = V_j/N$ for all $j = 1 .. J$.

First consider condition (a) from Section 5.3, consumer optimality. For a normal imputation and identical endowments of goods, the Walrasian budget constraint (13) is identical to the share-goods budget constraint (9). Any consumption bundle available to agent i in the Walrasian equilibrium is affordable in the share-goods economy, but no new bundle is affordable. Because the preferences and budget sets are unchanged, the bundles x_i^* for i = 1 .. I in the Walrasian equilibrium are also optimal in the share-goods economy.

Next consider condition (b) from Section 5.3, market clearing. Because consumption bundles and production plans are unchanged, market clearing for goods m = 1 .. M in the Walrasian economy implies that (5) is satisfied for the share-goods economy. Choose arbitrary ex post shares $\theta_{ijn} \geq 0$ with $\Sigma_i \theta_{ijn} = 1$ for all (j, n) so that (6) is satisfied. For example, one could choose $\theta_{ijn} = 1/I$ for all (j, n). Then choose the b_{in} using (3) to satisfy $x_{in}^* = \underline{x}_{in} + b_{in} + \Sigma_j \theta_{ijn} y_{jn}^*$ for all n. This ensures that the levels of consumption for each share good and each consumer are the same as in the Walrasian equilibrium. It is easy to check that (7) is satisfied: $\Sigma_i b_{in} = \Sigma_i x_{in}^* - \Sigma_i \underline{x}_{in} - \Sigma_i \Sigma_j \theta_{ijn} y_{jn}^* = 0$ for all n, due to (6) along with the market-clearing condition for goods n = 1 .. N in Walrasian equilibrium.

Finally, consider condition (c) in the definition of equilibrium for the share-goods economy, firm optimality. Given normal imputations, the firm valuation (11) for the share-goods economy is identical to the valuation (14) for the Walrasian economy. Moreover, each consumer i in the share-goods economy wants each firm j to maximize its value, as explained in connection with (11). The production plans y_j^* for j = 1 .. J are value-maximizing in the Walrasian economy, so condition (c) holds for the same plans in the share-goods economy.

This completes the proof that the production plans and consumption bundles from any Walrasian equilibrium can also be supported by a share-goods equilibrium.

5.5 What Does the Model Show?

Sections 5.2–5.4 show that in a competitive environment, control rights can be assigned to any set of input suppliers or output consumers without endangering unanimity or allocative efficiency. The results are highly general. Firms can have many inputs and outputs, and there can be trade-offs between labor and leisure. The level of flexibility is the same as in the standard Arrow-Debreu framework, where goods are distinguished by date, location, and state of the world. The results hold under any set of assumptions on preferences and technology that are sufficient for the existence of Walrasian equilibrium.

It follows that all adverse efficiency judgments with regard to the labor-managed firm must assume the presence of market imperfections, either overtly or otherwise. For the Ward-Domar-Vanek firm in Chapter 3, the problem is a missing labor market. For the horizon problem in Chapter 4, the problem is a missing market on which future income streams can be capitalized. Nothing intrinsic to the concept of workers' control requires that such imperfections be imposed.

The share-goods model also makes the point that market imperfections are central to normative disputes about labor-managed firms. Proponents of workers' control are not content to argue that this system is no worse than ordinary capitalism; they believe that it is better. Likewise, critics of workers' control are not content to argue that this system is no better than ordinary capitalism; they believe that it is worse. But with complete and competitive markets, the two systems are isomorphic. Thus, proponents and critics both need to identify specific departures from the world of complete and competitive markets in order to make their case.

An institutional rule requiring that certain inputs (e.g., labor) must be supplied to firms by consumers through shares, and that these shares must carry control rights, might seem to be an important constraint that would have serious efficiency consequences. But as was pointed out in Chapter 4, with complete and competitive markets this intuition is false. Indeed, it is equally false for the supply of labor and the supply of capital. Such institutional constraints on the set of feasible contracts are nonbinding.

Putting efficiency issues to one side, intuition suggests that transferring control rights from capital to labor leads to a redistribution of wealth. The share-goods model suggests how this could occur. A transfer of control rights could change the bargaining power of various groups of input suppliers, and therefore the distributional coefficients β_{jn} in the model. This is equivalent to a change in the share endowments of consumers in the Walrasian model and alters the wealth distribution if some firms have positive profit.

5.6 The Drèze Model of Labor Management

Drèze (1989, ch. 1) shows that an economy in which firms maximize value added per worker can achieve efficient allocations, even in the short run, when suitable rents are imputed to the nontraded assets used by firms. Indeed, any allocation supportable by a Walrasian equilibrium can also be supported in a labor-managed economy of this type (Drèze, 1989, 24). To replicate the Walrasian outcome, the imputed rent for each firm must be equal to the equilibrium profit the firm would enjoy in a Walrasian economy.

The key difficulty is with the assignment of rental fees to firms. Because these fees are analogous to fixed costs, one option would be for governments to collect lump-sum taxes from each firm. However, it is implausible that governments could gather the information needed to calculate the taxes correctly, in part because firm managers might not tell the truth about the production functions of their firms. Even with accurate data, the computational task would be comparable to the challenge facing a central planner.

It is possible that the required rental fees might emerge in a more decentralized fashion. Drèze points out that workers will queue for membership in LMFs where the rental fee is too low and leave LMFs where the fee is too high. But it is unclear how a disequilibrium in the labor market would push imputed rents to market-clearing levels. Without further institutional details, it is hard to see why LMFs would behave as if they faced market-clearing rental fees.

An alternative approach is to design institutions that induce LMFs to maximize profit rather than net income per worker. This removes the peculiar comparative static features of the WDV firm, so there is no longer any need to offset these peculiarities by imposing lump-sum taxes or fees. As we have seen, in a competitive world this can be done through membership markets. The price of membership is analogous to the rental fee proposed by Drèze, with one major exception: membership prices are generated in a decentralized fashion through the normal forces of supply and demand.

5.7 Postscript

Section 5.1 is new, and Sections 5.2–5.5 are based on a 1983 working paper (Dow, 1983). I revised this material to improve the organization, explain the arguments more clearly, and make the notation consistent with other chapters. Section 5.6 on the Drèze model is borrowed from Dow (1996a).

Despite extensive rewriting, the analysis in Sections 5.2–5.5 is substantively the same as in the 1983 paper, with one exception. The earlier paper allowed ex post shares θ_{ijn} to be negative in order to simplify the derivation of the equilibrium share prices V_{jn}. As explained in Section 5.3, here I impose a nonnegativity constraint $\theta_{ijn} \geq 0$. This does not affect any conclusions, and it slightly strengthens the results by showing that LMFs can achieve Walrasian allocations even under this additional constraint.

The 1983 working paper was my first foray into the theory of the labor-managed firm and was written independently of Sertel (1982), whose work I discovered after my own paper was largely complete. My thinking on this topic was strongly influenced by the literature on unanimity theorems for stock market economies, especially DeAngelo (1981) and the works cited there. The 1983 paper was never published in anything like its original form. One part morphed into my 1986 article in the *Journal of Comparative Economics*, represented here by Chapter 4. Another part became my 1996 article in *Economic Design*, represented here by Chapter 3. The general equilibrium framework is presented in this chapter for the first time.

I will conclude this part of the book with some speculation about why the WDV model became the default description of the labor-managed firm and why it has been so influential for almost sixty years. First, one must recall that the pioneers of this model, especially Ward (1958) and Domar (1966), did not use it to describe LMFs operating in the institutional context of Western market economies. The original model arose within the field of comparative economics, which focused on the contrast between the economic systems of the capitalist West and those of the Soviet Union, China, and other countries outside the Western orbit. Ward wanted to model the Yugoslav self-managed firm, and Domar wanted to model Soviet collective farms.

Both understood that the theoretical model had some odd features. Ward called attention to the lack of a labor market, and Domar observed that if such a firm received a lump-sum subsidy, its membership size would approach zero. To the extent that Vanek's (1970) general equilibrium analysis had an empirical referent, it was again the Yugoslav economy based on workers' self-management, although Vanek was a proponent of LMFs more broadly and regarded workers' control as a universal ideal.

During the 1970s, economists became increasingly interested in labor-managed firms, and the WDV model was widely used to study worker cooperatives in Western market economies. This occurred despite criticism of the WDV approach by Robinson (1967), Meade (1972), and others, who argued that it failed to capture the institutional realities of Western LMFs. It seems likely that the critics did not carry the day in part because they did not offer a simple and plausible alternative. As some philosophers of science have pointed out, you can't beat something with nothing.

It is also important to recall the state of microeconomic theory in the early 1970s. The study of asymmetric information was in its infancy. Pioneering papers on adverse selection (Akerlof, 1970), signaling (Spence, 1973), and moral hazard (Rothschild and Stiglitz, 1976) were just beginning to appear. Game theory was an esoteric art with few economic practitioners. Williamson's (1975) version of transaction cost economics had not yet arrived. Diamond (1967) had studied firm behavior in stock market economies, but this literature did not fully blossom until after 1975.

In the early 1970s, most economic theorists studied firms by assuming a plausible objective function, taking a derivative with respect to a choice variable, writing down a first order condition, and conducting a comparative static analysis. It would have been entirely natural to think about the problem in the following way: (a) there must be some behavioral difference between worker cooperatives and capitalist firms; (b) assuming that the firms have access to similar technology and operate in a similar market environment, any behavioral difference must reflect a difference in objective functions; and (c) the goal of maximizing income per worker seems to capture the egalitarian ideology motivating the creation of worker cooperatives. It is therefore easy to see why economists interested in LMFs during the 1970s and early 1980s would have treated the WDV model as a starting point. It is also easy to see why economists sympathetic to the LMF would have patched up the WDV model by introducing epicycles in an attempt to convince readers that LMFs weren't really as bad as the model made them appear.

It is harder to understand the continuing use of the WDV model in the 1990s and beyond, when the modern theory of the firm had taken shape and the shortcomings of the WDV model were well known. In several papers, Sertel (1982, 1987, 1991) and Dow (1986, 1996a) challenged the core of the model by showing that LMFs with competitive membership markets did not have perverse comparative static features. Other authors took up this idea (e.g., Stephen, 1984; Fehr, 1993). Dow (1986, 1993a) also showed that markets of this kind could eliminate the horizon problem emphasized by Pejovich (1969), Furubotn and Pejovich (1970), Furubotn (1971, 1976), and Jensen and Meckling (1979).

To a degree, the continued use of the WDV objective function can be attributed to simple inertia. Once a large literature has accumulated on a subject, and certain modeling strategies have become standard, it is difficult for an individual author, editor, or referee to abandon the conventional approach. "Normal science" takes over, and researchers add bells and whistles to the established theoretical framework.

Inertia, however, is not the whole story. The Sertel and Dow challenge was weak in a crucial respect. These authors only established that under ideal conditions, markets for membership would restore profit maximization in LMFs. This critique showed what was wrong with the WDV model, but the larger puzzle remained unresolved. Everyone working on the topic, including those who liked LMFs and those who did not, agreed that KMFs and LMFs differed in economically important ways. Showing that these two types of firms are isomorphic under perfect competition was therefore beside the point. This did not shed any light on the reasons for the asymmetries that existed in the real world. Even if it did nothing else, the WDV model at least asserted the existence of an asymmetry.

A further problem was empirical: LMF membership markets are substantially rarer than LMFs themselves. It was therefore reasonable to believe that such markets are unworkable in practice, even if the reasons were obscure. This undermined the Sertel and Dow critique by suggesting that the institutional design needed to rescue the LMF from WDV perversity was infeasible. Partly for this reason, I suspect, authors familiar with the Sertel and Dow results tended to treat them as theoretical curiosities.

Today, we are left with a dilemma. The WDV framework does not explain why firms controlled by labor suppliers maximize a ratio whereas firms controlled by capital suppliers maximize a total, it does not derive the firm's objective from the interests of its individual members, it is inconsistent with the institutional rules used by real LMFs, it is antiquated in relation to contemporary economic theory, and it does little to explain the real empirical differences between KMFs and LMFs.

At the same time, the critique of the WDV model based on the concept of LMF membership markets has clearly fallen short, and the workaday economist interested in LMFs still has no simple alternative to the WDV model. Unfortunately, I do not have a simple alternative to offer. The differences between the KMF and LMF are complex and cannot be captured within one model. But I do believe there is a way forward.

First, we need to catalog the empirical asymmetries between the two types of firms. This task is taken up in Chapters 6 and 7, which provide a set of facts or probable facts that can be used to constrain theoretical speculation. Second, we need to develop theoretical models that explain these facts. This necessitates a departure from the world of perfect markets, as well as the identification of a relevant asymmetry between capital and labor. A program of this kind is outlined at the end of Chapter 8 and pursued in the remainder of the book.

PART III

IMPERFECTION AND ASYMMETRY

6

Empirical Asymmetries I

6.1 Introduction

Before developing specific theoretical models, it is useful to take a step back and consider a fundamental question: what facts should a good theory of the labor-managed firm explain? The most obvious fact is that capital-managed firms are common, while labor-managed firms are rare. Although explaining this observation is clearly necessary, many theories purport to do so (see Chapter 8). By itself this criterion is too low a bar to be very helpful in discriminating among alternative theories.

A good theory should also explain other empirical patterns. These could include the distribution of LMFs across industries, the responses of LMFs to changes in input or output prices, the conditions under which LMFs are formed, the conditions under which LMFs fail, the design features of successful LMFs, and so on. Ideally, we want a theory that provides a unified explanation for a wide range of seemingly disparate observations.

This chapter and Chapter 7 catalog numerous important and robust generalizations about KMFs and LMFs that a good theory might be expected to explain. Of course, there is no way to provide a comprehensive review of the empirical literature on LMFs in only two chapters. I have therefore been selective and will explain later why I have focused on particular publications. For a review devoting more attention to econometric issues, see Pencavel (2013b). For a nontechnical survey of recent findings, see Pérotin (2016). For histories of the U.S. plywood cooperatives, the Mondragon cooperatives in Spain, and the Lega cooperatives in Italy, see Dow (2003, chs. 3–4).

This chapter deals with the aggregate rarity of LMFs and their distribution across industries, evidence about LMF comparative static behavior and objective functions, and comparisons of KMFs and LMFs with respect to productivity and wage distributions. In Chapter 7, I address other issues including LMF entry and exit, membership markets, the use of nonmember labor, possible underinvestment by LMFs, and possible benefits from clustering of multiple LMFs in a single geographic region. Chapter 7 concludes with an interpretive summary of the evidence presented in both chapters.

A great deal has been learned about the behavior of LMFs over the past fifteen years. Improvements in data and econometric methods have clarified a number of old issues and brought new ones to the forefront. As a consumer of empirical research, the results I find most interesting are normally those derived from large, nationally representative samples of firms where many industries or sectors are covered and one can compare the behavior of KMFs and LMFs operating in the same industry. Aggregate time series data on topics such as LMF birth and death rates are also of interest, as are panel datasets for firms in a specific industry. I am most readily persuaded by researchers who pay close attention to potential sources of endogeneity, reverse causality, and selection bias; who employ well-chosen instruments when necessary; who carry out robustness checks involving sample frames, variable definitions, and estimation techniques; and who are aware that a given empirical result could be consistent with more than one theoretical explanation.

By these criteria, several lines of research stand out. In a set of important articles between 2009 and 2016, Gabriel Burdín and his collaborators explored a wide range of topics using excellent data on Uruguayan worker cooperatives. Other recent research I find particularly valuable is that by Fathi Fakhfakh, Virginie Pérotin, and Monica Gago (2012) on worker cooperatives in France, and Jan Podivinsky and Geoff Stewart (2007, 2009) on LMF entry into U.K. manufacturing industries. John Pencavel, Luigi Pistaferri, and Fabinao Schivardi (2006) have done highly enlightening work on Italian worker coops. Other good recent work includes that by Pérotin (2006) on entry and exit of worker coops in France and by Saioa Arando, Monica Gago, Jan Podivinsky, and Geoff Stewart (2012) on worker coops in Spain. While it is less directly focused on LMFs, the work of Ran Abramitzky (2008, 2009, 2011) on the Israeli kibbutzim is careful and convincing. There has certainly been other worthy empirical work in recent decades, but these contributions represent the state of the art in terms of data quality, econometric sophistication, and robustness of results.

Having said this, I also want to recognize the pioneering empirical work on LMFs from the 1980s and 1990s by Avner Ben-Ner, Saul Estrin, Derek Jones, Stephen Smith, and Jan Svejnar, among others. Although later researchers may have had better data or more-advanced econometric tools, these authors blazed the trail and strongly influenced my thinking about the behavior and performance of LMFs. Also in the 1990s, Ben Craig and John Pencavel did path-breaking work on the U.S. plywood cooperatives. Craig and Pencavel performed a vital service by collecting and analyzing panel data on these unique LMFs, which have long been of interest to students of the subject and have unfortunately now succumbed to the overall decline of the plywood industry in the Pacific Northwest.

All of the results reported here are statistically significant at conventional levels unless otherwise stated. I generally summarize the data sources, the variables of interest, and the central results for a given publication with few evaluative comments. This is not because I believe all the papers discussed are of equal quality or importance. However, this is primarily a book about theory, not empirics, so I need to keep the discussion to a manageable length. Moreover, I prefer not to render sharp judgments on methodological matters beyond my competence. But the space I devote to publications is correlated with my perceptions of their quality and their relevance to the theoretical issues at hand.

6.2 Aggregate Rarity

One would like to have time series data for a range of countries on the economic importance of LMFs, measured by fraction of total firms, total employment, total assets, or total sales, with consistent definitions for all variables across countries and over time. Unfortunately, the available information is much more fragmentary. However, countries with the largest LMF sectors, in whatever way this may be measured, also tend to be the countries that have been intensively studied by LMF researchers. I therefore rely on an assortment of summary statistics from authors whose work will be reviewed in greater detail later. All figures refer to firms having the legal form of worker cooperatives (e.g., they do not include professional partnerships such as law firms). For convenience, I use the umbrella term "LMF," although from a theoretical standpoint this term includes a wider range of firms than just worker cooperatives. It can be safely assumed that developed economies not discussed here have proportionately smaller LMF sectors than those that are discussed.

Italy has the largest LMF sector among the developed economies. Bartlett et al. (1992) report that in 1981 Italy had more than 16,000 worker cooperatives that employed over 300,000 workers. Pencavel et al. (2006) report that the share of worker cooperatives as a fraction of Italian firms was 0.61% in 1981 and 1.02% in 1991. They observe that in 1996 worker cooperatives accounted for about 4% of total employment. Pérotin (2016) estimates that Italy had at least 25,000 worker coops in 2012.

Spain is famous in the literature on LMFs for its unique Mondragon system of worker cooperatives, which was established in the 1950s and continues to thrive today. However, even within the Basque Country that is the heartland for Mondragon, during 1995–2002 the number of LMF entrants was 1,005, while the number of KMF entrants was 46,282. Thus LMFs represented 2.1% of total entry (Arando et al., 2012). LMFs accounted for about 3% of the stock of firms in this region. Pérotin (2016) states that in 2012 there were about 17,000 worker cooperatives in Spain as a whole, which together employed about 210,000 people.

France also has a substantial LMF sector. Pérotin (2006) found that France had around 1,700 LMFs out of a total of 2.5 million firms. Fakhfakh et al. (2012) report that in 2011 there were about 2,000 worker cooperatives in France, employing about 46,500 people. The LMFs accounted for less than 1% of all firms with one or more employees. In 2013 the firm count was 2,600 and the employment count was 51,000 (Pérotin, 2016).

For the U.K. in 1985, Podivinsky and Stewart (2007) cite estimates for the total number of worker cooperatives ranging from 800 to 1,400, depending on the definitions used. During 1976–1985 there were 1,321 new LMF entrants, as compared with over 1.5 million new firms registering with the tax authorities. Some of these LMF entrants subsequently exited. During 1981–1983, over 9,000 new capitalist firms entered the U.K. manufacturing sector, but only 110 new LMFs entered this sector (Podivinsky and Stewart, 2009). Pérotin (2016) estimates that there are currently 500–600 worker coops in the U.K.

Using a representative sample for Uruguay during 1996–2005, Burdín and Dean (2009) found that about 3% of the workforce was employed in worker cooperatives. In a firm-level sample for 1997–2009, Burdín (2014) found that there were 223 LMFs out of a total of 29,125 distinct firms, so LMFs constituted about 1% of all firms in Uruguay.

The Israeli kibbutzim (the plural of kibbutz) are often discussed in the context of labor-managed firms, although they differ because they are full-fledged communities and not simply firms (see Section 6.7). In 2000 there were 268 kibbutzim in Israel, with 115,300 members, accounting for 2.3% of the Jewish population (Abramitzky, 2008).

These figures almost certainly represent upper bounds for developed economies. In most such economies, the LMF sector accounts for less than 1% of total private sector firms, employment, assets, and income.

6.3 Industry Distribution

Pencavel (2013b) remarks that labor-managed firms are common in professions such as accounting, law, medicine, and investment banking. Such firms usually take the legal form of partnerships. I return to the subject of partnerships in a different context in Chapter 11. Classifying professional partnerships as LMFs would add to the figures given in Section 6.2, but not by enough to alter the conclusion that the LMF sector is small. The research discussed in the rest of this chapter and the next deals with worker cooperatives rather than partnerships.

For Italy, Pencavel et al. (2006) observe that LMFs are more highly represented in the construction, transport, and service industries than elsewhere. In the sample of firms Pencavel et al. used for econometric work (see Section 6.4), the KMFs were concentrated in manufacturing, while the LMFs were more concentrated in construction and retailing.

For France, Fakhfakh et al. (2012) report that most LMFs are in manufacturing and construction but that the fraction of LMFs in service industries is growing rapidly. LMFs have a relatively strong presence in printing and publishing, but a weak presence in textiles and chemicals.

For the U.K., Podivinsky and Stewart (2007) find that during 1976–1985 almost all new LMFs entered in "other manufacturing"; "construction"; "distribution, hotels and catering, repairs"; "banking, finance, insurance, business services, and leasing"; "other services"; and "unclassified." Section 7.1 provides more information on LMF entry by industry for the U.K.

For Uruguay, Burdín and Dean (2009) observe that LMFs are more frequent in bus and taxi services, social services, and manufacturing than elsewhere in the economy. Formation of LMFs occurred mainly in the service sector between 1997 and 2005, and the historically high concentration in the transport sector declined accordingly. The LMFs in manufacturing most often arose through employee buyouts of KMFs. Burdín (2014) finds a relatively high concentration of LMFs in the service sector as compared with manufacturing, transport, and other.

In general, there does not appear to be any sharp difference in the distribution of KMFs and LMFs across broad sectors of the economy, defined at levels of aggregation like "services" or "manufacturing." To the extent that such differences exist, they are not robust across countries (Pérotin, 2016). However, at a more disaggregated level LMFs do seem to favor some industries over others (see Section 7.1).

The size distributions for KMFs and LMFs differ, with LMFs generally having a higher average number of workers than KMFs (contrary to widespread perceptions). For France, about 83% of conventional firms have less than 10 employees each, while the share of LMFs in this size class is about 55–60%. About 16% of conventional firms have 10–499 employees, while about 44% of LMFs are this large. Very small fractions of each firm population were in larger size classes (Fakhfakh et al., 2012). This tendency toward a higher average number of workers in LMFs is confirmed by the descriptive statistics provided for Italy by Pencavel et al. (2006) and for Uruguay by Burdín and Dean (2009).

6.4 Comparative Statics

As was discussed in Chapters 3–5, theorists have often claimed that LMF behavior deviates from profit maximization. This idea has been subjected to empirical tests. An early effort involved the U.S. plywood cooperatives (Berman and Berman, 1989). Other research has involved the U.S. plywood coops (Craig and Pencavel, 1992; Pencavel and Craig, 1994), Italian worker coops (Pencavel et al., 2006), and Uruguayan worker coops (Burdín and Dean, 2009).

Craig and Pencavel (1992) collected ten years of data (even-numbered years from 1968 to 1986) for 41 plywood firms in the state of Washington. These included 9 nonunionized conventional firms, 21 unionized conventional firms, and 11 cooperatives, with a total of 200 firm-year observations. For the conventional firms, hourly earnings, hours per worker, employment, and output responded in standard ways to variations in output price and the price of a major input (logs). For the cooperatives, on the other hand, point estimates indicated that hours and employment showed no response to output price, while real wages were strongly related to output price. The coops had positively sloped output supply functions with elasticities about half the size of those for conventional firms. The authors note, however, that they were unable to reject the null hypothesis of no difference in behavior across the three types of firms at conventional levels of statistical significance.

Pencavel and Craig (1994) used essentially the same data but with several more dependent variables: total worker hours, annual earnings per worker, and inputs of logs. Again the conventional firms responded in standard ways to prices, and again the coops adjusted earnings rather than employment or hours per worker. All firm types adjusted the input of logs and output of plywood. The elasticity of output with respect to output price for the cooperatives was roughly one-fourth of the corresponding elasticity for the conventional firms. As in their 1992 article, Pencavel and Craig caution that estimated standard errors were too large to permit confident inferences.

Pencavel et al. (2006) used a matched employer-worker panel for Italy involving a sample from the universe of workers in social security records. The authors had annual data for 1982–1994, with the number of individual workers averaging about 13,000 per year. The sample included about 2,000 LMFs and 150,000 KMFs. It was skewed toward firms that were larger, located in northern Italy, and creditworthy, but the included firms collectively accounted for more than half of total employment in Italy.

Product market shocks were defined by a deviation of the log of real sales from a time trend for the firm, industry, and region. Data were also available on wages, the cost of capital, and fixed costs (long-term debt), where dividends paid to LMF members were included in wages. For KMFs, the cost of capital and fixed costs had no effect on wages. For LMFs, these two variables had significant but quantitatively small effects on wages. Product market shocks had significant effects on wages for both KMFs and LMFs, but these effects were about two to three times larger in LMFs.

For KMFs, wages had the expected negative relationship with employment. For LMFs, the same relationship was insignificantly different from zero. The cost of capital had less effect on LMF employment than on KMF employment, and fixed costs had no effect on employment in either type of firm. Product market shocks did have some effect on employment in LMFs, but this was only a little more than half the size of the effect for KMFs. The cost of capital and product market shocks affected the demand for capital in similar ways for LMFs and KMFs, and fixed costs had little effect on demand for capital in either type of firm.

Burdín and Dean (2009) used a monthly panel data set from Uruguay that covered all cooperatives and their capitalist counterparts registered in social security records from April 1996 to December 2005. The data included wages, employment, and an industry-specific output price index. There was no information on hours of work or skill levels.

In general, wages were more flexible in LMFs than in KMFs. Output prices were positively related to wages for KMFs, but this effect was larger for LMFs. In the LMFs, output prices were only related to wages for the subset of workers who were members of the cooperative; there was no effect for hired nonmembers. For the KMFs, employment was negatively related to the wage and positively related to output price. For the LMFs, employment and wages moved in the same direction overall, but there was a significant negative relationship between employment and wages for nonmembers. Output price had no effect on employment, either for members or nonmembers. A large negative macroeconomic shock in 2002 had less effect on employment in LMFs than in KMFs.

Recent research by Alves et al. (2016) shows that for Uruguay both job creation and job destruction are lower in LMFs than in KMFs. For the LMFs, employment flows for nonmembers are higher than those for members.

Pencavel (2015) studied the relationship between wages and hours in LMFs using a data set for the U.S. plywood cooperatives similar to that of Pencavel and Craig (1994). He found that when real hourly wages increased, coops responded with a small reduction in hours worked, but annual earnings still increased. Using evidence from two firms that changed organizational form (one from LMF to KMF and the other conversely), Pencavel concluded that the gaps between actual and preferred hours worked were smaller in the cooperatives than in the conventional firms.

One cautionary remark that applies to much of the empirical literature on LMF comparative statics involves the role of wages. For an LMF, this is typically defined to be income per worker hour or some similar measure of the compensation actually received by LMF members. The problem is that such measures of compensation are endogenous for an LMF because the members are residual claimants. Regressing output on a "wage" defined in this way is like regressing output on the dividends paid to capital in a capitalist firm. In testing the effect of the wage on choice variables for an LMF, one should ideally define the wage as the external opportunity cost of labor (e.g., the wage rate in capitalist firms), which is exogenous to a competitive LMF. The same is true in testing the idea that LMFs maximize profit: one needs an external opportunity cost for labor in order to compute an economically meaningful profit for the LMF before tackling the question of whether the LMF maximizes profit. Some empirical researchers appreciate these issues and use lagged wages as instruments for the current wage, but others are less careful.

6.5 Objective Functions

Craig and Pencavel (1993) studied the objectives of the plywood cooperatives in the U.S. Pacific Northwest. The data were similar to those used by Craig and Pencavel (1992) and Pencavel and Craig (1994). In the 1993 article, Craig and Pencavel proposed a general objective function that gave weight to earnings, hours, and employment. For the key parameter (theta), a value of zero corresponded to employment maximization, a value of unity corresponded to profit maximization, and a value of positive infinity led to maximization of income per worker as in the Ward-Domar-Vanek model. The authors considered several production functions, including generalized Cobb-Douglas, quadratic, and translog. In all cases, the coops and the conventional firms were assumed to have the same production technology.

Craig and Pencavel found that no simple behavioral model adequately described the cooperatives. The estimated value of the parameter theta was between zero and unity. Therefore, to the extent that the coops deviated from profit maximization, they did so by placing a positive weight on employment rather than on income per worker. The authors concluded that there was little support for the WDV hypothesis, although they cautioned that the parameters were estimated imprecisely.

Pencavel and Craig (1994) used data on worker cooperatives and conventional firms in the U.S. plywood industry to test the behavioral restrictions implied by profit maximization, as well as behavioral restrictions implied by dividend maximization as in the Ward-Domar-Vanek model. For the conventional firms, they were unable to reject the sign, homogeneity, and symmetry restrictions implied by profit maximization. For the cooperatives, they were unable to reject the homogeneity, convexity, and symmetry restrictions implied by dividend maximization.

In response to potential criticisms that their tests lack power, Pencavel and Craig emphasized that their point estimates were remarkably similar for unconstrained models and for models with appropriate parameter restrictions. They also conducted experiments to see whether they could reject the null hypothesis that the conventional firms maximize dividends as in the WDV model, as well as the null hypothesis that coops maximize profit. The outcome of the first experiment was clear: conventional firms did not behave according to the WDV model. The outcome of the second experiment was less clear. The coops satisfied the sign restrictions implied by profit maximization, and it was not possible to reject homogeneity or symmetry restrictions at standard levels of statistical significance.

Thus "the co-ops appear to come closer to mimicking profit-maximizing behavior" than conventional firms do to mimicking WDV behavior (1994, 741). However, the authors pointed out that the wages paid by cooperatives were clearly not exogenous, as would be needed in order for the profit maximization hypothesis to be meaningful in this context.

Burdín and Dean (2012) apply techniques similar to those of Craig and Pencavel (1993) to data on worker cooperatives in Uruguay. The data set is similar to that used by Burdín and Dean in their 2009 article discussed earlier, in Section 6.4. They use a general objective function defined over employment and income per worker, with a parameter (theta) determining the weights assigned to these goals. The objective function can be written as a Cobb-Douglas function of total profit and total employment, where profit is income per worker minus opportunity cost per worker, all multiplied by employment. As in Craig and Pencavel (1993), a theta value near zero implies employment maximization, a theta value of unity implies profit maximization, and a theta value approaching positive infinity implies the maximization of income per worker. Burdín and Dean assume equal productivity of KMFs and LMFs as well as a competitive labor market.

The estimated value of theta varies from 0.70 to 0.91. This is inconsistent with the Ward-Domar-Vanek hypothesis that LMFs maximize income per worker. The coops in Uruguay put some weight on both employment and income, but the net effect is close to profit maximization. To the extent that LMFs deviate from profit maximization, they do so in the direction of employment maximization, not dividend maximization. Burdín and Dean also note that to the extent that LMFs may have productivity advantages, their point estimates represent an upper bound on the true value of theta and may understate the true importance of the employment goal. In general, these results are consistent with those of Craig and Pencavel (1993).

6.6 Productivity

Many writers have tried to compare the productivities of KMFs and LMFs using anecdotal evidence or small sample sizes. It is difficult to place much confidence in the resulting conclusions. It is also hard to infer much from the ratio of output to a specific input. For example, early researchers concluded that the U.S. plywood cooperatives had higher labor productivity than conventional firms in the 1950s and 1960s, but this seems to have reversed by the 1970s and 1980s. At the same time, the lower labor productivity of the coops in the latter period was at least partially offset by higher productivity in raw material use (Pencavel and Craig, 1994, 724–726).

The standard solution to such problems is to compare total factor productivity for KMFs and LMFs in the same industry. There has been much research along these lines. It has frequently been assumed that KMFs and LMFs in the same industry have the same production function except for a multiplicative productivity coefficient that could be higher or lower in LMFs. However, as will be discussed later, KMFs and LMFs in the same industry appear to have technologies that differ in more complicated ways, so this approach is less illuminating than one might have hoped.

A further complication identified by Craig and Pencavel (1995) is that firms may select into particular organizational forms depending upon anticipated productivity. For example, a firm might be organized as an LMF under idiosyncratic conditions where this organizational form happened to have unusually high productivity, and likewise for a firm organized as a KMF. The econometrician might be unable to observe the underlying conditions that accounted for the choice of organizational form in each case and thus might incorrectly infer that one type of firm had an intrinsic productivity advantage. However, it would not necessarily be true that one could increase the productivity of a KMF by converting it into an LMF or vice versa.

We do sometimes observe transitions between organizational forms. If a failing KMF is transformed into a successful LMF, one might argue that a productivity gain can be inferred. However, the subset of KMFs selected for conversion into LMFs is unlikely to be a random sample of all KMFs, so one cannot infer from such observations that the productivity of a randomly chosen KMF would rise if it were reorganized as an LMF.

This problem could be avoided if it were possible to choose a random sample of KMFs, transform them into LMFs, and study the consequences for productivity. In the absence of such direct experiments, one must hope that individual firms were organized as LMFs or KMFs for reasons independent of the inherent productivity of the two kinds of firms, so that something resembling random assignment prevails. This might be a plausible assumption for industries in which both types of firms have been competing for decades.

Craig and Pencavel (1995) carried out a pioneering comparison of productivity in KMFs and LMFs using the same data set for U.S. plywood firms as used by Craig and Pencavel (1992, 1993) and

Pencavel and Craig (1994). The results were based on Cobb-Douglas functional forms (quadratic and translog functions led to unsatisfactory results). Three types of mills were studied: conventional nonunionized, conventional unionized, and cooperative. The null hypothesis of no difference between the output elasticities for the unionized and cooperative mills could not be rejected at conventional levels, but the null hypothesis of no difference was rejected for the other two pairwise comparisons.

The key results (their table 8) involved predicted output levels for the three types of firms, taking as benchmarks the input levels actually chosen by each type of firm. This gave nine distinct output predictions (eighteen counting both the OLS and instrumental variable estimates). In every case, the worker cooperatives had higher predicted output than either type of conventional firm. Limiting attention to the input levels observed for coops and unionized firms, the productivity of the coops was higher by a factor between 6% and 14%. These differences would have been larger if the input levels used by nonunionized conventional firms had been considered. No standard errors were reported, and therefore it is unclear whether these differences are statistically significant.

Fakhfakh et al. (2012) compared the productivities of LMFs and KMFs in France using panel data sets for 1987–1990 (seven industries) and 1989–1996 (four industries). The data included about 7,000 firms each year, with about 500 fitting the definition of an LMF. This included the universe of French worker cooperatives having twenty or more employees, plus a representative sample of conventional firms. It is by far the largest sample for which systematic productivity comparisons have been undertaken.

Fakhfakh et al. (2012) noted that three out of four studies to estimate production functions for matched samples of LMFs and KMFs (Berman and Berman, 1989; Estrin, 1991; Craig and Pencavel, 1995) failed to detect any significant difference in total factor productivity when production functions for the two types of firms were required to differ only through an intercept term. The fourth (Jones, 2007) obtained nonrobust results. Fakhfakh et al. similarly found no significant productivity difference in most industries when the production functions were constrained to be identical except for an intercept.

However, Fakhfakh et al. found that in their sample, the production functions of LMFs and KMFs had systematic differences. When technologies were allowed to differ across the two types of firms but input levels were held constant, in some industries there would have been no significant difference in output depending on whether the LMF or KMF technology had been used. However, in those cases where a significant difference did exist, LMFs obtained more output using their own technology than they would have obtained if they had used the KMF technology. In several industries, KMFs would have produced more if they had been able to use the LMF technology. An effort to correct for the possibility that LMFs select into particularly suitable industries actually increased the estimated productivity advantage of the LMFs, perhaps because worker coops more often arise in industries where market conditions are poor (Pérotin, personal communication, July 2016).

The authors concluded that in most industries, LMFs are at least as productive as KMFs. They attributed the apparent differences in production technology to information and incentive effects. For example, in the majority of industries, the French LMFs had a lower proportion of managerial and supervisory staff than the conventional firms, with an insignificant difference in this variable for the other industries. This is consistent with a comment by Craig and Pencavel (1992) that the U.S. plywood cooperatives used fewer frontline supervisors than did similar conventional firms.

6.7 Wage Structure

Theory provides no clear prediction about whether income per worker should be higher in KMFs or LMFs. As Pencavel et al. (2006) note, such gaps can be influenced by nonpecuniary factors, risk, and unionism. They may also be influenced by differences in productivity, the willingness of LMF workers to sacrifice wages for the sake of collective investment, and the possible inclusion of returns to capital in the LMF "wage."

Empirical research has tended to focus less on the existence or direction of wage gaps and more on the question of whether LMF wage distributions are more compressed than wage distributions in KMFs. Some of this research has been motivated by Kremer's (1997) argument that if the productivity of the median LMF voter is lower than that of the mean voter, in equilibrium there will be redistribution from high-productivity members to low-productivity members. Unless high-productivity workers are locked into the LMF in some way or have an ideological commitment to the firm, there is a danger that they will flee to capitalist firms where they are paid their marginal product.

There is extensive anecdotal support for this idea. The Mondragon cooperatives in Spain, for example, have long debated the acceptable size of wage differentials among members (Dow, 2003, ch. 3). Initially, the highest wage was constrained to be no more than three times the lowest wage, although special bonuses to managers could push this up to a factor of 4.5. By 1987, the maximum wage was six times the minimum, but this still left top managers earning about half what they could obtain elsewhere. In 1991, the salaries of top managers were raised to 70% of the salary available in the outside market. It was widely believed that those managers who continued to work at Mondragon did so as a result of strong ideological beliefs.

Bartlett et al. (1992) provided evidence on this topic using a sample of 49 worker cooperatives and 35 conventional firms in north-central Italy in 1985–1986. The firms were matched by size and sector, all were in light manufacturing, and the average number of workers was about 100. About 65% of the coops had been created de novo, with most of the others formed through conversion of failed conventional firms. While average wages were similar for the two types of firms, the wage differentials in the coops were "sharply compressed" compared to the conventional firms, with managers receiving much lower pay in the coops relative to other firms. This compression was more pronounced for the subset of coops that had been created through conversion of failing conventional firms.

Craig and Pencavel (1995, 132–133) observed that collectively bargained contracts in conventional plywood firms in the U.S. Pacific Northwest imposed wages that differed by a factor of about 2.5 from the lowest- to highest-paid workers. While such differentials were narrow by most manufacturing standards, they were wide compared to the plywood cooperatives, where most workers received identical hourly wages.

The most systematic research on wage distributions within LMFs has been carried out by Burdín (2016), who uses panel data on Uruguayan workers registered for social security for at least one month during the period from January 1997 to April 2010. The sample has around 40,000 workers in each month. The data for individuals include daily wages, gender, age, and tenure, as well as information about job changes. The top and bottom 1% of the wage distribution are excluded.

Individuals can be matched to firms, where the data on firms include size and industry. The sample is restricted to private nonagricultural firms. The entire wage distribution within each firm is observed. The data include

type of firm, where worker-managed firms are defined to be firms registered as producer cooperatives in which the ratio of permanent employees
to members does not exceed 20%. LMFs are allowed to hire temporary
seasonal employees but must respect the 20% ratio in order for members to
be exempt from employer social security taxes. Roughly 3% of the individuals in the sample work in LMFs.

There is a small wage premium associated with employment in an
LMF, but this may include some capital income. Wage inequality is
systematically lower in LMFs: the Gini index of daily wages is on average
9.3 percentage points lower for LMFs than for conventional firms.
The ratio of mean to median wages is also systematically lower for
LMFs. In LMFs, the wage premium for the 0.2 quantile is 18%, while
the wage penalty for the 0.8 quantile is 4%. There is anecdotal evidence
that LMFs try to screen out low-ability applicants at the bottom end of
the wage distribution to limit adverse selection.

The primary caveat attached to these results is that workers may self-
select into LMFs according to unobservable traits that affect intrafirm pay
dispersion. Therefore, the relationship between LMF organization and
wage compression might not be causal. However, survey evidence
finds no significant difference in either wage compression or supervision
intensity between those LMFs that were created from scratch and those
that were created through the transformation of conventional firms. This
suggests that wage compression and lower supervisory intensity are intrinsic features of the LMF.

Voluntary quits in LMFs represent 72% of total separations (82% if
attention is limited to members). Restricting the sample to LMF members, a proportional hazard model indicates that members in the top
50% of the wage distribution are more than three times more likely to
exit than those in the bottom 50%. High-wage workers are less likely to
quit when redistribution is less intense, and founding members are less
likely to quit, perhaps because nonpecuniary motives are more important for these members. High-wage LMF members are also less likely to
quit when their outside options are less attractive, as indicated either by
a higher unemployment rate or a lower median wage in the capitalist
sector relative to the member's own wage. By contrast with LMF
members, workers having high relative wages within conventional
firms are less likely to quit.

Abramitzky (2008) has undertaken detailed research on the consequences of equal sharing within Israeli kibbutzim. The kibbutzim differ
from LMFs in that they are not just workplaces or firms; rather, they are full

rural communities in which individual members live, socialize, raise chil-
dren, and enjoy public goods. Accordingly, one must be cautious about
generalizing from the kibbutzim to LMFs, but Abramitzky's findings are of
interest because in a kibbutz all production activities are managed by the
membership, so there is a strong element of workers' control. About 80% of
production is industrial and 20% is agricultural (Abramitzky, 2011).

The data include linked census records on 1,577 individual kibbutz
members for 1983 and 1995, as well as kibbutz-level information about
equality, wealth, group size, ideology, and demographic variables. There is
coverage for 188 kibbutzim (more than 70% of the total number).
Unfortunately, it was not possible to link individual members with their
particular kibbutzim, but only with kibbutzim having similar locations.
The average kibbutz had roughly 400 members, who were employed in
a variety of industries. Wealthier kibbutzim and those with stronger
socialist ideology tended to maintain greater economic equality among
their members. Among those with equal sharing, the wealthier kibbutzim
tended to have lower overall exit rates.

Regression analysis suggested that among kibbutzim with equal sharing,
more-educated and more-skilled individuals were more likely to exit. For
example, having at least a high school education increased the probability
of exit by 9.8 percentage points. Those with high-skill occupations were
over 8 percentage points more likely to exit, and those with low-skill
occupations were over 9 percentage points less likely to exit relative to
the members in medium-skill occupations. "High skill" was defined to
mean those in managerial or academic occupations, while "low skill"
meant those working in unskilled industrial or service occupations
(Abramitzky, 2011).

In subsequent work, Abramitzky (2009) showed that high-skill individuals were more likely to leave kibbutzim than they were to leave other
rural localities that did not engage in redistribution. Furthermore, relative
to other members of the kibbutzim, high-skill members were disproportionately likely to exit both to rural locations and to urban locations. To the
extent that unobservable components of productivity show up in wages but
not in observed education or skill, there is evidence that individuals exiting
kibbutzim are also higher on such unobserved measures: the kibbutz
leavers who move to cities earn higher wages than similar individuals
already living in cities as well as other rural-to-city migrants. There is
also evidence that entrants to kibbutzim have lower wages than nonen-
trants or other city-to-rural migrants. This suggests negative selection with
respect to productivity among kibbutz entrants, despite an intensive

screening process designed to prevent this as well as the use of entry fees by some kibbutzim. Pre-entry wages appear not to have been observable to the kibbutzim in the screening process. No such negative selection was detected among migrants to rural nonkibbutz localities.

This concludes the survey of evidence about the aggregate rarity of LMFs, their distribution across industries, their comparative static behavior and objective functions, the productivity of LMFs relative to KMFs, and wage compression in LMFs relative to KMFs. Chapter 7 takes up a range of additional topics: rates of entry and exit for LMFs, evidence about membership markets, the possible degeneration of LMFs into KMFs, the possibility that LMFs underinvest relative to KMFs, and agglomeration of LMFs. Near the end of Chapter 7, I offer a synthesis of the lessons from the empirical work reviewed in Chapters 6 and 7.

7

Empirical Asymmetries II

7.1 Entry Rates

Most of the findings in Chapter 6 involved static snapshots of the labor-managed firm or studies of its response to short run shocks. Here I emphasize life-cycle questions relating to firm formation, survival, growth, and transformation. My review begins with evidence about entry rates and exit rates (Sections 7.1 and 7.2). I will continue with some observations about membership markets (Section 7.3), the possible degeneration of LMFs into KMFs (Section 7.4), and possible underinvestment by LMFs (Section 7.5). The last empirical topic is the geographic clustering of LMFs (Section 7.6). I conclude with some interpretive comments (Section 7.7).

Pérotin (2006) uses aggregate data on LMFs and conventional firms in France to compare entry and exit rates. I focus here on entry rates and defer the discussion of exit until Section 7.2. Data on entry are available for LMFs from 1971 to 2002 and for all firms in France from 1979 to 2002. Entry figures cover all industries and all sources of origin.

For LMFs, entry included creations from scratch, rescues of failing conventional firms, and conversions of financially sound conventional firms. From 1997 to 2001, 84% of entering LMFs were created from scratch and 7% were formed through conversion of failing conventional firms. For KMFs, entry included new firms, new subsidiaries, and new firms resulting from mergers and acquisitions. During 1979–2002, the average flow of new LMFs was 167 each year, while the average flow of new firms of all types was 263,460 each year. The average stock of LMFs in a typical year was 1,259, while the average stock of all firms was 2,235,000.

Econometric analysis revealed that LMF entry was markedly counter-cyclical. A one percentage point increase in unemployment was associated with a 5% increase in LMF entry, and a one percentage point increase in the GDP growth rate was associated with an 8–9% decrease in LMF entry. Both macroeconomic variables had the opposite effects on entry by conventional firms: higher unemployment led to less conventional entry, and higher GDP growth led to more conventional entry.

Membership in the Israeli kibbutz also seems to have been counter-cyclical over long periods. Abramitzky (2008, 1144) reports a negative correlation between kibbutz membership and the growth of GDP per capita for the period 1966–2000 and a similar negative correlation with the growth of NNP for the period 1922–1947.

Podivinsky and Stewart (2007) examine the determinants of LMF entry across a set of 90 U.K. manufacturing industries defined by the Standard Industrial Classification at the three-digit level of disaggregation. They use panel data for 1981–1985, so there are a total of 450 industry-year combinations. In 82% of these 450 combinations there was no LMF entry, and in 11.3% there was a single entrant.

LMF entry rates were lower for those industries with higher capital/labor ratios and higher risk, defined by variance of industry profit. Capital intensity was statistically significant for OLS and negative binomial models. Risk was not statistically significant for OLS but was significant in the negative binomial model. Results for a Poisson model were qualitatively identical to those for the negative binomial.

The economic magnitudes were quantitatively important. An increase of 0.01 in the capital/labor ratio (which had a mean of 0.052) was associated with a 19.5% decrease in LMF entry. A decrease of 0.1 in the measure of risk (which had a mean of 0.721) was associated with a 12% increase in LMF entry. Only one among the ten industries with the highest capital/labor ratios (brewing and malting) had LMF entry during 1981–1985, but eight of the ten industries with the lowest capital/labor ratios experienced LMF entry. LMFs entered just one of the ten industries that had the highest risk levels but entered seven of the ten industries that had the lowest risk levels.

The Podivinsky and Stewart 2007 study does not directly compare entry by LMFs and KMFs. In a subsequent article, Podivinsky and Stewart (2009) model the proportion of industry entrants that are LMFs. They define capitalist firms as those classified as "incorporated" in a database from the U.K. Office of National Statistics. The data are similar to those in the previous study except that the panel covers the period 1981–1983.

Industries where LMFs did not enter but KMFs did enter included mineral extraction, chemicals, office machinery, and motor vehicles. Almost 60% of LMF entry was in "paper, printing and publishing" and "clothing and footwear." Both are historically important areas of LMF activity in the U.K. Fractional logit regressions with random industry effects indicated that increased capital intensity and higher risk at the industry level were both associated with a lower proportion of LMF entrants.

7.2 Exit Rates

In addition to the results on LMF entry for France discussed in Section 7.1, Pérotin (2006) used the same data set to study LMF exit. She found that for 1979–2002, LMFs and conventional firms had similar annual exit rates (10% for the former and 11% for the latter). Greater LMF formation was associated with greater LMF exit two years later, which is unsurprising given that hazard rates generally peak in the first few years for most organizational forms (there is a similar pattern for KMFs; see Burdín, 2014).

With regard to the business cycle, Pérotin found that higher unemployment was associated with more LMF exit: a one percentage point rise in unemployment led to 7–12% more LMF exit. The GDP growth rate seemed to have no significant effect on LMF exit (by contrast with its effect on LMF entry). There was no sign that LMFs tended to exit in greater numbers during economic recoveries as some theorists have suggested. Neither unemployment nor GDP growth had a significant effect on exit for non-LMFs.

Burdín (2014) studied LMF survival rates in Uruguay using monthly firm-level panel data from January 1997 to July 2009 for 112 economic sectors. Sectors without LMFs were excluded. The populations of each firm type were obtained from government records. A worker-managed firm was defined as a firm legally registered as a producer cooperative in which the ratio of permanent employees to members did not exceed 0.2. These firms can hire temporary seasonal employees but must comply with the 0.2 ratio in order to avoid paying social security payroll taxes for their members (this tax must be paid for hired employees).

Burdín could observe when a new firm registered and when a firm was canceled (the latter was classified as a failure). He considered only the firms that entered during or after February 1997. The sample included 29,125 firms, of which 223 were LMFs. Of the producer cooperatives, 74% qualified as LMFs. About 11% of producer cooperatives that were active in 2009 had been formed through conversions of conventional firms. No information was available on mergers and acquisitions.

For both KMFs and LMFs, survival was associated with positive performance measured by wage and employment growth. LMFs had significantly less employment variability and more wage volatility than similar KMFs. The hazard rate had an inverted U shape for both KMFs and LMFs, reaching a maximum around the second year and then falling with age. In the econometric work, the starting wage was used as a proxy for firm quality, with controls for startup size and industry. The hazard of dissolution was about 29% lower for LMFs than KMFs after controlling for differences in taxes and excluding very small firms. There were no significant differences in survival for KMFs and LMFs in manufacturing or transport, but there was a large difference for services, which drove the overall results. Burdín suggests that this reflects an advantage for LMFs in industries with low capital intensity.

The results control for unobserved heterogeneity at the firm level and are robust to differences in sizes of the two types of firms, differences in tax rates, and conversions of LMFs into KMFs. Differences in tax treatment can explain some of the difference between KMF and LMF survival, but not all. The key caveats with respect to causality are that LMFs may tend to enter industries where their survival prospects are higher and may tend to attract unusually motivated or otherwise desirable workers.

Burdín suggests a number of possible interpretations. Higher LMF survival rates may reflect higher productivity, but it is not possible to measure productivity directly in this data set. LMF survival may be associated with greater wage flexibility, but this does not appear to be true in the data. Finally, LMF survival may be associated with greater employment stability. Burdín favors the latter interpretation because this variable does partly mediate the survival effect, even after possible endogeneity is taken into account. The benefits of employment stability may operate through investment in human capital, willingness to share information with managers, openness to innovation, and longer time horizons in relationships among workers or between workers and managers. This view is consistent with evidence for fewer supervisors, more mutual monitoring, and greater organizational innovation in Uruguayan LMFs compared to similar KMFs.

7.3 Membership Markets

Outside the U.S., markets for membership positions in LMFs are rare or absent. In some cases the charters of individual firms prevent such transactions, while in other cases there are broad legal restrictions. Mikami (2016) comments that in most countries cooperative law does not treat membership as an object to be sold on an open market. He reports that in Germany and Italy the sale of membership rights in cooperatives is legally prohibited, while in Spain, Sweden, and the U.K. the law requires membership transfers to be approved by the board of directors or a similar authority. According to Fakhfakh et al. (2012), legal rules prevent trading of membership shares in French LMFs. The Israeli kibbutzim studied by Abramitzky (2008, 1198–1199) do not have markets for membership. Members can exit at will and are entitled to a small exit payment but cannot cash out a share or take it with them. In the data set used by Burdín (2014, 207), fewer than 10% of Uruguayan LMFs are owned by their workforces through individual shares. I discuss the U.S. legal framework for professional partnerships in Chapter 11, but it suffices to remark that the other members of the firm must normally approve any partnership transaction.

Italian law specifies minimum and maximum amounts a member must pay upon joining a coop (Pencavel et al., 2006). Upon exit, he or she receives a refund on the entry fee plus interest, but the size of this refund is unrelated to expectations about the future value of membership in the firm. Practices with regard to entry fees and exit refunds seem broadly similar in most countries.

The U.S. plywood cooperatives had active markets for membership shares (see Pencavel, 2001, and Dow, 2003, ch. 3), although even here it was necessary for sales to be approved by the board of directors or through a vote of the entire membership. Other historical examples of such markets are known (Russell, 1985a; Dow, 2003, ch. 7). Craig and Pencavel (1992) provide the most detailed information on membership markets for the plywood cooperatives. They compute the discounted present value of a membership share using the price paid, the wages obtained by working in a cooperative, and the price at which the share could be sold upon exit. They compare this against the alternative present value that could have been obtained by investing the same amount of money in a savings account and working in a conventional plywood mill. Three of the cooperatives had enough information to permit detailed calculations. Depending on the specific firm and years, Craig and Pencavel found that membership shares were often substantially underpriced (prices below 70% of the "true" present value were not unusual). Craig and Pencavel suggest that this may reflect a lack of diversification because members were investing their financial wealth in the firm where they worked.

7.4 Degeneration

No one argues that successful capitalist firms tend to "degenerate" into workers' cooperatives. However, many writers have argued that successful workers' cooperatives degenerate into capitalist firms (Ben-Ner, 1984, 1988; Miyazaki, 1984; Dow, 2003, 221–224). The usual reason given is that LMF members have an incentive to replace departing members with hired employees who are paid a competitive wage and do not share in the (positive) profit of the firm. This does not occur with perfect membership markets where outsiders pay for their profit claims through an up-front fee. But if membership markets are imperfect, degeneration could occur (see Section 9.4). As an aside, I should remark that I dislike the pejorative connotations of the word "degeneration," but this term has long been used in the LMF literature and I reluctantly adopt it here.

Estrin and Jones (1992) investigated this issue using a panel data set with annual information for all 283 French worker cooperatives existing throughout the period 1970–1979. They supplemented this with a cross-sectional data set that included information on the total population of 541 such firms in 1979. The results showed a gradual decrease in the ratio of members to total workers early in the life cycle of a cooperative, followed by a gradual increase. The minimum tended to occur when an LMF had existed for about forty years. Degeneration was slower in LMFs created through the conversion of a KMF and less pronounced in more profitable firms (contrary to the expectations of most theorists who have written on the subject). The limited extent of degeneration may reflect the fact that in French cooperatives nonmembers are eligible for profit-sharing participation, so members may not derive any financial benefit by hiring nonmembers.

In a recent study, Fakhfakh et al. (2012) found no evidence for degeneration in French LMFs (see the discussion of their sample in Section 6.6). Of the employees who had been with a firm for at least two years, about 80–90% were members. However, as noted earlier, French law requires that nonmembers share in profit, so the temptation to replace members by nonmembers over time does not arise. Fakhfakh et al. (2012) also point out that in France it is legally difficult to transform an LMF into a KMF, so this potential avenue for degeneration is blocked as well.

Pencavel et al. (2006) report that a survey of Italian worker cooperatives carried out in the mid-1980s indicated that about 85% of coop workers were members. The nonmembers included apprentices and probationary workers. Most cooperatives distributed profit to members and nonmembers on the same terms. As in France, this institutional rule dampened any incentive for members to hire nonmembers.

Craig and Pencavel (1992, table 4) present relevant data for the U.S. plywood cooperatives during 1958–1982. These firms had membership markets, although the authors argue that membership rights were underpriced (see Section 7.3). Of the eleven cooperatives for which the membership ratio could be observed over twenty years or more, five had a large drop (more than ten percentage points) in the fraction of workers who were members. These firms provide examples of degeneration. However, of the remaining cooperatives, three had only minor declines in the membership ratio and three had increases. Thus, degeneration was not a universal feature of the plywood cooperatives.

Burdín and Dean (2009) examine the degeneration issue for Uruguayan LMFs. In order for these firms to qualify for tax benefits, they must keep the number of permanent nonmember workers at or below 20% of the number of members, although temporary workers are permitted. Their data make it possible to distinguish wages and employment for members and nonmembers within individual firms. As their dependent variable, Burdín and Dean use the change in the log of the ratio of hired workers to total employment for firm i in month j. They regress this on the change in the logged wage and the change in the logged output price. As one would expect from ordinary profit maximization toward hired labor, higher wages result in a smaller employment share for the hired workers. If higher profit increases the temptation to use hired workers, then a higher output price should result in a larger fraction of hired workers, but no significant positive relationship was found. Burdín and Dean conclude that there is no evidence for degeneration and suggest that it is prevented by taxation rules.

The importance of degeneration remains controversial. Pencavel (2013b, 466–468) believes that the phenomenon is real and cites evidence from the plywood cooperatives, the Mondragon cooperatives, and the Israeli kibbutzim. On the other hand, Pérotin (2006) states that French, Italian, and Spanish worker coops are all immune to degeneration for institutional reasons. The incentives for degeneration may vary with the circumstances, including whether members are more productive than hired employees (Ben-Ner, 1984). A related process may involve the formation of noncooperative subsidiaries by worker cooperatives or outsourcing of some activities to conventional firms, although data are scarce. In my opinion the general temptation is real, but in practice it can be (and often is) restrained through institutional mechanisms. For Italy and France, these restraints were sometimes written into law at the request of the cooperative movement (Pérotin, personal communication, July 2016).

7.5 Underinvestment

The claim that LMFs invest less than similar KMFs has been made almost since the beginning of the LMF literature (see Chapter 4). Various arguments have been made to support this claim. These include allegations that LMFs have low capital/labor ratios or small sizes as compared to similar KMFs. There are a number of distinct issues here: whether LMFs tend to be found in less capital-intensive industries, whether they are less capital intensive than KMFs in the same industry, and whether they expand at a slower rate than KMFs in the same industry. The evidence cited in Section 7.1 supports the first proposition. Here I focus on the latter two.

Berman and Berman (1989) found lower capital intensity among the LMFs in the U.S. plywood industry as compared with KMFs in this industry. Bartlett et al. (1992) and Jones (2007) obtained similar results for Italian LMFs, although survey evidence reported by Bartlett et al. indicated no difference between LMFs and KMFs in the time horizon used to evaluate investments. Bartlett (1994) found that Italian LMFs were more capital intensive than similar KMFs. Pencavel et al. (2006), using a large Italian sample, found that after controlling for industry, the capital/labor ratios of LMFs had a similar mean to KMFs but with more dispersion.

For France, Fakhfakh et al. (2012) found that when firm size was measured by the number of employees, there were no consistent firm size differences between LMFs and KMFs in the same industry. However, when firm size was measured by assets, LMFs were significantly smaller than KMFs in most industries. LMF capital/labor ratios were significantly lower in a minority of industries, with no significant difference in other industries. The authors of this study found that in all industries the growth rate of capital was at least as high for LMFs as for KMFs. They remark that "This evidence is not consistent with underinvestment, nor does it really fit a capital starvation hypothesis" (2012, 864).

According to Fakhfakh et al. (2012), French LMFs are required to plow back 25% of annual profit into collectively owned capital, although this lower bound seems not to be binding for many firms (the average is close to 45%). They cite the view of Estrin and Jones (1992, 1998) that such legal restrictions could help explain the apparent absence of underinvestment for French LMFs. They also suggest that rapid capital accumulation provides a form of insurance that preserves employment and maintains pay stability in economic downturns. In a much smaller sample, Bartlett et al. (1992) found that Italian LMFs reinvested 69–84% of profits. They argued that tax incentives discouraged these firms from distributing profit to individual workers. In general, Pérotin (2006) asserts that institutional rules prevent underinvestment in French, Italian, and Spanish LMFs.

7.6 Agglomeration

LMFs often cluster by industry, region, and time period (see Russell, 1985a, b, and Dow, 2003, ch. 10, for examples from the U.S.). One could imagine several reasons for this phenomenon. First, given the lack of information about LMFs, the success of a few such firms may inspire attempts at replication. Second, LMFs are more likely to thrive in regions where input suppliers, capital suppliers, customers, lawyers, and consultants have experience with this organizational form. Third, an LMF may receive technical support or capital from nearby LMFs or have some members with experience at other LMFs.

Federations can formalize and perhaps intensify these processes. The roles of the Mondragon system in Spain and the Lega federation in Italy are well known (Dow, 2003, chs. 3–4). Both have strong geographic focal points: the Basque region for Mondragon, and Emilia Romagna for the Lega. These are currently the two largest regional LMF concentrations (Arando et al., 2012).

Podivinsky and Stewart (2007) report rapid growth in the LMF sector in the U.K. from the mid-1970s through the mid-1980s. One explanation is that this was a period of high unemployment (as noted in Section 7.1, LMF formation tends to be countercyclical). However, Estrin and Pérotin (1987) argue that the most important impetus was support from the Industrial Common Ownership Movement (founded in 1971) and the Co-operative Development Agency (founded in 1978).

Arando et al. (2012) have tested the idea that LMFs benefit from agglomeration. These authors use data from the Basque region of Spain, which provide information on LMF entry by county, industry, and year during 1997–2002. There are 20 counties and 17 industries, yielding a panel with 2,040 data points. A simple calculation shows that within the Basque region LMFs are more geographically concentrated than KMFs.

For econometric work, Arando et al. use a negative binomial estimation method where the dependent variable is the number of LMF entrants by county, industry, and year. Independent variables include the stock of LMFs in the same county, industry, and in the previous year; the stock of LMFs in the same county and in the previous year but not in the same industry; and the stock of capitalist firms in the same county, industry, and in the previous year. Other controls include the level of employment in LMFs in the same county in the previous year; the county-level unemployment rate; and dummies for time, province, and broad industry categories.

LMF entry responds positively to the stock of existing LMFs in the same county and industry, and also to the stock of existing LMFs located in the same county but in a different industry. Both results are highly significant. An increase of 100 in the stock of LMFs is associated with an expected increase of 4.1% in LMF entry. The stock of KMFs has no significant effect on LMF entry. The authors conclude that there are nonindustry-specific agglomeration economies for LMFs (the estimation method does not permit an inference that industry-specific effects also exist, although this cannot be ruled out). No agglomeration economies flow from KMFs to LMFs.

7.7 An Interpretive Summary

In Chapter 19, I will attempt to explain most of the empirical patterns surveyed in Chapters 6 and 7 using a comprehensive theoretical framework. In the meantime, I offer a few preliminary remarks on the research reviewed in these chapters.

One noteworthy point is that LMFs have no visible disadvantage with respect to productivity or survival and sometimes exhibit advantages on these performance criteria (Sections 6.6 and 7.2). We can therefore reject any caricature of the LMF as a morass of organizational dysfunction. In most real LMFs, members do not shirk, fight over wages, or rebel against their supervisors; nor do real LMFs rapidly collapse or become KMFs.

Indeed, a reasonable conjecture is that higher LMF survival rates are explained in part by higher productivity of LMFs relative to KMFs in the same industry. Why LMFs would have a productivity advantage is a bit unclear, but the literature suggests a number of possibilities: gains from mutual monitoring and less use of supervisory labor, greater willingness of workers to share information with managers and vice versa, less conflict between workers and managers, and so on. Whatever the key advantages may be, they seem to be difficult for KMFs to replicate. Another possibility is that the productivity and survival advantages of LMFs reflect self-selection of unusually productive workers into LMFs rather than the features of the organizational structure itself (although in this case one still needs to explain why such workers prefer LMFs). But generally speaking, the evidence suggests that attempts to account for the rarity of LMFs should focus on the obstacles to their formation or on obstacles to the conversion of KMFs into LMFs rather than alleged deficiencies in day-to-day operations.

Another broad conclusion is that LMFs deviate from profit maximization in some systematic ways (Sections 6.4 and 6.5). In particular, they tend to respond to exogenous shocks by adjusting the incomes of their members rather than adjusting the quantities of inputs and outputs. One must be cautious about such claims, because LMFs with hired employees seem to treat them in much the same way as a KMF would. But there is little doubt that LMFs have smaller output elasticities than similar KMFs and are reluctant to lay off members. When they depart from profit maximization, it is in the direction of employment maximization rather than maximization of income per worker.

An old dogma holds that in a competitive market with free entry and exit, firms must maximize profit or at least behave as if they do, because if they deviate from such behavior, they will be driven out of the market by other firms that do maximize profit or behave as if they do (Alchian, 1950; Friedman, 1953). This claim has provoked a good deal of methodological debate and has been criticized from various angles (e.g., see Nelson and Winter, 1982). The empirical literature on LMFs shows the claim to be false. Despite systematic deviations from profit maximization, LMFs survive very well in competition with capitalist rivals. One possible reason is that LMFs tend to be more productive in ways that KMFs cannot replicate. Another is that LMFs tend to offer nonpecuniary benefits that KMFs cannot replicate.

What, then, are the barriers to LMF formation? Some evidence indicates that LMFs tend not to enter industries with high capital/labor ratios (Section 7.1). This is consistent with evidence about the cross-industry distribution of LMFs (Section 6.3) that suggests that LMFs occur relatively more often in construction, transport, services, and light manufacturing, and relatively less often in heavy manufacturing, mining, and other capital-intensive activities. One might therefore think that capital constraints are the main problem, and indeed many writers have taken this view.

While this is undoubtedly part of the story, there are complications. It is unclear whether KMFs and LMFs in the same industry have different capital/labor ratios (Section 7.5), as one might expect if LMFs were routinely starved for capital. Some authors find lower capital/labor ratios for LMFs, at least in some industries, or a tendency for LMFs to be smaller than similar KMFs when size is measured by capital assets, while other authors do not. There is little evidence that LMFs grow less rapidly than KMFs and some evidence that their rates of reinvestment out of internal cash flow can be quite high.

One possibility is that LMFs select into industries where capital constraints do not place them at a serious competitive disadvantage and do well in this subset of industries. To the extent that LMFs are obliged to use less capital than the KMFs in these industries, this is presumably outweighed by other competitive advantages for the LMFs. But at the same time, capital constraints could well account for the rarity of LMFs in more capital-intensive industries.

A related factor involves risk. There is evidently a tendency for LMFs to avoid industries where the variance in profit is high (Section 7.1). I will return to risk aversion as an explanation for LMF rarity in Chapter 8. Here, I want to address the fact that LMFs absorb economic shocks largely through variations in income rather than employment. Compared to KMFs, greater job stability in LMFs may better reflect worker preferences about how economic risks should be managed. Alternatively, LMFs may attract a subset of workers whose preference for job security is unusually strong.

Whatever the reasons for the emphasis on job security, this could be part of the explanation for findings of good LMF productivity performance. Long time horizons in relationships between coworkers, or between workers and managers, should foster more mutual monitoring, less need for supervision, greater willingness to share information, greater investment in firm-specific human capital, and the like (see Section 7.2). All of these phenomena are commonly reported in anecdotal accounts and survey research, and all are consistent with the proposition that LMFs can have productivity advantages over KMFs in those industries where both exist.

There is little doubt that LMFs have more compressed wage distributions than similar KMFs (Section 6.7). This is normally framed as a disadvantage: because LMFs have trouble committing themselves to not equalize incomes, high-productivity workers (e.g., top managers) are more likely to exit than would be true for a KMF and presumably are less likely to join the firm to begin with. But the other side of the coin is that workers at (and possibly below) the median wage enjoy a premium and therefore are less likely to exit as well as more likely to join. For this part of the workforce, a higher retention rate could enhance employment stability and reinforce any productivity advantages linked to the continuity of employment. If there is adverse selection in the labor market and more-productive workers have higher reservation wages, LMFs may attract a better applicant pool for frontline jobs than a comparable KMF because LMFs are more committed to maintaining a wage premium for this subset of workers.

Despite much theoretical discussion, the evidence for LMF "degeneration"—where successful LMFs replace departing members by hired workers and eventually resemble KMFs—seems mixed at best (Section 7.4). There are some clear anecdotal examples, but most econometric research fails to find a systematic tendency of this kind. One possible interpretation is that the theoretical temptation for an LMF to degenerate simply does not arise, at least under certain circumstances. Another is that while LMFs may be tempted to degenerate, many are subject to institutional constraints that prevent them from doing so. I will return to this issue in Chapter 9.

LMFs can be created in two ways: from scratch or through conversion of KMFs. Evidence on the relative importance of these two sources is scarce, although conversion was apparently the source for about 16% of LMFs in France (see Section 7.1) and about 11% in Uruguay (see Section 7.2). In the case of France, about 7% of LMFs were created by conversion of failing capitalist firms, and presumably the remaining 9% were created from financially healthy capitalist firms. Whether LMFs are created from scratch or by conversion, however, it seems that the obstacles to employee buyouts include informational asymmetries and public good problems, not just capital constraints. Two arguments point in this direction.

First, even in labor-intensive sectors, the rate of LMF entry is extraordinarily low (Sections 6.2 and 7.1). This suggests that capital constraints are not the only obstacle to LMF formation. One possibility is that LMFs exhibit agglomeration economies, and thus the rarity of LMFs itself constitutes an obstacle to LMF entry (Section 7.6). I suspect that a larger problem is the difficulty of capturing entrepreneurial rent by creating an LMF. A wealthy entrepreneur could establish an LMF if he or she wished to do so. Unless LMFs have systematically poor productivity, which is unlikely, there must be some other reason why entrepreneurs rarely create them. I will return to the problem of entrepreneurial rent appropriation in Chapter 10.

Second, it is implausible that the paucity of cases in which KMFs are transformed into LMFs can be explained entirely by capital constraints.

Again, one can easily explain why such conversions are rare if LMFs have systematically bad productivity, but suppose that we put this possibility to one side. If productivity can be improved by converting a KMF into an LMF, which should be true in some non-negligible fraction of cases, then capital suppliers in the KMF should want to help employees arrange the financing for a buyout, because both parties could be made better off through such a transaction. Partly for this reason, I suspect that the obstacles to employee buyouts include information and public good problems, not just capital constraints. I consider these issues in Chapters 12–13.

As the reader has no doubt guessed by now, I am an optimist with regard to the productivity and survival of LMFs. I am more agnostic about issues like degeneration and underinvestment. In Chapter 9, I argue that incentives along these lines tend to exist whenever membership markets are imperfect and that imperfection is the standard case. But experience shows that in the real world these problems have institutional fixes and are unlikely to threaten the viability of LMFs in any fundamental way.

I am more inclined to be a pessimist with regard to the creation of LMFs, either through formation from scratch or conversion of KMFs. Although both things happen in the real world, they are rare events. The rate of LMF creation is dwarfed by the rate of KMF creation, and the same is true for comparisons of the stocks of firms. Any serious attempt to encourage LMF formation needs to offer a diagnosis of why this is true and a prescription to remedy the problem. I will tackle the first of these tasks in Chapter 19 and the second in Chapter 20. The journey begins in Chapter 8 with a review of existing ideas about the rarity of LMFs.

The Rarity of Labor-Managed Firms

8.1 Introduction

Everyone agrees on one stylized fact: LMFs are rare by comparison with KMFs. It is easy to reject the null hypothesis that existing firms have been organized as KMFs or LMFs based on repeated tosses of a fair coin. Of course, there are many small firms in which entrepreneurs and family members supply both capital and labor. In such firms, it can be hard to determine whether control is based on the supply of one input or the other. But for firms large enough to have formal control structures, there is little debate about the relative frequency of KMFs and LMFs.

This chapter reviews theoretical explanations for the aggregate rarity of labor-managed firms. Although there are many theories, the most popular ones can be grouped into stories about (a) work incentives, (b) asset ownership, (c) capital constraints, (d) risk aversion, and (e) collective choice. This list is not exhaustive. For example, Mikami (2003, 2011) argues that monopoly or monopsony power can help determine whether capital suppliers, labor suppliers, or consumers hold control rights in firms. But to keep the discussion manageable, I limit attention to the five categories listed here.

Section 8.2 reviews these alternative explanations at a theoretical level. Section 8.3 assesses the plausibility of each explanation in light of the available evidence. In my view, ideas about capital constraints and collective choice will almost surely be important in any comprehensive explanatory framework, with asset specificity in a supporting role. I am unsure whether risk aversion adds much, but the jury is out. I believe that theories emphasizing deficient work incentives in LMFs are not supported by credible evidence and should be abandoned.

Section 8.4 argues that theories about capital constraints and collective choice are not wrong, but they are incomplete. My strategy is to include them in a larger theoretical edifice based upon the distinction between alienable capital and inalienable labor. To this end, I will elaborate on the principles of theory construction introduced in Section 1.3, and discuss the concept of alienability. Section 8.5 gives a road map to the rest of the book.

8.2 The Conventional Wisdom

The stories to be discussed in this section represent the conventional wisdom of economists on the subject of LMF rarity, in the sense that these stories are influential in the literature and are often mentioned by economists during casual conversations on the subject. Each is thought to be the most important explanation by a nonempty subset of economists. However, as I hope to show later, these stories are not mutually exclusive and several have something to contribute within a more comprehensive framework. For lengthier reviews, see Dow and Putterman (1999, 2000) and Dow (2003, chs. 8–9).

Work incentives. The first systematic attempt to explain the rarity of LMFs was provided by Alchian and Demsetz (1972). They noted that teamwork is often productive but makes it difficult to observe individual effort levels. Unless the pay of each worker is closely tied to that worker's effort, individual team members will shirk. The solution is to appoint a monitor who pays wages based on estimated effort. Shirking by the monitor is prevented by awarding this agent sole claim on the firm's residual income. The monitor manages the firm because the information obtained through monitoring can also be used to coordinate production activities. If the monitor is a capital supplier (perhaps due to the asset maintenance issues to be discussed later), the result is a KMF.

There are many theoretical and empirical objections to this story. I mention only a few here. First, vertical monitoring by a specialist may be less effective or more costly than horizontal monitoring among a group of coworkers (Putterman, 1984). Second, a monitor might be tempted to cheat by claiming that a worker's effort was low when in fact it was high (Eswaran and Kotwal, 1984; MacLeod, 1984; Andolfatto and Nosal, 1997). Third, it may be possible to motivate the team members through group bonuses or penalties, without any monitoring at all (Holmstrom, 1982). Fourth, shirking can be deterred in a repeated game if team members put

enough weight on future payoffs. The theoretical literature on these matters is at best inconclusive. I will argue that the Alchian and Demsetz (1972)
story is dubious on empirical grounds (see Section 8.3).

Asset ownership. Capitalist firms typically own some physical assets and
rent others. However, a number of authors have argued that (a) LMFs may
be unable to rent all of the productive assets they need and (b) LMFs could
have difficulty with collective asset ownership. If both problems arise
simultaneously, the LMF is clearly in trouble.

One difficulty with the rental of productive assets involves incentive
problems. If the workers who use an asset do not own it, they might
overuse it or neglect maintenance tasks. Moreover, it could be costly for
the outside owners of the asset to detect or punish abuse of this kind
(Alchian and Demsetz, 1972). This could motivate ownership of tools by
the individual workers who use them or collective ownership of larger
assets by the workforce as a whole.

A second difficulty involves bargaining problems. When physical assets
and the human capital of workers are specialized, the presence of sunk
costs creates a flow of quasi-rents. Having workers rent assets from outside
owners under these conditions can lead to costly ex post bargaining over
these quasi-rents (Klein et al., 1978; Williamson, 1985) and suboptimal ex
ante investment (Grossman and Hart, 1986; Hart and Moore, 1990). These
problems will be addressed at length in Chapters 14 and 15.

Both of these difficulties can be avoided by having the LMF own its
nonhuman assets collectively. However, this may lead to other problems.
The most obvious is that such assets have to be financed in some way. I will
return to this issue later. Alchian and Demsetz (1972) make a different
argument: assets owned collectively by an LMF may not be properly
maintained because no individual worker has an incentive to maintain
them. To avoid free rider problems associated with proper use and maintenance, it may be best to have a KMF in which one person owns the firm's
assets and monitors their use.

There is no clear reason why KMFs and LMFs would differ in their
ability to rent nonhuman assets from outside owners. But if we grant that
some nonhuman assets are difficult to rent for all firms, and therefore must
be owned by firms, then a comparison of collective asset ownership in
KMFs and LMFs becomes relevant. If we can show that the LMF has
defective investment incentives, poor maintenance incentives, or difficulties in financing collectively owned assets, such factors may help explain
the rarity of LMFs.

Wealth constraints. Perhaps the most common explanation for the rarity of LMFs is that workers lack the wealth needed to finance firms. This assumes that LMFs require start-up financing before they can begin to generate an internal cash flow. Because initial financing requirements are unlikely to be large when nonhuman assets can be rented, the wealth story is more persuasive when firms have problems renting productive assets from outside owners, either for incentive or bargaining reasons. The wealth story is also more persuasive for capital-intensive industries. Finally, the story requires some capital market imperfection that prevents workers from obtaining access to external financing on terms comparable to the opportunity cost of capital in the KMF.

Workers seeking loans to finance firms may encounter problems of moral hazard and adverse selection (Stiglitz and Weiss, 1981). The moral hazard problem arises when borrowers have incentives to take actions contrary to the interests of lenders after a loan contract has been signed. For example, workers might pursue risky projects if they can declare bankruptcy and leave lenders holding the bag. Eswaran and Kotwal (1989) argue that workers will be tempted to substitute inputs financed by loans for their own effort. LMF financing problems are likely to be aggravated when nonhuman assets are highly specialized, because such assets are not useful as loan collateral (Williamson, 1988).

An alternative to debt is for workers to sell nonvoting equity shares in order to attract capital without sacrificing control over the firm. But investors who lack control rights may fear that workers will use their decision-making powers in an opportunistic fashion, for example by raising wages at the expense of dividends (Putterman, 1993). Workers will therefore need to pay a premium for capital raised through nonvoting equity, disadvantaging LMFs relative to KMFs.

Adverse selection arises when some borrowers have better projects than others, it is impossible for lenders to distinguish between good and bad borrowers before issuing a loan, and the proportions of good and bad loan applicants are influenced by the terms of the loan contract. As a result, even workers with good projects may face credit rationing or high interest rates. Borrowers with good projects might try to signal their true quality by offering to put some of their own money at risk, but such strategies may be infeasible or very costly for poor workers. Lenders could screen potential borrowers to determine the quality of their projects, but this too may be costly.

KMFs may also face moral hazard and adverse selection problems in the capital market, so LMFs are not unique in this respect. But capitalists who are sufficiently rich have no need for external financing and can bypass these capital market imperfections when they create a firm. The relevant cost of capital in this case is the return that could be obtained by supplying capital to a financial market or using it in some other project.

Risk aversion. Another popular story about the rarity of LMFs is that workers are more risk averse than investors. Investors thus hold residual claims, bear risk, and insure workers through fixed wages. Investors manage the firm because only residual claimants have the right incentives for this task. Meade (1972), Kihlstrom and Laffont (1979), and Drèze (1989), among others, have advanced versions of this story.

The risk aversion argument reinforces ideas based on limited worker wealth and the imperfection of financial markets. Suppose that an LMF needs to own certain productive assets collectively. If workers are risk averse, they will not want to invest a large amount of their personal wealth in a single firm. Other things equal, LMF members would prefer to sell a portion of their claim on the firm's capital stock to outside investors and diversify their individual portfolios. This desire for diversification is more pressing when workers have firm-specific human capital. The diversification motive implies that the LMF must rely more heavily on external financing, with all the problems this already entails. Bonin et al. (1993) concluded that wealth constraints and risk aversion together are the central reasons for the rarity of LMFs. Bowles and Gintis (1996a) reached similar conclusions.

Two theoretical complications will be mentioned briefly. First, it is impossible to specify worker effort in a legally binding contract. A standard result from principal-agent theory is that workers in this situation will not receive full insurance from their employers (Holmstrom and Milgrom, 1994). Instead, employee compensation will be linked to the financial results of the firm, even though this exposes workers to some risk. But workers who bear risk have a stake in how the firm is managed. Given the common presumption in the literature that residual claimants will also be decision-makers, this poses a question about why workers would not participate in firm management.

Second, control rights themselves can provide a form of insurance. For example, suppose that a KMF would respond to a negative shock by firing workers. A similar LMF might respond by maintaining employment while spreading the economic pain across the workforce through reduced hours or lower hourly earnings. Given a choice, risk averse workers might prefer the LMF option and might be prepared to forego some financial diversification in order to obtain greater employment security.

Collective choice. Hansmann (1996) and others have argued that LMFs have greater difficulty in reaching collective decisions than KMFs because worker objectives tend to be more heterogeneous than those of investors. The idea is that capital suppliers unanimously support maximization of profit or present value, but workers have diverse attitudes toward effort, hours, income, job security, safety, social atmosphere, and other aspects of the workplace. Hansmann points out that majority voting among workers who have heterogeneous preferences is likely to run into a problem of cycling, where for every firm policy there is an alternative proposal that is preferred by a majority coalition. There are numerous solutions to the cycling problem, but each forces the LMF to incur costs that do not arise in a KMF.

The heterogeneity of worker preferences may also make LMFs an unstable mode of organization. Dow and Skillman (2007) argue that LMFs are vulnerable to takeover bids from outside investors that 51% of LMF members will accept. They also argue that KMFs are not equally vulnerable to takeover bids from employees. I will return to this issue in Chapter 12.

Another variation on the collective choice idea is that firms adopting the principle of "one worker, one vote" will suffer from excessive egalitarianism with respect to income distribution, because the median voter will favor redistribution from higher-productivity workers to lower-productivity workers (see Section 6.7). If high-ability workers confront wage compression in LMFs, they may prefer jobs at KMFs where they get their marginal products. It could be difficult for LMFs to devise credible institutional restraints on such behavior.

On the other hand, collective choice factors may actually advantage the LMF over the KMF. The characteristics of the workplace are local public goods for workers, and profit-maximizing firms do not usually offer an efficient supply of such public goods (Drèze and Hagen, 1978). The voting processes used in LMFs may therefore yield efficiency improvements relative to KMFs by aligning firm policies more closely with worker preferences. For example, Pencavel (2015) argues that the plywood cooperatives enabled members to bring actual work hours closer to their preferred hours.

8.3 Theory versus Evidence

For their influential literature survey, Bonin et al. (1993) chose the title "Theoretical and Empirical Studies of Producer Cooperatives: Will Ever the Twain Meet?" In 1993, this was a serious question. A large body of theoretical work on LMFs had accumulated, but the body of reliable empirical evidence was considerably smaller. Theorists were left free to speculate, and they did. Today the twain have moved much closer. The quantity and quality of empirical research on LMFs have increased, and the merits of various theoretical stories have come into sharper focus. This section outlines my current views in light of the evidence from Chapters 6 and 7. These differ in a few ways from the views I expressed on these topics in Dow (2003, chs. 8–9).

The work incentives story pioneered by Alchian and Demsetz (1972) has fallen by the wayside. One would think that if LMFs were rare because their effort incentives were weaker than those of similar KMFs, then LMFs would have lower productivity and lower survival rates. The first implication conflicts with evidence that LMFs have productivity at least as high as KMFs (see Section 6.6), and the second conflicts with the evidence that LMFs have survival rates at least as high as KMFs (see Section 7.2). More generally, the work incentives story is contradicted by a wealth of anecdotal evidence to the effect that LMF members work hard and have fewer front-line supervisors than do KMF employees. One might try to salvage the story by claiming that LMFs have adequate work incentives in the industries where they currently operate and avoid other industries where their poor work incentives would be a serious liability, but this is ad hoc. The burden clearly rests with proponents of the work incentives hypothesis to provide some credible evidence. Until they do, researchers are justified in discounting this hypothesis.

Hypotheses about asset ownership have not been subjected to systematic tests by LMF researchers. In general, it is hard to determine whether the assets used in a specific industry are especially vulnerable to maintenance or bargaining problems. To the extent that LMFs have difficulties with collective asset ownership beyond a need for financing, these might show up in the form of underinvestment. However, evidence on this issue is ambiguous (see Section 7.5). To the extent that asset ownership problems are manifested in a need for additional financing, one might expect LMFs to be rarer in industries where nonhuman assets are less easily rented or more highly specialized, but I am not aware of any strong evidence along these lines.

For the wealth constraint story, matters seem a bit clearer. The most persuasive evidence that LMFs confront capital constraints comes from the work of Podivinsky and Stewart (2007, 2009) described in Section 7.1. Using a large set of U.K. manufacturing industries in the early 1980s, these authors show that LMF entry was less common for more capital-intensive industries. It would be reassuring to have replications for other countries and time periods, but these econometric results are consistent with a good deal of impressionistic evidence and the intuition of most researchers in the field.

Another piece of intuition appears more questionable. Various writers (including this one) have asserted that LMFs tend to use less capital-intensive production techniques than KMFs operating in the same industry. However, Pencavel et al. (2006) did not find any significant difference in mean capital/labor ratios after controlling for industry, and Fakhfakh et al. (2012) found a significant difference (in the expected direction) only in a minority of industries. The latter authors accordingly express skepticism about the idea that LMFs are starved for capital (see Section 7.5).

One way to reconcile these findings with those of Podivinsky and Stewart is to argue that LMFs do not often enter industries where capital requirements are so large that financial constraints would be binding but do enter and compete effectively in industries where these constraints are nonbinding. For some industries where financial barriers are large but not prohibitive, LMFs might enter below efficient scale and accumulate capital rapidly after retained earnings become available. This is consistent with the observation that many LMFs plow back a large share of profit into growth (I thank Virginie Pérotin for this point).

Even if one grants that wealth constraints are important, this cannot be the entire story. As I argued in Section 7.7, limited worker wealth, even in combination with credit rationing, cannot explain why wealthy entrepreneurs do not create LMFs from scratch or why investors do not finance the conversion of KMFs into LMFs. Transactions of either kind could be attractive in cases where LMFs have productivity advantages over KMFs, and capital constraints should not be an obstacle in either case.

The risk aversion story remains in a confused state. Meade (1972) thought it obvious that workers were risk averse, could not diversify their labor across firms, and would want to avoid investing their financial wealth in the firms where they worked. He therefore argued that LMFs would be confined to industries where external shocks were not too severe. But as Bonin et al. (1993) observed, the U.S. plywood cooperatives faced large shocks to input and output prices. Craig and Pencavel (1995, 129, n. 13) state that volatility of plywood and timber prices "flatly contradicts Meade's (1972) assertion that a necessary condition for cooperative enterprises to thrive is an industry where 'the risk of fluctuations in the demand for the product must not be too great'" (p. 427). Along the same lines, Section 6.3 indicated that worker cooperatives are relatively common in the construction industry, which is well known for its exposure to business cycle risks. These observations and others (e.g., the willingness of U.S. employees to acquire equity shares in the firms where they work) persuaded me in the past that the risk aversion story was unlikely to be very important in explaining the rarity of LMFs (Dow, 2003, ch. 9).

Today, I am less sure. My uncertainty is based largely on the work of Podivinsky and Stewart (2007, 2009), who found that LMF entry was less common in industries with higher variance in profit, holding capital intensity constant (see Section 7.1). This seems to resurrect the Meade argument, or at least some variant of it. Matters would be clearer if these results could be replicated (or disconfirmed) for other countries and time periods, but in my revised assessment, the risk aversion story remains viable for the present.

Regarding the collective choice story, the situation is mixed. Based on the recent work of Burdín (2016) on Uruguay, along with related work by Abramitzky (2008, 2009, 2011), the argument that voting equilibrium leads to wage compression in LMFs appears incontrovertible (see Section 6.7). Whether this factor is important enough to explain the general rarity of LMFs is another matter. The conjecture by Hansmann and others about the role of heterogeneous worker preferences is consistent with considerable anecdotal evidence (see Dow, 2003, ch. 9). It would be useful to have an econometric test of the hypothesis that LMFs are less common in industries where firms' workforces are more heterogeneous or that LMFs less often enter such industries, other things being equal.

8.4 The Alienability Approach

The rest of the book tries to make some sense of the empirical patterns outlined in Chapters 6 and 7. To the extent possible, I want to absorb what is useful about the stories from Sections 8.2 and 8.3 into a larger theoretical structure. I hope to persuade the reader that these stories are incomplete as they stand but can be made complete (or at least more complete) by embedding them in an explanatory framework based upon the alienability of capital and the inalienability of labor. I begin this quest with a few conceptual points. These were sketched in Section 1.3, but the time has come for an elaboration.

The first point arises from Chapters 2–5. In a world of complete and competitive markets, suitably designed KMFs and LMFs are isomorphic: they exhibit identical static and dynamic behavior, and economies with each type of firm support identical resource allocations. To explain the empirical asymmetries between LMFs and KMFs, including the rarity of LMFs, one must study environments in which no such isomorphism arises. This requires some market imperfection, such as market power, asymmetric information, a lack of commitment devices, or other factors. In an interesting theory, the capital and labor markets must both be imperfect. If one is perfectly competitive, there is no reason for suppliers of that input to enjoy control rights. I call this the *imperfection principle*.

The second point is that if capital and labor were symmetric in all physical and institutional respects, and capital and labor markets had symmetric imperfections, we would not expect to find empirical asymmetries between KMFs and LMFs. For example, the distribution of KMFs and LMFs across industries would be random. A satisfactory theory must therefore identify relevant differences between capital and labor, show why KMFs and LMFs would be affected differently by a given set of market imperfections, and use these theoretical differences to explain the differences between KMFs and LMFs in the real world. I call this the *asymmetry principle*.

The third point is that one should avoid arbitrary institutional assumptions about the LMF that place it at a disadvantage relative to the KMF. To take a few examples, one should not assume the following: that LMFs must pay equal wages to all workers, that they must retain members regardless of their effort, or that they must make all decisions in group meetings rather than having specialized managers. Imposing ad hoc constraints on LMFs that are not imposed on KMFs begs the question. It is easy to understand why poorly designed LMFs are rare. A more interesting question is why even well-designed LMFs are rare.

A good theory should assume that LMFs can adopt any organizational practice KMFs can adopt, unless the practice conflicts in some explicit way with the definitional requirement of ultimate control by labor suppliers. The converse also applies: it should be assumed that KMFs can adopt any practice LMFs can adopt, unless it conflicts with the requirement of ultimate control by capital suppliers. Another way to put this is that intrinsic asymmetries between capital and labor have theoretical significance, while ad hoc asymmetries between KMFs and LMFs do not. I call this the *replication principle*.

I believe that the most fundamental difference between capital and labor is that capital is *alienable* while labor is *inalienable*. I will take some time to explain what this means. In most discussions of property rights and ownership, rights over an asset are "alienable" if these rights can be transferred from one person to another. Alienability in this sense has a strong legal flavor: the law might allow ownership rights over an asset to be transferred, or it might not. This is part of what I have in mind, but there are deeper issues.

My idea of inalienable labor is based on the physical impossibility of separating certain resources (time, skill, knowledge, experience) from the person who decides how these resources will be used. Whatever the law may say, it is physically impossible for me to transfer half of my time to you so that now I have twelve hours per day and you have thirty-six hours per day. It is also physically impossible, at least with present technology, to transfer a stock of human capital located in my brain directly into your brain. At best, one of us could educate the other, but instructors in classrooms everywhere know that this is a slow and unreliable process. The situation is different with nonhuman assets (machines, buildings, inventories, copyrights, stocks and bonds). There is no physical reason why ownership rights over resources of this kind cannot be transferred from one person or group to another. Moreover, the law generally facilitates such transfers.

This distinction has many economic implications. Several of these implications will play important roles in later chapters.

(a) One person can own unlimited nonhuman assets, but there are natural limits on one person's ownership of human assets such as time or skill.
(b) One person can own nonhuman assets in dispersed locations, but at a given point in time one person can only supply labor services at one location.
(c) Nonhuman assets can be purchased as a stock, or their services can be rented as a flow. Labor services can only be acquired as a flow.
(d) Nonhuman assets can be owned collectively by groups or organizations such as firms, while human assets cannot.
(e) Nonhuman assets can be used as loan collateral, while human assets cannot.

Whenever possible, I interpret empirical asymmetries between KMFs and LMFs as implications resulting from the alienability distinction between capital and labor. To the extent that this program succeeds, we will obtain a unified theory of the LMF rather than just a collection of disjointed theories explaining a collection of disjointed facts. In an ideal world, one would like to explain all of the empirical generalizations reviewed in Chapters 6 and 7. In practice, this is too ambitious, but I will argue that the alienability distinction accounts for a range of facts extending well beyond the mere rarity of LMFs. A synthesis along these lines will be proposed in Chapter 19.

A common heuristic device throughout the book will be to raise questions about the completeness of hypotheses like those in Sections 8.2 and 8.3. For example, if one argues that LMFs have trouble attracting capital, an obvious question is whether KMFs have any trouble attracting labor. If not, why is there an asymmetry? If so, why are the problems confronting the KMF in the labor market less consequential than the problems confronting the LMF in the capital market?

Similarly, if one argues that LMFs have problems with collective choice due to the heterogeneity of worker preferences, why don't KMFs have similar problems due to the heterogeneity of investor preferences? How do labor and capital markets generate the asymmetry? And if LMFs have problems with wage compression attributable to majority voting among workers, why don't KMFs have similar problems where a majority of shareholders redistributes dividends away from a minority?

Existing theories about the LMF are largely silent on such matters. One goal of the book is to show that it is possible to construct reasonable answers to these questions by exploiting the distinction between alienable capital and inalienable labor. Whether or not one accepts this particular approach, however, it would be desirable for future LMF theorists to develop the habit of asking, "Why the asymmetry?" This is useful in weeding out ad hoc explanations and pushes theory toward greater completeness.

8.5 A Road Map

Chapters 9–18 are organized around distinctive forms of market imperfection. Chapters 9–11 deal with appropriation problems that arise when control positions in firms are bought and sold on markets and insiders cannot fully capture the value of these positions to outsiders. I argue that due to the alienability distinction, markets for control rights in KMFs have fewer frictions than markets for control rights in LMFs. Chapter 9 shows that imperfections in LMF membership markets can account for the differences in comparative static behavior between KMFs and LMFs, the temptation for degeneration of LMFs into KMFs, and the temptation for underinvestment by LMFs. Chapter 10 shows that adverse selection involving entrepreneurial projects can cause entrepreneurs to create KMFs rather than more-productive LMFs. Chapter 11 argues that for adverse selection reasons, LMFs generally prohibit direct sales of control positions to replacement workers by departing members, while KMFs frequently allow open trading of control positions on anonymous markets.

Chapters 12 and 13 consider problems involving public goods. Two sources of market imperfection are considered: missing markets associated with an absence of state-contingent income claims (Chapter 12) and free rider issues associated with the creation of knowledge about firm productivity (Chapter 13). Again, in each case I claim that there are asymmetries connected with alienability. In Chapter 12, I argue that because capital is more mobile than labor, investors in a KMF are typically unanimous with respect to firm objectives whereas workers in an LMF are not. As a result, it is usually easier for investors to buy out LMFs than it is for employees to buy out KMFs. In Chapter 13, I argue that because workers usually face more severe free rider problems than investors, it is more difficult to convert KMFs into LMFs than vice versa.

Chapters 14–18 focus on what I broadly call "opportunism problems," which arise when individual agents can pursue their own self-interest at the expense of others due to the incompleteness or absence of legally binding contracts. Chapters 14 and 15 address the departures from perfect competition associated with firm-specific physical or human assets. Asset specificity can cause conflict between capital and labor suppliers over the distribution of quasi-rent within the firm. In general, KMFs will steer quasi-rent toward capital suppliers, while LMFs do the same for labor suppliers. Expectations about the outcome of this ex post conflict can affect the ex ante willingness of input suppliers to invest in specialized assets. This has implications for the viability of each type of firm. One solution consistent with the inalienability of labor is for LMFs to collectively own specialized nonhuman assets, but this raises issues involving worker wealth constraints and capital market imperfections.

Chapters 16–18 explore opportunism problems in a starker setting, where there are no contractual commitment devices. In the scenarios in all three of these chapters, input contributions and side payments must be enforced through repeated game mechanisms. Chapter 16 shows that in this environment, there is an isomorphism between firms where the capital stock is owned by outside investors and firms where it is owned collectively by workers. This result gives rise to several points. First, contrary to various claims in the literature, KMFs and LMFs sometimes provide identical work incentives. Second, LMFs are not always at a disadvantage when collective ownership of nonhuman assets is needed. Third, market imperfections are not sufficient to create asymmetries between KMFs and LMFs. Some distinction between capital and labor (such as alienability) is also required.

Chapter 17 develops a model comparing the temptation for KMFs to cheat employees by withholding wages with the temptation for LMFs to cheat investors by depreciating the capital stock and withholding rental or debt service payments. The main idea is that because capital is acquired as a stock whereas labor is acquired as a flow, LMFs are more tempted to behave opportunistically toward investors than KMFs are toward workers. For a two-period model with quadratic costs, I show that when up-front capital requirements are large enough, KMFs are viable while LMFs are not.

Chapter 18 considers adverse selection with respect to entrepreneurial projects and develops a model of the capital and labor markets where the numbers of KMFs and LMFs are endogenous. I show that the differing intertemporal structure of transactions involving capital and labor can create an incentive advantage for KMFs. In particular, when investors have up-front liquidity but workers do not, equilibria where all firms are KMFs can arise for a wider range of parameter values than when inputs are symmetric.

PART IV

APPROPRIATION PROBLEMS

9

Imperfect Appropriation

9.1 Introduction

Perfect membership markets were central to the isomorphism between capitalist and labor-managed firms in Chapters 3–5. This chapter examines LMF behavior when the current membership cannot fully appropriate the surplus generated by the firm. The main purpose is to determine whether imperfect appropriation is a promising way of explaining some empirical asymmetries from Chapters 6–7. I argue that imperfect appropriation can account for LMF comparative static rigidities (Section 6.4), as well as tendencies toward degeneration (Section 7.4) and underinvestment (Section 7.5). I also suggest reasons why imperfect appropriation is likely to be widespread among LMFs and why it is likely to be less severe among KMFs.

Section 9.2 models the LMF in a way that includes profit maximization and the Ward-Domar-Vanek hypothesis as special cases. I will show that when insiders cannot capture the entire surplus of the firm, the LMF has a lower output supply elasticity than a profit-maximizing firm. This is consistent with empirical evidence from Section 6.4.

Section 9.3 distinguishes between cases of expansion, where insiders recruit new members, and contraction, where the LMF reduces its labor input by having old members leave. The latter is problematic because if an LMF deviates from profit maximization in the course of contraction, some members will either have to leave involuntarily or stay involuntarily. Nevertheless, I show that an LMF with an internal power hierarchy can contract in a way that is consistent with the model developed in Section 9.2.

LMF degeneration is addressed in Section 9.4. I show that LMFs with imperfect appropriation have incentives to replace departing members with workers who receive a competitive wage and do not share in profit. This lends support to the idea that LMFs can degenerate into de facto KMFs over time through attrition among founding members (see Section 7.4). However, in practice LMFs have often avoided this problem through suitable legal or organizational rules.

LMF underinvestment is addressed in Section 9.5. The key question is whether imperfect appropriation can cause LMFs to grow more slowly than KMFs, even when LMFs have static productivity advantages (see Section 6.6). I show that this is indeed possible. Furthermore, LMFs could lose the growth race to KMFs or be converted into KMFs, even if LMFs generate more total surplus. The reason is that LMF insiders fail to internalize the surplus that will be appropriated by outsiders when they become members in the future. This offers a new perspective on traditional debates about underinvestment by LMFs (see Section 7.5). As for degeneration, the incentives for underinvestment pose a danger, but in practice LMFs have often developed successful institutional solutions.

Section 9.6 argues that several factors could cause imperfect appropriation to arise for LMFs. Section 9.7 is a short postscript, and Section 9.8 proves formal propositions.

9.2 Comparative Statics

In this section I investigate the following question: assuming that all labor in the LMF is supplied by members, and each member supplies a fixed number of hours, how do LMFs vary membership size in response to changes in their economic environment? This ignores other margins for adjustment. For example, if demand rises, the existing members could work longer hours or supply more effort per hour. An LMF could also hire nonmember workers and pay them a competitive wage, as a KMF would do. But membership size is fundamental to the theory of the LMF and is best studied in a setting where other adjustment strategies are suppressed. I treat expansion and contraction in a symmetric way in this section and discuss the differences between them in Section 9.3.

Consider an LMF with a twice continuously differentiable production function f(L) such that $f(0) = 0$, $f'(0) = \infty$, $f'(\infty) = 0$, and $f''(L) < 0$ for all $L > 0$. I assume that f(L) is unbounded as $L \to \infty$. Each member supplies one unit of labor, so firm membership size is equal to the labor input L. I ignore nonlabor inputs. These are of little interest if they can be acquired on competitive markets, because LMF members will follow the standard rules of profit maximization with respect to such inputs. The topic of central interest is the quantity of the input supplied by the agents who hold control rights within the firm.

Profit is defined to be

$$\pi(L;\ p,\ w,\ c) = pf(L) - wL - c \qquad (1)$$

where $p > 0$ is output price, $w > 0$ is the external wage, and $c > 0$ is fixed cost. All are parametric for the agents who control the firm. The function π is strictly concave in L and has a unique interior maximizer $L^{PMF}(p, w) > 0$. Profit is rising on the interval $L < L^{PMF}(p, w)$ and falling on the interval $L > L^{PMF}(p, w)$.

Proposition 1
Profit-maximizing firm:

(a) The labor input $L^{PMF}(p, w)$ for a profit-maximizing firm is increasing in p and decreasing in w. $L^{PMF}(p, w)$ is not affected by c.

(b) Maximum profit $\pi[L^{PMF}(p, w);\ p, w, c]$ is increasing in p and decreasing in (w, c).

(c) For any fixed $(w, c) > 0$, there is a unique output price $p_{min} > 0$ such that $\pi[L^{PMF}(p_{min}, w);\ p_{min}, w, c] = 0$.

These are textbook results, and proofs are omitted.

For comparisons with the WDV model from Chapter 3, define the dividend per worker-member to be

$$d(L;\ p,\ c) = [pf(L) - c]/L \qquad (2)$$

In the WDV model, the firm chooses L to maximize $d(L; p, c)$. It can be shown that there is a strictly positive value of L at which the first derivative with respect to L is zero and that whenever the first derivative is zero, the second derivative is negative. This implies that there is a unique labor input $L^{WDV}(p, c) > 0$ at which the dividend is maximized and that there are no other local maximizers or minimizers. The dividend is therefore rising on the interval $L < L^{WDV}(p, c)$ and falling on the interval $L > L^{WDV}(p, c)$.

Proposition 2
The Ward-Domar-Vanek firm:

(a) The labor input $L^{WDV}(p, c)$ for a WDV firm is decreasing in p and increasing in c. $L^{WDV}(p, c)$ is not affected by w.

(b) The maximum dividend $d[L^{WDV}(p, c); p, c]$ is increasing in p and decreasing in c.

These results are familiar from the LMF literature and will not be proven here. Upon substituting $L^{WDV}(p, c)$ into the production function $f(L)$, part (a) yields the famous (or infamous) backward-bending supply curve for the WDV firm.

The following results are also well known from the LMF literature.

Proposition 3
Comparison of profit-maximizing and WDV firms:
For any fixed $(w, c) > 0$, define p_{min} as in Proposition 1(c). This gives

(a) $L^{WDV}(p_{min}, c) = L^{PMF}(p_{min}, w)$
(b) $d[L^{WDV}(p_{min}, c); p_{min}, c] = w$
(c) $L^{WDV}(p, c) < L^{PMF}(p, w)$ whenever $p > p_{min}$

Part (a) says that when a PMF has zero profit, the PMF and its WDV twin use the same labor input. Part (b) says that when a PMF has zero profit, the maximum dividend for its WDV twin is equal to the external wage. Part (c) says that when a PMF enjoys a positive profit, its WDV twin uses less labor than the PMF does. The last result follows from (a) and the fact that labor input is increasing in output price for the PMF but decreasing in output price for the WDV firm.

Now let there be $L_0 > 0$ ex ante members of the LMF. These insiders choose the firm's ex post membership L. Suppose for concreteness that the insiders are considering expansion of the firm's membership. After L has been determined, the $L - L_0$ newcomers pay their membership fees, production occurs, and all ex post members receive $d(L; p, c)$. The L_0 ex ante members also share equally in the revenue from the membership fees paid by the $L - L_0$ newcomers.

For a given ex post membership size $L > L_0$, the maximum amount an outsider is willing to pay for membership is $d(L; p, c) - w$. By contrast with Chapters 3–5, here the market for membership positions may be imperfect, and outsiders may retain a positive surplus when they join the firm. The actual revenue the insiders collect from each new member is denoted by $\alpha[d(L; p, c) - w]$, where $\alpha \in [0, 1]$ is the fraction of the value of membership to an outsider that the insiders are able to appropriate. The LMF has no control over the appropriation factor α.

The total revenue collected from the L – L_0 new members is $\alpha[d(L; p, c) - w](L - L_0)$. This is divided equally among the L_0 insiders, so each insider receives

$$Z(L; p, w, c, \alpha, L_0) \equiv w + \alpha\pi(L; p, w, c)/L_0$$
$$+(1 - \alpha)[d(L; p, c) - w] \qquad (3)$$

In addition to the opportunity cost w, each insider receives a convex combination of the per capita profit $\pi(L; p, w, c)/L_0$ and the WDV surplus $d(L; p, c) - w$. Greater weight is placed on profit to the degree that the membership market comes closer to a competitive environment with $\alpha = 1$. Conversely, more weight is placed on the WDV objective as the appropriation factor approaches zero. Only cases with $p \geq p_{min}$ are interesting, because at any lower price, both $\pi(L; p, w, c)$ and $d(L; p, c) - w$ are negative for all L in (3) and the LMF cannot attract or retain members. The objective function in (3) differs from some of the objective functions used in the empirical research reviewed in Section 6.5, which treat the maximization of employment and maximization of income per worker as polar cases, with profit maximization intermediate between these two goals. By contrast, the function Z assigns positive weight only to profit and income per worker.

Now consider fixed values of (p, w, c) such that $p \geq p_{min}$ so profit is nonnegative. Z is increasing in L on the interval $L < L^{WDV}$ because both π and d are increasing on this interval. Likewise, Z is decreasing in L on the interval $L > L^{PMF}$ because both π and d are decreasing. Thus, there cannot be a global (or local) maximum of Z outside $[L^{WDV}, L^{PMF}]$. Z takes on a maximum value in this interval due to the compactness of the interval and the continuity of Z as a function of L, so there must be a global maximizer for Z in this interval. However, the global maximizer may not be unique, or there could be multiple local maximizers and minimizers in the interval $[L^{WDV}, L^{PMF}]$.

The central problem in addressing these questions is that the strict concavity of Z on the interval $[L^{WDV}, L^{PMF}]$ is not guaranteed. The profit function π is globally concave, but the dividend function d is not. The dividend is strictly concave in a neighborhood of L^{WDV}, but for large L it is strictly convex because d is positive and approaches zero as L approaches infinity. In this region, a small value of α would make Z strictly convex.

Some results can be obtained even without concavity, but the most convenient approach is to place bounds on the values of the parameters (p, w, c).

Proposition 4

Strict concavity of Z:

Choose a fixed $(p, c) > 0$, and let $d^{max}(p, c) \equiv d[L^{WDV}(p, c); p, c] > 0$ be the maximum dividend as in Proposition 2(b). There is a nonempty, nondegenerate wage interval $[w^{min}(p, c), d^{max}(p, c)]$ such that for any fixed $w \in [w^{min}(p, c), d^{max}(p, c)]$, the following results hold:

(a) The profit $\pi(L; p, w, c)$ is nonnegative on the interval $[L^{WDV}, L^{PMF}]$ associated with (p, w, c).

(b) The dividend $d(L; p, c)$ is at least equal to the wage w on the same interval.

(c) The dividend $d(L; p, c)$ is strictly concave in L on the same interval.

(d) The function Z is strictly concave in L on the same interval.

(e) There is a unique labor input $L(p, w, c, \alpha, L_0) \in [L^{WDV}, L^{PMF}]$ at which the first order condition for a maximum of Z holds.

(f) The labor input $L(p, w, c, \alpha, L_0)$ is the unique global maximizer of Z.

A proof is provided in Section 9.8. The key idea is that when w is close to the maximum dividend d^{max}, the profit-maximizing labor input L^{PMF} (p, w) is close to the Ward-Domar-Vanek labor input $L^{WDV}(p, c)$ and the dividend function is strictly concave on the interval $[L^{WDV}, L^{PMF}]$. This situation is depicted in Figure 9.1.

Given the exogenous parameters (p, w, c, α), one question of interest is whether there is some membership size L_0 such that the existing members would not deviate to a different membership size. Using the notation of Proposition 4(f), this is true if

$$L_0 = L(p, w, c, \alpha, L_0) \qquad (4)$$

In this case, the current membership size L_0 is also the desired membership size, in the sense that it maximizes the objective function Z.

A firm size L_0 satisfying (4) will be called an *equilibrium membership*. From Proposition 4, we have $L(p, w, c, \alpha, L_0) \in [L^{WDV}(p, c), L^{PMF}(p, w)]$ regardless of L_0. This implies that in searching for an equilibrium membership size, we can confine attention to values of L_0 in this interval.

Proposition 5

Existence and uniqueness of equilibrium membership size:

Assume that the conditions in Proposition 4 are satisfied.

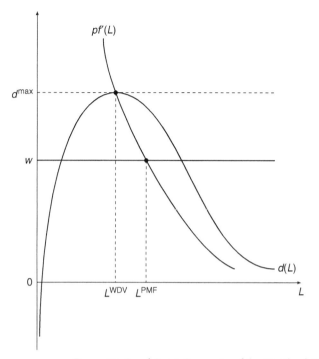

Figure 9.1 Local Strict Concavity of the Dividend Function

(a) $L(p, w, c, \alpha, L_0)$ is continuous and strictly decreasing in L_0.
(b) For fixed (p, w, c, α), there is a unique $L_0 \in [L^{WDV}(p, c), L^{PMF}(p, w)]$ such that (4) holds. Furthermore:

   (i) If $\alpha = 0$, the value of L_0 satisfying (4) is L^{WDV}.
   (ii) If $0 < \alpha < 1$, the value of L_0 satisfying (4) has $L^{WDV} < L_0 < L^{PMF}$.
   (iii) If $\alpha = 1$, the value of L_0 satisfying (4) is L^{PMF}.

A proof is provided in Section 9.8. Part (a) follows from the fact that as L_0 increases, less weight is placed on the profit component of Z in (3), and this decreases the optimal labor input. Part (b) follows from (a) and the fact that $L(p, w, c, \alpha, L_0)$ is in $[L^{WDV}, L^{PMF}]$.

The optimal labor input $L(p, w, c, \alpha, L_0)$ satisfies the first order condition

$$Z'(L; p, w, c, \alpha, L_0) \equiv \alpha\pi'(L; p, w, c)/L_0 + (1-\alpha)d'(L; p, c) = 0 \qquad (5)$$

where primes indicate differentiation with respect to L. Let $L^E = L_0 = L$ (p, w, c, α, L_0) be the equilibrium firm size. Substituting L^E in (5) gives

$$pf'(L^E) = \alpha w + (1 - \alpha)[pf(L^E) - c]/L^E \qquad (6)$$

When $\alpha = 1$, this reduces to the first order condition for profit maximization, and when $\alpha = 0$, it reduces to the first order condition for the WDV firm.

The next task is to study the determinants of the equilibrium firm size L^E. It is easy to sign the comparative static effects of (p, w, c) on L^E when output elasticity is a constant.

Proposition 6
Comparative statics for equilibrium membership size:
Suppose that $f(L) = L^\eta$ so that $\eta \equiv f'(L)L/f(L)$ is a constant with $0 < \eta < 1$. Let $L^E(p, w, c, \alpha)$ be the function implicitly defined by treating (6) as an identity. Then

(a) L^E is increasing in p when $\alpha > 1-\eta$, unaffected by p when $\alpha = 1-\eta$, and decreasing in p when $\alpha < 1-\eta$.
(b) L^E is decreasing in w whenever $\alpha > 0$ and unaffected by w when $\alpha = 0$.
(c) L^E is increasing in c whenever $\alpha < 1$ and unaffected by c when $\alpha = 1$.

In place of a formal proof, I use a graphical approach. Rearranging (6) implies that L^E is located at the intersection of the functions $p[\alpha - (1-\eta)]L^\eta$ and $\alpha wL - (1-\alpha)c$. Figure 9.2 depicts the high-appropriation case $1-\eta < \alpha < 1$. The graph indicates that L^E increases in response to a higher p, a lower w, or a higher c. Figure 9.3 depicts the low-appropriation case $0 < \alpha < 1-\eta$. Here L^E increases in response to a lower p, a lower w, or a higher c. The boundary case $\alpha = 1-\eta$ yields $L^E = (1-\alpha)c/\alpha w$ so p has no effect on L^E.

Proposition 6 unifies the theory of profit maximization with the theory of the Ward-Domar-Vanek firm through the appropriation factor α. When insiders appropriate enough surplus from outsiders, the LMF expands in response to a positive demand shock, yielding an upward sloping supply curve. When insiders appropriate too little surplus, the LMF contracts in response to a positive demand shock. At the boundary between these cases, the firm has no quantity response to output price.

Whenever the appropriation factor is positive, the LMF has some response to the outside wage, and the quantity effect goes in the usual profit-maximizing direction. This effect strengthens as the appropriation factor rises and terminates in the behavior of the PMF for perfect

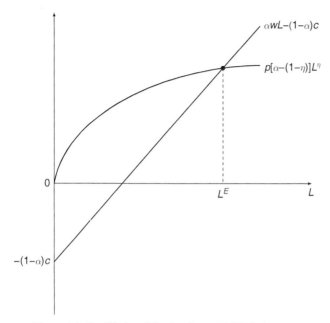

Figure 9.2 Equilibrium Membership with High Appropriation $(1 - \eta < \alpha < 1)$

appropriation. Likewise, whenever the appropriation factor is below unity, the LMF has some response to fixed cost, and the quantity effect goes in the WDV direction. This effect strengthens as the appropriation factor declines and terminates in the behavior of the WDV firm for zero appropriation.

Empirical researchers have been particularly interested in the supply elasticity of the LMF, motivated in part by the possibility of a backward-bending supply curve in the WDV model. There is no compelling evidence for negative supply elasticities, but it has sometimes been impossible to reject the null hypothesis that LMFs have a zero quantity response to demand conditions. When output is positively correlated with output price or some other index of demand, researchers generally find that supply is less elastic for LMFs than for similar KMFs (see Section 6.4).

This is readily explained under the assumption that LMFs suffer from imperfect appropriation while KMFs either do not or do so to a lesser degree. In the simple model developed here, the supply elasticity for each type of firm is equal to the product of two factors: the elasticity of output

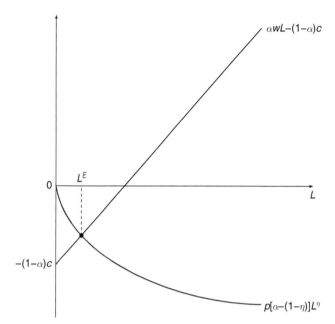

Figure 9.3 Equilibrium Membership with Low Appropriation $(0 < \alpha < 1 - \eta)$

with respect to labor input (η) and the elasticity of labor input (L) with respect to output price (p). Let η be an identical technological constant for LMFs and KMFs. For a profit-maximizing firm, the elasticity of labor input with respect to output price is $1/(1-\eta)$, so the supply elasticity for a PMF is $\eta/(1-\eta)$. Assuming that KMFs maximize profit, this is also the KMF supply elasticity. Upon treating (6) as an identity, differentiating with respect to p, and carrying out some algebra, one can establish for the high-appropriation case where $1-\eta < \alpha < 1$ that the LMF supply elasticity is positive but smaller than $\eta/(1-\eta)$. Thus it seems reasonable to interpret the evidence for lower supply elasticities in LMFs than KMFs as prima facie evidence for weaker appropriation of firm surplus by insiders in LMFs as compared with KMFs.

The comparative static effects of (p, w, c, α) on equilibrium firm size L^E can often be signed without the assumption of constant output elasticity used in Proposition 6. This can be done by combining the first order condition for the LMF's maximization problem with the equilibrium condition in (4). (I thank Gil Skillman for pointing this out.) Due to space constraints, I will not pursue the details here.

9.3 Expansion versus Contraction

When an LMF is contemplating expansion, there is a clear distinction between the roles of insiders and outsiders. Informational asymmetries or other factors could prevent insiders from capturing all of the surplus from transactions with outsiders, and there is no reason why insiders and outsiders must have equal payoffs. It is also easy to imagine that a group of identical insiders would have unanimous preferences with respect to the firm's expansion policy.

Contraction is different. In a model where workers have identical preferences and productivities, there is no evident reason why one ex ante member should leave the firm while another stays. Furthermore, individual members are indifferent between leaving and staying only under special conditions to be studied later on. When members are not indifferent, decreasing the size of the firm generally requires that someone be forced to leave involuntarily or forced to stay involuntarily. The institutional rules governing real LMFs are not typically compatible with either of these scenarios.

To see the issues involved, let there be L_0 incumbent members, and suppose that this group is considering a reduction in the firm's labor input to $L < L_0$. Thus L members stay while $L_0 - L > 0$ members leave. First, suppose that there is sufficient solidarity among the L_0 incumbents that all ex post income will be shared equally among this group, regardless of whether the income is generated within the firm or on the external labor market. Total ex post income is $pf(L) - c + w(L_0 - L)$ where c is fixed cost and w is the external wage as in Section 9.2. Maximization of this aggregate income is clearly equivalent to maximization of the firm's profit. Because the L_0 incumbents share total income equally and the initial membership size L_0 is predetermined, profit maximization is supported unanimously.

To avoid this implication, one must introduce some friction that prevents equal sharing. For example, one could assume that it is impossible to write binding contracts under which the $L - L_0$ workers who leave the firm must share their wage income from the outside labor market with the L workers who remain in the firm. In what follows, I assume that full pooling of internal and external incomes is infeasible.

Instead, suppose that there is a system of transfers where agents who leave the firm receive a severance payment (t) at the time of their departure. Each leaver gets the total income $w + t$, and the aggregate payment to all departing members is $t(L_0 - L)$. The latter burden is shared equally among the L members who stay. Each stayer thus receives the dividend $d(L)$ from

Section 9.2 minus $t(L_0 - L)/L$, the stayer's share in the total severance cost. The size of the transfer t can depend upon the number of agents who stay and leave, so I will write it as $t(L)$.

Straightforward algebra shows that if the severance payment $t(L)$ is determined so that individual workers are indifferent between staying and leaving, this payment must be $t(L) = \pi(L)/L_0$, and each individual worker must have the payoff $w + \pi(L)/L_0$. Thus, each worker gets the external wage plus a per capita claim on firm profit. Accordingly, the ex ante members unanimously support profit maximization with respect to the choice of L.

In order to avoid profit maximization, one has to abandon the idea that members are indifferent between staying and leaving. One way to do this is to choose severance payments so that stayers receive the payoff Z from Equation (3). Fix the appropriation factor α as in Section 9.2. We want to construct the transfers $t(L, \alpha)$ so that each worker who leaves gets $w + t(L, \alpha)$ and each worker who stays gets

$$d(L) - (L_0 - L)t(L, \alpha)/L = w + \alpha\pi(L)/L_0 + (1 - \alpha)[d(L) - w] \equiv Z(L, \alpha) \qquad (7)$$

The left-hand side is the dividend received by each ex post member minus the share of that member in the total severance payments $(L_0 - L)t(L, \alpha)$. The right-hand side is the objective function Z from (3), with some arguments omitted for simplicity. Solving for the severance payment to an individual leaver yields

$$t(L, \alpha) = \alpha\pi(L)/L_0 \qquad (8)$$

In contrast to the case where leavers and stayers are equally well off, here the leavers get the external wage plus a fraction of per capita profit, where the fraction is equal to the appropriation factor α. Under imperfect appropriation ($\alpha < 1$), the stayers are better off than the leavers.

With severance payments determined according to (8), any worker who expects to stay in the firm wants the ex post input L to maximize $Z(L, \alpha)$ as in Section 9.2. Thus, in principle the objective $Z(L, \alpha)$ can be extended to cover contraction as well as expansion. But due to the conflicting interests of leavers and stayers, it is unclear whether it makes any sense to impute this objective to the firm as a whole. To address this problem, one must spell out a process through which control rights of individual workers are exercised in a way that determines both the ex post labor input L and the status of each worker as a stayer or leaver. To rationalize the objective function $Z(L, \alpha)$, it is also necessary for the control structure to give the stayers authority over L.

I will briefly sketch a procedure that satisfies these conditions. The appropriation factor α, the severance payments $t(L, \alpha)$, and the function $Z(L, \alpha)$ are treated as fixed in what follows. Let the L_0 incumbent workers form a continuum on $[0, L_0]$ and assign each individual worker a rank $r \in [0, L_0]$. A worker's rank is unrelated to her preferences or productivity and represents her power within the firm (for concreteness, imagine that it is an index of seniority). A lower numerical value of r implies a higher degree of power or seniority. Let the grand coalition of incumbents be $N \equiv [0, L_0]$, let the set of stayers be $S \subseteq N$, and let the set of leavers be N-S. Assume that for a given ex post labor input L, the coalition of stayers is always $S = [0, L]$, so members with the greatest power or seniority remain in the firm. Each member of S receives the dividend d(L) and contributes equally to the transfers $t(L, \alpha)$ paid to the leavers in N-S, as described in (7) and (8).

Suppose that a stayer coalition forms, starting with the highest-ranked members of the firm. These stayers can invite workers of slightly lower rank to join the stayer coalition if this raises the incomes of the existing stayers. For example, if the current stayers are $S = [0, L]$ and there is $\varepsilon > 0$ such that $Z(L+\varepsilon, \alpha) > Z(L, \alpha)$, the existing stayers are willing to extend their coalition to $S' = [0, L+\varepsilon]$. The stayer coalition reaches equilibrium size when any extension of the coalition to lower-ranked workers would decrease the incomes of the existing members. Assuming that $Z(L, \alpha)$ has a global maximum at some $L^* \in (0, L_0)$, no coalition S smaller than $S^* = [0, L^*]$ could be an equilibrium, because the members of S would want to include enough additional members to reach S^*. No coalition larger than S^* could be an equilibrium, because once S^* has been reached, there is no incentive for the members of S^* to issue further invitations to nonmembers.

A model along these lines can potentially justify the use of an objective function like $Z(L, \alpha)$ for both expansion and contraction of an LMF. It can also provide strategic foundations for the WDV hypothesis of dividend maximization in the special case where $\alpha = 0$ holds in (7). In this case, (8) indicates that there are no severance payments to the leavers, who receive only the external wage.

Several caveats must be stated immediately. First, there is no known LMF with a strongly hierarchical power structure of this kind. Real LMFs give members equal votes. Second, there are few if any LMFs where members can be expelled involuntarily for a reason other than poor performance. Third, even if an LMF did have a control structure like the one described here, high-ranking members would not necessarily be bound by the specified rules governing severance payments.

Another problem is that the economic factors leading to imperfect appropriation for expansion may be quite different from those operating in the case of contraction. For example, when the firm is expanding, it is reasonable to assume that insiders know more about the true value of the firm than do outsiders. Chapters 10 and 11 will argue that such informational problems can lead to imperfect appropriation. It is less plausible that when the firm contracts, there would be similar informational asymmetries among the insiders. It seems more plausible in this case that appropriation issues would center on differences in bargaining power among individuals or factions within the firm. There is no general reason why the appropriation factor α must be identical for expansion and contraction.

Virtually without exception, real LMFs have institutional rules that prevent one subset of members from expelling another subset of members against their will. If LMF property rights prohibit involuntary expulsion, then payments to departing members must make them at least indifferent between staying and leaving. As noted previously, indifference implies unanimous support for profit maximization. When there are frictions that prevent this result, no one will leave, even if contraction would be profitable for the firm taken as a whole. Hence, labor inputs will be downwardly rigid. This reinforces the tendency for relatively inelastic output supply responses when the firm expands, and is consistent with evidence that quantity adjustments are weak or absent in LMFs (see Section 6.4).

9.4 Incentives for Degeneration

Many authors have argued that profitable LMFs tend to degenerate into KMFs over time because when individual members leave through normal turnover, continuing members will prefer to replace them by hiring employees who are paid the external wage, rather than bringing in full members (for citations to the literature, see Section 7.4). The reason is simple: new members receive a claim on profit while hired hands do not.

The modeling framework from Section 9.2 can be applied to this issue. Suppose that there are L_0 insiders and their desired labor input is $L(\alpha, L_0) > L_0$. The labor demand $L(\alpha, L_0)$ is obtained from maximization of the objective function $Z(L; \alpha, L_0)$ in (3), where some arguments of Z are suppressed. This situation might arise because L_0 was initially an equilibrium firm size but the parameters (p, w, c) have shifted in a way that makes expansion desirable or because the firm initially had a membership above L_0 but some individual members left due to relocation, retirement, or other exogenous events.

As explained in Section 9.2, if the L_0 incumbents adjust membership upward to $L(\alpha, L_0)$, then each incumbent will receive $Z(L; \alpha, L_0) = w + \alpha\pi(L)/L_0 + (1-\alpha)[d(L) - w]$, where I abbreviate $L = L(\alpha, L_0)$. Now suppose instead that the additional labor input $L(\alpha, L_0) - L_0 > 0$ is obtained by hiring nonmember employees who are paid the external wage w and have no claim on profit. In the latter case, each of the L_0 insiders gets $[pf(L) - c - w (L - L_0)]/L_0 = w + \pi(L)/L_0$.

Comparing the two payoffs, we find that with perfect appropriation ($\alpha = 1$), the insiders are indifferent between recruiting new members through the sale of membership positions and hiring the same amount of labor at the external wage. But with imperfect appropriation ($\alpha < 1$), the insiders strictly prefer nonmember labor, because $\pi(L)/L_0 > \pi(L)/L = d(L) - w$. This is a strong conclusion: LMFs face temptations for degeneration except in the empirically unlikely case where the membership market is perfect ($\alpha = 1$).

Whether this temptation poses a serious risk to the viability of LMFs is a matter for debate. As discussed in Section 7.4, some authorities believe that degeneration has been a significant problem for the plywood cooperatives, the Mondragon cooperatives, and others, while other authorities find little empirical evidence for this phenomenon. At least in some cases, institutional rules appear to have forestalled degeneration. Many LMFs face legal restrictions on the amount of nonmember labor they can hire or have self-imposed constitutional restrictions on the use of nonmember labor. Others are legally required to share profit with nonmembers or give employees the option of becoming full members at any time for a nominal fee. Such rules can prevent degeneration, though they may bring rigidities of other kinds. Another factor tending to limit degeneration is that hired employees may be less productive than members, either due to differences in personal characteristics or incentives, and this may give insiders a reason to recruit full members even when appropriation is imperfect.

To the extent that LMFs do use some hired employees, this helps alleviate the comparative static rigidities discussed in Sections 9.2 and 9.3. LMFs can be expected to treat such employees in the same way that KMFs do and to follow the standard rules of profit maximization in hiring them or laying them off in response to market shocks. The output supply elasticity of such an LMF may resemble that of a profit-maximizing firm, at least over some range, both for expansion and contraction.

9.5 Incentives for Underinvestment

As discussed in Chapter 4, there is a long tradition of arguments to the effect that LMFs will underinvest by comparison with similar KMFs. Empirical evidence on this issue is inconclusive (see Section 7.5). Here I show that imperfect appropriation can lead to LMF underinvestment as well as conversion of LMFs into KMFs, even when LMFs have static productivity advantages and generate more total surplus.

Consider a firm with the capital stock K. Capital and labor are combined in fixed proportions, so the number of workers supplying labor to the firm is L = K. The external payoffs of workers and investors are both normalized at zero.

In a KMF, there is an investor who receives the dividend $\pi_K > 0$ per unit of capital in each period. I assume that KMF employees do not obtain rents. In an LMF, the workforce collectively owns the firm's capital stock. The LMF's dividend per unit of capital in each period, which is also the dividend per worker, is $\pi_L > 0$.

Time is discrete. Individuals maximize the present values of their consumption streams using the common discount factor $\delta \in (0, 1)$. Firms solve optimization problems of the form

$$\max \sum_{t=0}^{\infty} \delta^t [\pi - I(g_t)]K_t \quad \text{with respect to } (g_0 .. g_t ..)$$
$$\text{subject to } K_{t+1} = g_t K_t \text{ for all t, with } K_0 \text{ given} \tag{9}$$

The choice variable g_t is called the growth policy of the firm in period t, and $I(g_t)$ is the cost of adjusting the firm's capital stock. I consider only stationary solutions where the firm adopts the same growth policy in every period. Investment expenditure per unit of capital is a quadratic function of the firm's growth policy: $I(g) \equiv \upsilon(g - \tau)^2$ where $\upsilon > 0$ and $0 < \tau < 1$. The assumption $\tau < 1$ implies that over time the firm's capital stock will decay toward zero in the absence of investment expenditures.

Investment incentives in the KMF. If KMF shares are traded on a competitive stock market, the firm's owners in each period will unanimously support present value maximization. Let A_K be the maximized present value of a unit of capital in the KMF. This present value satisfies the stationarity condition

$$A_K = \max_g [\pi_K - I(g) + g\delta A_K] \tag{10}$$

For an arbitrary growth factor g, the present value of one unit of capital A_K equals this period's cash flow $\pi_K - I(g)$ plus the discounted value of g units of capital in the next period, each having the value A_K. Upon choosing g optimally in (10), the KMF growth policy is

$$g_K = 1/\delta - [(1/\delta - \tau)^2 - \pi_K/\upsilon]^{1/2} \qquad (11)$$

and the maximized present value of a unit of KMF capital is

$$A_K = 2\upsilon(g_K - \tau)/\delta \qquad (12)$$

When the dividend π_K is positive, we have $g_K > \tau > 0$. Net expansion ($g_K > 1$) and the requirement that g_K be a real number together imply

$$(1/\delta - \tau)^2 - (1/\delta - 1)^2 < \pi_K/\upsilon \le (1/\delta - \tau)^2 \qquad (13)$$

There are always positive values of the ratio π_K/υ satisfying these inequalities.

Investment incentives in the LMF. For simplicity I assume that there is complete turnover in the membership of the LMF in each period (the members work for one period and then retire). Let v be the price paid by each new LMF member upon joining the firm. The present value A_L of a typical LMF member satisfies

$$A_L = \max_g[\pi_L - I(g) + \delta g v] \qquad (14)$$

Each member receives π_L in the current period and pays the per capita investment cost $I(g)$. An investment $I(g)$ in period t creates g jobs in period t+1 per-period t member. The revenue from membership fees paid by new recruits is shared equally among the members from period t, each of whom therefore receives gv at the start of period t+1. Because the firm cannot charge incoming members more than the present value of membership, we have $0 \le v \le A_L$. If $v < A_L$, then memberships are sold at a discount and newcomers enjoy a rent. Write $v \equiv \alpha A_L$ where α is the fraction of the membership value that is captured by the insiders. Then (14) becomes

$$A_L - \max_g[\pi_L \quad I(g) + \delta g \alpha A_L] \qquad (15)$$

As in earlier sections, the appropriation factor α is an exogenous parameter.

Current LMF members favor investment policies that maximize the present value of their membership rights. For this reason, the membership unanimously supports the LMF growth policy associated with (15):

$$g_L = 1/\alpha\delta - [(1/\alpha\delta - \tau)^2 - \pi_L/\upsilon]^{1/2} \qquad (16)$$

The maximized present value of membership in the LMF is

$$A_L = 2\upsilon(g_L - \tau)/\alpha\delta \tag{17}$$

An LMF that sells memberships at their full value ($v = A_L$ or equivalently $\alpha = 1$) adopts the same growth policy as in (11) if KMFs and LMFs have equal productivity per unit of capital (i.e., $\pi_K = \pi_L$). Suppose instead that new workers pay less than the full value of their membership rights ($\alpha < 1$). This implies that the effective discount factor $\alpha\delta$ used to compute the LMF growth policy is smaller than the discount factor δ used by the KMF. Thus the LMF places insufficient weight on future dividends, and the growth factor g_L is less than g_K when the two firms have equal static productivity ($\pi_K = \pi_L$).

Private and social values. Define the social values of the KMF and LMF (per unit of capital) as follows:

$$B_K \equiv \sum_{t=0}^{\infty} \delta^t g_K{}^t[\pi_K - I(g_K)] = [\pi_K - I(g_K)]/(1 - \delta g_K) \tag{18a}$$

$$B_L \equiv \sum_{t=0}^{\infty} \delta^t g_L{}^t[\pi_L - I(g_L)] = [\pi_L - I(g_L)]/(1 - \delta g_L) \tag{18b}$$

Assuming that workers receive no rent in a KMF, the private and social values coincide for the KMF and $A_K = B_K$. When $\alpha = 1$, the same is true for an LMF: future surpluses are fully capitalized into the entry fees paid by new members and hence $A_L = B_L$. However, when $\alpha < 1$, the social value B_L for the LMF exceeds the private value A_L. The private and social values diverge because outsiders gain rents upon joining the firm, so insiders fail to capture the full social value of the returns from their investment expenditures. I ignore distributional concerns here and focus solely on aggregate surplus.

Comparisons of KMFs and LMFs. The interesting case occurs when LMFs have a productivity advantage over KMFs ($\pi_K < \pi_L$), because then there is a trade-off between static and dynamic factors. This may be an empirically relevant case given the evidence that productivity in LMFs is often at least as high as in similar KMFs (see Section 6.6).

The following theorem establishes that LMFs can be socially preferred even when they grow less rapidly than KMFs and have a lower private value per unit of capital. The proof involves lengthy algebraic manipulations and is omitted.

LMF Dominance Theorem. Assume that the LMF has a static productivity advantage so that $0 < \pi_K < \pi_L$.

(a) There is a unique value of α (denoted by α^g) for which the growth rates of the KMF and LMF are equal ($g_K = g_L$).
(b) There is a unique value of α (denoted by α^P) for which the private values of the KMF and LMF are equal ($A_K = A_L$).
(c) Either

    (i) There is a unique value of α (denoted by α^s) for which the social values of the KMF and LMF are equal ($B_K = B_L$); or
    (ii) $B_K < B_L$ for all $\alpha \geq 0$. In this case, define $\alpha^s \equiv 0$.

(d) It can be shown that $0 \leq \alpha^s < \alpha^P < \alpha^g < 1$.
(e) It can be shown that

$$g_L \gtrless g_K \text{ when } \alpha \gtrless \alpha^g;$$
$$A_L \gtrless A_K \text{ when } \alpha \gtrless \alpha^P;$$
$$B_L \gtrless B_K \text{ when } \alpha \gtrless \alpha^s.$$

To interpret this theorem, call $G \equiv [\alpha^g, 1]$ the interval of *LMF growth dominance*; call $P \equiv [\alpha^P, 1]$ the interval of *LMF private dominance*; and call $S \equiv [\alpha^s, 1]$ the interval of *LMF social dominance*. The theorem gives $G \subset P \subset S$. This has several implications:

    (i) At high values of α where insiders appropriate most of the value of membership, the LMF dominates in all three ways.
    (ii) At somewhat lower values of α, the LMF dominates with respect to private and social value, but the KMF dominates with respect to growth rate. Ignoring the possible creation of new firms, this means that KMFs will account for most of the economy in the long run, even though LMFs have higher private and social value. In order to prevent KMFs from taking over the economy, it is necessary to convert KMFs into LMFs. Given perfect capital markets, this will occur because there are private gains from the conversion of a KMF into an LMF.
    (iii) At still lower values of α, the LMF dominates with respect to social value, but the KMF dominates with respect to both growth rate and private value. This prevents conversion of KMFs into LMFs. Instead, there are private incentives to transform LMFs into KMFs despite the social superiority of LMFs.
    (iv) At very low values of α, LMFs could discount membership rights so heavily that LMFs lose their social advantage over KMFs. However, when $\alpha^s = 0$, even LMFs with open admission policies are socially preferred to KMFs.

Two key conclusions can be drawn from this simple model. First, LMFs may have higher static productivity than similar KMFs but undervalue investment returns in a dynamic setting. When this is so, the easiest hurdle for the LMF to surmount is that of social superiority. It is more difficult for the LMF to yield the same private value as a KMF and hardest of all for the LMF to win a growth contest against a KMF.

Second, even when it is socially desirable to convert a KMF into an LMF, there may be no private incentive to do so. Indeed, if future worker cohorts will capture some surplus, it may be privately beneficial for current LMF members to transform their firm into a KMF in order to enjoy a capital gain. Such conversions sacrifice the interests of future LMF members and can be socially perverse when the static productivity of the KMF is inferior to that of the LMF. Some skepticism about the efficiency of private organizational arrangements is therefore warranted.

9.6 Sources of Imperfect Appropriation

Sections 9.2–9.5 investigated the effects of imperfect appropriation. Here I briefly survey potential causes. Later chapters will explore these hypotheses in greater detail.

Employees of profit-maximizing firms often receive rents. These may arise from efficiency wages to provide effort incentives, reduce costly worker turnover, or attract a better applicant pool. Employees may also capture rents by bargaining with firms when search is costly or skills are specialized. One might think that such frictions could also enable outsiders to gain rents when joining an LMF and that this may lead to imperfect appropriation by LMF insiders. Although all of this could be true, the problem is that such reasoning does not identify an asymmetry between KMFs and LMFs. Indeed, the replication principle suggests that LMF insiders could copy whatever strategies KMF insiders use to cope with these issues.

A more promising approach is to consider the contrast between LMF membership markets and KMF stock markets. Each market has an intertemporal structure: an outsider pays something today in exchange for insider status tomorrow. However, these markets differ in ways that can be linked to the alienability distinction between capital and labor. As I pointed out in Section 1.3, the alienability of capital implies that investors in a KMF can come and go without any change in the firm's physical inputs, because ownership of productive nonhuman assets is readily transferred from one person or group to another. But when workers in an LMF come and go, this does change the firm's physical inputs, because the identities of the labor suppliers change.

This point becomes important when workers are heterogeneous with respect to their skills or preferences. In particular, if there is adverse selection among membership applicants, insiders may be unwilling to permit open trading in LMF membership rights. I will pursue this idea in Chapter 11.

A related point developed in Chapter 10 is that there may be adverse selection on the firm side, where outsiders cannot observe the true value of the membership positions offered by insiders. This is especially likely for newly formed LMFs or for those without a long track record. In this case, outsiders will only be willing to pay membership prices corresponding to the value of the average LMF, which might be well below the values of the best LMFs. This keeps insiders in the latter firms from appropriating the full value of membership.

A natural question is why this is any different from adverse selection problems where outside investors cannot observe the true value of a KMF. One part of the answer is that equity shares on stock markets are highly divisible and traded continually, while membership rights in LMFs are lumpy and only traded when a worker switches firms. Moreover, investors around the world can participate in markets for KMF shares, while workers wanting to participate in an LMF membership market must have suitable skills and often must either live near the firm or be willing to move there. Consequently, the volume of trade is much greater for KMF equity shares, which encourages specialists to engage in research on the value of these shares. Outsiders can pay for such research, so there is a good deal of information built into the stock market value of a KMF. There is no comparable market for information about LMF membership rights.

Because markets for LMF membership are thin, they may not be competitive in the usual sense. Instead, there may be only a few plausible candidates for a position in an LMF. If so, membership transactions could involve bilateral bargaining between insiders and outsiders, with private information on each side.

Another appropriation problem involves the lack of liquidity of LMF membership rights. Due to the thinness of membership markets, an outsider will know that if cash is urgently needed at some point in the future or if it becomes necessary to relocate, a long time may pass before a replacement worker can be found. This is quite different from a KMF stock market, where equity shares can often be converted into cash very quickly. A candidate for LMF membership will also understand that future membership candidates will have similar concerns. This will lower the price others will be prepared to pay in the future, which reduces what the candidate is prepared to pay today. These liquidity issues exacerbate the problems insiders face in capturing surplus from membership transactions.

One partial solution to this problem is for the LMF to assure its members that it is ready to buy back membership positions at a guaranteed price and that it will take on the burden of finding replacement workers when necessary. As I will explain in Chapter 11, this may be required in any case, because allowing departing LMF members to sell their positions directly to replacement workers can lead to major adverse selection problems. However, KMFs do not have to make similar commitments and often permit trading of their equity shares on anonymous markets.

A different explanation sometimes advanced for the imperfection or absence of membership markets is that workers have little personal wealth and cannot afford to pay membership fees. I am skeptical that this can be the full explanation. First, even workers with limited wealth could be asked to pay something, and it is in the interest of insiders to get what they can. Second, in labor-intensive industries with free entry, the equilibrium price of membership is near zero, so the claim that workers cannot afford to pay it is implausible. Third, many worker cooperatives do ask members to pay a fee upon entry, and these fees are sometimes substantial but are not necessarily set at a market-clearing level. For these reasons, I suspect that LMF membership markets face obstacles that go beyond wealth constraints. These include the appropriation issues discussed earlier.

9.7 Postscript

The material in this chapter is new, with one exception. The model in Section 9.5 is based on the book chapter "Democracy versus Appropriability: Can Labor-Managed Firms Flourish in a Capitalist World?" (Dow, 1993a). This appeared in a volume of conference proceedings from a meeting in June 1991 at the Swedish Collegium for Advanced Study in the Social Sciences. I have simplified and shortened the original presentation. The 1993 version extended the model to cases where employees can capture rents in KMFs and where LMF members remain in the firm for more than one period.

9.8 Appendix

Proof of Proposition 4

Choose an arbitrary (p, c) > 0. This determines the dividend function d(L; p, c) and thus its unique maximizer L^{WDV}(p, c). At this labor input, the first order condition implies that the second derivative of the dividend function d″[L^{WDV}(p, c); p, c] is negative (primes indicate derivatives with respect to L). Choose some L^{max}(p, c) > L^{WDV}(p, c) such that d″[L; p, c] < 0 for all L ∈ [L^{WDV}(p, c), L^{max}(p, c)]. This is possible because d″[L; p, c] is continuous in L. Nothing in this paragraph depends on w, because the external wage does not appear in the dividend function.

Now let w^{max}(p, c) ≡ d^{max}(p, c) ≡ d[L^{WDV}(p, c); p, c] be the maximum dividend. It can be shown that L^{PMF}(p, w^{max}) = L^{WDV}(p, c). The proof is the same as for the standard result involving p_{min} in Proposition 1, except that here we are arbitrarily fixing the price p and deriving the zero profit wage w^{max} rather than arbitrarily fixing the wage w and deriving the zero profit price p_{min}. For w < w^{max}, the profit-maximizing labor input L^{PMF}(p, w) is a continuously decreasing function of w at the fixed price p, with L^{WDV}(p, c) < L^{PMF}(p, w). Define w^{min}(p, c) so that L^{PMF}(p, w^{min}) ≡ L^{max}(p, c), where L^{max}(p, c) was chosen as in the previous paragraph. This is always possible because L^{PMF}(p, w) → ∞ as w → 0 for the fixed p. We have w^{min}(p, c) < w^{max}(p, c) because we chose L^{max}(p, c) > L^{WDV}(p, c). This construction ensures that for any w ∈ [w^{min}(p, c), w^{max}(p, c)] we have d″[L; p, c] < 0 for all L ∈ [L^{WDV}(p, c), L^{PMF}(p, w)].

Now consider each point of Proposition 4.

(a) Choose any (p, w, c) with w ∈ [w^{min}(p, c), d^{max}(p, c)]. The profit π(L; p, w, c) is increasing on [L^{WDV}, L^{PMF}], so it suffices to show that π(L^{WDV}; p, w, c) ≥ 0. But w ≤ d^{max}(p, c) ≡ d[L^{WDV}(p, c); p, c]. This implies π(L^{WDV}; p, w, c) ≥ 0.

(b) The dividend d(L; p, c) is decreasing on [L^{WDV}, L^{PMF}], so it suffices to show that d[L^{PMF}; p, c] ≥ w. This is true iff π(L^{PMF}; p, w, c) ≥ 0, so the maximum profit is nonnegative. But we know that the maximum profit is zero when w = d^{max}(p, c), and the maximum profit must be strictly positive at any lower wage level.

(c) The dividend d(L; p, c) is strictly concave in L on [L^{WDV}, L^{PMF}], because when w ∈ [w^{min}(p, c), d^{max}(p, c)], we have L^{WDV}(p, c) ≤

$L^{PMF}(p, w) \le L^{max}(p, c)$. The dividend is strictly concave on $[L^{WDV}(p, c), L^{max}(p, c)]$ by construction of $L^{max}(p, c)$.

(d) From Equation (3), the function Z is strictly concave in L on $[L^{WDV}, L^{PMF}]$ if both $\pi(L; p, w, c)$ and $d(L; p, c)$ are strictly concave on this interval. But $\pi(L; p, w, c)$ is strictly concave globally, and $d(L; p, c)$ is strictly concave because of (c).

(e) From the compactness of $[L^{WDV}, L^{PMF}]$ and the continuity of Z in L, the function Z has a maximum value on $[L^{WDV}, L^{PMF}]$. The first order condition must hold at the associated value of L. The first derivative of Z cannot be zero at any other point in the interval, because the second derivative is strictly negative throughout.

(f) $L(p, w, c, \alpha, L_0)$ satisfies the necessary first order condition and sufficient second order condition for a maximum, and Z is strictly concave on $[L^{WDV}, L^{PMF}]$, so this labor input is the unique maximizer of Z on this interval. Because both π and d are increasing in L on $[0, L^{WDV}]$ and these functions are continuous, the value of Z is less than $Z(L^{WDV})$ for all $L < L^{WDV}$. Because both π and d are decreasing in L on $[L^{PMF}, \infty)$ and these functions are continuous, the value of Z is less than $Z(L^{PMF})$ for all $L > L^{PMF}$. Therefore $L(p, w, c, \alpha, L_0)$ is the unique global maximizer of Z.

Proof of Proposition 5

(a) Continuity follows from the Theorem of the Maximum. To show that $L(p, w, c, \alpha, L_0)$ is strictly decreasing in L_0, differentiate Z with respect to L in (3), set the derivative equal to zero, treat it as an identity that implicitly defines $L(p, w, c, \alpha, L_0)$, and differentiate this identity with respect to L_0. The result follows from the facts that $L(p, w, c, \alpha, L_0) \in [L^{WDV}, L^{PMF}]$ for all L_0; $\pi' > 0$ on this interval, $d'' < 0$ on this interval under the conditions of Proposition 4, and $\pi'' < 0$ globally.

(b) For $L_0 = L^{WDV}$, we have $L_0 \le L(p, w, c, \alpha, L_0)$. For $L_0 = L^{PMF}(p, w)$, we have $L_0 \ge L(p, w, c, \alpha, L_0)$. Because $L(p, w, c, \alpha, L_0)$ is continuous and strictly decreasing in L_0, there is a unique $L_0 \in [L^{WDV}, L^{PMF}]$ such that $L_0 = L(p, w, c, \alpha, L_0)$.

(i) If $\alpha = 0$, then the first order condition for maximization of Z is the same as the first order condition for maximization of the dividend d. This implies $L(p, w, c, 0, L_0) = L^{WDV}$ for all L_0. Therefore we must have $L_0 = L^{WDV}$ in (4).

(ii) If $0 < \alpha < 1$, then if L^{WDV} and L^{PMF} are distinct, neither can satisfy the first order condition for the maximization of Z. Hence $L(p, w, c, \alpha, L_0) \neq L^{WDV}$ and also $L(p, w, c, \alpha, L_0) \neq L^{PMF}$. Because $L(p, w, c, \alpha, L_0) \in [L^{WDV}, L^{PMF}]$, we therefore have $L^{WDV} < L(p, w, c, \alpha, L_0) < L^{PMF}$.

(iii) If $\alpha = 1$, then the first order condition for maximization of Z is the same as the first order condition for maximization of the profit π. This implies $L(p, w, c, 1, L_0) = L^{PMF}$ for all L_0. Therefore we must have $L_0 = L^{PMF}$ in (4).

10

Firm Formation with Adverse Selection

10.1 Introduction

An important puzzle about labor-managed firms is why wealthy entrepreneurs do not create them (see Sections 7.7 and 8.3). This question is particularly significant if one believes that LMFs would have higher productivity than similar KMFs, at least in enough cases to matter. The usual answer to this question in the literature is deceptively simple. Suppose that a newly created firm would have profit $\pi > 0$, and assume that this profit is the same whether the firm is organized as a KMF or an LMF. An entrepreneur who has access to this profit opportunity and creates a KMF gets the full amount π. If the entrepreneur creates an LMF with n members and these members share profit equally, the entrepreneur only gets π/n. Clearly, the entrepreneur prefers to create a KMF.

As it stands, this argument is unconvincing. If the entrepreneur chose to create an LMF, she could charge a membership fee equal to π/n, collect this amount from each of n workers, and capture the entire profit π. Such payments could be secured by competitive bidding among potential members. This is analogous to the case where an entrepreneur offers equity shares in a KMF to investors. If an LMF had even a minimal productivity advantage over a KMF, the entrepreneur would be better off creating an LMF.

Nevertheless, there is a nugget of truth in the idea that entrepreneurs have trouble appropriating profit from an LMF. When workers cannot observe the true quality of the entrepreneur's project, they may not be willing to pay much for control rights in an LMF. As a result, the entrepreneur may prefer to create a KMF even if an LMF would be more productive, because the entrepreneur captures a larger fraction of a smaller social surplus in a KMF. I will develop this argument in this chapter.

It will be convenient here to assume that capital supply is unproblematic because the entrepreneur is wealthy enough to invest whatever amount may be needed, whether the firm is a KMF or an LMF. A less wealthy entrepreneur, or one seeking diversification, may confront adverse selection problems like those discussed later even if she creates a KMF, because she will need to recruit outside investors who do not observe the value of her project in advance. I also assume that workers can afford to pay any membership fees that may be required. Consideration of capital constraints will be postponed until Chapters 17–19.

The entrepreneur is a worker as well as an investor, is always a member of the firm's control group, and decides how many other workers (if any) will be offered control rights. I refer to all workers with control rights, including the entrepreneur, as *members* of the firm. Members have access to all information held by the entrepreneur about firm technology, and this increases productivity. At the same time, members have bargaining power and appropriate equal shares of firm profit. I treat workers' control as a matter of degree, where some workers may become members whereas others become employees. The latter do not have access to proprietary information, are told what to do, and receive a competitive wage. If the entrepreneur decides not to offer control positions to anyone else, I interpret this as a KMF in which all profit goes to the entrepreneur.

Whether an entrepreneur shares control depends on informational asymmetries about the value of control rights. When most new projects are good, so adverse selection problems are minor, uninformed workers may be willing to pay large amounts to become members, and this may offset most of the effects from the bargaining that will occur after control positions have been assigned. In this case, an entrepreneur with a good project will create an LMF. But if most new projects are bad, workers will not offer much for control rights, and an entrepreneur with a good project will create a KMF instead.

In a separating equilibrium, good and bad entrepreneurs propose control groups of different sizes. Uninformed workers can draw inferences from these proposals about the quality of the entrepreneur's project. I show that a separating equilibrium always exists and always yields a KMF.

In a pooling equilibrium, the two types propose control groups of the same size, and outsiders must rely on their prior beliefs about project quality. Pooling equilibrium can lead to some degree of workers' control, but this depends on the severity of adverse selection. When most projects are bad, a pooling equilibrium again yields a KMF. As the average quality of projects improves, additional pooling equilibria emerge in which more workers become members. But even when almost all projects are good, there can be pooling equilibria with low levels of membership and productivity. The equilibrium level of participation depends on worker beliefs, which may be fragile.

Section 10.2 introduces assumptions about production, and Section 10.3 briefly discusses bargaining issues. The main results are in Section 10.4. Section 10.5 uses the model to explain why entry by U.S. plywood cooperatives ceased in the 1950s. Section 10.6 connects the results from the model with the larger themes of the book. Section 10.7 is a postscript, and proofs of all formal propositions are in Section 10.8.

10.2 Production Issues

Consider an entrepreneur with a good project who faces a horizontal demand curve at a price of p per unit up to a maximum total demand of N units. This situation could arise because the entrepreneur offers a new good for which there are N potential consumers, each with the reservation price p. Alternatively, the entrepreneur may have a superior technique for producing an existing good where the current technique has a constant average cost equal to p. A unit of output requires one unit of labor, and each unit of labor is supplied by a distinct worker. All agents are risk neutral.

The number of workers with control rights is $n \in \{1 .. N\}$. I label the workers so that $i = 1 .. n$ have control rights while $i = n+1 .. N$ do not. The entrepreneur always has control rights. Average cost is $c(n)$, which is less than p for all n. Total profit is

$$\pi(n) = [p - c(n)]N \qquad (1)$$

This function has two important features.

$$0 < \pi(n) < \pi(n+1) \qquad \text{for all } n = 1 .. N - 1 \qquad \text{and} \qquad \text{A1}$$

$$\pi(n)/n > \pi(n+1)/(n+1) \qquad \text{for all } n = 1 .. N - 1 \qquad \text{A2}$$

A1 says that total profit is higher when more workers have control rights. A2 says that profit per member falls as the size of the control group rises. This means that bargaining effects dominate productivity effects from the entrepreneur's point of view. If $\pi(n)/n$ is increasing in n, the entrepreneur always prefers a larger control group. This case is less interesting, and I ignore it in the discussion that follows.

Production can be modeled in various ways that yield A1 and A2, and it will not matter how this is done. For example, workers with control rights who understand the production technology could receive noisy signals about the true state of the world and aggregate this information to choose production methods (see sections 6 and 7 of Dow, 1988). In a model of this kind, expected profit is an increasing function of the number of signals so A1 holds, and at least eventually the marginal gain from another signal falls so A2 holds when the control group is large enough.

10.3 Bargaining Issues

When the entrepreneur has a good project, workers who have control rights will bargain over the distribution of the profit $\pi(n)$. Once workers have control positions and understand the firm's technology, they are on an equal footing with the entrepreneur, and therefore each member of the control group receives $\pi(n)/n$. This would not be true if the entrepreneur could make strategic commitments before other workers gain control rights in ways that give the entrepreneur a lasting advantage in bargaining power. I ignore this complication here (see Dow, 1985, 1988, and 1989, for models along these lines).

In a more explicit bargaining model, we would need to say why the disagreement point is the origin $(0, 0 .. 0)$. One rationale is to suppose that each member of the control group threatens to disclose the firm's proprietary technology publicly unless her demands are met. Disclosure would destroy the rent $\pi(n)$ by allowing free entry. Alternatively, a member of the control group could threaten to establish a rival firm, a situation where competition among firms would destroy the rent. A third approach is to use a dynamic framework in which the rent vanishes with positive probability in each period, perhaps because another entrepreneur independently replicates the new technology. If no rent can be appropriated until an agreement is reached, a limit argument shows that the outcome is the symmetric Nash bargaining solution with the origin as the disagreement point (Binmore, Rubinstein, and Wolinsky, 1986).

10.4 Equilibrium Organizational Form

We now consider how an entrepreneur (E) organizes the firm. E has a project that may be good or bad. If the project is good, E faces the profit function $\pi(n)$ and chooses $n \in \{1 .. N\}$. If the project is bad, profit is zero for any choice of n. E knows whether the project is good or bad, but the other agents cannot see this in advance. If everyone knew with certainty that E's project was good, E would establish an LMF by setting $n = N$ and appropriate all of the resulting profit $\pi(N)$ by selling membership positions. However, if adverse selection occurs, E may have insufficient incentive to create an LMF.

To formalize these ideas, consider the following sequence of events.

(a) Nature decides whether the project is good or bad. A good project occurs with probability θ. The true quality is revealed only to E.

(b) E chooses a number of agents $n \in \{1 .. N\}$ to become members of the firm. This always includes E and may include another $n-1$ agents as well.

(c) After observing E's choice of n, many uninformed workers bid for membership. E grants control rights to the $n-1$ workers offering the largest membership fees, with randomization in case of ties. These workers pay their fees, which become sunk.

(d) Members other than E, if any, find out whether the project is good or bad. Each member (including E) receives $\pi(n)/n$ if the project is good and zero if it is bad.

I assume that it is impossible to write contracts under which the agents settle up after the true value of membership is revealed. If such contracts were feasible, entrepreneurs with good projects would set $n = N$ and promise to refund membership fees in the event that the project turned out to be bad, knowing that no refund would have to be paid. This would eliminate the effect of the parameter θ on organizational form.

Let $\mu(n)$ be the probability that uninformed workers assign at step (c) to the event that E's project is good. Competition among uninformed agents implies that the workers who become firm members receive zero surplus, so each pays E the membership fee

$$m(n) = \mu(n)\pi(n)/n \qquad (2)$$

When E chooses to have n members, E's total revenue from these fees is

$$M(n) = (n-1)m(n) = \mu(n)(n-1)\pi(n)/n \qquad (3)$$

Let E_g denote an entrepreneur with a good project, and let E_b denote an entrepreneur with a bad project. The payoffs of these two types are

$$U_g(n) = \pi(n)/n + M(n) \qquad \text{and}$$
$$U_b(n) = M(n) \qquad (4)$$

Thus good entrepreneurs receive both a profit share and membership revenue, while bad entrepreneurs receive only what they can get by selling membership positions.

Two kinds of equilibria can arise: separating (SE) and pooling (PE). Let n_g be the number of members chosen by E_g, and let n_b be the number chosen by E_b. SE has $n_g \neq n_b$, while PE has $n_g = n_b$.

Proposition 1
Separating equilibrium: A separating equilibrium always exists. Every SE has $n_g = 1$ and $n_b \geq 2$. This outcome can be supported by beliefs $\mu(1) = 1$ and $\mu(n) = 0$ for $n \geq 2$. The resulting payoffs are $U_g(n_g) = \pi(1)$ and $U_b(n_b) = 0$.

This proposition shows that there is always an equilibrium in which entrepreneurs with good projects create KMFs. Those with bad projects try to sell membership rights, but the equilibrium fee is zero. A separating equilibrium thus eliminates the bad projects, but the potential productivity gain from worker participation in good projects is lost.

The analysis of pooling equilibrium is more complex. Let $n_g = n_b = n_p$ where Bayes' rule requires $\mu(n_p) = \theta$.

Lemma 1
(a) If a deviation $n' < n_p$ is profitable for E_b, then it is also profitable for E_g.
(b) If a deviation $n' > n_p$ is profitable for E_g, then it is also profitable for E_b.

Because a downward deviation is never profitable for E_b unless it is also profitable for E_g, such deviations should not be interpreted by the uninformed workers as a reason to assign higher probability to E_b. Similarly, an upward deviation should never result in a higher probability for E_g. This motivates the following restriction on beliefs.

$$\text{(a)} \quad \mu(n) \geq \theta \text{ for all } n < n_p \qquad \qquad \text{A3}$$

$$\text{(b)} \quad \mu(n) \leq \theta \text{ for all } n > n_p$$

Now define the function

$$\phi(n, \theta) \equiv \theta\pi(n) + (1 - \theta)\pi(n)/n \qquad (5)$$

Proposition 2
Pooling equilibrium: The choice n_p can be supported by a pooling equilibrium consistent with A3 if and only if $\phi(n,\theta) \leq \phi(n_p,\theta)$ for all $n \leq n_p$.

This can be done using the beliefs $\mu(n) = \theta$ for all $n \le n_p$ and $\mu(n) = 0$ for all $n > n_p$. The resulting payoffs are $U_g(n_p) = \phi(n_p, \theta)$ and $U_b(n_p) = \theta(n_p - 1)\pi(n_p)/n_p$.

Upward deviations from n_p can be deterred using the pessimistic beliefs $\mu(n) = 0$ for $n > n_p$, which ensure that such deviations generate zero membership revenue. This deters E_b, because this type only cares about membership fees, and from Lemma 1 it also deters E_g. Now consider downward deviations. If E_g can be deterred from such a deviation then by Lemma 1, E_b is also deterred. The beliefs $\mu(n) = \theta$ are the most pessimistic permitted by A3 and yield the lowest membership revenue to a deviator. Subject to this constraint, E_g can be deterred from a downward deviation if and only if $\phi(n, \theta) \le \phi(n_p, \theta)$ for all $n \le n_p$.

Existence of at least one PE is guaranteed because $n_p = 1$ satisfies the condition in Proposition 2. From an economic standpoint this outcome is identical to an SE, because in each case an entrepreneur with a good project becomes the sole controller of the firm while one with a bad project receives a zero payoff. However, Proposition 2 also opens up the possibility that control rights could be awarded to additional agents ($n_p \ge 2$).

Write $\phi^*(\theta) \equiv \max \{\phi(n, \theta) \text{ for } n = 1 .. N\}$, and let $n^*(\theta)$ be the largest n such that $\phi(n, \theta) = \phi^*(\theta)$. No choice $n_p > n^*(\theta)$ can satisfy the condition in Proposition 2, but $n^*(\theta)$ does satisfy this condition and some $n < n^*(\theta)$ may also satisfy it (in addition to $n = 1$).

Lemma 2

If n_p° and n_p^1 both satisfy the condition in Proposition 2 with $n_p^\circ < n_p^1$, then n_p^1 is Pareto superior to n_p°.

Pooling equilibria can be Pareto ranked because of these factors: (a) uninformed workers receive zero ex ante surplus in any PE, (b) good entrepreneurs do at least as well with increased worker participation by the condition in Proposition 2, and (c) bad entrepreneurs strictly prefer increased worker participation due to the additional membership revenue it provides.

In the best scenario, each value of θ is associated with a pooling equilibrium that supports the Pareto efficient outcome $n^*(\theta)$. Assuming that this is true, we study the effect of varying the parameter θ, which captures the severity of the adverse selection problem.

Proposition 3

Adverse selection and organizational form: There are finitely many points $\{\theta_a, \theta_b, .. \theta_z\}$ with $0 < \theta_a < \theta_b < .. < \theta_z < 1$ such that

(a) $n^*(\theta) = 1$ for $\theta < \theta_a$, and $n^*(\theta) = N$ for $\theta \geq \theta_z$

(b) $n^*(\theta)$ is constant on each of the half-open intervals $[\theta_a,\theta_b)$, $[\theta_b,\theta_c)$ ..
$[\theta_y,\theta_z)$

(c) $n^*(\theta)$ is larger on intervals with higher values of θ

The equilibrium payoffs for E_g and E_b are

$$V_g(\theta) = \phi^*(\theta) \equiv \max\{\phi(n, \theta) \text{ for } n = 1 .. N\}$$
$$V_b(\theta) = \theta[n^*(\theta) - 1]\pi[n^*(\theta)]/n^*(\theta)$$

$V_g(\theta)$ is positive, continuous, nondecreasing, and convex on $0 \leq \theta \leq 1$. $V_b(\theta)$ is strictly increasing in θ.

The shape of $V_g(\theta)$ is shown in Figure 10.1 for N = 3. This function is the upper envelope of the lines $\phi(n, \theta)$ defined by fixed values of n, where the increasing steepness of $V_g(\theta)$ reflects upward jumps in $n^*(\theta)$ at θ_a and θ_b.

Proposition 3 shows that when the average quality of projects is sufficiently low, a good entrepreneur creates a KMF. It is not worthwhile

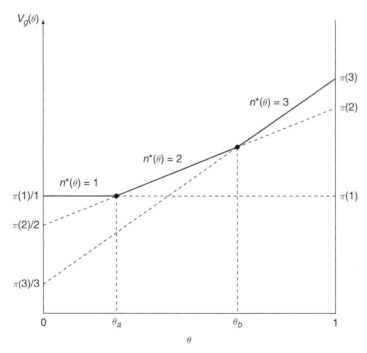

Figure 10.1 The Payoff Function $V_g(\theta)$ for a Pooling Equilibrium (N = 3)

to have any worker participation, because the entrepreneur must share profit with the workforce ex post and cannot extract enough ex ante compensation due to adverse selection. As the average quality of projects rises, workers become willing to pay more for membership. The entrepreneur captures a larger fraction of the benefits from worker participation and offers membership to more workers. If the probability of a good project is close enough to unity, the entrepreneur offers control rights to all workers and the firm becomes a full-fledged LMF.

The main results can now be summarized. A separating equilibrium always leads to a KMF: an entrepreneur with a good project hoards information about the production technology, tells workers what to do, and receives all profit. The productivity gains from worker participation are lost. There is a pooling equilibrium that leads to the same result, but there could also be pooling equilibria where workers in addition to the entrepreneur obtain control rights. If Pareto efficient equilibria are always selected, workers' control becomes more extensive as adverse selection becomes less severe. However, the possible existence of multiple pooling equilibria supported by different worker beliefs implies that high-participation outcomes cannot be taken for granted.

10.5 The Plywood Cooperatives

The plywood cooperatives of the U.S. Pacific Northwest have been among the most intensively studied labor-managed firms (see Pencavel, 2001, and Dow, 2003, 50–57, for historical accounts and references). These firms gradually vanished as the overall plywood industry (both cooperatives and conventional firms) declined across the region. But for much of the last century, coops competed success-fully with conventional rivals and compared favorably with respect to productivity (see Section 6.6).

The results from Section 10.4 shed light on an important episode in the history of these cooperatives. About twenty plywood cooperatives were formed in the 1940s and early 1950s. This new entry occurred during a postwar boom in housing construction and was stimulated at least in part by an expectation of rapid capital gains on membership shares. The new cooperatives were often organized by outside promoters who knew little about the industry and had no intention of working in a plywood mill. Two such efforts resulted in criminal trials for securities fraud and mail fraud, with the promoters receiving jail terms. Around this same time, the formation of new plywood cooperatives came to an abrupt halt, with no known entry by coops after 1955 (Berman, 1967, 113–116; Dow, 2003, 52).

Several points in this story are of interest.

(a) Both LMFs and KMFs entered the industry in large numbers prior to 1955, and the LMFs were clearly able to compete effectively against KMFs.

(b) Entry of new LMFs stopped after 1955, although the previously created LMFs survived and prospered for many decades afterward.

(c) Entry of KMFs continued unabated (about 90 new conventional plywood mills were established in the region during 1956–1972).

These events strongly suggest that LMF entry did not stop due to any inherent defect in LMFs themselves or any dramatic change in the industry as a whole. A more plausible explanation is that the widely publicized instances of fraud in the mid-1950s altered the beliefs of prospective LMF members. Despite a record of economic success for existing LMFs, potential members could no longer assume that the entrepreneurs responsible for creating new LMFs were trustworthy.

Once it became known that some entrepreneurs had bad projects, entrepreneurs with good projects could not induce workers to pay up front for membership rights. A pooling equilibrium that had supported LMF entry collapsed and was replaced by an equilibrium where all firms were organized as KMFs. This occurred despite the highly visible presence of successful coops. Indeed, members of existing coops often became quite wealthy by selling their shares to outside investors. The entry of labor-managed firms was thus sensitive to information conditions, while the entry of conventional firms evidently was not.

10.6 Conclusion

The model in this chapter helps explain the low rate of LMF formation from scratch, even by wealthy entrepreneurs who face no capital constraints. An entrepreneur interested in creating an LMF would have to appropriate its surplus through membership fees, and this is problematic when workers cannot readily distinguish good projects from bad ones. Information asymmetry of this kind is likely to be significant when new firms are being organized. An entrepreneur can avoid this problem by creating a KMF, which can be attractive even when an LMF would have higher productivity and total profit.

Nothing in this story requires limited worker wealth or imperfect capital markets. The argument goes through even if workers are wealthy enough to buy LMF membership shares at their true value. Of course, workers may be too poor to pay such prices, which could aggravate the problem. But I want to stress that appropriation problems involving the sale of LMF control positions play an independent role and may prove decisive even in the absence of capital constraints.

The distinction between capital and labor with respect to alienability is significant for the model in several ways. First, endowments of financial wealth or other nonhuman assets have no upper bound, so there is no reason why a sufficiently wealthy entrepreneur cannot create any type of firm (KMF or LMF) she may prefer. Second, there are natural upper bounds on endowments of time, skill, knowledge, and the ability to supply effort. Because labor comes in person-sized packages, a firm that needs a large input of labor also needs a large number of individual workers. For this reason, an entrepreneur who creates an LMF must engage in membership transactions in order to capture firm profit. Third, the inalienability of labor means that individual workers participate directly in the production process and obtain valuable information by doing so. This can give LMFs a productivity advantage over KMFs, because control rights enable workers to bring their information to bear on managerial decisions.

Firms can have different levels of worker participation in decision-making due to (a) multiple equilibria for a given degree of adverse selection and (b) the varying severity of adverse selection across firms and industries. Firms with zero or low levels of worker participation need not have unobserved characteristics that make participation especially unproductive or costly. Worker participation in decision-making might be very valuable in such firms if it could be implemented, but firms and workers might be trapped in a bad equilibrium where workers do not trust the promises made by entrepreneurs, investors, or managers. This may make it impossible to compensate the latter for losses in bargaining power that they will experience once workers gain control.

I have assumed here not only that control rights give workers bargaining power, but also that the bargaining effect outweighs the productivity effect from the standpoint of entrepreneurs. Hybrid firms like those in Section 1.6 may arise in the opposite case, where the productivity effect is larger, so entrepreneurs introduce some level of worker participation even if they do not receive any side payments from workers. For example, entrepreneurs may use suggestion boxes to raise productivity because there is no danger that workers will acquire bargaining power in this context, and thus there is no need for the entrepreneur to receive any compensation payment. Even if participation does give workers a degree of bargaining power, the productivity effect may dominate over some range. Examples could include membership of employees on certain committees or a promise to provide employees with credible accounting data.

A labor-managed firm gives its members a very high degree of bargaining power in relation to a founding entrepreneur, who becomes just another member. For example, it is hard to imagine in this case that the entrepreneur could hide significant technological information from other members. Therefore, bargaining considerations would usually be top of mind for an entrepreneur contemplating the creation of an LMF.

A number of empirical predictions flow from the model. First, LMFs are more likely to be created if most recent entrants in the same industry have succeeded. Workers who observe a series of successes will be more confident in the quality of the next project and more willing to pay the entrepreneur for a claim on the firm's profit. This strengthens the entrepreneur's incentive to create an LMF. This "track record" effect could arise even if earlier entrants were not LMFs. However, if workers are specifically concerned with the record of past LMF success when forming beliefs about future LMFs, this effect can help explain LMF agglomeration within industries or geographic areas (see Section 7.6).

Another implication involves the life cycles of firms. Suppose that the average quality of new projects is low, so entrepreneurs with good technologies create KMFs. Over time it may become clear to workers that these firms have solid foundations, that their product niches are profitable, and that the entrepreneurs are not of the fly-by-night variety. If so, employees should become more willing to acquire profit shares and entrepreneurs should become more willing to offer control rights to the workforce.

Movements toward greater worker participation may be slow. A long time may have to elapse before a project can be judged a success or failure with any confidence. A run of good or bad luck may mask the true merits of a project for years, or a project may require investments that pay off only over decades. Accordingly, participatory practices will probably be less extensive and introduced more slowly in industries where projects involve a high variance in profit or lengthy investment cycles.

Furthermore, the fact that past projects have succeeded is no guarantee that future projects will succeed. Sophisticated employees will recognize that adverse selection can recur with each new round of innovation and that entrepreneurs, investors, or managers may take the money and run if they have a bad project in the current round. This danger may be mitigated by reputational effects or the repeated nature of the relationships within the firm, but it is unlikely to vanish entirely. On a related note, I argue in Chapter 13 that employee buyouts of KMFs are obstructed by uncertainties about the productivity a firm would have as an LMF and by free rider problems among employees with respect to the acquisition of information on this subject.

10.7 Postscript

This chapter is based on a previously published book chapter called "Worker Participation and Adverse Selection" (Dow, 2010). The book—entitled *Industrial Organization, Trade, and Social Interaction* and published by University of Toronto Press—featured the proceedings from a 2008 conference held in honor of B. Curtis Eaton at Simon Fraser University in Vancouver. I am grateful for comments on earlier versions of the paper from Saul Estrin and participants at the SFU conference, as well as from members of the Association for Comparative Economic Studies, the International Association for Employee Participation, and the Alberta Industrial Organization Workshop. The Social Sciences and Humanities Research Council of Canada provided financial support.

The original version of the paper emphasized hybrid firms like those described in Section 1.6, along with the productivity benefits from worker participation in such firms. Labor-managed firms were discussed, but to a lesser degree. I have shortened the paper substantially and refocused it around the implications for LMFs.

10.8 Appendix

Proof of Proposition 1

Suppose that $n_g \neq n_b$ with $n_g \geq 2$. Bayes' rule gives $\mu(n_g) = 1$, and it follows from (3) that $M(n_g) > 0$. Bayes' rule also gives $\mu(n_b) = 0$, so $M(n_b) = 0$. Since E_b can deviate to n_g and obtain $M(n_g) > 0$, this cannot be an equilibrium. Therefore $n_g = 1$ and $n_b \geq 2$ must hold in every SE. Now let $n_g = 1$, and consider any $n_b \geq 2$ where $\mu(n) = 0$ for all $n \geq 2$. It is unprofitable for E_g to deviate to any $n' \geq 2$, because $M(n') = 0$ and thus $U_g(n') = \pi(n')/n' < \pi(1) = U_g(1)$ using (3), (4), and A2. It is unprofitable for E_b to deviate to any $n' \neq n_b$, because $U_b(n_b) = U_b(n') = 0$ from (3) and (4). This shows that $n_g = 1$, $n_b \geq 2$, $\mu(1) = 1$, and $\mu(n) = 0$ for $n \geq 2$ is an SE. The payoffs follow from (3) and (4).

Proof of Lemma 1

(a) Consider any $n' < n_p$. If E_b prefers n' to n_p, then $M(n') > M(n_p)$ by (4). A2 and $n' < n_p$ imply $\pi(n')/n' + M(n') > \pi(n_p)/n_p + M(n_p)$. Hence E_g also prefers n' to n_p by (4).

(b) Consider any $n' > n_p$. If E_g prefers n' to n_p, then $\pi(n')/n' + M(n') > \pi(n_p)/n_p + M(n_p)$ by (4). A2 and $n' > n_p$ imply $M(n') > M(n_p)$. Hence E_b also prefers n' to n_p by (4).

Proof of Proposition 2

Sufficiency. Suppose that $\phi(n,\theta) \leq \phi(n_p,\theta)$ for all $n \leq n_p$. Set $\mu(n) = \theta$ for $n \leq n_p$ and $\mu(n) = 0$ for $n > n_p$. First consider some upward deviation $n' > n_p$. For any $n' > n_p$ we have $M(n') = 0$ due to (3). However, $M(n_p) \geq 0$, so no upward deviation can be profitable for E_b due to (4). Lemma 1 then implies that no upward deviation is profitable for E_g either. Next, consider some downward deviation $n' < n_p$. If no such deviation is profitable for E_g, then from Lemma 1 no such deviation is profitable for E_b either. For any $n' < n_p$, E_g has the payoff $\phi(n',\theta)$ due to (3), (4), and $\mu(n') = \theta$. But at n_p this agent has the payoff $\phi(n_p,\theta)$ where $\phi(n',\theta) \leq \phi(n_p,\theta)$, so no downward deviation can be profitable for E_g. Thus n_p can be supported by a pooling equilibrium. The payoffs are derived from (3) and (4).

Necessity. Suppose that $\phi(n',\theta) > \phi(n_p,\theta)$ for some $n' < n_p$. E_g's payoff from n_p is $\phi(n_p,\theta)$. E_g's payoff from n' is $\pi(n')/n' + M(n') \geq \phi(n',\theta) > \phi(n_p,\theta)$ where the first inequality follows from (3), (4), and A3. Because a deviation to n' is profitable for E_g, the choice n_p cannot be supported by a pooling equilibrium consistent with A3.

Proof of Lemma 2

From (4), the equilibrium payoffs of E_b are $M(n_p^\circ)$ and $M(n_p^1)$. Using (3), A1, A2, and the Bayesian requirement $\mu(n_p^\circ) = \mu(n_p^1) = \theta$, we have $M(n_p^\circ) < M(n_p^1)$ whenever $n_p^\circ < n_p^1$. The equilibrium payoffs of E_g are $\phi(n_p^\circ,\theta)$ and $\phi(n_p^1,\theta)$. Because n_p^1 is supported by a PE, it satisfies the condition in Proposition 2, and hence $n_p^\circ < n_p^1$ implies $\phi(n_p^\circ,\theta) \leq \phi(n_p^1,\theta)$. Uninformed agents are indifferent between PE with n_p° and n_p^1 because they receive zero expected surplus in both cases.

Proof of Proposition 3

Consider $\phi(n,\theta) = \theta\pi(n) + (1-\theta)\pi(n)/n$ as a function of θ for a fixed choice of n. The resulting line L_n has a left intercept $\pi(n)/n$ at $\theta = 0$, a right intercept $\pi(n)$ at $\theta = 1$, and the slope $\pi(n)(1 - 1/n)$. There are N such lines corresponding to $n = 1 .. N$, and lines with larger values of n have steeper slopes (see Figure 10.1 for the case $N = 3$).

Since L_1 has the largest left intercept among all L_n, there is an interval $[0, \theta_a)$ on which L_1 lies above all L_n with $n \geq 2$, where

$\theta_a \equiv$ the smallest θ such that $\phi(1, \theta) = \phi(n, \theta)$ for some $n \geq 2$.

Whenever $N \geq 2$, we have $0 < \theta_a < 1$ because the right intercept of L_N exceeds the right intercept of L_1 so that L_1 and L_N intersect at an interior point $\theta \in (0, 1)$. By definition, $n^*(\theta) = 1$ is the unique maximizer of $\phi(n,\theta)$ at any $\theta \in [0, \theta_a)$. Moreover, $n^*(\theta) = 1$ is a maximizer (although not unique) at θ_a. Now define

$A \equiv$ the largest $n \geq 2$ such that $\phi(1, \theta_a) = \phi(n, \theta_a)$

Because the largest maximizer is selected at each θ, it follows that $n^*(\theta_a) = A$.

Because the slopes of the lines L_n are strictly increasing in n and $\phi(n,\theta_a) \leq \phi(A,\theta_a)$ for all $n \leq A$, the lines L_n for $n < A$ all lie strictly below the line L_A on $(\theta_a,1]$. Thus no $n < A$ is a candidate to maximize $\phi(n,\theta)$ on $(\theta_a,1]$. If $A = N$, then $\theta_a = \theta_z$ and this part of the proof is finished. If $A < N$, then observe that $\phi(n,\theta_a) < \phi(A,\theta_a)$ for all $n = A+1 .. N$. This follows because otherwise we contradict the definition of θ_a or the definition of A. Thus, there is an interval (θ_a,θ_b) on which L_A lies above all L_n with $n \geq A+1$, where

$\theta_b \equiv$ the smallest θ such that $\phi(A, \theta) = \phi(n, \theta)$ for some $n \geq A + 1$

Whenever $N \geq A+1$, we have $\theta_a < \theta_b < 1$ because the right intercept of L_N exceeds the right intercept of L_A so that L_1 and L_N intersect at an interior point $\theta \in (\theta_a, 1)$. By definition, $n^*(\theta) = A$ is the unique maximizer of $\phi(n,\theta)$ at any $\theta \in (\theta_a, \theta_b)$. Moreover, $n^*(\theta) = A$ is a maximizer (although not unique) at θ_b. Now define

$B \equiv$ the largest $n \geq A + 1$ such that $\phi(A, \theta_b) = \phi(n, \theta_b)$

Because the largest maximizer is selected at each θ, it follows that $n^*(\theta_b) = B$.

This procedure can be repeated as many times as necessary for $n = C, D \ldots$ At most there are $N-1$ points of the form $\theta_a, \theta_b .. \theta_z$ at which two or more n are indifferent. Hence, at most there are

N intervals of the form $[0,\theta_a)$, $[\theta_a,\theta_b)$, .. $[\theta_z,1]$. These have the property that $n^*(\theta) = 1$ is chosen on $[0,\theta_a)$, $n^*(\theta) = A$ is chosen on $[\theta_a,\theta_b)$, and so on, with $1 < A < B < C$ .. and $n^*(\theta) = N$ chosen on $[\theta_z,1]$. The maximizer is unique in the interior of each interval and also at the endpoints $\theta = 0$ and $\theta = 1$.

The function $V_g(\theta)$ is positive for all $\theta \in [0,1]$ due to A1; it is continuous because it is the maximum of continuous functions; it is nondecreasing because $\pi(n) \geq \pi(n)/n$ for all n; and it is convex because $\phi(n,\theta)$ is linear in θ when n is held constant, but optimal adjustments in n may yield a larger payoff as θ varies. The payoff for E_g follows from (4), the fact that E_g receives $\phi(n_p, \theta)$ in any PE, and the fact that we are setting $n_p = n^*(\theta)$ for each $\theta \in [0, 1]$. The payoff for E_b is obtained by substituting $n^*(\theta)$ and $\mu(n^*(\theta)) = \theta$ in (4). This payoff is increasing due to A1, A2, and the fact that $n^*(\theta)$ is nondecreasing.

11

Partnership Markets with Adverse Selection

11.1 Introduction

We have seen in Chapter 10 that an entrepreneur may not want to create a labor-managed firm because adverse selection can make it impossible to capture the full value of the firm by selling LMF membership rights to workers. This chapter makes a related point: an existing LMF may have trouble using a membership market to handle worker turnover. An important difference is that in Chapter 10, the outsiders lacked information about the quality of the entrepreneurial project, while in this chapter, the insiders lack information about the productivity of potential LMF members.

Due to the inalienability of labor, the LMF must alter the identities of the workers who supply labor whenever membership transactions occur. If insiders are unsure about the productivity of outsiders, this creates problems for membership markets. The same is not true for KMFs. Because capital is alienable, the firm's physical assets can remain the same when one investor sells equity shares to another investor on a stock market. LMF membership markets are consequently vulnerable to adverse selection involving worker characteristics, while KMF membership markets do not generally have parallel problems involving investor characteristics.

This asymmetry accounts for a key feature of economic organization. Ownership positions in large corporations are routinely traded on anonymous markets without prior approval from any other shareholder. By contrast, professional partnerships and worker cooperatives require an insider to obtain permission from the other insiders before selling membership rights to an outsider. In some cases, such transactions are simply prohibited.

These ideas have a long pedigree. In the following passage from *The Wealth of Nations*, coming just before his famous diatribe against the joint stock company, Adam Smith distinguishes a partnership from a corporation by stressing the different procedures through which members are replaced.

[I]n a private copartnery, no partner, without the consent of the company, can transfer his share to another person or introduce a new member into the company. Each member, however, may, upon proper warning, withdraw from the copartnery and demand payment from them of his share of the common stock. In a joint stock company, on the contrary, no member can demand payment of his share from the company; but each member can, without their consent, transfer his share to another person, and thereby introduce a new member. (Adam Smith, [1776] 1994, 799)

One need only substitute "LMF" for "copartnery" and "KMF" for "joint stock company" to see the relevance of Smith's observations. Here I assume that firms are legally organized as partnerships, but the economic arguments apply equally well to worker cooperatives.

In the English common law tradition, systematized by the Partnership Act of 1890, partnerships have no legal identity distinct from that of their individual members. In the absence of an explicit contrary agreement, no one can be introduced as a partner without the consent of all other members of the firm (Prime and Scanlan, 1995, 178). If anyone retires from a partnership at will, this dissolves the firm (Prime and Scanlan, 1995, 276). Partnership agreements entitling an outgoing member to choose a successor, although legally possible, are rarely adopted (Banks, 1990, 229). Parallel default rules on turnover among partners exist in Australia and New Zealand (Graw, 1996), Canada (VanDuzer, 1997, ch. 2), and France and Germany (Banks, 1990, 21–25).

Until the 1990s, the Uniform Partnership Act (UPA), which governed partnerships in almost all U.S. states, required a firm to dissolve upon withdrawal by any individual (Hillman, 1995; Hynes, 1995). The UPA did not even allow partners to waive their right to bring about dissolution. Revisions in the 1990s sought to provide more organizational stability by substituting an "entity" theory of partnership under which a business unit can survive the departure of individual members. But the default is still for the partnership to dissolve upon withdrawal by a single partner. This ensures that the continuing members hold veto rights over the choice of a successor.

As was discussed in Section 7.3, similar policies are found in worker cooperatives. In some countries, legal rules prevent any sale of membership rights. In other countries, such transactions are allowed, but only if other members agree. Even in the latter case, individual LMFs often choose not to have a membership market. In the U.S. plywood cooperatives, a majority of worker-owners generally had to approve any membership transaction (Craig and Pencavel, 1992; Pencavel and Craig, 1994; Pencavel, 2001).

The most obvious reason why partners might insist upon unanimous consent, or at least a majority vote, before accepting a new colleague is that they are concerned with the quality of the candidate. Applicants vary in skill, judgment, motivation, and collegiality, among other things. For firms where net income is shared, decision-making is joint, and personal liability is unlimited, it is unsurprising that incumbents pay close attention to the characteristics of new applicants. To grasp why freely transferable partnership positions are rare, an academic economist need only imagine a system in which colleagues can sell their professorships to the highest bidder.

Allowing membership transactions to take place on an open market often imposes a negative externality on the continuing members, because the departing member finds it attractive to sell to a low-quality successor. If the continuing members would not have made the same decision, the joint payoff of the parties is reduced. In theory, this problem can be eliminated by having continuing members bribe departing members to recruit their successors differently. But if it is costly to negotiate agreements of this sort, the partners will prefer to have continuing members retain control over vacancies.

Such arrangements are less vital when individuals contribute cash or property to an enterprise, rather than labor services, because informational asymmetries often matter less for nonhuman inputs. One example involves limited partnerships in the real estate, oil and gas, cable television, and equipment leasing industries. An active secondary market for such partnership positions has existed in the United States since the 1980s (Wollack and Donaldson, 1992; Denning and Shastri, 1993; Allen, 1995; Barber, 1996). Limited liability partners do not participate in firm operations, lack voting rights, and are viewed by tax authorities as "passive" investors. In this context, adverse selection issues appear negligible by comparison with firms where the partners contribute professional skills and participate in business decisions.

In closely held corporations, share transactions sometimes require prior approval from other owners due to the prominent role of each individual shareholder in managerial decision-making. KMFs may well confront adverse selection problems in the market for equity shares when the number of investors is small, each investor has significant power, and investors have heterogeneous preferences or abilities. However, KMFs with publicly traded shares do not confront such problems, because no individual investor has a decisive role. Exceptions typically arise only when corporate control is at stake.

Section 11.2 describes the formal model. There are two types of workers: high productivity (type a) and low productivity (type b). Partnerships consist of two workers who share profits equally. Vacancies are filled by having incumbents announce prices for admission to their firms. Section 11.3 studies equilibria where outsiders can observe the productivity of firms, and thus can infer the type of the partner with whom they will be matched, but where insiders cannot observe the productivity of unattached outsiders.

Section 11.4 shows that control over vacancies by continuing workers dominates control by departing workers. When departing workers hold property rights over their positions, they sell out to whomever will pay the most. Due to adverse selection, this is a low-quality agent. If the continuing worker would have done the same, as is sometimes true, it does not matter whether the continuing or departing worker holds property rights over the vacancy. But if the continuing worker would have chosen a low membership price in order to attract high-quality applicants, the joint payoff of the partners is larger when property rights over the vacancy are assigned to the continuing worker.

Section 11.5 examines incentives for endogenous separations between partners. I show that market transactions always reduce aggregate surplus when adverse selection is severe. This provides a rationale for the prohibition of membership markets. However, market sorting can increase aggregate surplus when adverse selection is mild, provided that most existing firms have low productivity and/or involuntary separations are rare.

Section 11.6 develops some connections with other chapters, and Section 11.7 is a postscript. Proofs of selected formal propositions are provided in Section 11.8.

11.2 The Model

Production in a partnership requires two workers, who share profit equally. All workers are risk neutral. There are two kinds of workers: type a (high quality) and type b (low quality). An individual agent's type is not verifiable in court. At least one worker must have prior experience in the same firm due to a need for firm-specific skills (see Chapters 14 and 15).

These skills can be readily transmitted from an incumbent to a novice, but two incumbents cannot sell the firm to two novices.

Per-person income (g) in a firm depends symmetrically on worker types, with

$$0 < g_{bb} < g_{ab} = g_{ba} < g_{aa} \qquad\qquad A1$$

The subscripts indicate the types of the two partners (not differentiation). The per-person marginal product of worker quality when one worker is fixed at type b is $\Delta g_b \equiv g_{ab} - g_{bb}$. The marginal product of quality when one worker is fixed at type a is $\Delta g_a \equiv g_{aa} - g_{ab}$. I assume $\Delta g_a > \Delta g_b$ throughout. For example, a talented lawyer's advice about difficult cases raises the productivity of colleagues, and this effect is likely to be stronger when these colleagues are also highly talented. Such complementarities often arise in team production tasks with a division of labor. Under full information, this encourages the formation of firms in which the partners have similar ability levels (Sherstyuk, 1998).

The workers have outside options worth $r_a > 0$ and $r_b > 0$, which are interpreted as the payoffs from self-employment. I assume $\Delta r \equiv r_a - r_b > 0$ so better workers have better self-employment opportunities. For example, a lawyer who is unusually productive in a team is also unusually productive when self-employed. Moreover, $g_{ab} > r_a$ and $g_{bb} > r_b$ so every worker wants to join a firm even if the match will involve a type b colleague. The higher return from membership in a firm is due to the quasi-rents associated with earlier investments by firms in physical assets, proprietary data, client contacts, or brand-name reputation (Carr and Mathewson, 1990).

The total number of firms is small relative to the number of workers of each type, so in principle firms could be staffed entirely by high-quality workers or entirely by low-quality workers. Workers not currently in firms pursue solo careers but are available for recruitment if a vacancy arises. I often use uppercase letters A or B for incumbents in firms and lowercase letters a or b for unattached workers.

Among unattached workers, the fraction μ have high productivity and the fraction $1-\mu$ have low productivity, where $0 < \mu < 1$. I treat μ as exogenous. Unattached workers know their own types, but incumbents do not see this. All agents see the productivities of existing firms and so can infer whether both partners are type A, both are type B, or there is one partner of each type. For a framework where μ is endogenous and the unattached workers cannot observe the productivities of firms, see Dow (2014).

I assume throughout that

$$0 < \Delta g_b < \Delta g_a < \Delta r < 2\Delta g_b \qquad \text{A2}$$

The first two inequalities have already been discussed. The inequality $\Delta g_a < \Delta r$ says that the income gap between good and bad workers is always greater in self-employment than in firms. This is plausible for two reasons. First, the productivity gain from high ability must be shared in a firm but not in self-employment (g is a per-person payoff). Second, productivity differentials are likely to be muted in a firm if income sharing leads to lower effort by both types. The inequality $\Delta r < 2\Delta g_b$ implies that AB firms provide more total surplus than BB, and together with $\Delta g_b < \Delta g_a$ implies that AA firms provide more surplus than AB. Hence, under full information all matches would be AA.

A2 implies that any partnership offer attractive to type a workers is attractive to type b as well, so there is no equilibrium where only high-quality workers apply. To formalize this point, let $s_a(p, \theta) = \theta g_{aa} + (1-\theta)g_{ab} - r_a - p$ be the surplus for an unattached type a worker from a match with an incumbent believed to be type A with probability θ, given an admission price of p. Let $s_b(p, \theta) = \theta g_{ab} + (1-\theta)g_{bb} - r_b - p$ be the corresponding surplus for a type b worker. A2 gives $s_b(p, \theta) > s_a(p, \theta)$ for all p and θ. Thus, any offer yielding nonnegative surplus for unattached type a workers must yield positive surplus for type b, regardless of the price and beliefs involved.

11.3 Price Determination

Consider one firm with a vacancy. Assume that the incumbent has a known type. For example, if unattached workers observed incomes g_{aa} before a match dissolved, then the incumbent must be type A, while if incomes were g_{bb}, then the incumbent must be type B. The incumbent chooses a price p that an outsider must pay to join the firm. Next, each unattached worker decides whether to apply for the position. Such workers apply whenever joining the firm would yield nonnegative surplus. The incumbent randomly selects a worker from the resulting applicant pool. This worker pays the entry fee and becomes a partner in the firm.

Suppose that the incumbent is type A. Outsiders of both types apply when $p \le g_{aa} - r_a$, only outsiders of type b apply when $g_{aa} - r_a < p \le g_{ab} - r_b$, and neither type applies when $g_{ab} - r_b < p$. Notice that the second of these intervals is nonempty due to $\Delta g_a < \Delta r$ from A2. The incumbent wants to extract the maximum membership revenue and thus chooses either $p = g_{aa} - r_a$ to attract both types or $p = g_{ab} - r_b$ to attract only type b. It is always better to choose one of these prices than a price so high that no one will apply. I assume that if the incumbent is indifferent, the price is set at a level that attracts both types.

For $p = g_{aa} - r_a$, the incumbent receives the total expected surplus $\mu g_{aa} + (1-\mu)g_{ab} + (g_{aa} - r_a) - r_a$, where the terms involving μ are expected partnership income given that both types apply, the term in the second set of parentheses is the price paid by the outsider, and r_a is the opportunity cost of the incumbent. For $p = g_{ab} - r_b$, the incumbent receives the surplus $g_{ab} + (g_{ab} - r_b) - r_a$, because only type b workers apply, giving the partnership income g_{ab} with certainty. As before, the price of the vacancy is in parentheses and the incumbent's opportunity cost is subtracted. A comparison of these payoff expressions determines the price preferred by the incumbent. A parallel analysis applies when the incumbent is type B. This yields the following results.

Proposition 1
Price determination:
Define $\mu_A° \equiv \Delta r/\Delta g_a - 1$ and $\mu_B° \equiv \Delta r/\Delta g_b - 1$, where $0 < \mu_A° < \mu_B° < 1$.

(a) A type A incumbent chooses $p = g_{aa} - r_a$ and attracts both types when $\mu_A° \leq \mu$. Such an incumbent chooses $p = g_{ab} - r_b$ and attracts only type b when $\mu < \mu_A°$.
(b) A type B incumbent chooses $p = g_{ab} - r_a$ and attracts both types when $\mu_B° \leq \mu$. Such an incumbent chooses $p = g_{bb} - r_b$ and attracts only type b when $\mu < \mu_B°$.

The proof involves easy algebra and is omitted. When adverse selection is mild (high-quality workers are abundant so μ is above $\mu_B°$), all incumbents find it profitable to set a low membership price in order to attract good workers. When adverse selection is severe (high-quality workers are scarce so μ is below $\mu_A°$), all incumbents find it profitable to set a high membership price and attract only low-quality workers. At intermediate values of μ, type A incumbents attract both types, while type B incumbents attract only type b.

Now consider a more subtle problem. Suppose that the unattached workers see per-person income g_{ab} before the existing partnership dissolves and thus know that the firm has members of type AB. However, when dissolution occurs, the existing partners can choose who will retain membership in the firm and outsiders cannot directly observe whether the continuing incumbent is type A or B. We need to determine the type of worker who stays in the firm and the price this worker charges when filling the vacancy.

Conditional on an AB separation, whether for exogenous reasons or as a result of a voluntary decision by the partners, let there be three steps:

(i) The existing partners decide whether A or B will be the continuing incumbent. This choice maximizes the joint payoff of the partners.
(ii) The continuing incumbent chooses a price at which the vacancy will be filled.
(iii) Each unattached worker decides whether to apply, and as before the incumbent randomly selects one outsider from the resulting applicant pool.

This leads to the following result.

Lemma 1
Dissolution of AB matches: Whenever an AB match dissolves, the continuing incumbent is B.

A formal proof is omitted, but I will sketch the reasoning. Suppose that the continuing incumbent is A. This agent sets some price p that either attracts both unattached types or only type b, depending on the price and the beliefs of the unattached workers about the type of the incumbent (where these beliefs could depend on the price). It can be shown that the joint payoff of the partners must be larger when the continuing incumbent is B, given that B announces the same price and attracts the same applicant pool as A. This occurs because the gain from having A rather than B be self-employed exceeds the gain from having A rather than B remain in the firm. Thus there is no equilibrium where A is the continuing incumbent. However, there is an equilibrium where B is the continuing incumbent, the unattached workers believe the incumbent is B with probability 1 for every price, and the incumbent B announces the price described in Proposition 1(b).

11.4 Property Rights

Vacancies may arise in partnerships for exogenous reasons such as relocation, or endogenously because the total surplus of the partners can be increased by separation. It is standard practice that whenever a vacancy arises, the continuing partner sets the terms on which an outsider can join. One explanation for this pattern runs as follows.

The departing worker is indifferent toward the quality of a replacement, because this has no effect on the payoff from self-employment. If the departing worker owns the vacancy, he or she chooses the highest price at which anyone will apply. Due to adverse selection, this implies that a low-quality worker is recruited. However, if the continuing worker owns the vacancy, he or she internalizes the tradeoff between a low membership price and a high-quality applicant pool. When the continuing worker wants a high price and attracts only low-quality applicants, it does not matter who owns the vacancy. But when the continuing worker wants a low price in order to attract high-quality applicants, ownership of the vacancy by the continuing worker maximizes the joint payoff of the partners, while ownership by the departing worker does not.

In theory, the departing worker could own the vacancy and the continuing worker could bribe the departer to set a low price when this is necessary to achieve joint payoff maximization. However, such arrangements involve negotiation and enforcement costs. These costs can be avoided by committing the firm to a system in which the continuing worker owns the vacancy. The next proposition formalizes these ideas.

Proposition 2
Property rights over vacancies: Assume that continuing workers cannot bribe departing workers to alter the membership price announced for a vacancy. Let an existing partnership dissolve, where the departing worker may be of either type.

(a) If either

> (i) the continuing worker is A and $\mu_A{}^\circ < \mu$ or
> (ii) the continuing worker is B and $\mu_B{}^\circ < \mu$

then having the continuing worker own the vacancy yields a strictly larger joint payoff to the partners than having the departing worker own the vacancy.

(b) If either

> (i) the continuing worker is A and $\mu \leq \mu_A{}^\circ$ or
> (ii) the continuing worker is B and $\mu \leq \mu_B{}^\circ$

then having the continuing worker own the vacancy yields the same joint payoff to the partners as having the departing worker own the vacancy.

A proof is provided in Section 11.8. In part (a), the continuing worker strictly prefers to attract type *a* applicants, while the departing worker would fail to do so. In part (b), the continuing worker attracts only type b applicants or is indifferent about attracting type *a* applicants, so it does not matter who owns the vacancy. Because ownership of vacancies by continuing workers dominates, in the rest of the chapter I assume that this system of property rights prevails. The pricing strategies from Section 11.3 therefore apply.

11.5 Welfare Analysis

In this section, I explore two questions. First, we want to know whether existing partnerships ever dissolve voluntarily. Second, we want to know whether membership transactions raise or lower aggregate surplus. I will show that AA and AB partnerships never dissolve voluntarily but that BB partnerships do. I will also show that when adverse selection is severe enough (sufficiently low μ), transactions in the membership market unambiguously decrease aggregate surplus. But when the adverse selection problem is mild (sufficiently high μ), market sorting can sometimes increase aggregate surplus.

Assume that if two partners want to preserve a match, it remains intact with the probability $\rho \in (0, 1)$ but ends involuntarily with the probability $1-\rho$. This may occur, for example, if one partner must relocate. Matches end voluntarily when the sum of the payoffs of their members can be raised by having one partner pursue self-employment while the other stays in the firm and recruits a replacement. I assume that the nonhuman assets lending continuity to the firm (such as client lists or brand names) can be inherited by either partner regardless of the reasons for separation. Thus when an AB partnership dissolves, Lemma 1 applies, and the continuing incumbent is always B.

Lemma 2
Voluntary separation:

(a) AA partnerships always strictly prefer continuation of the match.
(b) AB partnerships always strictly prefer continuation of the match.
(c) BB partnerships strictly prefer separation if $\mu > \mu_B^\circ$ and are indifferent between continuation and separation otherwise.

A proof is given in Section 11.8. Parts (a) and (b) trace to A2, which ensures that self-employment never has a large enough payoff for the departing worker to offset the fact that type b workers will be included in the applicant pool when the resulting vacancy is filled. Part (c) derives from the fact that separation is profitable for BB if the incumbent strictly prefers to attract type *a* workers. Otherwise, separation and recruitment of a new partner is equivalent to continuation with the existing partner.

Now let $\pi = (\pi_{aa}, \pi_{ab}, \pi_{bb})$ be an initial distribution of firm types. Transactions in the membership market update π to give a final distribution $\pi' = (\pi_{aa}', \pi_{ab}', \pi_{bb}')$. For the sake of compactness in notation, let μ_A be the probability that an A incumbent recruits an unattached worker of type *a*, and let μ_B be the probability that a B incumbent recruits an unattached worker of type *a*. These probabilities are obtained from Proposition 1 and do not depend on the initial match (AA, AB, or BB). For simplicity, I assume that the BB partnerships dissolve in case of indifference in Lemma 2(c). This gives

$$\begin{aligned}
\pi_{aa}' &= [\rho + (1-\rho)\mu_A]\pi_{aa} \\
\pi_{ab}' &= (1-\rho)(1-\mu_A)\pi_{aa} + [\rho + (1-\rho)\mu_B]\pi_{ab} + \mu_B\pi_{bb} \\
\pi_{bb}' &= (1-\rho)(1-\mu_B)\pi_{ab} + (1-\mu_B)\pi_{bb}
\end{aligned} \tag{1}$$

To see how these equations arise, consider the first one. There are two sources of AA firms in the final distribution π'. First, there are existing AA firms that stay intact with probability ρ. Second, there are existing AA firms that dissolve involuntarily with the probability $1-\rho$ where the incumbent has the probability μ_A of recruiting a new type *a* member. AA matches cannot be obtained in any other way, because when AB and BB matches dissolve, the incumbent is always B. The reasoning is similar for the other two equations. The parameters μ_A and μ_B will be discussed in the context of Proposition 3.

The surpluses per firm at the initial distribution π and the final distribution π' are

$$\begin{aligned}
W &= \pi_{aa}(2g_{aa} - 2r_a) + \pi_{ab}(2g_{ab} - r_a - r_b) + \pi_{bb}(2g_{bb} - 2r_b) \\
W' &= \pi_{aa}'(2g_{aa} - 2r_a) + \pi_{ab}'(2g_{ab} - r_a - r_b) + \pi_{bb}'(2g_{bb} - 2r_b)
\end{aligned} \tag{2}$$

Define the changes in market share for each firm type by $\Delta\pi_{aa} \equiv \pi_{aa}' - \pi_{aa}$, $\Delta\pi_{ab} \equiv \pi_{ab}' - \pi_{ab}$, and $\Delta\pi_{bb} \equiv \pi_{bb}' - \pi_{bb}$. The resulting change in surplus per firm is

$$\begin{aligned}
\Delta W \equiv W' - W &= \Delta\pi_{aa}(2g_{aa} - 2r_a) + \Delta\pi_{ab}(2g_{ab} - r_a - r_b) \\
&\quad + \Delta\pi_{bb}(2g_{bb} - 2r_b) \text{ or} \\
\Delta W &= -\pi_{aa}(1-\rho)(1-\mu_A)(2\Delta g_a - \Delta r) - \pi_{ab}(1-\rho)(1-\mu_B) \\
&\quad (2\Delta g_b - \Delta r) + \pi_{bb}\mu_B(2\Delta g_b - \Delta r)
\end{aligned} \tag{3}$$

Proposition 3

Welfare comparisons: From Proposition 1, three cases can arise.

(a) *Severe adverse selection:* $\mu < \mu_A^\circ$ so A and B incumbents both attract only type b unattached workers. This gives $\mu_A = \mu_B = 0$. A2 yields $\Delta W < 0$ in (3) if there are some AA or AB firms, and $\Delta W = 0$ if all firms are BB.

(b) *Moderate adverse selection:* $\mu_A^\circ \leq \mu < \mu_B^\circ$ so A incumbents attract both types of unattached workers while B incumbents attract only type b unattached workers. This gives $\mu_A = \mu$ and $\mu_B = 0$. A2 yields $\Delta W < 0$ in (3) if there are some AA or AB firms, and $\Delta W = 0$ if all firms are BB.

(c) *Mild adverse selection:* $\mu_B^\circ \leq \mu$ so both types of incumbents attract both types of unattached workers. This gives $\mu_A = \mu_B = \mu$. From (3), we have

$$\Delta W = \pi_{bb}\mu(2\Delta g_b - \Delta r) - (1 - \rho)(1 - \mu)[\pi_{aa}(2\Delta g_a - \Delta r) + \pi_{ab}(2\Delta g_b - \Delta r)]$$

For a given μ, this yields $\Delta W > 0$ if π_{bb} is sufficiently close to unity and/or $1-\rho$ is sufficiently close to zero.

No proof is required apart from the preceding algebra. The upshot is that market sorting decreases total surplus when adverse selection is severe or moderate. Such sorting may increase total surplus when adverse selection is mild, but only under certain conditions.

To see the mechanics of Proposition 3, consider cases (a) and (b). At least some of the AA matches that split involuntarily result in AB matches, but there is no flow of new AA matches. Consequently the market share of AA firms must shrink, decreasing welfare. AB matches that dissolve involuntarily have type B incumbents from Lemma 1. These all result in BB matches, which also decreases welfare. Finally, the dissolving BB matches result in type B incumbents, who only recruit type b workers and thus maintain the existing supply of low-surplus BB matches. Because AB splits result in BB matches, the BB market share must grow as long as some AB firms exist.

In case (c), aggregate surplus can rise for a given value of μ. This only happens when the initial share of BB firms is large enough and/or involuntary separations are rare enough. When π_{bb} is close to unity, there is a large potential benefit from the conversion of BB matches into AB matches. This can occur in case (c) because B incumbents attract unattached workers of both types. When $1-\rho$ is close to zero, the AA or AB matches are unlikely to dissolve, which limits the welfare loss from this source. However, aggregate surplus can still fall in case (c) if the initial market shares for AA and AB firms are large enough relative to the other parameters in the model.

11.6 Conclusion

The key message from this chapter is that due to the inalienability of labor and the alienability of capital, LMF membership markets encounter adverse selection problems involving worker characteristics, while KMF stock markets do not generally confront any similar problems with adverse selection among investors. Given the importance of LMF membership markets as a way of achieving isomorphism between LMFs and KMFs (see Chapters 3–5), this asymmetry is a cause for concern.

Chapter 9 showed that imperfect membership markets can lead to asymmetries between LMFs and KMFs in comparative statics and investment behavior. Chapter 10 showed that adverse selection can discourage entrepreneurs from creating LMFs because imperfect membership markets prevent entrepreneurs from fully appropriating rents from innovation. The present chapter extended these ideas by showing that LMFs face adverse selection issues when workers come and go from the firm. One implication is that LMFs (whether they are professional partnerships or worker coops) will adopt property rights systems where continuing members control the admission of replacement members. This is consistent with universal practice in such firms and contrasts sharply with the common practice in KMFs of allowing equity shares to be traded on anonymous public markets.

The welfare analysis in Section 11.5 suggests that there may even be a rationale for shutting down LMF membership markets entirely, because such transactions tend to reduce aggregate surplus when adverse selection is significant. This conclusion requires some qualification because market sorting can increase surplus when adverse selection is mild and other special conditions are satisfied. Nevertheless, it is interesting given that some countries ban the sale of membership rights in cooperatives (see Section 7.3).

Of course, a full policy analysis would also have to take account of the benefits of membership markets. For example, Section 9.5 indicated that a missing membership market could cause LMFs to be converted into KMFs even when this reduces aggregate surplus. One would also need to consider institutional rules that might help cope with the absence of a membership market, such as restrictions on nonmember hiring to prevent degeneration or a minimum level of saving out of cash flow to prevent underinvestment.

A potential objection to the conclusions reached in this chapter is that there may be ways of overcoming adverse selection problems in LMF membership markets, and therefore I have painted a starker picture than is really warranted. For example, perhaps high-quality applicants could signal their type, or incumbents could screen new workers by requiring a probationary period before promotion to full partner. But signaling and screening are costly and do not eliminate information asymmetries entirely. Academic records, for example, shed little light on character traits such as honesty or willingness to help one's coworkers. Moreover, there is empirical evidence that adverse selection is a problem for professional partnerships despite their use of such mechanisms (Spurr, 1987; O'Flaherty and Siow, 1995; Landers et al., 1996).

Another solution is for incumbents to assign low-productivity newcomers a lower profit share ex post. But when productivity is unverifiable, the incumbents could do the same thing to high-productivity newcomers. This firm-side moral hazard problem can be avoided through the use of promotion tournaments, but tournaments have poor incentive features when cooperation among junior members is important. Perhaps the incumbents could invest in a reputation for fairness toward newcomers having high productivity, but the feasibility of this approach undoubtedly varies with the circumstances.

A final way to alleviate adverse selection problems is through regulation. Leland (1979) argues that quality standards imposed by professional associations can be justified in this way, a view contested by Ryoo (1996). Even when such quality regulation exists, it is likely to be a coarse filter that only screens out the worst practitioners, leaving ample scope for adverse selection among the remaining population.

This chapter ignored capital market problems by assuming that firms already had any nonhuman assets needed for production. This facilitated the investigation of adverse selection problems specific to LMFs. However, a fuller comparison of KMFs and LMFs requires attention to the capital market. Investments in nonhuman assets are studied in Chapters 15, 17, and 18. Before turning to these issues, I consider market imperfections involving public good problems in Chapters 12 and 13.

11.7 Postscript

This chapter is based on "Partnership Markets with Adverse Selection," published in the *Review of Economic Design* (Dow, 2014). A complete working paper existed in 2001, the manuscript was accepted for publication in 2007, and it appeared electronically in

2013 and in print in 2014. The published article was extensively revised for this volume.

The formal model in Sections 11.2–11.5 has been simplified by changing two assumptions. First, I assume here that unattached workers can observe the productivity of an existing partnership and therefore can determine whether the match is AA, AB, or BB. This differs from Dow (2014), where I assume that unattached workers do not see this and must therefore form beliefs about the types of incumbents (the adverse selection problem is bilateral). Second, I assume here that the fraction of unattached workers who have high productivity (μ) is exogenous. In Dow (2014), this was determined in market equilibrium, which led to a much more complicated analysis.

Earlier drafts of this chapter were presented at Simon Fraser University, the University of British Columbia, McMaster University, the University of New South Wales, the University of Sydney, Australian National University, Wesleyan University, the University of Connecticut, and annual meetings of the Canadian Economics Association and Western Economics Association. The Social Sciences and Humanities Research Council of Canada supplied financial support, and Teodora Cosac and Ken Carlaw provided research assistance.

This paper was written independently of Levin and Tadelis (2005). These authors consider information asymmetries between consumers of professional services like law, who have trouble determining the quality of the services they receive, and the firms that supply such services, who know the true quality. Levin and Tadelis focus on the choice between partnerships and corporations as alternative organizational forms and argue that partnerships are sometimes better able to solve the information problem because they can credibly commit to high service quality. This article has added interest for students of the LMF because the authors cite Ward (1958) to provide intuition for their model.

11.8 Appendix

Proof of Proposition 2

Suppose that the continuing incumbent is A and $\mu_A{}^\circ \leq \mu$ in Proposition 1(a) so A attracts both types. With incumbent ownership of the vacancy, the joint payoff of the partners is $\mu g_{aa} + (1\text{-}\mu)g_{ab} + (g_{aa} - r_a) + \underline{r}$, where the second expression in parentheses is the price chosen by the incumbent and $\underline{r}$ is the external payoff of the departing member (the type of this member is irrelevant). With departer ownership of the vacancy, the price is $g_{ab} - r_b$ where only type b is attracted, because this exceeds the price $g_{aa} - r_a$ at which both types are attracted due to $\Delta g_a < \Delta r$ from A2. The joint payoff, then, is $g_{ab} + (g_{ab} - r_b) + \underline{r}$, where again the expression in parentheses is the price. Some algebra shows that the joint payoff is larger under incumbent ownership when $\mu_A{}^\circ < \mu$ and that the joint payoffs are equal when $\mu = \mu_A{}^\circ$.

Now continue to suppose that the continuing incumbent is A, but assume that $\mu < \mu_A{}^\circ$ in Proposition 1(a) so A attracts only type b. With incumbent ownership, the joint payoff of the partners is $g_{ab} + (g_{ab} - r_b) + \underline{r}$. With departer ownership, the price is $g_{ab} - r_b$ where only type b is attracted, because this exceeds the price $g_{aa} - r_a$ at which both types are attracted. In this case the joint payoff of the partners is $g_{ab} + (g_{ab} - r_b) + \underline{r}$. Therefore the joint payoff is identical regardless of who owns the vacancy.

These arguments give the results in Proposition 2(a)(i) and 2(b)(i). When B is the continuing incumbent, the argument is similar.

Proof of Lemma 2

   (a) The members of an AA match get $2g_{aa}$ by staying together. If they separate and the incumbent attracts both types of workers, their total payoff is $\mu g_{aa} + (1-\mu)g_{ab} + (g_{aa} - r_a) + r_a$, where the second expression in parentheses is the price and r_a is the external payoff of the departing worker. Their total payoff together is larger due to $(1-\mu)\Delta g_a > 0$. If the incumbent attracts only type b, their total payoff is $g_{ab} + (g_{ab} - r_b) + r_a$. Their total payoff together is larger due to $\Delta r < 2\Delta g_a$ from A2.

   (b) The members of an AB match get $2g_{ab}$ by staying together. If they separate, B becomes the incumbent as in Lemma 1. If B attracts both types of workers, their total payoff is $\mu g_{ab} + (1-\mu)g_{bb} + (g_{ab} - r_a) + r_a$. Their total payoff together is larger due to $(1-\mu)\Delta g_b > 0$. If B attracts only type b, their total payoff is $g_{bb} + (g_{bb} - r_b) + r_a$. Their total payoff together is larger due to $\Delta r < 2\Delta g_b$ from A2.

   (c) The members of a BB match get $2g_{bb}$ by staying together. If they separate and the incumbent attracts both types of workers, their total payoff is $\mu g_{ab} + (1-\mu)g_{bb} + (g_{ab} - r_a) + r_b$. Their total payoff from separation is strictly larger when $\mu_B{}^\circ < \mu$, as in Proposition 1(b). Their total payoffs together and apart are equal when $\mu_B{}^\circ = \mu$. If they separate and the incumbent only attracts type b, which occurs when $\mu < \mu_B{}^\circ$ in Proposition 1(b), the total payoff is $g_{bb} + (g_{bb} - r_b) + r_b$. This is identical to the total payoff from staying together.

PART V

PUBLIC GOOD PROBLEMS

12

Collective Choice and Investor Takeovers[*]

12.1 Introduction

When markets are complete and competitive, consumption and production plans are determined independently. In their roles as consumers, individual agents want the largest possible income, because this gives them the largest possible budget set. In their roles as controllers of firms, individual agents want each firm to maximize profit or net market value, because this maximizes their incomes. This logic underpins the isomorphic relationship between capital-managed firms (KMFs) and labor-managed firms (LMFs) developed in Chapters 2–5.

In the real world, there is no such isomorphism. As we saw in Chapters 6–8, there are numerous asymmetries between real KMFs and LMFs. Chapter 10 argued that one reason for the general rarity of LMFs is that entrepreneurs lack incentives to create them. This chapter considers another reason: LMFs sometimes sell out to external investors and become KMFs. Examples can be found among U.S. plywood cooperatives (Pencavel, 2001) and professional partnerships in advertising, investment banking, and health care (Hansmann, 1996).

In Section 9.4, I considered one mechanism through which LMFs could become KMFs: the process of degeneration where departing LMF members are replaced by hired hands. In Section 9.5, I also showed that LMF underinvestment can create incentives for members to sell out to investors and transform the firm into a KMF. In both cases, the underlying problem was incomplete surplus appropriation by LMF insiders.

This chapter investigates a different causal mechanism through which LMFs can become KMFs, one involving collective choice. We argue that

* This chapter is based on material coauthored with Gilbert L. Skillman.

unanimity toward firm policies is achieved automatically for KMFs through competitive market conditions, in a way that LMFs typically do not enjoy. The difference arises from a mobility asymmetry linked to the alienability of capital and inalienability of labor. When unanimity does not prevail in LMFs, some majority of LMF members will usually be tempted to sell out to profit-maximizing investors. We do not obtain symmetric results for the conversion of KMFs into LMFs. Under reasonable conditions, investors in KMFs achieve unanimity and KMFs are not bought out by workers.

We start from the fact that markets are incomplete and that firms offer differentiated product attributes, workplace attributes, and state-contingent incomes. In this context, consumption opportunities for stakeholders generally depend on the production decisions of individual firms. Accordingly, input suppliers may want the firms in which they hold control rights to pursue goals other than the maximization of net market value.

To put the same point another way, in a world of incomplete markets, any change in a firm's production plan typically yields direct consumption effects in addition to the familiar wealth effect. If the consumption effects differ across agents, a collective choice problem can arise among the decision-makers within the firm. For example, stakeholders may disagree over the nature of the firm's products, the working conditions it provides, the riskiness of its net income, or the temporal pattern of net income.

A number of writers have attempted to explain the allocation of enterprise control rights by appealing to transaction costs associated with collective choice. In particular, Hansmann (1996, chs. 5–6) has argued that LMFs face higher costs of reaching collective decisions than do KMFs, which helps account for the rarity of LMFs. In Hansmann's view, KMF investors are nearly unanimous in their support for value maximization, while LMF members have diverse preferences. Thus LMFs can thrive only when conditions such as small scale or low task differentiation limit the scope for disagreement among workers. Benham and Keefer (1991) and Gordon (1999) have expressed similar views.

A point sometimes overlooked in the LMF literature is that standard unanimity theorems from finance could rule out preference heterogeneity in both KMFs and LMFs. Makowski (1983a,b) shows that even with incomplete markets, the consumption effects of firm decisions vanish and unanimity with respect to value maximization is restored if all agents believe that marginal rates of substitution are unaffected by an individual firm's production plan. Hart (1979a,b) shows that such competitive conjectures are rational when each firm is small enough relative to the potential market for its shares. In Hart's model, consumption effects approach zero as the number of potential share buyers becomes large. The firm's stakeholders will then unanimously support value-maximizing production plans. Nothing in the literature indicates why these theoretical results would not apply to LMFs using tradeable membership shares.

This insight is the point of departure for our contribution. We argue that financial capital is highly mobile, while the inalienable nature of human capital ensures substantial mobility costs for workers. The competitiveness conditions identified by Makowski and Hart can be approximated only in markets for financial capital. The inalienability of labor rules out a scenario in which individual LMFs are vanishingly small relative to the potential market for their shares. This asymmetry is reflected in the robustness of equity markets as compared with the rarity and thinness of markets for membership in LMFs.

We develop this idea using a two-period stock market model, augmented to allow simultaneous trade in both capital and labor shares. This dual markets approach has not previously been used to study control rights in firms, but it is essential in understanding how asymmetries between KMFs and LMFs can arise despite the apparent parallelism of the relevant asset markets. The standard conception of asset market equilibrium is then bolstered by a condition we term "sustainability against takeover" by outside coalitions. This enables us to establish a basic asymmetry: LMFs are prone to takeover by investor coalitions unless the preferences of their members satisfy highly restrictive conditions, while KMFs are sustainable against takeover by worker coalitions under much less stringent conditions. Our conclusions about the differential sustainability of LMFs and KMFs do not require any assumption about the incidence of transaction costs.

Our argument bears some relation to the analysis of product differentiation by Drèze and Hagen (1978). Their main result (labeled Theorem 1) shows that the product characteristics chosen by profit-maximizing firms are Pareto efficient only under severe restrictions on consumer preferences. This is consistent with our analysis, but we make the stronger point that even when LMFs achieve Pareto efficient allocations, they remain prone to takeover by profit-seeking investors if they depart from profit maximization. On the other hand, unanimously profit-maximizing KMFs that fail to attain Pareto efficiency can be sustainable against worker takeover. Unlike Drèze and Hagen, we do not take the goals of firm owners as given, but instead derive them from the underlying structure of capital and labor markets.

The analysis is organized as follows. In Section 12.2, the model is presented and conditions ensuring existence and differentiability of share market equilibria are stated in Propositions 1 and 2. The linkage between the competitiveness of share markets and the nature of shareholder objectives is developed in Section 12.3. We introduce the notion of sustainability against takeover in Section 12.4 and contrast the sustainability of KMFs and LMFs. Proposition 3 shows that LMFs are prone to investor takeover unless members have preferences that are virtually unanimous, while Proposition 4 shows that KMFs are sustainable against worker takeover under realistic conditions.

Section 12.5 discusses empirical implications. The theory is shown to account for a number of facts about the incidence and behavior of LMFs, and helps explain employee buyouts of KMFs when these occur. Section 12.6 is a short postscript. The proofs of the formal propositions are quite lengthy and can be found at www.cambridge .org/9781107132979.

12.2 The Model

We modify the two-period stock market model pioneered by Diamond (1967) to include both capital and labor shares. There are finitely many agents, partitioned into two classes K and L depending on whether the agent is endowed with capital or labor; no one is endowed with both. We write $i \in K$ for capital suppliers and $i \in L$ for labor suppliers. There is an exogenously given set of firms indexed by $f \in F$.

Endowments

There are two periods, $t = 0$ and 1. In period $t = 0$, each $i \in K$ has an endowment $\underline{K}_i > 0$ of a capital good and each $i \in L$ has an endowment $\underline{L}_i > 0$ of hours. Each $i \in K$ also has an endowment of (ex ante) *capital shares* in firms $(\underline{\kappa}_{i1}, \underline{\kappa}_{i2}, .. \underline{\kappa}_{iF}) \in R_+^F$, with $\Sigma_{i \in K} \underline{\kappa}_{if} = 1$ for all $f \in F$. There is a parallel system of ex ante *labor shares* where each $i \in L$ has the share endowment $(\underline{\lambda}_{i1}, \underline{\lambda}_{i2}, .. \underline{\lambda}_{iF}) \in R_+^F$, with $\Sigma_{i \in L} \underline{\lambda}_{if} = 1$ for all $f \in F$.

Consumption

The consumption of individual i in period 0 is x_{i0}. Consumption at $t = 1$ is state contingent, with uncertain states indexed by $s \in S$. Let x_{is} be state-s consumption for agent i, so i's *consumption plan* is $x_i = (x_{i0}, x_{i1}, .. x_{iS}) \in R_+^{S+1}$.

Preferences over consumption plans are represented by utility functions $u_i: R_+^{S+1} \to R$ that are strictly increasing, strictly quasi-concave, and twice continuously differentiable in R_+^{S+1} with finite derivatives.

Production

Because there are no endowments of the state-contingent period-1 goods, these goods must be produced by firms. Firm $f \in F$ produces the output vector $y_f^1 = (y_{f1}, y_{f2}, .. y_{fS}) \in R_+^S$ in period 1 using capital and labor inputs (k_f, l_f) acquired in period 0. The firm's *production plan* is denoted by $y_f = (k_f, l_f, y_f^1) \in R_+^{S+2}$. Input requirements are given by $k_f = l_f = g_f(y_f^1)/2$, where $g_f: R_+^S \to R_+$ is increasing and continuously differentiable with $g_f(0) = 0$. Whenever k_f or l_f is finite, the set of feasible output vectors y_f^1 is bounded.

Policies

The fraction of output distributed to firm f's labor suppliers as a group (in every state) is $\mu_f \in [0,1]$, with $1-\mu_f$ paid out to capital suppliers. We refer to $\phi_f = (y_f^1, \mu_f)$ as the *policy* of firm f and denote the vector of firms' policies by ϕ.

Markets

Markets operate only in period 0. All agents secure claims on period-1 goods via shares in firms. There are two types of output claims, both associated with the supply of an input: capital shares κ_{if} indicating capital supplier i's claim on firm f, and labor shares λ_{if} indicating labor supplier i's claim on the same firm. We call κ_{if} and λ_{if} "ex post shares" to distinguish them from the ex ante share endowments $\underline{\kappa}_{if}$ and $\underline{\lambda}_{if}$. We also use κ_{i0} and λ_{i0} to denote period-0 consumption. The resulting portfolios are $\kappa_i = (\kappa_{i0}, \kappa_{i1} .. \kappa_{iF}) \in R_+^{F+1}$ and $\lambda_i = (\lambda_{i0}, \lambda_{i1} .. \lambda_{iF}) \in R_+^{F+1}$, with $\kappa = \{\kappa_i\}_{i \in K}$ and $\lambda = \{\lambda_i\}_{i \in L}$.

Portfolios induce consumption bundles according to the following mapping

$$
\begin{aligned}
x_{i0} &= \kappa_{i0} &&\text{and} \\
x_{is} &= \sum\nolimits_{f \in F} \kappa_{if}(1 - \mu_f)y_{fs} &&\text{for all } s \in S \text{ and } i \in K
\end{aligned} \tag{1a}
$$

$$
\begin{aligned}
x_{i0} &= \lambda_{i0} &&\text{and} \\
x_{is} &= \sum\nolimits_{f \in F} \lambda_{if}\mu_f y_{fs} &&\text{for all } s \in S \text{ and } i \in L
\end{aligned} \tag{1b}
$$

In our framework, shares reflect commitments to supply inputs as well
as claims on the resulting output. If firm f has the total capital requirement
$k_f = g_f(y_f^1)/2$, then purchasing the capital share κ_{if} entails an obligation to
supply $\kappa_{if}g_f(y_f^1)/2$ units of capital to firm f, and likewise purchasing the
labor share λ_{if} entails an obligation to supply $\lambda_{if}g_f(y_f^1)/2$ units of labor. It is
therefore natural to rule out short sales. This feature of the model leads to
a physical restriction on feasible portfolios because it must be possible to
comply with all input supply obligations simultaneously. Thus portfolios
need to satisfy

$$\sum\nolimits_{f \in F} \kappa_{if} g_f(y_f^1)/2 \leq \underline{K}_i \quad \text{all } i \in K \qquad (2a)$$

$$\sum\nolimits_{f \in F} \lambda_{if} g_f(y_f^1)/2 \leq \underline{L}_i \quad \text{all } i \in L \qquad (2b)$$

Any physical endowment not supplied to firms is converted into the
period-0 consumption good on a one-for-one basis. We define consump-
tion sets (relative to fixed firm policies ϕ) by $\Omega_i^K = \{\kappa_i \geq 0 : \Sigma_f \kappa_{if}g_f/2 \leq \underline{K}_i\}$ for
all $i \in K$ and $\Omega_i^L = \{\lambda_i \geq 0 : \Sigma_f \lambda_{if}g_f/2 \leq \underline{L}_i\}$ for all $i \in L$.

Agents can sell off their ex ante shares in firms ($\underline{\kappa}_{if}$ or $\underline{\lambda}_{if}$) in exchange for
period-0 consumption. The price of a capital share in firm f is p_f, and the
price of a labor share is q_f. The price of the period-0 consumption good
is $p_0 \equiv q_0$. The price vectors facing agents are $p = (p_0, p_1 .. p_F) \in R_+^{F+1}$ and
$q = (q_0, q_1 .. q_F) \in R_+^{F+1}$ for K and L, respectively. The budget constraints
for the two types of agents are given by

$$p\kappa_i \leq W_i^K(p, q) \equiv p_0\underline{K}_i + \sum\nolimits_{f \in F}(1 - \underline{\mu}_f)\kappa_{if}v_f \quad \text{for all } i \in K \text{ and} \quad (3a)$$

$$q\lambda_i \leq W_i^L(p, q) \equiv q_0\underline{L}_i + \sum\nolimits_{f \in F}\underline{\mu}_f\lambda_{if}v_f \qquad \text{for all } i \in L \qquad (3b)$$

where $v_f \equiv p_f + q_f - p_0g_f(y_f^1)$ is the net market value of firm f ($\underline{\mu}_f$ is defined
later).

To see how these constraints arise, first consider a firm f organized solely
by some individual investor $i \in K$. This investor can obtain $p_f - p_0g_f/2$ by
selling off the firm's ex ante capital shares, where p_f is the price of the pure
financial claim on period-1 consumption associated with firm f's capital
shares and $p_0g_f/2$ is the cost of satisfying the firm's capital requirements,
expressed as foregone period-0 consumption. Although the ex post owner
of a capital share must supply capital inputs to the firm, the resulting loss in
consumption is borne by the ex ante owner through the price of capital
shares. If the ex ante owner keeps some or all capital shares and personally
supplies this input, again the opportunity cost falls on the ex ante owner.

For this reason it is convenient to define prices so that the cost of firm f's capital input is deducted from the value of the ex ante owner's endowment in (3a).

By virtue of organizing the firm, investor i is also endowed with the firm's ex ante labor shares. Because $i \in K$ has no endowment of this input, firm f can only obtain labor if these shares are sold to one or more workers. The investor receives $q_f - q_0 g_f / 2$ through such transactions, where q_f is the price paid for the period-1 consumption claim associated with a labor share and $q_0 g_f / 2$ is foregone period-0 consumption resulting from the ex post owner's supply obligation. Again, the cost of labor supplied to firm f falls ultimately on the ex ante owner even though this agent does not personally provide any of this input, and share prices are defined so that this cost is deducted from the value of the ex ante owner's endowment.

The founder of the firm thus captures the overall net market value v_f from the sale of ex ante capital and labor shares. The set of feasible portfolios is unaffected by whether the founder supplies inputs directly or sells shares to other agents who take on this role. When $i \in K$ is the sole founder, we set $\underline{\mu}_f = 0$ and $\underline{\kappa}_{if} = 1$ in (3), with $\underline{\kappa}_{jf} = 0$ for all $j \in K$ such that $j \neq i$. The analysis is symmetric when some individual worker $i \in L$ is the sole founder of firm f. In that case we set $\underline{\mu}_f = 1$ and $\underline{\lambda}_{if} = 1$ in (3), with $\underline{\lambda}_{jf} = 0$ for all $j \in L$ such that $j \neq i$.

More generally, firm f could be organized by a coalition consisting of some capital suppliers and some labor suppliers. The net market value v_f is then divided by its founders through a bargaining process we do not model here. Let $\underline{\mu}_f$ be the fraction of net firm value v_f captured by labor suppliers as a group, and let $1 - \underline{\mu}_f$ be the fraction captured by capital suppliers as a group, where $(1 - \underline{\mu}_f) \underline{\kappa}_{if}$ is the share of v_f obtained by an individual investor $i \in K$ and $\underline{\mu}_f \underline{\lambda}_{if}$ is the share obtained by an individual worker $i \in L$. Assigning the ex ante capital shares in proportion to $\underline{\kappa}_{if}$ and the ex ante labor shares in proportion to $\underline{\lambda}_{if}$ implies that the generalized ownership shares $(1 - \underline{\mu}_f) \underline{\kappa}_{if}$ and $\underline{\mu}_f \underline{\lambda}_{if}$ in (3) reflect the bargaining power of the agents with respect to the entrepreneurial rent for firm f.

From (2) and (3), the budget sets for each type of agent are

$$B_i^K(p, q) \equiv \{\kappa_i \in \Omega_i^K : p\kappa_i \leq W_i^K(p, q)\}$$
$$B_i^L(p, q) \equiv \{\lambda_i \in \Omega_i^L : q\lambda_i \leq W_i^L(p, q)\}$$

Define $\underline{\kappa}_{i0} \equiv \underline{K}_i - \Sigma_f (1 - \underline{\mu}_f) \underline{\kappa}_{if} g_f(y_f^1)$ and $\underline{\lambda}_{i0} \equiv \underline{L}_i - \Sigma_f \underline{\mu}_f \underline{\lambda}_{if} g_f(y_f^1)$ to be physical endowments net of agent i's endowed share in the cost of each firm's production plan. We impose two restrictions on the production plans (y_f) of firms:

Ex ante feasibility (EAF): $\underline{\kappa}_{i0} > 0$ for all $i \in K$ and $\underline{\lambda}_{i0} > 0$ for all $i \in L$
Ex post feasibility (EPF): $\Sigma_{f\in F} \, g_f(y_f^1)/2 < \Sigma_{i\in K} \, \underline{K}_i$ and $\Sigma_{f\in F} \, g_f(y_f^1)/2 < \Sigma_{i\in L} \, \underline{L}_i$

EAF says that each agent can cover her ex ante share in firm costs by liquidating part of her input endowment. Because the price vectors p and q are nonnegative, this ensures that each consumer has positive wealth in (3a) and (3b). EPF ensures that the aggregate endowments are large enough to implement all production plans simultaneously.

Time Sequence

Agents with ex ante control rights in each firm establish a tentative policy for that firm. If there is a takeover market, coalitions lacking control rights in a given firm can now bid to acquire such rights. If there is no takeover market or no bid is accepted, the original policies stand, but otherwise they are modified according to the terms of successful bids. After policies are fixed, markets for capital and labor shares open and inputs are supplied in proportion to ex post shares. Production takes place in period 1. Finally, the realized state-contingent outputs are divided as specified by firm policies and the ex post share allocation.

For given policies ϕ let $U_i(\kappa_i)$ be the utility function induced over κ_i for $i \in K$ by (1a). Similarly, let $U_i(\lambda_i)$ be the utility function induced for $i \in L$ by (1b).

A *share market equilibrium* relative to fixed policies ϕ is a set of portfolios (κ^*, λ^*) and a nonnegative price vector $(p, q) \neq \underline{0}$ (with $p_0 \equiv q_0$) having the following properties.

Optimization

<u>E1a</u>   For each $i \in K$, $\kappa_i{}^*$ maximizes $U_i(\kappa_i)$ subject to $\kappa_i \in B_i{}^K(p, q)$
<u>E1b</u>   For each $i \in L$, $\lambda_i{}^*$ maximizes $U_i(\lambda_i)$ subject to $\lambda_i \in B_i{}^L(p, q)$

Market Clearing

<u>E2a</u> $\Sigma_{i\in K} \, \kappa_{i0}{}^* + \Sigma_{i\in L} \, \lambda_{i0}{}^* = \Sigma_{i\in K} \, \underline{K}_i + \Sigma_{i\in L} \, \underline{L}_i - \Sigma_{f\in F} \, g_f$
<u>E2b</u>   For each $f \in F$, $\Sigma_{i\in K} \, \kappa_{if}{}^* = 1$
<u>E2c</u>   For each $f \in F$, $\Sigma_{i\in L} \, \lambda_{if}{}^* = 1$

Proposition 1
Existence: Fix any firm policies ϕ satisfying EAF and EPF. A share market equilibrium exists relative to ϕ.

Proposition 2
Differentiability: Suppose that there is a share market equilibrium with the following properties.

(a) All shares are non-null: that is, $0 < \mu_f < 1$ and $y_f^1 \neq \underline{0}$ for all $f \in F$.
(b) The output vectors $\{y_f^1\}$ for $f \in F$ are linearly independent.
(c) For each $i \in K$ and $i \in L$ there is a neighborhood around current prices and policies in which the set of binding constraints on portfolio choice does not change.
(d) The Jacobian matrix resulting from differentiation of the aggregate excess demands for shares is nonsingular at the equilibrium.
Then in a neighborhood of the current policies ϕ, the share prices (p, q) are continuously differentiable functions of firm policies.

Assumption (a) ensures that all prices are strictly positive, while (b) guarantees that optimal portfolios are unique for given prices and policies. This implies that the number of firms cannot exceed the number of states; linear independence of output vectors is a generic feature of firm policies in this situation. Assumption (c) avoids the problem that arbitrarily small changes in parameters could move an agent from zero to positive share-holdings in a firm or vice versa. Along with a standard strengthening of strict quasi-concavity to ensure the sufficiency rather than just the necessity of second order conditions, this implies that the portfolios are continuously differentiable in prices and policies. Finally, (d) permits the use of the implicit function theorem. Assumptions (c) and (d) can be regarded as the "typical" case, but a formal genericity proof is beyond the scope of this paper.

12.3 Market Structure and Policy Preferences

As discussed in Section 12.1, differences in mobility costs lead to differences in the structures of the capital and labor markets. The market for each firm's capital shares is competitive because an investor encounters no cost in shifting financial capital across firms, and an individual firm is negligible relative to the economy as a whole. Thus no single firm can alter the implicit prices of state-contingent consumption for investors. However, each firm is significant in the market for its own labor shares due to costly worker mobility, and its policies can affect the prices for period-1 consumption that implicitly confront workers participating in this market. We generally picture labor markets as geographically localized, but the operative notion of "distance" could also reflect costly searches or mismatches in skill.

It will frequently be necessary in what follows to consider the preferences of agents toward local policy changes in some firm f. Given fixed policies for all other firms, the maximized utility of $i \in K$ as a function of the policy ϕ_f can be written

$$
\begin{aligned}
T_i(\phi_f) = &\ U_i[\kappa_i*(\phi_f); \phi_f] + \eta_i*(\phi_f)[\underline{K}_i - g(\phi_f)\kappa_i*(\phi_f)/2] \\
&+ \theta_i*(\phi_f)[W_i^K(p(\phi_f), q(\phi_f), \phi_f) - p(\phi_f)\kappa_i*(\phi_f)]
\end{aligned}
\tag{4a}
$$

where U_i is the utility function over capital shares induced by equation (1a); $\kappa_i*(\phi_f)$ is an optimal portfolio in the share market equilibrium associated with policy ϕ_f; η_i* is the Kuhn-Tucker multiplier for the physical input constraint in (2a), with $g = (g_0, g_1 .. g_F)$ and $g_0 \equiv 0$; and θ_i* is the multiplier for the budget constraint defined by (3a). Multipliers for the nonnegativity constraints on capital shares can be ignored by assumption (c) of Proposition 2. Due to the structure of the budget constraint, firm f's policy influences agent i's wealth W_i^K only through the net values $v_h(\phi_f) = p_h(\phi_f) + q_h(\phi_f) - g_h(\phi_f)$ for $h \in F$ rather than the prices p_h and q_h separately, where we have now set $p_0 \equiv q_0 \equiv 1$. The counterpart to (4a) for $i \in L$ is

$$
\begin{aligned}
T_i(\phi_f) = &\ U_i[\lambda_i*(\phi_f); \phi_f] + \eta_i*(\phi_f)[\underline{L}_i - g(\phi_f)\lambda_i*(\phi_f)/2] \\
&+ \theta_i*(\phi_f)[W_i^L(p(\phi_f), q(\phi_f), \phi_f) - q(\phi_f)\lambda_i*(\phi_f)]
\end{aligned}
\tag{4b}
$$

The effects on the utility of an agent $i \in K$ of changing firm f's policy variables y_{fs} and μ_f are given respectively by

$$
\begin{aligned}
\partial T_i / \partial y_{fs} = &\ \theta_i*(1 - \underline{\mu}_f)\underline{\kappa}_{if}(\partial v_f / \partial y_{fs}) + \theta_i* \sum_{h \neq f}(1 - \underline{\mu}_h)\underline{\kappa}_{ih}(\partial v_h / \partial y_{fs}) \\
&+ \kappa_{if}*[(1 - \mu_f)u_{is} - \eta_i*(\partial g_f / \partial y_{fs})/2 - \theta_i*(\partial p_f / \partial y_{fs})] \\
&- \theta_i* \sum_{h \neq f}\kappa_{ih}*(\partial p_h / \partial y_{fs})
\end{aligned}
\tag{5a}
$$

$$
\begin{aligned}
\partial T_i / \partial \mu_f = &\ \theta_i*(1 - \underline{\mu}_f)\underline{\kappa}_{if}(\partial v_f / \partial \mu_f) + \theta_i* \sum_{h \neq f}(1 - \underline{\mu}_h)\underline{\kappa}_{ih}(\partial v_h / \partial \mu_f) \\
&- \kappa_{if}*\left[\sum_s u_{is}y_{fs} + \theta_i*(\partial p_f / \partial \mu_f)\right] - \theta_i* \sum_{h \neq f}\kappa_{ih}*(\partial p_h / \partial \mu_f)
\end{aligned}
\tag{6a}
$$

where u_{is} is the partial derivative of the utility function u_i with respect to consumption x_{is} in state s. The first line in each of Equations (5a) and (6a) is the *wealth effect*, which we split into a direct effect on firm f's own net

value v_f and an indirect effect on the values of other firms. The wealth effect
is analogous to the budget set dominance effect in Chapters 2–5, although
in these chapters the policy of a given firm only influenced its own
value. The second line in each of (5a) and (6a) is the *consumption effect*,
which again has direct and indirect components. The consumption effect
captures changes in utility resulting from changes in the implicit prices of
state-contingent output.

The corresponding derivatives for $i \in L$ are

$$\partial T_i/\partial y_{fs} = \theta_i * \underline{\mu}_f \underline{\lambda}_{if}(\partial v_f/\partial y_{fs}) + \theta_i * \sum_{h \neq f} \underline{\mu}_h \underline{\lambda}_{ih}(\partial v_h/\partial y_{fs})$$
$$+ \lambda_{if}*[\mu_f u_{is} - \eta_i*(\partial g_f/\partial y_{fs})/2 - \theta_i*(\partial q_f/\partial y_{fs})]$$
$$- \theta_i * \sum_{h \neq f} \lambda_{ih}*(\partial q_h/\partial y_{fs}) \quad (5b)$$

$$\partial T_i/\partial \mu_f = \theta_i * \underline{\mu}_f \underline{\lambda}_{if}(\partial v_f/\partial \mu_f) + \theta_i * \sum_{h \neq f} \underline{\mu}_h \underline{\lambda}_{ih}(\partial v_h/\partial \mu_f)$$
$$+ \lambda_{if}*\left[\sum_s u_{is} y_{fs} - \theta_i*(\partial q_f/\partial \mu_f)\right] - \theta_i * \sum_{h \neq f} \lambda_{ih}*(\partial q_h/\partial \mu_f) \quad (6b)$$

where again in each equation the first line represents the wealth effect and
the second line represents the consumption effect from a given policy
change.

Now consider a local policy change $d\phi_f = (dy_{f1} .. dy_{fS}, d\mu_f)$. The change
in firm f's net market value resulting from $d\phi_f$ is $dv_f = \Sigma_s (\partial v_f/\partial y_{fs})dy_{fs} + (\partial v_f/\partial \mu_f)d\mu_f$. The effect on agent i's utility is given by $dT_i = \theta_i*dw_{if} + dz_{if}$,
where θ_i*dw_{if} is the wealth effect from $d\phi_f$ and dz_{if} is the consumption
effect. Notice that the change in wealth dw_{if} includes both the direct effect
from dv_f and indirect effects through dv_h for $h \neq f$.

We next state our key assumption: competitive conjectures (CC).

CC   Markets for capital shares are perfectly competitive in the sense of
Hart (1979a,b) and Makowski (1983a,b), while markets for labor
shares are not.

CC implies that the consumption effect of firm f's policy on investor i's
utility in (5a) and (6a) is zero, so all investors evaluate policy changes
in firm f solely by their wealth effects. But workers generally differ both
with respect to the sign of the consumption effect dz_{if} from a local
policy change $d\phi_f$ and the relative size of the consumption and wealth
effects. We assume that workers cannot be assigned to firms in such
a way that the workers in each firm have identical tastes (otherwise, no
collective choice issues arise for LMFs). This requires scale economies
sufficient to rule out one-person firms and either (a) more worker types

than firms, (b) significant costs to the market matching of workers based on preference profiles, or (c) both.

To justify our claim that capital share markets are perfectly competitive, we need to link our model with Hart (1979a). The assumptions used by Hart are either implied by our framework or consistent with it, but due to space limitations we will not delve into technical details. Instead, we take a more intuitive approach.

Interpret the model in Section 12.2 as describing a geographic region containing finitely many capital suppliers, labor suppliers, and firms. Suppose that there are r identical regions of this kind. Capital moves freely across regions, but workers can supply labor only to firms in their region. Suppose for the moment that all regions are "capitalist"— that is, all firms are KMFs with $\mu_f = 0$ for all f, so workers have no ex ante claim on the net market value of any firm. The prices of labor shares (q_f) for firms in a particular region are determined solely by the policies of the firms in that region, the preferences of the local workers, and the time endowments of these workers. The policies of firms in other regions are irrelevant because local workers cannot supply labor to such firms and worker wealth is unaffected by capital share prices. Fix the policies of all firms.

Now interpret each $i \in K$ from Section 12.2 as a "type" of investor in Hart's sense, where all investors of a given type have identical preferences and wealth. Regions are replicated by increasing r. As r goes to infinity, each firm becomes negligible relative to the aggregate capital market because its output is constrained by the labor endowment of its own region. In the limit economy no firm can influence the implicit prices of state-contingent output facing investors, and capital share prices are

$$p_f(\phi_f) = \max_{i \in K_*} \{ \Sigma_{s \in S} z_{is}(x_i)(1 - \mu_f) y_{fs} \} \tag{7}$$

where $z_{is}(x_i) \equiv u_{is}(x_i)/u_{i0}(x_i)$ is type i's marginal rate of substitution between state s and period 0, and the maximization is over the set K^* of investor types whose consumption bundles x_i have positive measure in the limit economy defined by Hart (1979a). Each type's bundle x_i is independent of any individual firm's policy ϕ_f because each firm is small and can affect the consumption of only finitely many investors. Some implications of this pricing formula are developed by Makowski (1983a,b) and Makowski and Pepall (1985).

Against this backdrop we add a new region where some firms are LMFs with $\mu_f > 0$. This reflects the fact that the LMF sector is small relative to the aggregate economy, which is dominated by capitalist firms. Although LMFs may have some ability to affect the implicit prices facing workers in a local labor market, they must attract investors who have access to a perfectly competitive capital market. The policies of firms in the LMF region have a negligible effect on the capital market as a whole, so the pricing formula for capital shares given by (7) applies to this region as well.

The prices in (7) are well defined but could be nondifferentiable. This is true at the policy ϕ_f only if $\Sigma_{s \in S} z_{is}(x_i)(1-\mu_f)y_{fs} = \Sigma_{s \in S} z_{js}(x_j)(1-\mu_f)y_{fs}$ for two distinct investor types $i \neq j$, implying $\Sigma_{s \in S} \Delta z_s(1-\mu_f)y_{fs} = 0$ where $\Delta z_s \equiv z_{is} - z_{js}$. The output vector $(1-\mu_f)y_f^1$ for capital suppliers as a group is therefore orthogonal to $\Delta z \neq \underline{0}$ and lies in a subspace of dimension $S-1$. If there are finitely many investor types, there are only finitely many such subspaces, and p_f is differentiable at almost all ϕ_f. We assume differentiability in the discussion that follows.

12.4 Takeover Bids and Sustainability

Suppose now that before share markets open, the ex ante shareholders of firms can be bought out by alternative coalitions who will implement policies differing from those of the initial owners. We will show that the asymmetric structure of capital and labor markets discussed in Section 12.3 affects the viability of KMFs and LMFs in asymmetric ways. In particular, LMFs are prone to takeover by wealth-maximizing investors except under highly restrictive conditions, while KMFs are sustainable against takeover by worker coalitions under conditions that seem likely to be met in practice.

Let the *control group* C_f for firm f be the set of agents entitled to vote on firm f's policies. A necessary condition for membership in C_f is that an agent have a positive ex ante stake in the firm—that is, $(1-\mu_f)\kappa_{if} > 0$ for $i \in$ K or $\mu_f\lambda_{if} > 0$ for $i \in$ L. Voting rights may be confined to a proper subset of the ex ante shareholders. A firm is defined to be a KMF if $C_f \subseteq K$ and all i with $\kappa_{if} > 0$ have a vote. Likewise, an LMF has $C_f \subseteq L$ and all i with $\lambda_{if} > 0$ have a vote. In each case, votes are proportional to the endowments κ_{if} or λ_{if}. It is natural to suppose that KMFs have $\mu_f = 0$ and LMFs have $\mu_f = 1$ (agents without voting rights also lack ex ante claims on the firm's net market value), but this is not essential.

A majority rule equilibrium in the sense of Plott (1967) is defined as follows. The policy ϕ_f^* is a *majority rule equilibrium* in firm f if for any local deviation $d\phi_f$ there is some majority coalition $M \subseteq C_f$ such that no $i \in M$ is strictly better off when $d\phi_f$ is implemented. A majority coalition is a subset $M \subseteq C_f$ having 50% or more of the total votes in firm f. A deviation $d\phi_f$ from the status quo can be blocked by any such M if all members of M vote against it. Each $i \subseteq C_f$ votes against $d\phi_f$ unless this deviation strictly increases her utility. This equilibrium concept has previously been applied to collective choice in firms by Sadanand and Williamson (1991) and deMarzo (1993).

An equilibrium of this sort does not generally exist when voters have heterogeneous preferences and the policy space has high dimensionality. Kramer (1973) has shown that the restrictions on preference profiles needed to guarantee majority rule transitivity do not differ significantly from the condition of identical preferences. Further, McKelvey (1979) demonstrates that when majority rule intransitivity obtains, it may be extreme, in the sense that majority decisions can cycle over virtually all alternatives in the relevant choice set.

For our purposes it is unimportant how status quo policies are determined, because all we need in this discussion is the generic nonexistence of majority rule equilibrium in LMFs (for a discussion of policy equilibrium in a related context, see Magill and Quinzii, 1996, ch. 6). Thus we simply assume the existence of some collective choice procedure that defines a tentative policy ϕ_f for each $f \in F$. In order to stress that transaction costs of the Hansmann sort are not essential to our story, we further suppose that this choice procedure costlessly picks a policy that is Pareto efficient relative to the preferences of the control group C_f, given the policies of all other firms. This biases the analysis in favor of LMF viability and hence strengthens our conclusions about the vulnerability of such firms to takeover bids.

Let a market for control rights open in period 0 after tentative policy decisions have been made but before these policies are finalized. Transactions on this market involve takeovers, which occur when a bidding coalition buys a majority of the shares owned by the ex ante control group. After the takeover market closes, the policies of successful takeover coalitions are adopted, and tentative policies become final otherwise.

Let B_f be a coalition seeking to take over firm f, where $B_f \cap C_f = \varnothing$. A control group C_f is sustainable only if there are no gains from trade between the outsider group B_f and any strict voting majority M of the insider group C_f (for related ideas, see Hart, 1977). A *takeover bid* for firm f consists of a firm valuation $v_f{}'$ at which B_f offers to buy all ex ante shares held by a particular strict majority M, together with a local policy change $d\phi_f$ that B_f promises to adopt if it gains control. All members of M must expect $(v_f', d\phi_f)$ to increase their utilities for the bid to succeed. Each member of B_f contributes a positive fraction of the payment to M and acquires a corresponding claim on the firm's new market value.

Formally, the control group C_f is *sustainable against takeover by B_f* when there is no feasible bid $(v_f', d\phi_f)$ such that

T1   All $i \in M \subseteq C_f$ for some strict majority M of the control group C_f increase their utility by selling their ex ante shares at price v_f' when $d\phi_f$ is implemented; and

T2   All $i \in B_f$ increase their utility by acquiring the ex ante shares of M at price v_f' when $d\phi_f$ is implemented.

If the coalition B_f can commit itself to arbitrary policy changes, either contractually or by reputation, $d\phi_f$ is unrestricted. Otherwise $d\phi_f$ must be confined to a subset of credible proposals. Because we are interested in local changes and takeover bids are formulated by coalitions rather than individuals, the usual notion of subgame perfection is difficult to apply. An approach that is similar in spirit is to require that $d\phi_f$ make all members of B_f strictly better off once this coalition takes control. Thus when commitment is impossible, the proposal $d\phi_f$ is said to be *credible* if $dT_i > 0$ for all $i \in B_f$ where dT_i is the change in utility induced by $d\phi_f$ after B_f has acquired control and the side payment v_f' is sunk.

Proposition 3
Sustainability of LMFs: Consider an LMF and any takeover coalition $B_f \subseteq K$ consisting entirely of investors with a zero ex ante capital share for all firms in the LMF's labor market.

(a) Suppose that takeover coalitions can commit themselves to arbitrary policy changes. The control group $C_f \subseteq L$ is sustainable against takeover by B_f if and only if its tentative policy ϕ_f^M is a majority rule equilibrium.

(b) Suppose that takeover coalitions cannot commit themselves to arbitrary policy changes and bids must therefore be credible. The control group $C_f \subseteq L$ is sustainable against takeover by B_f if and only if there is no policy change $d\phi_f$ that induces $dv_f > 0$ and makes some strict majority $M \subseteq C_f$ better off.

Proposition 3(a) says that if commitment to policy changes is feasible, an LMF with individually tradeable shares will be taken over by outside investors unless it has achieved a majority rule equilibrium. But we know from the discussion earlier in this section that this is very unlikely. Such an equilibrium can only arise if a share-weighted majority of worker-members has essentially identical preferences toward the firm's policies. The problem for the LMF is that some frustrated majority is generally willing to bribe a coalition of outside investors to implement a new policy.

The prospects for LMF viability are less bleak when outside investors can credibly commit only to policy changes that increase the market value of the firm. Proposition 3(b) says that in this case an LMF is sustainable as long as there is no way to increase firm value that is supported by a majority of the current members. A fortiori, the firm is sustainable if it is already maximizing its market value. But takeover bids that target nonvalue-maximizing LMFs also fail as long as any policy change that wealth-maximizing investors can credibly deliver would be opposed by some majority of the firm's insiders.

Proposition 4

Sustainability of KMFs: Consider a KMF with a tentative policy ϕ_f^* that maximizes its market value v_f. Assume that each investor $i \in C_f$ has a zero ex ante capital share for all other firms in the same labor market as firm f. The following results hold whether or not a takeover coalition B_f can commit to arbitrary policy changes.

(a) The control group $C_f \subseteq K$ is sustainable against takeover by any coalition B_f that includes an outside investor $i \in K$ who has a zero ex ante capital share for all firms in the same labor market as firm f.

(b) The control group $C_f \subseteq K$ is sustainable against a worker coalition $B_f \subseteq L$ if and only if for every local policy change $d\phi_f$ there is some $i \in B_f$ whose utility does not increase when $d\phi_f$ is adopted.

The first message of Proposition 4 is that a capitalist firm generally faces a threat of takeover only from worker coalitions. Because KMFs are already value-maximizing, there are no gains from trade between inside and outside investors. The only caveat is that the firm could be vulnerable to a takeover coalition consisting entirely of investors with ex ante claims on firms $h \neq f$ operating in the same local labor market. Such investors may want to implement policies that decrease one firm's value in order to increase the value of another firm. The assumptions of Proposition 4 rule out such indirect wealth effects.

Worker coalitions could take over a KMF in order to pursue consumption goals at the expense of value maximization. For a buyout to succeed, the takeover coalition must unanimously agree on the desirability of some local policy shift. If it does, commitment issues are irrelevant because the change is automatically credible. In principle, a single employee with a sufficiently large endowment could buy out a KMF for consumption purposes, because one-person coalitions never have internal disagreements. A two-person partnership (again assuming sufficient resources) could also achieve unanimity as long as relative bargaining power is well established. But a realistic view of worker wealth and credit markets suggests that labor coalitions must usually be sizable in order to take over large firms. We return to this point in Section 12.5.

Proposition 4 does not require that workers participating in a takeover bid intend to work in the firm ex post ($\lambda_{if}{}^* > 0$). It might appear that only employees of firm f could obtain consumption benefits by changing its policy so that viable takeover coalitions could only emerge from within this subset of workers. This is not correct, because the consumption effects in (5b) and (6b) include terms involving the prices of labor shares for other firms, which could be nonzero even though $\lambda_{if}{}^* = 0$. In a monopolistically competitive labor market, a worker who does not supply labor to firm f might want to change its policies in order to change the price of labor shares at some firm h ≠ f where she does plan to work.

This complication cannot arise for monopsony (one firm per labor market), because then $\lambda_{if}{}^* = 0$ implies a zero consumption effect. But even without monopsony, a KMF will generally be open to takeover only by its own employees, because workers will seldom buy a firm that does not employ them merely to influence prices elsewhere in the local labor market.

12.5 Conclusion

Several factors not captured in our formal analysis tend to reduce the likelihood of a worker takeover beyond what is described in Proposition 4. First, small employee groups with parallel consumption interests may encounter liquidity problems in buying out capital-intensive KMFs, while larger coalitions that could potentially overcome such problems may be unable to agree on firm policies. Second, when unanimity cannot be achieved, coalition size is likely to matter due to transaction costs of the sort emphasized by Hansmann (1996). Again, this makes it less likely that a large employee coalition could take over a KMF but has no effect on investors who want to take over an LMF. Finally, collective bargaining is often a good substitute for control rights from the standpoint of KMF employees who want to pursue consumption goals within the firm, as long as the consumption benefits involved can be specified and enforced contractually. But there is no real alternative to takeover for investors who want to reorganize an LMF in a wealth-enhancing direction.

The theory developed here is consistent with numerous stylized facts about labor-managed firms. Among these is the emphasis LMFs often give to achieving homogeneity among the membership with respect to rewards, skills, attitudes, and organizational roles (Rothschild and Whitt, 1986, 95–100). Our framework also accounts for the tendency of LMFs to cluster in craft manufacturing and professional services. The small scale of such firms facilitates informal side payments among workers, while a uniform occupation promotes homogeneity of attitudes and beliefs. It is probably also not a coincidence that some LMFs demand conformity to religious or ideological principles, recruit from particular ethnic groups, or have a cohesive group of founders who share a common vision of the firm's objectives.

These patterns are also consistent with the transaction cost framework of Benham and Keefer (1991) and Hansmann (1996). However, in contrast to these writers, we show that LMFs concerned with organizational stability will limit preference heterogeneity even if the cost of collective decision-making is zero. More fundamentally, we trace the difference in heterogeneity between investors and workers to differences in the structure of capital and labor markets, which in turn can be traced to differences in alienability.

Our theory does not assert that KMFs are never taken over by their employees, but it highlights the need for a uniform motivation within the takeover coalition. From this perspective it is interesting that employee buyouts tend to occur disproportionately often in KMFs facing financial difficulties (Dow, 2003, ch. 10). The prospect of a plant closing or bankruptcy likely affects many employees in a parallel way and thus gives rise to takeover coalitions that might lack cohesion at other times. The fact that employee buyouts are more common in troughs of the business cycle (Ben-Ner and Jun, 1996) is consistent with the idea that collective bargaining is a poor substitute for takeover when bankruptcy is likely.

Our theory also highlights a tension between the organizational stability of LMFs and reliance on tradeable membership rights. Most LMFs forego membership markets (see Section 7.3) despite theoretical arguments favoring such markets (see Chapters 3–5). One possible explanation is that if LMFs want to avoid takeover bids, they may want to prohibit internal majorities from selling their voting rights. This may mean banning the sale of membership rights completely, because otherwise an outside investor could gain control through a series of bilateral bargains with individual members.

As discussed in Sections 6.6 and 7.2, LMFs often have good productivity and survival performance compared to KMFs. But LMF success stories generally involve muted forms of worker participation, with representative rather than direct democracy, delegation of decisions to hired managers, and the like. Our theory suggests that this is not an accident and that LMF advocates may have to compromise between democratic participation and organizational stability.

12.6 Postscript

This chapter is a lightly edited version of an article entitled "Collective Choice and Control Rights in Firms" coauthored with Gilbert L. Skillman and published in the *Journal of Public Economic Theory* (Dow and Skillman, 2007). We began work on this topic in fall 1992 while we were both visitors at the Swedish Collegium for Advanced Study in the Social Sciences (SCASSS) at the University of Uppsala. Gil deserves equal credit for whatever is good in this chapter and equal blame for whatever is not.

We received research support from SCASSS, the Social Sciences and Humanities Research Council of Canada, the University of Alberta, Simon Fraser University, and Wesleyan University. We also thank seminar audiences at the Universities of Alberta, British Columbia, Massachusetts, Victoria, and Winnipeg; Brown and Simon Fraser Universities; and Union College for helpful comments. All opinions are our own.

13

Free Riding and Employee Buyouts

13.1 Introduction

The theory in Chapter 12 dealt with the objectives of the firm. When markets for state-contingent income are missing, the production plans of firms resemble public goods in the sense that the choice of such a plan can affect the welfare of a number of agents in a nonexclusive and nonrivalrous fashion. Here I consider another way in which public good issues can arise within firms, where the public good is now information about what firm productivity would be under alternative organizational arrangements. By contrast with Chapter 12, I am not concerned with the firm's objectives, but rather with free rider problems that can block transitions from one organizational form to another.

The productivity of LMFs is often at least as high as the productivity of KMFs in the same industry (see Section 6.6). The same is true for LMF survival rates (see Section 7.2). These findings strongly suggest that LMFs are not rare because they fail the test of market competition. We must therefore investigate other features of LMF demography. Specifically, we need to consider the possibilities that (a) LMFs are rarely created from scratch, (b) LMFs are often converted into KMFs, or (c) KMFs are rarely converted into LMFs. Of course, LMFs could be rare for a combination of these reasons.

Chapter 10 studied one obstacle to the creation of LMFs from scratch: difficulties in appropriating entrepreneurial rent through LMF formation. Earlier chapters have also identified possible reasons for the conversion of LMFs into KMFs. Chapter 9 argued that imperfect appropriation of surplus by LMF insiders could have this result, either through degeneration or investor takeover. Chapter 12 argued that investor takeovers could occur due to collective choice problems in

LMFs. This chapter focuses on the reverse process: conversion of KMFs into LMFs. Because KMFs are widespread, LMFs can only remain rare if conversions of this kind are rare.

Most existing LMFs appear to have been created from scratch. The fraction of worker cooperatives formed by conversion of KMFs has been estimated at roughly 16% in France and 11% in Uruguay (see Sections 7.1 and 7.2). Anecdotal evidence suggests that within the small subset of LMFs arising through conversion of conventional firms, most involve KMFs in financial distress (Ben-Ner and Jun, 1996; Dow, 2003, ch. 10). Few LMFs arise through buyouts of successful KMFs, even though at any point in time successful KMFs are probably much more numerous than KMFs on the brink of failure.

One barrier to transformation of successful KMFs into LMFs may involve capital constraints. It is easier for employees to buy out failing KMFs than successful ones, for the simple reason that failing firms are cheaper and workers need not invest as much of their own wealth to acquire them. Workers may also have strong motivations to buy out a failing firm if their current wages, benefits, or working conditions are better than what they could obtain on the external labor market.

However, if a KMF is financially healthy and everyone knows that productivity could be increased through conversion to an LMF, it is unclear why capital constraints would impede an employee buyout. Although employees might lack the wealth needed to buy the firm all at once, presumably the existing investors would like to finance such a transaction, because the employees and investors could both be made better off. Adverse selection issues where lenders have less information than borrowers should be irrelevant if the investors are already knowledgeable about the firm.

One response to this argument involves commitment problems: perhaps investors would hesitate to finance a buyout because the employees might not repay a loan after the firm has been reorganized as an LMF. A second response involves risk aversion: even if financing is available, perhaps employees want diversified portfolios. I defer discussion of these two issues until Chapters 17–19. A third response is that the employees may be unable to agree on the policies the firm should pursue, as was suggested in Chapter 12.

This chapter studies a different problem: employees, managers, and investors are all likely to have some uncertainty about whether and by how much the productivity of a firm could be increased by transforming it from a KMF into an LMF. The answer could depend on the firm's location, industry, technology, size, idiosyncratic features of firm-specific physical or human assets, and the like. It is necessary to expend time, effort, and other resources in order to discover or estimate what productivity would be after the firm has been converted into an LMF. Prudent employees will not trust optimistic forecasts from the KMF investors or managers, so they will need to do their own research.

The problem is that reliable information about the profitability of an employee buyout is a public good from the standpoint of employees. An individual worker or a small group of workers has little incentive to investigate the potential profitability of a buyout, because most of the gains will flow to other workers. There is no easy way to overcome this problem by having a single worker, or a small group, capture most of the gains. If a subset of workers invested resources in learning about potential productivity gains, bought the firm, and then tried to charge other employees a price to participate, the latter would harbor the same skepticism that employees in general would have about such claims if they were made by investors or managers. Thus, a free rider problem will limit the supply of reliable information. This problem will be more severe in firms with larger workforces, and it can arise even if the productivity of the KMF is common knowledge.

Section 13.2 presents a model in which a KMF can potentially be converted into an LMF, where the profitability of the KMF is known but its profitability as an LMF is a random variable. Section 13.3 uses an aggregate welfare criterion to derive the efficient level of worker effort in learning about LMF profitability. Section 13.4 examines Nash equilibrium when individual workers decide how much effort to contribute. Section 13.5 establishes that the Nash effort is usually less than the socially optimal effort, so too few KMFs are transformed into LMFs. Section 13.6 discusses two subjects: (a) asymmetries between conversions of KMFs into LMFs and conversions in the opposite direction and (b) potential remedies for the free rider problem. Section 13.7 is an appendix containing proofs of the formal propositions.

13.2 The Model

Consider a KMF with profit $\pi_K > 0$. The firm has one investor and employs n workers, where n > 1. Everyone is risk neutral. The KMF pays each of its employees a competitive wage, which is normalized to zero. The firm can be converted into an LMF by having the employees pay the amount π_K to the investor. Any surplus beyond π_K goes to the employees. The employees contribute equally to the cost of the buyout. If an LMF is created, the workers collectively own its capital stock and share equally in its profit.

A1   All agents have the same prior belief that if the firm is converted into an LMF, it will have profit π_L with probability $\lambda \in (0, 1)$ and zero profit with probability $1-\lambda$ where $0 < \lambda\pi_L < \pi_K < \pi_L$.

At the outset it is unattractive to convert the firm into an LMF due to $\lambda\pi_L < \pi_K$. However, the employees can gather additional information by engaging in research about the firm's profitability as an LMF. Let $e_i \geq 0$ be the effort expended by employee $i = 1 .. n$ on such research, and let $E \equiv \Sigma e_i$ be total effort. It is impossible to contract on effort, because this is not verifiable in court, but all workers observe E.

Research generates a signal available to all workers, which may be either good (G) or bad (B). Signals are accurate with probability $p(E) \in [1/2, 1]$ so that

$$
\begin{aligned}
p(E) &= \Pr(\text{signal} = G|\text{LMF profit} = \pi_L) \\
&= \Pr(\text{signal} = B|\text{LMF profit} = \text{zero}) \\
1 - p(E) &= \Pr(\text{signal} = B|\text{LMF profit} = \pi_L) \\
&= \Pr(\text{signal} = G|\text{LMF profit} = \text{zero}) \quad (1)
\end{aligned}
$$

I adopt the following assumptions about research into LMF profitability.

A2   The function $p(E)$ is twice continuously differentiable with $p(0) = 1/2$ and $p(\infty) = 1$, where $p'(E) > 0$ is finite for all $E \geq 0$, $p'(\infty) = 0$ and $p''(E) < 0$ for all $E > 0$.

If total research effort is zero, the signal provides no new information. The accuracy of the signal is an increasing and strictly concave function of total effort.

Let $q_G(E)$ be the posterior probability that an LMF is profitable given a good signal, with $q_B(E)$ as the corresponding posterior probability for a bad signal. Thus

$$
\begin{aligned}
q_G(E) &= \lambda p(E)/[\lambda p(E) + (1 - \lambda)(1 - p(E))] \\
q_B(E) &= \lambda[1 - p(E)]/[\lambda(1 - p(E)) + (1 - \lambda)p(E)]
\end{aligned} \quad (2)
$$

Conditional on a good signal, the expected value of the firm as an LMF is $q_G(E)\pi_L$, and conditional on a bad signal, the expected value of an LMF is $q_B(E)\pi_L$. We have $q_B(E) \leq \lambda$ for all $E \geq 0$, so the firm is never converted when the signal is bad.

Given a good signal, it is profitable to convert the firm into an LMF when $q_G(E) \geq \pi_K/\pi_L$. From (2), this condition holds when

$$p(E) \geq p_0 \equiv 1/\{1 + [\lambda/(1 - \lambda)](\pi_L/\pi_K - 1)\} \qquad (3)$$

The threshold $p_0 > 1/2$ is the lowest signal accuracy at which it is profitable to buy out the firm when the signal is good. There is an effort level $E_0 > 0$ such that $p(E_0) = p_0$. For $E \in [0, E_0)$, the firm is never bought out even if the signal is good; for $E = E_0$, the employees are indifferent if the signal is good; and for $E > E_0$, the employees strictly prefer a buyout if the signal is good. I assume throughout that a buyout occurs in the case of indifference.

13.3 Welfare Maximization

To determine the socially efficient effort level, I will begin by defining the gross surplus $S(E)$. For $E \in [0, E_0)$, the firm is never converted and gross surplus is π_K. For $E \geq E_0$, the firm is converted if the signal is good but not otherwise. In this situation, $S(E)$ depends on the accuracy of the signal as follows:

$$
\begin{aligned}
S(E) &\equiv \pi_K && \text{for } 0 \leq E \leq E_0 \\
S(E) &\equiv \lambda p(E)\pi_L + \lambda[1 - p(E)]\pi_K \\
&\quad + (1 - \lambda)p(E)\pi_K + (1 - \lambda)[1 - p(E)](0) && \text{for } E_0 \leq E \quad (4)
\end{aligned}
$$

The first term in the second line of (4) reflects the case where an LMF is profitable, the signal is correct, and conversion occurs. The second reflects the case where an LMF is profitable but the signal is incorrect and conversion does not occur. The third arises for the case where an LMF is not profitable, the signal is correct, and no conversion occurs. The fourth arises where an LMF is not profitable, the signal is incorrect, and a mistaken conversion occurs. The coefficient of $p(E)$ is positive in the second line of (4) due to A1, so $S(E)$ is increasing on $E \geq E_0$.

The gross surplus function is shown in Figure 13.1. The function is continuous at E_0, because at this point the expected profit from an LMF is equal to actual profit from the KMF. A nonconvexity arises because signals are ignored to the left of E_0 but exploited to the right of it. The derivative $S'(E)$ is undefined at E_0. As E approaches infinity, $S(E)$ approaches $\lambda\pi_L + (1-\lambda)\pi_K$ because $p(E)$ approaches unity, signals

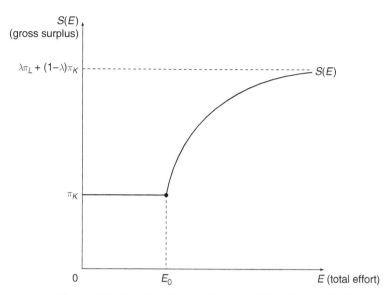

Figure 13.1 Gross Surplus as a Function of Total Research Effort

become perfect, and the firm is transformed into an LMF if and only if an LMF is profitable in expectation.

Let $c > 0$ be the cost per unit of research effort. Social welfare (or net surplus) is

$$W(E, c) \equiv S(E) - cE \qquad (5)$$

For a fixed cost parameter c, welfare is decreasing in E on the interval $[0, E_0)$ because $S(E) = \pi_K$ is constant. Effort is wasted on this interval because signals are never used. Welfare is strictly concave on $E \geq E_0$ because $p(E)$ is strictly concave from A2.

For a given $c > 0$, consider the constrained problem

$$\max W(E, c) \quad \text{subject to } E \geq E_0 \qquad (6)$$

This has a unique finite solution, denoted by $E(c)$, because $S(E)$ is strictly concave on the relevant interval and $S'(E) \to 0$ as $E \to \infty$ due to A2 and (4). Define $c_0 \equiv S'(E_0) > 0$ to be the right derivative at E_0. For $c \geq c_0$ we have a corner solution $E(c) = E_0$ and for $c < c_0$ we have an interior solution $E(c) > E_0$. In the latter case, $S'[E(c)] \equiv c$, $E(c)$ is decreasing in c, $E(c) \to \infty$ as $c \to 0$, and $E(c) \to E_0$ as $c \to c_0$.

Define $W^*(c)$ for a given $c > 0$ to be maximum welfare when E is unconstrained:

$$W^*(c) \equiv \max W(E, \ c) \text{ subject to } E \geq 0$$
$$= \max\{W(0, \ c); W[E(c), \ c]\} \quad\quad (7)$$
$$= \max\{\pi_K; W[E(c), c]\}$$

The second and third lines follow from the fact that no $E \in (0, E_0)$ is optimal, because all such effort levels give $S(E) = \pi_K$ but have unnecessary costs. Thus it suffices to compare $W(0, c) = \pi_K$ against the maximum welfare $W[E(c), c]$ from the constrained problem (6).

Proposition 1
Welfare maximization: Define the unique cost c^* by $W[E(c^*), c^*] \equiv \pi_K$, where $0 < c^* < c_0$.

(a) When $c < c^*$, the unique solution in (7) is $E(c)$, the solution from the constrained problem in (6). When $c = c^*$, $E = 0$ and $E = E(c^*)$ both solve (7) and there are no other solutions. When $c > c^*$, the unique solution in (7) is $E = 0$.
(b) The function $W^*(c)$ is continuous. For $c \leq c^*$, $W^*(c) = W[E(c), c]$ where $E(c)$ solves the constrained problem in (6), $W^*(c)$ is decreasing, and $W^*(c) \to \lambda\pi_L + (1-\lambda)\pi_K$ as $c \to 0$. For $c \geq c^*$, $W^*(c) = \pi_K$.

The intuition behind this proposition is provided in Figure 13.2. The shaded area shows where $W(E, c) \geq \pi_K$. For $c < c^*$, the optimal effort $E(c)$ corresponds to the dashed curve in the graph. Along this curve, the first order condition $S'(E) \equiv c$ applies, $E(c) > E_0$ is an interior solution in the constrained problem (6), and $W^*(c) > \pi_K$. At the threshold $c = c^*$, $W(E, c^*) = \pi_K$ can be obtained either from $E(c^*) > E_0$ or $E = 0$, while all other effort levels yield lower welfare. For $c > c^*$, $W(E, c) < \pi_K$ holds for all $E > 0$, but π_K can still be obtained from $E = 0$, so zero effort is socially optimal.

13.4 Nash Equilibrium

In this section, I assume that the individual workers $i = 1 .. n$ choose their own effort levels $e_i \geq 0$, with total effort determined by $E = \Sigma e_i$. Each worker faces the same cost parameter $c > 0$ per unit of research effort. I use (e_i, e_{-i}) for the vector of worker efforts, where $e_{-i} \equiv (e_1 .. e_{i-1}, e_{i+1} .. e_n)$ is the effort vector for workers other than i. As in Section 13.3, when $E < E_0$, the firm never becomes an LMF. When $E \geq E_0$, the firm is converted into an LMF if the signal is good. In this case, each worker pays π_K/n to the investor.

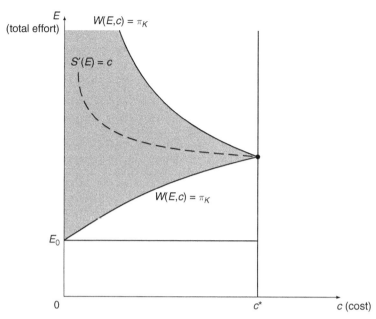

Figure 13.2 Socially Optimal Effort as a Function of Research Cost

Worker i's utility function is

$$u_i(e_i, e_{-i}) = -ce_i \qquad \text{for } 0 \leq E \leq E_0 \qquad \text{and}$$
$$u_i(e_i, e_{-i}) = \lambda p(E)(\pi_L - \pi_K)/n + \lambda[1 - p(E)](0) + (1 - \lambda)p(E)(0)$$
$$+(1 - \lambda)[1 - p(E)](-\pi_K/n) - ce_i \qquad \text{for } E \geq E_0 \qquad (8)$$

where $E = e_i + \Sigma_{j \neq i} e_j$. The utility function for worker i is continuous at $E = E_0$. In the second line of (8), the first term reflects cases where the LMF is profitable, the signal is correct, and upon conversion each worker enjoys the profit π_L/n but must pay π_K/n to the investor. The fourth term reflects mistaken conversions where the LMF is not profitable, the signal is incorrect, and each worker pays π_K/n to the investor but gains no profit from the LMF. In other situations, no conversion occurs and the worker gets the KMF wage, which is normalized at zero.

From the first line in (8), it is never a best reply for worker i to choose any effort level $e_i > 0$ that results in $E \leq E_0$. We can therefore confine attention to strategy choices involving either $e_i = 0$ or $e_i > 0$ with $E > E_0$. Furthermore, worker i can always guarantee $u_i \geq 0$ by setting $e_i = 0$. This gives zero utility when the efforts of the other workers give $0 \leq E \leq E_0$. It gives strictly positive utility when the efforts of the other workers result in $E > E_0$, because then a good signal leads to conversion, gross surplus satisfies $S(E) > \pi_K$, and the second line in (8) is positive.

For each worker $i = 1 \, .. \, n$, Equations (4) and (8) give

$$nu_i(e_i, e_{-i}) + \pi_K = S(E) - nce_i \qquad (9)$$

where $E = e_i + \Sigma_{j \neq i} \, e_j$. This implies that worker i's individual effort choice e_i maximizes gross surplus minus a cost involving the parameter nc, rather than the parameter c that is relevant for welfare maximization in Section 13.3. Due to $n > 1$, a worker behaves as if the private cost of accurate information is higher than the social cost. We also have

$$\pi_K + \sum u_i = S(E) - cE = W(E, c) \qquad (10)$$

The sum of the payoffs to the investor and all workers adds up to net surplus, which is the welfare index maximized in Section 13.3. It follows that total worker utility is positive if and only if welfare exceeds the KMF profit π_K.

I limit attention to symmetric Nash equilibria and indicate the equilibrium effort of each worker by e^N. Total equilibrium effort is $E^N = ne^N$. The first task is to identify conditions under which zero effort is a Nash equilibrium. This is easily done using (9). If all other workers supply zero effort, then $e_i = E$. It is a best reply for worker i to set $e_i = E = 0$ if and only if this maximizes $S(E) - ncE = W(E, nc)$. This is the same as welfare maximization except that the social cost c is replaced by the private cost nc.

Proposition 2
Zero Nash effort: Define c^* as in Proposition 1. A Nash equilibrium with total effort $E^N = 0$ exists iff $c \geq c^*/n$.

The next task is to determine conditions under which there is a Nash equilibrium where each worker has $e^N > 0$ in equilibrium. A necessary condition for this is $E^N = ne^N > E_0$. If instead $0 < E^N \leq E_0$, then from (4) gross surplus is $S(E^N) = \pi_K$. This is also the gross surplus if worker i deviates to $e_i = 0$. However, from (9) the deviation enables worker i to increase utility by avoiding a positive effort cost, so this cannot be an equilibrium.

Another necessary condition is $S'(E^N) = nc$. If we had $E^N > E_0$ but this first order condition did not hold, then from (9) worker i could raise utility through a small increase or decrease in e_i while maintaining $E > E_0$. There cannot be more than one E^N satisfying this condition, so there is at most one Nash equilibrium with positive effort.

A third necessary condition is $W(E^N, c) \geq \pi_K$. This is required because a worker i can always get nonnegative utility by deviating to $e_i = 0$. Therefore, equilibrium utility must be nonnegative. This is true for every worker, so (10) implies that the equilibrium welfare must be at least π_K. The next proposition gives existence and uniqueness results.

Proposition 3

Positive Nash effort: Let $c_0 \equiv S'(E_0) > 0$ be the right derivative at E_0, and define c^* as in Proposition 1. Define the total effort $E^N(c)$ for $0 < c < c_0/n$ using $S'[E^N(c)] \equiv nc$. Define the unique cost c^K by $W[E^N(c^K), c^K] = \pi_K$, where $0 < c^K < \min \{c_0/n, c^*\}$.

(a) When $0 < c \leq c^K$, there is a unique symmetric Nash equilibrium with positive total effort. The equilibrium total effort $E^N(c)$ has $E^N(c) > E_0$, and $E^N(c)$ is decreasing in c. For $c < c^K$, equilibrium worker utility is positive, $W[E^N(c), c] > \pi_K$, and welfare $W[E^N(c), c]$ is decreasing in c. At $c = c^K$, equilibrium worker utility is zero.

(b) When $c^K < c$, there is no symmetric Nash equilibrium with positive total effort.

Proposition 3 can be explained graphically using Figure 13.3. As in Figure 13.2, the area where $W(E, c) \geq \pi_K$ is shaded in the graph. The dashed curve indicates the locus $S'(E) \equiv c$, along which welfare W is maximized with respect to E for a given c. The curve $S'(E) \equiv nc$ shows the points satisfying the first order condition for Nash equilibrium. Due to $n > 1$, this curve lies below the locus $S'(E) \equiv c$.

In equilibrium it is necessary that worker utility be nonnegative, which from (10) requires $W(E, c) \geq \pi_K$. The heavy part of the $S'(E) \equiv nc$ curve shows the points satisfying this requirement. The cost c^K in Proposition 3 corresponds to the point on the locus $S'(E) \equiv nc$ at which $W(E, c) = \pi_K$, so equilibrium welfare is equal to KMF profit. Worker utility is positive for equilibria in the interior of the shaded region, while worker utility is zero at the boundary. There is no equilibrium with positive effort when $c > c^K$, because in this case $S'(E) \equiv nc$ implies $W(E, c) < \pi_K$ and from (10) worker utility would be negative.

13.5 Equilibrium and Efficiency

This section unifies the results on welfare maximization from Section 13.3 with those for Nash equilibrium from Section 13.4. Recall that $W(E, c)$ is social welfare for an arbitrary cost c and total effort E as in (5), while $W^*(c)$

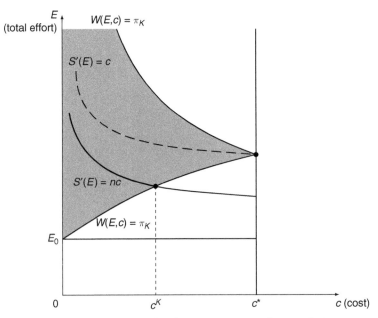

Figure 13.3 Nash Effort as a Function of Research Cost

is maximum social welfare at the cost c when E is chosen optimally as in
(7). Also recall that $E_0 > 0$ is the minimum total effort such that a good
signal results in conversion of the firm into an LMF.

Proposition 4
Equilibrium and efficiency: Define $c_0 \equiv S'(E_0)$ as in Proposition 3, define
$E(c)$ for $0 < c < c_0$ using $S'[E(c)] \equiv c$, and define $E^N(c)$ for $0 < c < c_0/n$
using $S'[E^N(c)] \equiv nc$. Define c^* and c^K as in Propositions 1 and 3.
We have $0 < c^*/n < c^K < \min \{c_0/n, c^*\} < c_0$. Confining attention to
symmetric Nash equilibria, the following results hold.

(a) For $c \in (0, c^*/n)$, the unique Nash effort $E^N(c)$ satisfies $E_0 < E^N(c) <$
    $E(c)$, with $\pi_K < W[E^N(c), c] < W^*(c)$.
(b) For $c \in [c^*/n, c^K]$, there are two Nash equilibria: one with $E_0 < E^N(c)$
    $< E(c)$ and the other with $E^N = 0$. For the equilibrium with $E_0 < E^N$
    (c), we have $\pi_K \leq W[E^N(c), c] < W^*(c)$, where the first inequality is
    strict for $c < c^K$ and the equality holds at $c = c^K$. For the equilibrium
    with $E^N = 0$, we have $\pi_K = W(E^N, c) < W^*(c)$.
(c) For $c \in (c^K, c^*)$, the unique Nash effort is $E^N = 0$, with $\pi_K = W(E^N, c)$
    $< W^*(c)$.

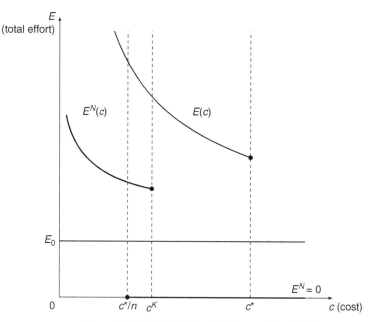

Figure 13.4 Socially Optimal Effort and Nash Effort

(d) For $c \geq c^*$, the unique Nash effort is $E^N = 0$, with $\pi_K = W(E^N, c) = W^*(c)$.

Proposition 4 shows that a symmetric Nash equilibrium always exists. For low costs as in case (a), the Nash equilibrium is unique and involves positive total effort. For intermediate costs as in case (b), there is one equilibrium with positive effort and another with zero effort. For higher costs as in cases (c) and (d), the Nash equilibrium is unique and involves zero effort.

Figure 13.4 shows the relationship between equilibrium effort and efficient effort. Total research effort in Nash equilibrium is always lower than the effort that maximizes social welfare, except at very high cost levels as in (d), where effort is zero for both. In case (a), the Nash effort is positive but too small; in (b) the Nash effort is too small even if it is positive, and it could also be zero; and in (c) the Nash effort is uniquely zero, while the efficient effort is positive.

When Nash effort is positive, as in case (a) or the equilibrium with positive effort in (b), some conversions occur, but the accuracy of signals about LMF profitability is too low, and welfare maximization requires greater total research effort. When $\lambda > 1/2$ so more than half of all KMFs would be profitable as LMFs, this additional effort would increase the fraction of KMFs converted into LMFs.

When the Nash effort is zero, as may occur in case (b) and always occurs in case (c), employees never buy out KMFs. In both of these cases, welfare maximization implies a positive probability of conversion. Only in case (d), where costs are very high, does the Nash effort coincide with efficient effort. In sum, the model supports the idea that even though we rarely observe the conversion of successful KMFs into LMFs, social welfare could be enhanced by increasing the rate at which such conversions occur.

13.6 Conclusion

I have shown that uncertainty about LMF productivity, and free rider problems that interfere with the resolution of this uncertainty, can help explain why few KMFs are bought out by employees, even when capital constraints do not bind. But there is an obvious question: why doesn't a symmetric problem arise for conversions of LMFs into KMFs? And if it does, how can the model explain the prevalence of KMFs?

The key point is that the number of investors required to buy out an LMF need not be similar to the number of employees required to buy out a KMF. The inalienability of labor imposes natural limits on the endowments of individual workers, so a firm wanting a large labor input must employ numerous workers. This can cause substantial free rider problems among employees. However, there is no limit on the capital endowment of an individual agent. A single investor who is wealthy enough could supply all of the capital used by the firm. Such an investor could observe the productivity of an LMF and would have private incentives to engage in the socially optimal amount of research to estimate what the firm's productivity would be as a KMF. If one investor lacked the wealth to buy out the LMF unilaterally, or wanted to maintain diversification across firms, it might be possible to assemble a small coalition of like-minded investors for whom the free rider problem would be minimal. Assuming that the probability distribution over productivity is similar for KMFs and LMFs in the same industry, or even if mean LMF productivity is somewhat higher, the fact that conversions of KMFs into LMFs are systematically more difficult than those in the opposite direction can help explain the overall rarity of LMFs.

The most obvious way in which employees could try to overcome the free rider problem is by contracting on research effort about potential LMF productivity. I ruled this out by assuming that individual research efforts are unverifiable, which parallels the usual assumption that other forms of worker effort are unverifiable. One solution might be to hire a consultant who specializes in such research. However, to the extent that this requires individual employees to incur search, bargaining, monitoring, or enforcement costs, the free rider problem persists. Another solution might involve repetition of the game. However, it seems unlikely that repeated games would be relevant for one-time decisions about organizational form.

Conversion of a KMF into an LMF would be less problematic if one person or a small group captured the surplus from a buyout. I argued in Section 13.1 that it would be difficult for KMF investors to appropriate the gains from conversion to an LMF, because employees would distrust claims from investors about the allegedly high productivity of an LMF. If such claims turned out to be false after a buyout, the employees might have little recourse. If the employees must guard against opportunism on the part of investors by incurring costs to verify productivity assertions, we are back to the previous problem.

For the same reason, it is unlikely that a small subset of employees could do the necessary research, buy out the firm, and then persuade other workers to make large up-front payments in exchange for LMF membership. Such scenarios can lead to adverse selection problems like those studied in Chapter 10 for LMFs created from scratch. In general it seems difficult to avoid the need for most or all employees to participate in the research process and for credible information to be widely shared among the workforce.

These problems are more easily solved when workers already have a labor union or some other form of collective organization. A union with the authority to collect dues from individual members and use these funds for common purposes could potentially overcome the free rider problem. In practice, employee buyouts often involve unions that study the potential benefits to their membership and bargain with investors over the terms of the transition (see Dow, 2003, ch. 10).

Of course, one is not limited to solutions that can be devised by private agents. A government has its own toolkit. It is probably infeasible to subsidize employee research effort directly, because this is not verifiable. But governments could support research that is complementary to research carried out by employees in individual firms and useful for workers across a number of firms or industries. They could also subsidize the services of consultants or promote collective organization for workers. Finally, governments could tax KMFs and subsidize LMFs. Such measures would promote employee research about productivity gains from buyouts, make LMFs more common, and quite possibly increase aggregate welfare. Other policy options will be considered in Chapter 20.

13.7 Appendix

Proof of Proposition 1

I first show that $c^* \in (0, c_0)$ exists and is unique. There is no $c \geq c_0$ with $W[E(c), c] = \pi_K$, because all such c have $E(c) = E_0$, and therefore $W[E(c), c] = S(E_0) - cE_0 < S(E_0) = \pi_K$. Thus I confine attention to the case $0 < c < c_0$. Here, the constrained problem (6) has a unique interior solution $E(c) > E_0 > 0$ where $E(c)$ is defined by $S'[E(c)] \equiv c$. The function $W[E(c), c]$ is continuous due to the theorem of the maximum and decreasing due to the envelope theorem. The fact that $E(c) \to E_0$ as $c \to c_0$ implies $W[E(c), c] \to \pi_K - c_0 E_0 < \pi_K$ as $c \to c_0$. We also have $W[E(c), c] = S[E(c)] - cE(c) < S[E(c)] < \lambda\pi_L + (1-\lambda)\pi_K$ because $S(E)$ is increasing and $S(\infty) = \lambda\pi_L + (1-\lambda)\pi_K$. I next show that $W[E(c), c] \to \lambda\pi_L + (1-\lambda)\pi_K$ as $c \to 0$. Choose any $\varepsilon > 0$. I will show that there is $\delta > 0$ such that $0 < c < \delta$ implies $\lambda\pi_L + (1-\lambda)\pi_K - W[E(c), c] < \varepsilon$. Because $S(E) \to \lambda\pi_L + (1-\lambda)\pi_K$ as $E \to \infty$, we can choose some $\underline{E}$ such that $\lambda\pi_L + (1-\lambda)\pi_K - S(\underline{E}) < \varepsilon/2$. Let $\delta = \varepsilon/2\underline{E} > 0$. This ensures that $\lambda\pi_L + (1-\lambda)\pi_K - [S(\underline{E}) - c\underline{E}] < \varepsilon$ for all $c \in (0, \delta)$. Observe that $W[E(c), c] \geq S(\underline{E}) - c\underline{E}$ for all such c because $E(c)$ is optimal for the given c while $\underline{E}$ may not be. Therefore $\lambda\pi_L + (1-\lambda)\pi_K - W[E(c), c] < \varepsilon$ for all $c \in (0, \delta)$, as was to be shown. Due to (i) the continuity and monotonicity of $W[E(c), c]$; (ii) the limit results; and (iii) $\lambda\pi_L + (1-\lambda)\pi_K > \pi_K$ from A1, there is a unique $c^* \in (0, c_0)$ such that $W[E(c^*), c^*] = \pi_K$.

(a) The fact that $W[E(c), c]$ is decreasing for $c \in (0, c_0)$ implies $W[E(c), c] > \pi_K$ for all $c < c^*$. This implies that when $c < c^*$, the unique solution in (7) is $E(c)$. When $c = c^*$, $W[E(c^*), c^*] = W(0, c^*) = \pi_K$. No other E can give $W(E, c^*) \geq \pi_K$, because $E(c^*)$ is the unique maximizer in the constrained problem (6) and $0 < E < E_0$ gives $W(E, c^*) = \pi_K - c^*E < \pi_K$. Thus $E(c^*)$ and $E = 0$ both solve (7), and there are no other solutions. When $c > c^*$, we have $W[E(c), c] < \pi_K$ and $W(0, c) = \pi_K$, so the unique solution in (7) is $E = 0$.

(b) Continuity of $W^*(c)$ follows from the continuity of $W[E(c), c]$ and the continuity of the max operator in (7). From part (a), $0 < c \leq c^*$ implies $W^*(c) = W[E(c), c]$, which is decreasing by the envelope theorem. We have $W^*(c) \to \lambda\pi_L + (1-\lambda)\pi_K$ as $c \to 0$ because we have already shown that $W[E(c), c] \to \lambda\pi_L + (1-\lambda)\pi_K$ as $c \to 0$. Finally, from part (a), $c \geq c^*$ implies $W^*(c) = \pi_K$ because $E = 0$ is optimal and $W(0, c) = \pi_K$ for all $c > 0$.

Proof of Proposition 2

From (9), there is a Nash equilibrium with $E^N = 0$ iff $e_i = E = 0$ maximizes $S(E) - ncE = W(E, nc)$. From (7), this is true iff $W[E(nc), nc] \leq \pi_K = W(0, nc)$. From Proposition 1(a), this is true iff $nc \geq c^*$ or $c \geq c^*/n$.

Proof of Proposition 3

As explained in the text, a Nash equilibrium with $E^N > 0$ must have both $E^N > E_0$ and $S'(E^N) = nc$. The equality is consistent with $E^N > E_0$ iff $nc < c_0$ or $c < c_0/n$. Thus the latter is a necessary condition for the existence of any such Nash equilibrium.

Define $E^N(c)$ for $c \in (0, c_0/n)$ using $S'[E^N(c)] \equiv nc$, and consider the social welfare level $W[E^N(c), c] = S[E^N(c)] - cE^N(c)$ for $0 < c < c_0/n$. Total differentiation gives $dW/dc = n(n-1)c/S'' - E^N(c) < 0$ because $S'' < 0$ from A2 and (4), so welfare is decreasing in c.

There are two possible cases: (i) $c^* < c_0/n$ or (ii) $c^* \geq c_0/n$. In case (i), recall from Proposition 1 that $W[E(c^*), c^*] = \pi_K$ where $S'[E(c^*)] = c^*$, and any $E > 0$ with $E \neq E(c^*)$ has $W(E, c^*) < \pi_K$. Because $0 < E_0 < E^N(c^*) < E(c^*)$ due to $n > 1$, we have $W[E^N(c^*), c^*] < \pi_K$. In case (ii), we have $E^N(c) \to E_0$ as $c \to c_0/n$ and so $W[E^N(c), c] \to \pi_K - c_0E_0/n < \pi_K$ as $c \to c_0/n$. Due to continuity, these results show that $W[E^N(c), c] < \pi_K$ for all values of c sufficiently close to min $\{c_0/n, c^*\}$.

Next we want to show that there is some c^Y with $0 < c^Y < $ min $\{c_0/n, c^*\}$ such that $W[E^N(c^Y), c^Y] > \pi_K$. If this is true, the continuity and monotonicity of $W[E^N(c), c]$ ensure the existence of a unique c^K with $c^Y < c^K < $ min $\{c_0/n, c^*\}$ such that $W[E^N(c^K), c^K] \equiv \pi_K$. From the proof of Proposition 1, as $c \to 0$, we have $W[E(c), c] \to S(\infty) = \lambda\pi_L + (1-\lambda)\pi_K > \pi_K$. This implies that there is some $c^Z > 0$ with $W[E(c^Z), c^Z] = S[E(c^Z)] - c^Z E(c^Z) > \pi_K$, and moreover we can choose c^Z to be small enough that $c^Z < $ min $\{c_0/n, c^*\}$. Write $E^Z = E(c^Z)$ so $S(E^Z) - c^Z E^Z > \pi_K$. From the definition of the function $E(c)$ we have $S'(E^Z) = c^Z = nc^Z/n$. Thus $E^Z = E^N(c^Z/n)$. At the cost $c^Y = c^Z/n$ we have $W[E^N(c^Y), c^Y] = W[E^N(c^Z/n), c^Z/n] = S(E^Z) - (c^Z/n)E^Z > S(E^Z) - c^Z E^Z = W[E(c^Z), c^Z] > \pi_K$. Thus there is a cost c^Y with $0 < c^Y < $ min $\{c_0/n, c^*\}$ such that $W[E^N(c^Y), c^Y] > \pi_K$. This proves the existence of a unique c^K with $0 < c^K < $ min $\{c_0/n, c^*\}$ such that $W[E^N(c^K), c^K] \equiv \pi_K$.

(a) Choose any $c \in (0, c^K]$. I will prove that it is a Nash equilibrium for each worker $i = 1 .. n$ to set $e_i = E^N(c)/n$. There are two possibilities: (i) a deviation by an individual worker i to $e_i = 0$ may yield $E = (n-1)E^N(c)/n \geq E_0$ or (ii) this deviation may yield $E = (n-1)E^N(c)/n < E_0$. In case (i), the utility function u_i in (9) is strictly concave in e_i for $e_i \geq 0$, and the first order condition $S'[E^N(c)] = nc$ is sufficient for a maximum with respect to e_i. Thus we have a Nash equilibrium. In case (ii), no deviation by worker i that yields $E \geq E_0$ can increase utility u_i, for the same reason as in case (i). A deviation with $e_i > 0$ and $E < E_0$ gives less utility than the deviation $e_i = 0$ due to (8). Therefore it suffices to show that the deviation $e_i = 0$ does not increase utility. This deviation gives $S(E) = \pi_K$, so (9) implies $u_i = 0$. If worker i does not deviate, (10) and the symmetry of the effort levels imply that this worker receives $u_i = [W(E^N(c), c) - \pi_K]/n \geq 0$, where the inequality follows from $0 < c \leq c^K$; $W[E^N(c^K), c^K] \equiv \pi_K$; and the fact that $W[E^N(c), c]$ is decreasing in c. The equilibrium is unique because the solution of $S'(E^N) \equiv nc$ is unique, and this condition is necessary for any Nash equilibrium with positive total effort $E^N > 0$. We have $E^N(c) > E_0$ because $c \leq c^K < \min \{c_0/n, c^*\} \leq c_0/n$. $E^N(c)$ is decreasing in c due to $S'' < 0$ from A2 and (4). We have already shown that $W[E^N(c), c]$ is decreasing in c. The remaining statements follow from (10), the symmetry of the equilibrium efforts, and the definition of c^K.

(b) Choose any $c > c^K$. As explained in the text, two necessary conditions for a symmetric Nash equilibrium with positive total effort $E^N > 0$ are $E^N > E_0$ and $S'(E^N) = nc$. Together these imply $c < c_0/n$. Assume that these conditions are satisfied and each worker $i = 1 .. n$ sets $e_i = E^N/n$. From the definition of c^K, the definition of the function $E^N(c)$, and the fact that $W[E^N(c), c]$ is decreasing on the interval $0 < c < c_0/n$, we have $W[E^N(c), c] < \pi_K$. From (10) and the symmetry of effort levels, the latter inequality implies $u_i < 0$ for all i. But as explained in the paragraphs of the text following (8), any worker i can get non-negative utility by deviating to $e_i = 0$. This shows that there is no such Nash equilibrium.

Proof of Proposition 4

We have $c^* < c_0$ from Proposition 1 and $c^K < \min \{c_0/n, c^*\}$ from Proposition 3. We need to establish $c^*/n < c^K$. Suppose instead that $c^K \leq c^*/n$. From Proposition 1, we have $W[E(c^*), c^*] = \pi_K$. From the definition $W[E^N(c^K), c^K] = \pi_K$, the fact that $c^K \leq c^*/n < c_0/n$, and the fact that $W[E^N(c), c]$ is decreasing for $c < c_0/n$ (see the proof of Proposition 3), we have $W[E^N(c^*/n), c^*/n] \leq \pi_K$. Now observe from the definitions of the functions $E(c)$ and $E^N(c)$ that $E^N(c^*/n) = E(c^*)$. Substituting this into previous results gives $W[E(c^*), c^*/n] \leq \pi_K = W[E(c^*), c^*]$, which implies $S[E(c^*)] - (c^*/n)E(c^*) \leq S[E(c^*)] - c^*E(c^*)$. But this is false because $n > 1$. Therefore it must be true that $c^*/n < c^K$.

(a) The characterization of Nash equilibrium follows from Propositions 2 and 3(a), where $E^N(c) < E(c)$ occurs because $S'[E^N(c)] = nc$ and $S'[E(c)] = c$. The welfare results follow from Propositions 1 and 3(a), along with $E^N(c) \neq E(c)$.

(b) The characterization of Nash equilibrium follows from Propositions 2 and 3(a), where $E^N(c) < E(c)$ as in part (a). The welfare results follow from Propositions 1 and 3(a), along with $E^N(c) \neq E(c)$.

(c) The characterization of Nash equilibrium follows from Propositions 2 and 3(b). The welfare results follow from Proposition 1.

(d) The characterization of Nash equilibrium follows from Propositions 2 and 3(b). The welfare results follow from Proposition 1.

PART VI

OPPORTUNISM PROBLEMS I

Transaction Cost Economics

14.1 Introduction

One useful definition of the firm is that it is a set of agents supplying inputs to a common production process, where the activities of the agents are organized through an authority structure and the resulting outputs are sold on a market. The inputs may include labor, capital, raw materials, and so on. The role of authority as the defining feature of the firm dates to Coase (1937), who offered the first coherent theoretical explanation for the existence of firms—namely, that they arise when the transaction costs of organizing production through authority are less than the transaction costs of organizing production through markets. Coase's approach remained dormant for decades, but it was revived by Oliver Williamson, whose book *Markets and Hierarchies* (1975) proved to be extremely influential. Williamson shared a Nobel Prize in 2009 for his work on firm organization.

I am not concerned in this book with the reasons for the existence of firms, which I take for granted. The question here involves the locus of control: among the members of the firm, who has ultimate authority over production and why? Because scholars in transaction cost economics (TCE) have had a good deal to say on this topic, it is worth reviewing this approach and the resulting explanations for the dominance of the capital-managed firm. I will treat the writings of Williamson from the 1970s and 1980s as the canonical exposition of TCE.

The present chapter is organized as follows. First, I sketch some key concepts in Section 14.2. This is followed by a critical assessment in Section 14.3, where I stress the fact that authority can be used in self-interested ways. Input suppliers who enjoy control rights within a firm are therefore likely to disregard some costs their decisions impose on input suppliers who lack control rights. Implications for work organization are

developed in Section 14.4. The notion that prevailing governance structures necessarily have good efficiency features is disputed in Section 14.5.
Specifically, I argue against the inference that because labor-managed firms
are rare, they must be inefficient. Section 14.6 closes with a postscript on
some matters of intellectual history.

14.2 Conceptual Framework

Williamson (1975) starts with two postulates about human nature. First,
humans are boundedly rational in the sense of having limited abilities to
process information and foresee future events. The main theoretical role of
this postulate is to justify the idea that contracts are usually incomplete.
If complete contracts were feasible, every aspect of the production process
could be negotiated in advance through arms-length transactions, and we
would be back to the world of complete and competitive markets in
Chapters 2–5. The problem of contractual incompleteness is usually
greater when agents make longer-term investments, because there are
more future events for which foresight could fail.

Bounded rationality is not the only possible rationale for incomplete
contracts. Others include high costs of negotiating complicated legal agreements and high costs of reliable third party enforcement. I return to these
points in Chapters 16–18. In any case, contracts do not spell out what every
agent must do in every potential state of the world. Accordingly,
agents need a governance structure to determine how gaps in contracts
will be filled as events unfold. Firms accomplish this through authority
relationships.

The second postulate is that humans are prone to opportunism.
In Williamson's usage, this goes beyond ordinary self-interest to include
guile or deception. Opportunism is most likely to matter in situations of
"small numbers." When a party to a transaction has ready access to many
alternative partners who are good substitutes for one another, as in competitive markets, opportunism is usually of little concern. The scope for
opportunism expands as the number of available partners shrinks, and may
be large under bilateral monopoly. It is a special hazard when small
numbers are combined with "impacted information," where at least one
transacting party has important private knowledge.

In practice, small numbers conditions tend to be associated with asset
specificity. If all of the inputs used by a firm have close substitutes available
on external markets, the agents involved can renegotiate their contracts
whenever an unforeseen event occurs, and reliance on authority can be

replaced by reliance on spot markets. However, many assets used by firms (both physical and human) are mutually specialized, in the sense that their value when used together inside the same firm exceeds the sum of their values when used separately elsewhere in the economy. Once mutually specialized assets exist, the owners of the assets must bargain over a pool of quasi-rent (the difference between total revenue when the assets are used together and total revenue when they are used separately). The bargaining problem tends to be more challenging when agents have private information.

Three fundamental concepts in TCE are transactions, governance structures, and transaction costs. The core hypothesis of this research program is that "transactions are assigned to and organized within governance structures in a discriminating (transaction-cost economizing) way" (Williamson, 1981a, 1564). I examine each concept in turn.

Transactions. TCE accepts Commons's dictum that the transaction is the basic unit of analysis (Williamson, 1975, 254; Teece, 1980, 234). A transaction occurs "when a good or service is transferred across a technologically separable interface" (Williamson, 1981a, 1544). This technological definition often becomes rather elastic in practice, because "the 'appropriate' level of transactional detail is not well defined and may vary with circumstances" (Williamson, 1976, 102). Long-lived physical assets may give rise to transactions consummated only over decades (Goldberg, 1976; Williamson, 1976).

Williamson (1979, 246–247) identifies three dimensions along which transactions can vary: the specificity of the assets required to execute the transaction, the frequency with which the transaction recurs, and the level of uncertainty surrounding its execution. It is useful to think of these (and possibly other) dimensions as defining a characteristics space within which a given transaction can be located. Williamson (1979, 253) develops this idea diagrammatically. A transaction's location in this space summarizes its content for the purposes of further analysis. Once concrete transactions have been mapped onto points of the characteristics space, the task is to find a governance structure, chosen from some set of feasible structures, that is best suited to each point in the space.

Governance structures. The transaction is the substrate upon which governance structures are superimposed. Governance structures are implicit or explicit contractual arrangements (Williamson, 1979) used by the parties to a transaction to effect adaptations as circumstances change. Such structures can be arrayed on a spectrum according to the degree of autonomy maintained by the parties involved. Discrete transactions are at one extreme, and hierarchical transactions are at the other, with hybrids such as franchising and joint ventures in between (Williamson, 1985, 83). Employment relationships are at the hierarchical end of the spectrum and are generally agreed to be central to the firm.

Although authority relations are fundamental to the distinction between firm and market, these relations arise endogenously through the bargains reached among initially autonomous agents rather than through crude coercion. Authority relations are internal features of the contracts (implicit or explicit) accepted in the market. Authority is limited to an "area of acceptance" (Simon, 1976, 133–134), and contracting agents retain the right to terminate the relationship.

Transaction costs. Assume that transaction characteristics and a set of feasible governance structures have each been specified, and consider the definition of transaction costs. Numerous writers have attempted either to distinguish transaction costs from more-conventional costs or to argue that no such distinction is tenable. I offer an interpretation meant to be consistent with the usage of transaction cost theorists themselves.

Everyone agrees that transaction costs must be evaluated comparatively, varying governance structures while holding constant the transaction to be implemented. Or, as Williamson (1975, 20) puts it, "Only to the extent that frictions associated with one mode of organization are prospectively attenuated by shifting the transaction, or a related set of transactions, to an alternative mode can a failure be said to exist." Therefore, we can just as well refer to the net benefits of a governance structure, relative to feasible alternatives, rather than the transaction costs of the structure.

The TCE literature usually assumes wealth maximization, so it is natural to value foregone resources by computing a sum of compensating variations in monetary units. In my definition, the transaction cost arising when a given governance structure is used for a transaction is the total monetary value of the resources sacrificed by *not* applying a Pareto efficient structure to that transaction. Thus, governance structures are compared using a potential Pareto improvement (or Kaldor-Hicks) test.

One must also identify the specific types of benefits or costs associated with the use of a governance structure. This is necessary in order to distinguish transaction costs from mundane production costs. Williamson calls for a study of the "comparative costs of planning, adapting, and monitoring task completion under alternative governance structures"

(1981a, 1544, emphasis deleted). Both ex ante and ex post transaction costs arise. Ex ante, there are "costs of drafting, negotiating, and safeguarding an agreement." Ex post, in addition to the standard administrative setup and operating costs, there are "maladaption costs incurred when transactions drift out of alignment," "haggling costs incurred if bilateral efforts are made to correct *ex post* misalignments," and "bonding costs of effecting secure commitments" (Williamson, 1985, 20).

From this exposition, it is clear that the gross benefit of a governance structure is the value of the adaptations to changing circumstances that the structure makes possible. The other items on the list are merely resources needed to effect these adaptations in an incentive-compatible way and are deducted to compute the net benefit of a governance structure. Governance structures are to be judged by their capacity to provide a "better" transaction in the potential Pareto improvement sense.

The main conceptual difficulty is that a "better" transaction must in some way be a different transaction. This undermines the premise that the transaction under discussion is fixed, while governance structures can be varied to assess the transaction costs of each structure. To avoid circularity, one must distinguish the "details" of the transaction, which are subject to sequential adaptation in ways that vary from one governance structure to another, from the "general" features of the transaction, which are invariant.

14.3 The Use and Abuse of Authority

In TCE, firm organization is explained by identifying net benefits from organizing certain transactions through authority, as compared with bargaining between autonomous agents. Williamson's discussion of the functions of authority is the most comprehensive, but his views parallel those of Klein, Crawford, and Alchian (1978) and Teece (1982). In *Markets and Hierarchies*, Williamson describes three ways in which firm organization can restrain the opportunism that would otherwise infect market exchange.

Appropriability. By depriving agents of independent profit streams, firms ensure that "the parties to an internal exchange are less able to appropriate subgroup gains, at the expense of the overall organization (system)." Opportunism is mitigated because "the terms of trade are circumscribed," and "compensation (including promotions) can be easily varied by the general office to reflect noncooperation" (1975, 29).

Monitoring. Informational asymmetries are mitigated in firms because "internal organization can be more effectively audited." Internal auditors are not limited solely to written records, and when "audits of operating divisions are made by the general office, [a] stigma is not attached to such disclosure" (1975, 29).

Conflict resolution. "Internal organization realizes an advantage over market mediated exchange in dispute settling respects," because with limited appropriability and suitable incentive systems, "parties are more inclined to adapt cooperatively" (1975, 29). Also, firms are "able to settle many such disputes by appeal to fiat" (1975, 30).

In each of these cases, authority at a higher level is invoked as a means to restrain opportunism among subordinate agents. This illustrates a more general point: transaction cost theorists tend to see authority primarily as a *remedy* for opportunism rather than a device that might be *abused* in an opportunistic fashion. Little attention is given to the danger that those in positions of authority might use the data obtained through internal audits to gain strategic advantages over lower-level parties, impose self-serving incentive systems, or use fiat to settle disputes in ways that suit themselves.

This omission is puzzling, because transaction cost analysis itself indicates that a potential for opportunistic abuse is intrinsic to authority relations. It is widely recognized that hierarchy concentrates information at a central node for decision-making purposes (Arrow, 1974, 68–70). This implies that information is impacted at the top as *an explicit principle of organizational design* when authority relations are used. A situation of small numbers and impacted information is precisely the case in which transaction cost theory suggests that opportunism poses the greatest difficulties (Williamson, 1975, ch. 2).

It is important to recognize that in the present context, bargaining cannot be relied upon to curb abuses of authority. In TCE, the firm exists precisely because bargaining is too costly relative to authority. For this reason, one cannot appeal to the Coase Theorem and assume that agents who might be harmed by an opportunistic abuse of authority will bribe the perpetrators to desist. In a world of positive transaction costs, the assignment of control rights within the firm has real allocative consequences, much as the assignment of property rights has real allocative consequences when externalities exist (Coase, 1960).

The fact that authority can be abused in self-interested ways is fundamental to the question of who should hold authority within the firm, and therefore is crucial to this book. Either control rights can be assigned to capital suppliers, who will sometimes abuse their authority at the expense of labor suppliers, or else control rights can be assigned to labor suppliers, who will sometimes abuse their authority at the expense of capital suppliers. We need to know which of these problems is more serious and why.

14.4 Work Organization

Oliver Williamson and Henry Hansmann have both applied TCE to the question of why labor-managed firms are rare. I begin by reviewing the work of Williamson and then turn to that of Hansmann. For a related discussion, see Dow (2003, s. 6.3).

Radical economists have maintained that hierarchy does not serve primarily to promote efficiency, but rather to exploit workers (Marglin, 1974, 1982; Gintis, 1976; Edwards, 1979; Bowles, 1985). In his own analysis of work organization, Williamson disputes the idea that "bosses exploit workers and hierarchy is the organizational device by which this result is accomplished" (1980, 7). He concludes instead that capitalist authority relationships outperform the worker peer group (the closest thing to a labor-managed firm in Williamson's discussion) on transaction cost dimensions. While his performance criteria account for such forms of worker opportunism as malingering and equipment abuse (1980, 23), he includes no performance measure that captures the idea of employer opportunism. As a result, his analysis sidesteps the very features of work organization the radical writers sought to address.

Examples of employer opportunism include distortion or hoarding of information about the product market (Klein, Crawford, and Alchian, 1978; Hashimoto, 1981), or the magnitude of labor costs relative to other firms (Willman, 1982), as well as the unilateral introduction of technological innovations that undercut labor's bargaining position (Dow, 1985; Skillman and Ryder, 1993). If dysfunctions of this sort had been included, the peer group organization, which involves democratic checks on such behavior, would have tied or outranked the capitalist authority relationship on Williamson's own evaluation scheme (1980, 29).

A recognition that opportunistic behavior can occur on both sides of an authority relationship has figured in several commentaries on TCE, including those by Goldberg (1980), Perrow (1981, 1986), Putterman (1981, 1984), Jones (1982), and Willman (1982). But more is at stake than the simple fact that employers and employees both suffer from moral flaws. The deeper problem is that authority establishes the structural preconditions under which employer opportunism can flourish: small numbers, impacted information, and a tool (decision by fiat) tailor-made for the unilateral pursuit of self-interest.

Appealing to higher authorities as a solution only displaces this problem. What is needed to limit opportunism by authorities is reciprocal monitoring by subordinates and a capacity to impose sanctions when abuses are detected. As Putterman puts it, echoing Williamson's own diagnosis of the worker peer group, "If workers are . . . tied to firms, and if managers, 'having more complete information', have a 'strategic advantage over everyone else', and 'inordinate influence over both the value and factual premises of other members of the group', why should workers relinquish all controls over management?" (1984, 178–179). It is indeed striking that in discussing the peer group (1975, 52) and the "iron law of oligarchy" (1975, 127), Williamson clearly recognizes issues of leadership opportunism, only to lose sight of the problem when analyzing the capitalist firm.

In a reply to Putterman (1981), Williamson questions the value of granting workers a check on managerial authority, saying, "The intrusion of operating into strategic decision making (or the reverse) can easily impair performance . . . [A]lthough some of the worker participation literature seems to presume extensive involvement of workers in strategic affairs, this can come at a high cost. In the degree to which efficiency is highly valued, worker participation programs will recognize the hazards and attempt to provide safeguards against 'excessive' strategic involvement" (1981b, 282–283).

While this is a valid concern, several points should be made. First, when workers gain relevant knowledge from operating activities, tapping this knowledge by involving workers in strategic decisions may offer net benefits. Second, it is not vital for workers to engage in strategic decision-making in order for them to evaluate overall managerial performance and remove inept or abusive managers. Finally, actors at the strategic level may behave opportunistically toward actors at the operating level. When this is ignored, the potential benefits from checks on authority are also ignored.

Williamson (1985, 302–304) later conceded that worker representation on the board of directors might be necessary to secure a flow of credible information to workers about firm profitability, although he wanted to confine employees to nonvoting seats. To this extent, Williamson acknowledged that the dangers of managerial opportunism toward workers are real. Shareholders, however, were said to need more than just information; they required the power to replace managers.

When it came to labor-managed firms, the founders of the transaction cost school never fully implemented their program of comparative contractual analysis. One might have expected (a) an appreciation of the danger that authority could be abused, whoever happened to have it; (b) a comparison of the costs of such abuse, depending on whether authority was held by capital or labor suppliers; and (c) an argument that characteristics of capital and labor are relevant in assessing these transaction costs. The literature of the time did not pursue this agenda. The closest approach was Williamson's (1985, ch. 12) argument that investors are more vulnerable to expropriation than workers and therefore more in need of control rights as a safeguard.

A different story about the rarity of LMFs comes from Hansmann (1988, 1990a, 1990b, 1996). My summary will be brief; interested readers should see Dow (2003, 124 and 200–206) for additional information. Hansmann's starting point is that workers tend to have heterogeneous preferences about the goals of the firm, while investors are nearly unanimous in favoring the maximization of profit or stock market value. As a result, an LMF faces difficult collective choice problems and tends to have higher transaction costs than a similar KMF. The transaction costs of the LMF vary with factors such as the size of the firm and the homogeneity of the workforce, which can help explain the incidence of LMFs across industries. The need to limit transaction costs is said to explain various design features of successful LMFs, such as intensive screening of members, avoidance of an extensive division of labor, limited skill or wage differentials, use of representative rather than direct democracy, and delegation of decision-making to managers.

Because collective choice problems have already been addressed in Chapter 12, I will only highlight a few points. First, the asserted difference in the degree of preference heterogeneity for workers and investors cannot just be assumed; it must be derived from deeper characteristics of the labor and capital markets. Without foundations of this kind, it is unclear why the unanimity theorems from the finance literature would not carry over to LMFs with membership markets. Second, collective choice could help explain the rarity of LMFs even without transaction costs, because problems of this kind can lead to asymmetries in the conversion of LMFs into KMFs and vice versa. Finally, although transaction costs associated with collective decision-making may be a part of the story about LMF rarity, many LMFs seem to have overcome these problems through good organizational design, at least to the extent that they do not have obvious productivity deficits relative to their KMF rivals.

14.5 Efficiency and Causality

The transaction cost program owes its "distinctive powers" to "its unremitting emphasis on efficiency" (Williamson and Ouchi, 1981, 367). Indeed, TCE adherents often infer the efficiency of a governance structure directly from its existence. This inference then motivates a search for the efficiency benefits provided by the structure. If this search terminates in a reasonable story, the theorist declares that the existence of the structure has been explained.

Belief in the efficiency of observed governance structures leads to functionalist explanatory statements: governance structure X exists because efficiency requirements dictate X for transactions of type Y. Causal explanations, on the other hand, describe how later structures have emerged out of earlier ones. The status of functionalist theory in the social sciences has long been a matter of heated debate. Here I examine two causal mechanisms that transaction cost theorists might use to justify a presumption that governance structures are efficient: intentionality and competition. Both run into difficulties.

Intentionality. The simplest argument is that the transacting parties consciously choose a governance structure based upon an explicit assessment of the transaction costs associated with each feasible structure. Before any transaction occurs, the parties foresee the frictions likely to emerge under alternative structures, including the cost of restraining ex post opportunism to an optimal degree, and agree to implement efficient procedures for making all subsequent decisions. This is consistent with Williamson's view that "the parties to a contract are hard-headed and ... the ramifications of alternative contracts are intuited if not fully thought through" (1985, 38).

Unfortunately, intentionality arguments collide with the transaction cost school's bounded rationality postulate. If agents cannot cope with contracts featuring complex contingencies (Williamson, 1975, 24), it seems doubtful that they can determine which decision-making procedure will be efficient in adapting to future circumstances. To put the point differently, if transaction costs reflect the value of adaptations to future events, including unforeseen events, then the parties cannot know at the outset what transaction costs they face. Knowledge of this kind would require cognitive abilities sufficient for comprehensive contracting, but this has been ruled out on bounded rationality grounds.

The intentionality approach also runs afoul of the opportunism postulate if ex ante contracting involves small numbers and impacted information. Transaction costs include not just ex post costs, such as those of administration and contract enforcement, but also the ex ante costs of finding trading partners, negotiating contracts, and so on. When these costs are large, they may severely limit the set of potential ex ante partners. Accordingly, there is no reason to suppose that the hazards of small numbers bargaining with impacted information are absent ex ante. If such bargaining leads to maladaptation ex post, as TCE authors claim, then it should have the same effect ex ante, when the governance structure is chosen. To put it a bit paradoxically, the fact that ex ante transaction costs are positive may prevent transaction cost minimization. In this sense, TCE lacks a coherent theory of governance structure formation.

Competition. Elster (1983) suggests that functionalist explanations in biology are warranted by the known workings of natural selection. However, he argues that there is no feedback mechanism of comparable power and universality that can serve as the basis for functionalist reasoning in the social sciences. Nevertheless, transaction cost theorists often view market competition as a suitable analog to natural selection. As Williamson puts it,

The argument relies in a general background way on the efficacy of competition to preserve a sort between more and less efficient modes and to shift resources in favor of the former. This seems plausible, especially if the relevant outcomes are those which appear over intervals of five or ten years rather than in the very near term. This intuition would nevertheless benefit from a more fully developed theory of the selection process. (1985, 22–23)

As Langlois (1984) notes, this intellectual strategy is appealing because it is compatible with the bounded rationality assumption used elsewhere in TCE.

It is possible, of course, to *define* the efficiency of a governance structure by its capacity to survive in competition with alternative structures (Goldberg, 1980, 251). But I will assume that the independent efficiency criterion suggested in Section 14.2 pertains, so the efficiency of surviving structures is not just tautological. Two distinct claims may then be advanced: (a) that competition from successful firms will induce imitation and learning among other firms, encouraging the diffusion of efficient organizational forms; or (b) that firms with efficient structures will simply eliminate firms having inefficient ones. Williamson (1975, 172) uses both types of arguments to explain the spread of the multi-divisional corporate structure, for example.

Nelson and Winter (1982, ch. 6) identify various assumptions that are needed in order to reconcile evolutionary dynamics with orthodox concepts of profit maximization and equilibrium. Parallel issues arise in the context of TCE, as Williamson recognizes (1985, 23). Without pursuing the details here, I observe that the credibility of economic selection arguments depends heavily on circumstances. When firms engage in simple recurrent tasks in competitive markets with frequent entry and exit, selection may well remove inefficient modes of organization expeditiously. On the other hand, when firms engage in complex idiosyncratic activities in concentrated markets where entry and exit are rare, skepticism is warranted. Putting these broad issues aside, two additional points require attention: intraorganizational power and appropriation biases.

With regard to power, Williamson recognizes that selection pressures may be resisted. He remarks that "more efficient modes will eventually supplant less efficient modes—though entrenched power interests can sometimes delay the displacement" (1985, 236). But Williamson and Ouchi (1981, 363–364) claim that over sufficiently long periods, the distribution of power within firms becomes endogenous and is determined by efficiency needs.

This view does not seem compatible with the TCE emphasis on asset specificity. Once idiosyncratic assets are in place, the parties are locked into a relation of bilateral exchange. For this reason, the parties may behave in a strategic fashion, resulting in substantial inefficiency, without any agent having an incentive to recontract externally. This is so even in long run competitive equilibrium, with zero ex ante profit for potential entrants. In a formalization of this idea, Dow (1985) shows that input suppliers may seek to impose inefficient technologies that transfer rents or quasi-rents away from other input suppliers. Such strategic behavior need not be self-limiting. Thus, asset specificity can insulate authority structures from the discipline of competitive markets.

With regard to appropriation, it is essential to distinguish between aggregate payoffs and the payoffs of individual agents. A central dogma of TCE is that only the aggregate transaction cost of a governance structure, *not* the distribution of these costs among agents, affects the likelihood that the structure will be adopted. The problem is that there may not be any economic unit that precisely internalizes the total transaction cost for a specific exchange. This is clearly true ex ante before a governance structure has been created, when individual agents necessarily bear their own costs of search or contract negotiation. It may also be true ex post if multiple agents share in the rents or quasi-rents generated by whatever governance structure is adopted.

The outcomes from market selection do not reflect costs and benefits arising at the level of the economy as a whole. They only reflect private payoffs for the economic units selected upon, much as natural selection acts on genes or organisms, not species or ecosystems. Without full internalization of transaction costs (or full appropriation of the net benefits from a governance structure) by the economic units subject to selection, the selection mechanism becomes decoupled from the maximization of aggregate surplus.

Consider the labor-managed firm. Those skeptical of the LMF often claim that LMFs must be inefficient because they rarely arise spontaneously in market economies (Jensen and Meckling, 1979). Indeed, skepticism of this sort has been framed explicitly in transaction cost language (Williamson, 1985, 322–324). However, the Panglossian faith that prevailing organizational forms are efficient ignores possible appropriation biases.

Assume for the sake of argument that, compared with a KMF, an ongoing LMF yields large transaction cost savings, perhaps because it adapts more easily to changing circumstances. Assume also that the benefits of any governance structure, KMF or LMF, flow at least proximately to the agents holding control rights within that structure. Then the governance benefits of the LMF will inevitably be diffuse, flowing in some measure to each worker in the firm. But the benefits of the KMF (smaller by assumption) can be concentrated in the hands of a single investor by bringing all nonhuman assets under an umbrella of common ownership.

If an entrepreneur cannot internalize the social benefits of the LMF by charging entry fees that reflect the benefit each member will receive, the only other way to derive governance benefits from the LMF is to participate in the firm as a coequal member. But only a small fraction of the aggregate social benefit of the LMF can be appropriated by a single agent in this way, in contrast to the ability of an individual investor to appropriate a large share of the aggregate social benefit of the KMF. The link between selection and efficiency is broken by appropriation biases, because no unit of

economic selection bears all of the costs and benefits of the LMF governance structure. With positive transaction costs there is no reason to
suppose that LMFs will spring to life of their own accord (even if their
net social benefits are larger than those of KMFs), any more than one
would expect selection mechanisms to eliminate negative externalities,
deficient public good supply, or monopoly power in an environment
where transaction costs are positive.

14.6 Postscript

This chapter draws extensively from the article "The Function of
Authority in Transaction Cost Economics," originally published in the
Journal of Economic Behavior and Organization (Dow, 1987). I am grate-
ful for comments on the 1987 version from Sid Winter, Charles Perrow,
Richard Nelson, Louis Putterman, and Richard Langlois. I have edited
the original article for style, clarity, and content, deleting outdated
passages and adding new sentences or paragraphs where needed.
To the extent possible, I tried to preserve the spirit of the debates around
TCE in the 1980s. Williamson (1987) published a response to my article.
My later writings on TCE include Dow (1993b, 1996b, 1997) as well as
section 6.3 of Dow (2003).

On a personal note, Williamson and I were faculty colleagues at Yale
University during 1983–1986 and continued to meet occasionally afterward. We sometimes discussed TCE, LMFs, and related issues. I enjoyed
these conversations, but Williamson did not want to give up efficiency as
a way of explaining governance structures, and I did not want to give up
the possibility that LMFs could have efficiency advantages despite their
rarity. Nevertheless, my encounter with TCE had a lasting influence,
much of which is visible in this book. Williamson's ideas about incomplete contracts, authority structures, and asset specificity were simply too
important to ignore.

My criticism of the view that markets select efficient governance
structures led to the material in Section 9.5 of this book, where I argue
that due to appropriation problems, KMFs may win the evolutionary race
even if they generate less aggregate surplus than do LMFs. Another
influence from TCE can be found in Chapter 10, where I translated my
1987 argument about ex ante transaction costs into an adverse selection
story about the difficulty of appropriating entrepreneurial rent through the
establishment of LMFs. The analysis of collective choice problems in
Chapter 12 owes a debt to Hansmann's research mentioned in

Section 14.4, although Skillman and I wanted to redirect the study of LMF collective choice problems away from TCE in favor of ideas derived from finance. The concepts of asset specificity and appropriation led to the model in Chapter 15, where I argue that KMFs can prevail in equilibrium even if they generate less total surplus. My focus on self-enforcement in Chapters 16–18 was inspired in part by Williamson's stress on incomplete contracts. I replaced Williamson's bounded rationality justification for the incompleteness of contracts with a justification based on the absence of enforcement by third parties, which facilitated the use of game-theoretic methods.

The most fundamental element of my 1987 critique was the idea that authority could be used in self-interested ways. As I emphasized in the original article, the LMF is specifically designed to restrain the abuses of managerial authority that workers often suffer in KMFs. To ignore this is to miss the whole point. However, I took seriously Williamson's (1985, 1988) argument that investors might also be vulnerable to abuse in LMFs. This became central to my way of thinking about capital market imperfections and their implications for the rarity of LMFs. The reader will see the results of this line of reasoning in Chapters 17 and 18.

15

Firm-Specific Investments

15.1 Introduction

The comparison between capitalist and labor-managed firms is a special
but paradigmatic case of a broader question: given free entry, why do some
organizational forms survive in equilibrium while others do not? One
plausible hypothesis is that the surviving modes of organization yield
a larger total surplus than potential alternatives. This is the answer offered
by transaction cost economics, as discussed in Chapter 14.

In fact, there is no necessary relationship between the size of the surplus
from an organizational form and its long run viability. To see why, suppose
that production requires an initial investment in a specialized asset, and
assume that it is impossible to sign binding contracts about this investment
(perhaps it is too costly to write down all technologically relevant characteristics of the asset). Now consider two organizational forms, A and
B. Firms of type A yield a large aggregate surplus after the specialized asset
is in place but prevent asset owners from capturing any of this ex post
surplus. Firms of type B yield a smaller aggregate surplus but direct most of
it to the asset's owners. Given the constraint that the prospective surplus
recipients in type A firms cannot sign a contract where they pay the
investors to create the asset, the ease with which investors can capture
surplus in a type B firm is decisive and these firms will prevail in
equilibrium.

The application to labor-managed firms is straightforward. Suppose that
the asset is a factory and workers cannot construct a factory themselves, but
LMF members can lease a factory from outside investors. After the factory
has been built, the LMF workers would choose output, working conditions,
the intensity of equipment use, and similar variables. These control rights

could enable the workers to capture a large fraction of the firm's ex post surplus at the expense of the factory owners. Investors who anticipate this problem will be reluctant to build a factory in the first place.

The investors could create a KMF instead, where they run the firm and capture any resulting surplus. This might yield less aggregate surplus than an LMF, but at least the factory would be built. After the KMF exists, employees could conceivably pay the investors to switch from a KMF to an LMF if this would increase total surplus. But if the LMF leases the factory after this organizational transition, the owners of the factory may have little incentive to maintain it, because they may have difficulty in capturing a return on their maintenance expenditures and the LMF members may be unable to sign a legally binding contract under which they pay for maintenance costs. This problem is essentially identical to the previous problem of convincing investors to build a factory for an LMF.

Define quasi-rent to be firm revenue minus the sum of the opportunity costs of the input suppliers after firm-specific investments have been made. The firm's governance structure typically affects the distribution of quasi-rent among individual input suppliers. At least to a first approximation, quasi-rent tends to flow toward the agents with control rights. When firm-specific investments are noncontractible, the expected distribution of quasi-rent ex post will affect the willingness of input suppliers to make these investments ex ante. For example, if investments in firm-specific skills are noncontractible, workers might be unwilling to make such investments in a KMF because they cannot capture any of the incremental quasi-rent this generates. However, workers in an LMF might readily make similar investments because they can use control rights to appropriate most of the incremental quasi-rent resulting from their investments in training. The general point is that all agents who invest in noncontractible firm-specific assets, whether these involve physical or human capital, must be willing to participate in the firm even without any ex ante compensation for their investment expenditures. Organizational forms that violate this ex ante participation constraint will not flourish in the long run, regardless of their potential ex post productivity (Dow, 1993b).

I will begin by investigating how control rights and bargaining power interact to determine the distribution of quasi-rent between investors and workers. I will then study investment in firm-specific assets and implications for the viability of KMFs and LMFs. The model has the following structure. In the KMF, the owners of physical assets hire workers, choose output, and keep the firm's net income. These roles are reversed in the LMF. In either type of firm, events unfold in three stages. At the *investment* stage, the agents decide whether to invest in firm-specific assets. If all necessary investments are made, at the *bargaining* stage the hired input negotiates its own remuneration. In the KMF this is the wage paid to labor, while in the LMF it is the fee paid to the physical asset owners. At the *production* stage, the firm's controllers choose an output level.

The analysis shows that two general cases can arise. When the controlling input has high costs at the production stage, and therefore a weak position at the bargaining stage, quasi-rent is shared between capital and labor. This can motivate investments in firm-specific assets by both capital and labor suppliers. But when the controlling input has low costs at the production stage, and therefore a strong position at the bargaining stage, all quasi-rent goes to the controllers. In this case, noncontrolling input suppliers have no incentive to make firm-specific investments.

The consequences for market equilibrium under conditions of free entry run as follows. When one input is specialized and the other is generic, control rights go to the specialized input. When both inputs are specialized, control rights go to the input with the weaker bargaining position (i.e., higher costs at the production stage). This somewhat counterintuitive result arises because control rights function as a substitute for bargaining strength. Giving control to the weaker input ensures that both input suppliers appropriate some quasi-rent, which induces specialized investments by both parties. I will show that equilibrium organizational forms sometimes maximize total surplus, but equilibrium can also involve excessive output from each firm, too little entry, and the appropriation of ex ante rents by hired inputs. In particular, KMFs can prevail even when LMFs would yield a larger total surplus.

Section 15.2 describes assumptions about the economic environment. Section 15.3 considers the output decisions of a capitalist firm, and Section 15.4 considers wage bargaining in a capitalist firm. Section 15.5 extends these results to labor-managed firms and presents conditions under which each type of firm survives in the long run under free entry. Section 15.6 discusses situations where the market equilibrium does not maximize aggregate surplus, and Section 15.7 is a postscript.

15.2 The Economic Environment

Throughout this chapter I assume that investments in firm-specific assets are noncontractible. Several additional contracting frictions will also be important.

Output is noncontractible. Without this assumption, the agents would always choose output to maximize surplus and then bargain over its distribution. For similar reasons, I rule out contracts in which output-related costs (such as effort costs) directly borne by noncontrolling agents are shifted to the agents with control rights. Instead, I assume that payments to the noncontrolling inputs are invariant with respect to output. This restriction is appropriate when courts cannot verify output quality, for example.

Hired inputs cannot promise to forgo bargaining in exchange for side payments. Section 15.3 will show that total surplus in the KMF varies with the wage. This effect would be of no interest if input suppliers could simply adopt whatever wage maximizes total surplus and then divide the resulting pie through side payments. I rule this out by assuming that if investors try to bribe workers to accept such a deal, workers can just pocket the bribe and resume negotiations. Under these conditions, it is impossible for agents to avoid the allocative consequences of wage bargaining. By the same token, I assume that LMFs cannot bribe the owners of physical assets to refrain from opportunistic bargaining over the rental fee charged for the use of their assets.

Capital and labor supply cannot be integrated. Bargaining inefficiencies between buyers and sellers are frequently avoided through vertical integration (Klein et al., 1978; Williamson, 1985; Grossman and Hart, 1986; Hart and Moore, 1990). Similar problems could be avoided here if investors supplied labor to KMFs or if workers supplied physical assets to LMFs. I assume that the first solution is ruled out by scale factors or the investor's demand for leisure, while the second is ruled out by limits on worker wealth and capital market imperfections. Therefore capital and labor are supplied by distinct agents. I will return to these issues near the end of the chapter.

15.3 Output Choice in the Capitalist Firm

Call the input suppliers in the capitalist firm K and L. These can be regarded as coalitions of individual agents—for example, shareholders and a labor union. I abstract from input substitution by assuming a Leontief technology. The reservation payoffs of K and L are normalized at zero. At the production stage, K chooses output subject to the constraint that L's payoff be nonnegative. This labor participation constraint is ex post in nature, because it arises after firm-specific assets have been created.

It should not be confused with the ex ante participation constraint to be discussed in Section 15.5.

The utility functions for K and L at the production stage are

$$u_K(q, w) = pq - z_K q^2 - w$$
$$u_L(q, w) = w - z_L q^2 \tag{1}$$

where $q \geq 0$ is output and $w \geq 0$ is the wage. The wage is parametric in this section, but it will be endogenized through bargaining in Section 15.4. The price $p \geq 0$ is parametric for an individual firm but will be endogenized using market equilibrium conditions in Section 15.5. The expression $z_K q^2$ is depreciation on physical assets, and $z_L q^2$ is the disutility of effort, with $z_K > 0$ and $z_L > 0$. A more general model with strictly convex cost functions is used in Dow (1993c).

The sum of the payoffs in (1) gives the quadratic surplus function

$$\begin{aligned} s(q) &\equiv u_k(q, w) + u_L(q, w) \\ &\equiv pq - z_K q^2 - z_L q^2 \end{aligned} \tag{2}$$

I use the terms "surplus" and "quasi-rent" interchangeably. Surplus is strictly concave in output, increasing from zero at $q = 0$ to a maximum level $s^* > 0$ at the output $q^* > 0$ and then decreasing to zero again at $q_0 > q^*$. With complete contracts, the firm would choose output to maximize total surplus at the production stage. I depart from this framework by assuming that the costs $z_K q^2$ and $z_L q^2$ are borne privately by the respective input suppliers. A capital-managed firm cannot sign contracts under which investors bear the disutility of worker effort, and a labor-managed firm cannot sign contracts under which workers bear the depreciation costs incurred by asset owners.

For a given wage, K chooses output to solve

$$\max\{pq - z_K q^2 - w\} \text{subject to } q \geq 0 \text{ and } z_L q^2 \leq w$$

The unconstrained optimum is $q = p/2z_K$, which is feasible for wage levels at or above $w_K \equiv z_L(p/2z_K)^2$. This output is excessive because K ignores effort costs. At any wage below w_K, the labor participation constraint binds and output is $q = (w/z_L)^{1/2}$. Writing K's output choice as $q_K(w)$, we therefore have

$$\begin{aligned} q_K(w) &= (w/z_L)^{1/2} &&\text{for } 0 \leq w \leq w_K \\ q_K(w) &= p/2z_K &&\text{for } w_K \leq w &&\text{where} &&w_K \equiv z_L(p/2z_K)^2 \end{aligned} \tag{3}$$

Increasing the wage on the interval $[0, w_K]$ relaxes L's participation constraint and raises output. This effect vanishes for wage levels beyond w_K where output becomes constant.

Substituting (3) into (1), we obtain indirect utilities as functions of the wage:

$$\begin{aligned} v_K(w) &= u_K[q_K(w), w] \\ v_L(w) &= u_L[q_K(w), w] \end{aligned} \tag{4}$$

There are two cases, depending on whether or not the participation constraint is binding.

$$\begin{aligned} \text{If} \quad 0 \le w \le w_K \quad &\text{then} \quad v_K(w) = s[q_K(w)] \\ & \qquad\qquad v_L(w) - 0 \\ \text{If} \quad w_K \le w \quad &\text{then} \quad v_K(w) = s_K + w_K - w \\ & \qquad\qquad v_L(w) = w - w_K \end{aligned} \tag{5}$$

where I write $s_K \equiv s(p/2z_K)$ for total surplus when K's output choice is unconstrained.

The functions v_K and v_L are shown in Figures 15.1 and 15.2. These two graphs have the following common features. To the left of w_K, L's payoff is zero because the participation constraint binds. K therefore appropriates the full surplus $s[q_K(w)]$. This surplus attains a maximum of s^* at the wage w^*, which induces K to choose the optimal output q^*. Wage increases beyond w^* raise output and lower surplus until w_K is reached. To the right of w_K in each figure, the participation constraint for labor is irrelevant. K's unconstrained output choice is implemented and total surplus is constant at s_K. Variations in the wage on this interval only redistribute this fixed surplus between K and L. To the right of w_0, K's payoff becomes negative.

Figures 15.1 and 15.2 differ with respect to the sign of the surplus s_K arising when K's output choice is unconstrained. It is easy to show that

(i) $\quad s_K > 0 \quad$ when $\quad z_K > z_1$
(ii) $\quad s_K = 0 \quad$ when $\quad z_K = z_L$
(iii) $\quad s_K < 0 \quad$ when $\quad z_K < z_L$

In case (i), K has a weak incentive to overproduce and K's unconstrained output $p/2z_K$ is below the output $q_0 = p/(z_K + z_L)$ at which total surplus is zero. In case (ii), these outputs coincide. In case (iii), K has a strong incentive to overproduce and K's unconstrained output $p/2z_K$ is above the level q_0 at which total surplus is zcro.

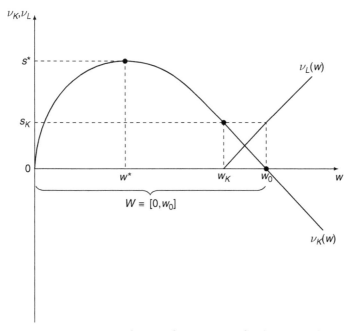

Figure 15.1 Indirect Utility Functions for the KMF When $s_K > 0$

Figure 15.1 corresponds to case (i), where s_K is positive. This implies that there is an interval $[w_K, w_0]$ on which K and L both have strictly positive payoffs. Figure 15.2 corresponds to the case (iii), where s_K is negative. In this situation, the labor participation constraint binds throughout the relevant wage interval $[0, w_0]$, so L cannot get a positive payoff on this interval.

15.4 Wage Bargaining in the Capitalist Firm

This section develops a model of the process by which wages are determined in the capitalist firm. I first consider the case $s_K > 0$, as in Figure 15.1, because this leads to more-complex bargaining issues. The case $s_K \leq 0$ will be discussed afterward.

When $s_K > 0$, the set of utility pairs generated by wage offers in the interval $W \equiv [0, w_0]$ is nonconvex, implying that the Nash bargaining solution cannot be used. I turn instead to an alternating-offers game of the Rubinstein (1982) type, where K opens with some proposal $w \in W$ that L either accepts or rejects. If L rejects this offer, L makes a counterproposal

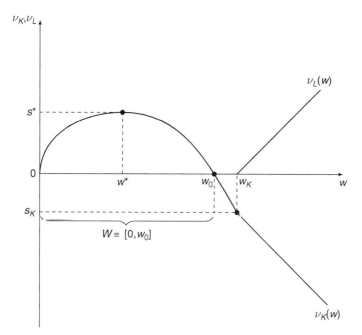

Figure 15.2 Indirect Utility Functions for the KMF When $s_K < 0$

in the following period, which K accepts or rejects, and so on. If this process ends with an acceptance, the accepted wage becomes binding and production occurs. Otherwise, each agent gets a zero payoff. Both agents discount the future.

The analysis is straightforward if wage offers are confined to the interval $[w_K, w_0]$ in Figure 15.1, because then a pie of fixed size is being divided. It is well known that the Rubinstein game has a unique perfect equilibrium in this case (Osborne and Rubinstein, 1990). However, when offers throughout the interval $W \equiv [0, w_0]$ are admissible, total surplus varies and neither utility function is strictly monotonic in the wage. This environment generates many subgame perfect equilibria, some of which give L a zero payoff.

There is nevertheless a strong intuition that wage bargains should lie in the range (w_K, w_0) where both payoffs are positive. Any bargaining strategy such that L accepts a zero payoff is dominated by an otherwise identical strategy where L rejects proposals of this kind and instead insists on a positive payoff. If L does hold out for a positive payoff, K is better off with an agreement in (w_K, w_0) than with perpetual deadlock.

For brevity, I will skip over some technical details at this point and move directly to the key results (readers wanting further information should see Dow, 1993c). Assume that agents discount future payoffs, equilibrium bargaining strategies are stationary, and existing proposals are accepted in situations of indifference. Under these conditions, there are only two subgame perfect equilibria for the bargaining game.

The first equilibrium is an extended Rubinstein solution (ERS), which is identical to the usual Rubinstein solution but permits any wage offer in the entire interval $W \equiv [0, w_0]$ rather than just the truncated set $[w_K, w_0]$ where total surplus is constant. All wage proposals by K or L lie in the interior of the truncated set, even though this restriction is not imposed a priori. Letting the time between successive bargaining proposals approach zero, the identity of the first mover becomes irrelevant and the equilibrium wage is

$$w^{ERS} = \alpha_K w_K + \alpha_L w_0 \qquad (6)$$

where $\alpha_K \equiv \rho_L/(\rho_K + \rho_L)$, $\alpha_L \equiv \rho_K/(\rho_K + \rho_L)$, ρ_K is the continuous-time discount rate for K, and ρ_L is the continuous-time discount rate for L. Thus the wage will be lower when L is more impatient to achieve an agreement. This is a standard result from noncooperative bargaining theory (Binmore, Rubinstein, and Wolinsky, 1986).

The second equilibrium will be called the residual claimant optimum (RCO). In this case, L accepts any wage offer from K. Accordingly, K demands the wage w^* and only accepts wage proposals that are at least as attractive as the maximum surplus s^* received with a one-period delay. L's own wage proposal is arbitrary because L has no reason to make acceptable offers: any wage acceptable to K has zero utility for L.

There is a clear basis for selecting the ERS equilibrium when both equilibria exist. The strategies of K and L in the ERS equilibrium are undominated, but L's strategy in any RCO equilibrium is dominated. Accordingly, I assume that the ERS solution occurs when $s_K > 0$, as in Figure 15.1. Substituting the wage bargain back into (5) gives KMF payoffs for the case where $s_K > 0$.

If $s_K > 0$ (*or equivalently* $z_K > z_L$)   then $v_K^{KMF} = \alpha_K s_K$

$$v_L^{KMF} = \alpha_L s_K \qquad (7a)$$

In this case, output is excessive and quasi-rent is shared between the two parties.

Now consider the situation where $s_K \leq 0$, as in Figure 15.2, so K's incentive to overproduce is strong. Here the bargaining problem disappears, because L's payoff is identically zero on the wage interval $[0, w_0]$. Intuition suggests the result w^*. It can be shown that no ERS equilibrium exists in this case, so the question of dominated strategies does not arise and any equilibrium must be of the RCO variety. As the time lag between successive wage offers approaches zero, K's acceptance set shrinks to w^*. Assuming that L makes proposals acceptable to K when L is indifferent, in the limit the wage w^* is the unique equilibrium result. Substituting w^* back into (5) gives KMF payoffs for the case where $s_K \leq 0$.

$$\text{If } s_K \leq 0 \ (\textit{or equivalently } z_K \leq z_L) \quad \text{then} \quad v_K^{KMF} = s*$$
$$v_L^{KMF} = 0 \qquad (7b)$$

In this case, output is efficient and K appropriates all quasi-rent.

There is a sharp discontinuity in the bargaining outcome at the transition from $s_K > 0$ to $s_K \leq 0$ (this occurs at $z_K = z_L$, where the parties have identical cost functions). The wage drops abruptly from w_K to w^*, output drops from K's unconstrained choice $p/2z_K$ to the surplus-maximizing level $q^* = p/2(z_K + z_L)$, and surplus jumps up from s_K to s^*. The reason is that a nonconvex utility possibility set is replaced by a convex one at $s_K = 0$.

The following terminology provides a convenient shorthand. I will say that K's bargaining position is *weak* when (7a) and Figure 15.1 apply, because in this case K must share quasi-rent with L. This corresponds to the situation where $z_K > z_L$ so that K has higher costs at the production stage and weak incentives to overproduce. I will say that K's bargaining position is *strong* when (7b) and Figure 15.2 apply, because then K appropriates the total surplus of the firm. This corresponds to $z_K < z_L$ so that K has lower costs at the production stage and strong incentives to overproduce.

To avoid possible confusion, notice that the concept of bargaining position is not the same as the concept of bargaining power. The strength or weakness of a bargaining *position* is determined by the costs z_K and z_L at the production stage. An input supplier's bargaining *power* (relevant only for the ERS equilibrium) is given by the parameter α_K or α_L, which is determined by the rates of time discount ρ_K and ρ_L, as explained after (6).

15.5 Equilibrium Organizational Form

We can now return to the question posed in Section 15.1: what determines the equilibrium mode of organization? First, a brief discussion of the LMF is required. In such a firm, labor is the residual claimant and has control over output, while capital is the hired input and lacks control. Due to this role reversal, the payoff functions from (1) are replaced by

$$u_K(q,\ r) = r - z_K q^2$$
$$u_L(q,\ r) = pq - z_L q^2 - r \qquad (1')$$

where $r \geq 0$ is the rental fee paid by L for the use of K's physical assets. Because K and L cannot contract on the intensity with which assets are used, r is a lump-sum transfer that does not vary with output. This restriction on LMFs is motivated by Klein et al. (1978), Jensen and Meckling (1979), and Putterman (1988a,b), who stress the cost to absentee owners of monitoring the use or abuse of physical assets.

Due to the symmetry of the KMF and LMF, the analysis from Sections 15.3 and 15.4 goes through for the LMF with an interchange of subscripts. Because the surplus function s(q) from (2) does not depend on organizational form, the surplus-maximizing output q^* remains the same. The unconstrained investor output $p/2z_K$ is replaced for the LMF by the unconstrained worker output $p/2z_L$ that maximizes the payoff u_L in $(1')$.

Let $s_L \equiv s(p/2z_L)$ be the surplus generated by L's unconstrained output choice. The equilibrium payoffs v_K^{LMF} and v_L^{LMF} from bargaining over K's rental fee are symmetric to those listed in (7) for the KMF with bargaining over L's wage. For easy reference, I list the LMF payoffs here.

If $s_L > 0$ (*or equivalently* $z_L > z_K$)   then $v_K^{LMF} = \alpha_K s_L$

$$v_L^{LMF} = \alpha_L s_L \qquad (8a)$$

If $s_L \leq 0$ (*or equivalently* $z_L \leq z_K$)   then $v_K^{LMF} = 0$

$$v_L^{LMF} = s* \qquad (8b)$$

To highlight the fact that output choices and the resulting surplus depend on the output price p, I denote the surplus-maximizing output, the unconstrained KMF output, and the unconstrained LMF output by $q^*(p)$, $q_K(p)$, and $q_L(p)$, respectively. The corresponding surplus levels are denoted by $s^*(p)$, $s_K(p)$, and $s_L(p)$.

In order for quasi-rents to arise in equilibrium, at least one factor supplier must incur a sunk setup cost at the investment stage. These costs will be denoted by $y_K \geq 0$ and $y_L \geq 0$. For instance, y_K could be the sunk cost associated with a factory, while y_L could be a sunk cost from specialized worker training. I assume that these expenditures cannot be transferred from one input supplier to the other. In the terminology of

Section 15.1, investments in firm-specific assets are noncontractible. I ignore the case $y_K = y_L = 0$, because then free entry drives price to zero in the product market. For simplicity, firm-specific investments are lumpy (all or nothing) rather than continuous. Finally, I assume that even if one input is generic and has no sunk cost, there is still a bilateral bargaining problem after the investment stage due to frictions in input markets not modeled here. It will be shown that even under this assumption, generic inputs never have control rights.

A viable organizational form must give both input suppliers nonnegative ex ante payoffs, so that entrepreneurs can attract all of the required inputs.

Definition
The KMF is *viable* at a price p if $v_K^{KMF}(p) \geq y_K$ and $v_L^{KMF}(p) \geq y_L$. The LMF is viable at a price p if $v_K^{LMF}(p) \geq y_K$ and $v_L^{LMF}(p) \geq y_L$.

Viability means that all ex ante participation constraints are satisfied simultaneously at the price p. This motivates the following definition of market equilibrium.

Definition
Let p_K be the lowest price at which the KMF is viable, and let p_L be the lowest price at which the LMF is viable. The KMF is the *equilibrium organizational form* if $p_K < p_L$. Conversely, the LMF is the equilibrium form if $p_L < p_K$. If $p_K = p_L$, then the KMF and LMF can coexist in equilibrium.

When a given organizational form provides both capital and labor suppliers with positive ex ante payoffs, entrepreneurs create more firms of that type and entry occurs. Entry by new firms places downward pressure on price. The equilibrium organizational form is the one that can survive this competitive pressure in the long run.

The bargaining results from Section 15.4 can be used to determine the minimum price at which each organizational form is viable. I will assume that $z_K \neq z_L$ in the following discussion in order to avoid the consideration of boundary cases. In interpreting the following proposition, it is important to recognize that the definition of a weak or strong bargaining position does not depend on organizational form. The input with the higher production cost always has a weak position, and the input with the lower production cost always has a strong position.

Proposition
Viability of organizational forms: Let $i = K, L$ be the controlling input who chooses output at the production stage, and let j be the

noncontrolling input who receives a lump-sum payment (w or r) determined at the bargaining stage. The lowest price p_i for which the iMF is
viable is derived as follows.

(a) Suppose that the controlling input i has a *weak* bargaining position
    ($s_i > 0$ or $z_i > z_j$). Then p_i satisfies the condition $s_i(p_i) = \max\{y_K/\alpha_K,$
    $y_L/\alpha_L\}$.
(b) Suppose that the controlling input i has a *strong* bargaining position
    ($s_i < 0$ or $z_i < z_j$). Then when $y_j > 0$, the iMF is never viable; but when
    $y_j = 0$, the price p_i satisfies $s^*(p_i) = y_i$.

Proof
In part (a), we use (7a) and (8a). K's ex ante payoff in the iMF is $\alpha_K s_i(p) - y_K$, and L's ex ante payoff in the iMF is $\alpha_L s_i(p) - y_L$. Because $s_i(p)$ is
monotonic, the lowest price p_i at which both ex ante payoffs are non-
negative satisfies the condition in part (a).

In part (b), we use (7b) and (8b). The controlling input's ex ante payoff is
$s^*(p) - y_i$, and the noncontrolling input's ex ante payoff is $-y_j$. If $y_j > 0$,
the iMF is never viable, because the noncontrolling input's ex ante payoff
is negative at all output prices. If $y_j = 0$, the noncontrolling input's ex
ante payoff is zero at all output prices. Because $s^*(p)$ is monotonic, the
lowest price p_i at which the ex ante payoff of the controlling input is
nonnegative satisfies the condition in part (b).

The main lessons of the proposition are twofold. First, giving control to
the weak input ensures that both input suppliers will receive some quasi-
rent. This is necessary in equilibrium if both inputs have positive setup
costs, but it implies that firms produce too much output, because the
controlling input does not internalize the costs borne by the
noncontroller. Second, giving control to the strong input implies that all
surplus goes to the controller. This forces the controller to internalize costs
borne by the noncontroller and implies that firms have efficient output
levels. However, strong inputs can have control in market equilibrium only
when the weak (noncontrolling) input is generic, because if this input has
positive setup costs, these cannot be recouped ex post.

I develop these ideas more formally in two corollaries.

Corollary 1
When the weak input i is specialized ($y_i > 0$), that input always has
control in equilibrium, whether or not the strong input j is also
specialized.

	K weak *L* strong ($z_K > z_L$)	*K* strong *L* weak ($z_K < z_L$)
K specialized *L* generic ($y_K > y_L = 0$)	KMF (Corollary 1)	KMF (Corollary 2)
K generic *L* specialized ($y_L > y_K = 0$)	LMF (Corollary 2)	LMF (Corollary 1)
both specialized ($y_K > 0, y_L > 0$)	KMF (Corollary 1)	LMF (Corollary 1)

Figure 15.3 Equilibrium Organizational Forms

Proof

Suppose that $z_i > z_j$, so i is weak. If i has control, part (a) of the proposition gives $s_i(p_i) = \max \{y_K/\alpha_K, y_L/\alpha_L\}$. The fact that i is weak implies that j is strong. But if j has control and j is also strong, interchanging the subscripts in part (b) shows that the jMF is never viable because i cannot recoup $y_i > 0$. Therefore in equilibrium the weak input has control.

Corollary 2

When the strong input i is specialized ($y_i > 0$) but the weak input j is not ($y_j = 0$), the strong input always has control in equilibrium.

Proof

If the weak input j has control, part (a) of the proposition gives $s_j(p_j) = y_i/\alpha_j$. If the strong input i has control, part (b) gives $s^*(p_i) = y_i$. Because $s^*(p) > \alpha_i s_j(p)$ for all $p > 0$, we have $p_i < p_j$. Therefore in equilibrium the strong input has control.

Figure 15.3 summarizes the implications of the corollaries for KMFs and LMFs. With specialized capital and generic labor, control always goes to capital. The resulting output is excessive if K is weak and efficient if K is strong. Conversely with specialized labor and generic capital, control always goes to labor, where output is excessive if L is weak and efficient if L is strong. When both of the inputs are specialized, in equilibrium control is assigned to the weak input, because otherwise it would be impossible for this input to recoup its setup cost. Output is always too large in this case.

It may seem paradoxical that when both inputs are specialized, the weak input has control rights. However, there is a natural intuition. If both input suppliers must receive positive quasi-rent, in market equilibrium the same input cannot enjoy *both* control rights *and* a strong bargaining position, because then the controlling input would seize all quasi-rent ex post, and the noncontrolling input would be unwilling to invest ex ante. Giving control to the weak input solves this problem, because control rights compensate for a weak bargaining position. Both the weak controller and the strong noncontroller can simultaneously appropriate some quasi-rent, so both are willing to invest in the firm.

From the standpoint of aggregate surplus maximization, entry is efficient when $s^* - y_K - y_L = 0$, so output is efficient and neither input enjoys an equilibrium rent. This can occur in equilibrium if only one of the inputs is specialized and that input is also strong. But it cannot occur when both inputs are specialized, for two reasons. First, output is too large and surplus is not maximized. Second, one of the inputs gains an ex ante rent when $y_K/\alpha_K \neq y_L/\alpha_L$. The rent goes to the input with the lower of these two ratios. Entry ceases prematurely because in equilibrium the return on investments in specialized assets has already fallen to zero for the input that does not get a rent. If enough entry occurred to eliminate the rent for the input with the lower ratio of sunk cost to bargaining power, the ex ante payoff for the input for the higher ratio would become negative.

15.6 Surplus Maximization

KMFs can prevail in equilibrium even when LMFs would yield a larger surplus. This occurs when capital is weak and both inputs are specialized, as in the bottom left cell of Figure 15.3. In this case KMFs prevail, but because L is strong, conversion to an LMF after firm-specific assets have already been created would yield more surplus. To this extent, the model vindicates those who argue that LMFs could be desirable despite their marginal status. But the comfort to LMF advocates is tempered by the fact that a symmetric argument applies to LMFs: some LMFs might yield a larger total surplus if they were converted into KMFs. This is true for the bottom right cell of Figure 15.3.

Under the bargaining mechanism examined here, hired inputs may queue for employment when equilibrium organizational forms fail to maximize total surplus. For example, suppose that capital is weak and capital is specialized but labor is not (the top left cell in Figure 15.3). The KMF prevails in equilibrium, but firm output is too large, labor has a rent $\alpha_L s_K > 0$, and workers queue for jobs.

If employers could require workers to bid competitively for jobs in this situation, employers would be compensated ex ante for the rent $\alpha_L s_K$ and the labor market would clear. This would help overcome the problem of suboptimal entry, because investors would now capture the entire surplus s_K. But even so, the ex post participation constraint for labor would remain nonbinding at the production stage, leading to excessive output and a surplus of s_K rather than s^*.

Taking the noncontractibility of output as given, the problem boils down to one of noncontractible investment. In the scenario under consideration, if the KMF were to be replaced by an LMF, surplus would be maximized at the production stage because L is strong and would internalize the depreciation costs borne by asset owners. The reason this does not occur is that LMFs cannot induce investors to provide firm-specific physical assets. If such investments were contractible, an entrepreneur could organize an LMF and pay the investors to supply these assets. However, even if K and L both know the characteristics of the assets supplied by K, a court might be unable to verify these characteristics, or the contracts might be too costly or complex for the parties to formulate in the first place.

Once a capitalist firm has been established and specialized assets are already in place, there are incentives to reassign control rights to labor if the LMF would generate a larger surplus. But when capital does not appropriate any quasi-rent as a hired input and physical investments are noncontractible, there is no incentive for outside asset owners to maintain the firm's capital stock after it is reorganized as an LMF. This undermines the long run survival of the LMF. Employee takeovers of KMFs tend to involve firms that are in financial difficulty, and maintenance of the existing capital stock (whether by outsiders or workers themselves) is seldom a central concern under such circumstances.

The analogous problem for capitalist firms, that of inducing workers to acquire specialized skills, is frequently solved by having employers bear training costs or by means of informal training on the job. Because skills can often be maintained simply by using them, incentives for the maintenance of such assets seldom pose a serious dilemma for the capitalist firm. An LMF could therefore be reorganized as a KMF if this increases total surplus, without necessarily threatening the maintenance of specific human capital.

An alternative scenario is for K to create any required assets unilaterally and then sell LMF membership rights to workers. Upon paying a competitive membership price to K, workers would get claims on the firm's profit stream, the right to manage the firm, and the right to negotiate a rental fee for the use of the physical assets belonging to K. If the membership market functions smoothly and the LMF maximizes surplus, K will extract the surplus $s^*(p)$ ex ante and voluntarily incur the sunk cost y_K when $s^*(p) \geq y_K$. Entry decisions will be optimal and output will be chosen correctly ex post. Because workers receive a zero ex ante payoff net of membership fees, the labor market clears.

This approach removes the need for third-party verification, because prospective LMF members can now directly inspect the firm's assets before deciding whether to pay the membership fee demanded by K. However, incentives for K to maintain or expand the firm's capital stock remain problematic. Also, as we have seen in Chapters 10 and 11, LMF membership markets are vulnerable to information asymmetries because workers may not be able to observe the true value of the assets supplied by K.

Finally, LMFs might combine the roles of capital and labor supplier by treating physical assets as the collective property of the enterprise. Under this solution, the LMF no longer hires capital from outside owners, and therefore the bargaining problem vanishes. One potential objection is that LMFs with collective capital ownership will underinvest (see Section 9.5), although the evidence for this phenomenon is thin. Another is that LMF members will free ride on the maintenance of collective assets (Alchian and Demsetz, 1972). A third objection is the usual one that workers may lack the wealth required to supply their own capital. I will return to the latter problem in Chapters 17 and 18.

15.7 Postscript

This chapter is a simplified and extensively rewritten version of the article "Why Capital Hires Labor: A Bargaining Perspective," originally published in the *American Economic Review* (Dow, 1993c). I am grateful to Gil Skillman, Louis Putterman, Sam Bowles, Herb Gintis, and Margaret Duncan for discussions of the original paper. Marcel Boyer, Christophe Deissenberg, and Rick Szostak provided helpful advice on early drafts.

The main changes here are the use of quadratic cost functions rather than general convex cost functions, a more casual treatment of technical bargaining issues, and (one hopes) clearer economic intuition. Readers interested in the previously unpublished proofs of the formal propositions in Dow (1993c) can find them at www.cambridge.org/9781107132979.

Scholars in transaction cost economics have long pointed out that the bargaining costs arising under bilateral monopoly (say, between a firm producing a good and another firm that uses the good as an input) can be avoided by placing the firms under common ownership (Klein et al., 1978; Williamson, 1979). In the present context, bargaining can likewise be avoided by having the same agents supply both capital and labor. I discussed this in 1993 but failed to stress the essential point: due to the inalienability of labor, it is impossible for investors to own workers and thus to contribute both inputs, but there is no parallel obstacle preventing workers from owning physical assets. If bargaining between separate capital and labor suppliers is problematic, this is a strong reason why LMFs with collective asset ownership should prevail, and one needs an equally strong reason why LMFs have offsetting liabilities that make them rare.

There is also an empirical question: what facts, if any, does the model explain? The model is consistent with the dominance of KMFs in industries where physical assets are firm specific while skills are generic. It also predicts the emergence of LMFs, or at least a nontrivial employee role in KMF governance, in industries where skills are firm specific but physical assets are generic. One can certainly argue that physical assets are generic for law firms, taxi services, and a wide range of other activities where LMFs are common. But it is not clear that lawyers and taxi drivers make significant firm-specific investments in human capital (it seems more likely that their skills would be transferable across many firms), so the relevance of the model is debatable. In general, the empirical literature has not identified any robust correlation between the specificity of physical or human assets and the locus of control, so for now such relationships remain speculative.

The model in this chapter assumes that decisions about output and investment are not subject to contracts enforced by third parties, but it treats agreements about payments to the hired inputs (the wage in KMFs, the rental fee in LMFs) as binding once they have been negotiated. In Chapters 16–18, I move to a repeated game setting where input levels and side payments are enforced by the input suppliers themselves. As I hope to show in Chapters 17 and 18, this is a useful framework for studying the intertemporal implications of alienable capital and inalienable labor.

I conclude with a note on terminology. As mentioned in Chapter 14, the concept of "opportunism" introduced to transaction cost economics by Oliver Williamson involves the pursuit of self-interest with guile. In Chapters 16–19, I apply this term to any pursuit of self-interest by one agent at the expense of others in a context where such behavior is not restrained by legally binding contracts. Guile may or may not be relevant. In this usage, "opportunism" is simply strategic behavior when the interests of agents conflict.

PART VII

OPPORTUNISM PROBLEMS II

16

Asset Ownership and Work Incentives

16.1 Introduction

There are strong economic reasons why individual workers should own their own tools. This guarantees that workers will pay attention to maintenance, and it avoids costly monitoring or bargaining with an outsider who has no direct role in production. Precisely because it is so easy to see why a carpenter would own a hammer or a farmer would own a tractor, it is puzzling that large physical assets such as factories are not jointly owned by the workers who use them. This is especially true when asset maintenance is hard for outsiders to observe or when use of the asset requires specialized skills.

One popular approach to this puzzle is to identify incentive benefits that could arise from outside ownership. Alchian and Demsetz (1972) argue that firms require a central owner with strong incentives to monitor asset use, because otherwise individual workers would free ride on joint assets by depreciating them excessively. Holmstrom (1982) suggests that an outside asset owner can provide effort incentives by imposing group penalties on employees when team output is too low. Holmstrom and Milgrom (1991, 1994) show that outside ownership can be attractive if it is desirable for workers to have low-powered effort incentives.

Here I explore the interactions between asset ownership and work incentives in a repeated game framework where effort supply and side payments are both self-enforced. Incentives are provided ultimately by the threat that employment relationships will end through quitting or firing. The model allows flexible transfers in each period, before and after production, as well as transfers at the start of each new employment relationship. It also incorporates match-specific investments in physical assets and skills. In this sense, the model builds on Chapter 15, because the match-specific investments studied here are conceptually similar to the firm-specific investments examined in that chapter.

Two organizational forms are compared: outside ownership, in which someone external to the production team owns the firm's physical assets, and joint ownership, in which the firm's workforce owns these assets. For each case, I characterize the payoff frontier determined by the effort levels and profit distributions that are supportable through self-enforcing equilibria. In general, these frontiers differ and depend on search parameters.

Despite these apparent asymmetries, the two ownership systems are equivalent. For every point along the second-best frontier of an outside ownership economy, there is a point on the frontier of a joint ownership economy that gives all agents identical present values. Conversely, for every point along the frontier of a joint ownership economy, there is a point on the frontier of an outside ownership economy that gives identical present values. This isomorphism arises because as long as inputs are unchanged in an ownership transition, the temptations to deviate from the equilibrium path are also unchanged. Furthermore, the total surplus resulting from a continuation of relationships among the input suppliers stays constant. This conservation of surplus across ownership structures makes it possible to devise an incentive scheme that supports the original input vector under the new ownership system. The present values of the agents are unchanged because any differences in the division of profit are precisely offset by differences in the bundling or unbundling of the factor payments received by the agents.

If capital is scarce, in the sense that job vacancies can be filled more rapidly than workers can find jobs, then total welfare is maximized when workers receive all profit in each firm. If labor is scarce, then total welfare is maximized when asset owners receive all profit in each firm. This counter-intuitive result arises because suppliers of the scarce input are tempted to break off relationships prematurely. In order to avoid deviations of this kind, the more abundant input must appropriate profit. However, the required profit distribution can be implemented under either ownership regime. Furthermore, when an allocation is second best in an outside ownership economy, it is impossible to obtain a Pareto improvement by switching to joint ownership, and vice versa.

These isomorphism results are important to the themes of this book in several ways. First, as discussed in Chapters 4, 9, 14, and 15, the literature on labor-managed firms has seen a good deal of controversy over the merits or defects of collective asset ownership. Various writers have claimed that such arrangements are costly or infeasible, and have concluded that productive assets must be owned by outsiders (capitalists). Thus it is interesting that in at least one economic environment where there is no obvious reason to expect such a result, asset ownership is neutral with respect to resource allocation.

As noted earlier, many authors have argued that asset ownership is closely related to effort incentives for workers. In one of the first attempts to explain the capitalist firm using economic theory, Alchian and Demsetz (1972) claimed that capitalists would both own the firm's physical assets and monitor worker effort, because in the context of team production, collective asset ownership by workers would lead to free riding (see Section 8.2). Similarly, Holmstrom (1982, 325) remarks: "the fact that capitalistic firms feature separation of ownership and labor implies that the free-rider problem is less pronounced in such firms than in closed organizations like partnerships." By contrast with Alchian and Demsetz (1972), Holmstrom (1982) does not derive his conclusion from monitoring considerations, but rather from the idea that external owners can use group bonuses or penalties that would be infeasible in a worker partnership with a balanced budget.

Holmstrom (1982) assumes that an outside asset owner can sign a binding contract with workers in which wages depend upon output. His approach has been criticized for neglecting moral hazard by the owner, who might cheat the employees (Eswaran and Kotwal, 1984; Andolfatto and Nosal, 1997). In this chapter, I assume that there are no legally binding contracts, so all side payments (such as wages) are self-enforced and all moral hazard issues are bilateral. This overturns Holmstrom's conclusion and demonstrates that outside ownership does no better (or worse) than joint ownership in solving free rider problems.

More generally, the model in this chapter highlights the dangers in trying to study ownership regimes or effort incentives for a single firm in isolation. Self-enforcement leads to fundamental incentive externalities across firms. A worker's incentive to supply effort in the present firm depends on the payoff from quitting or firing, which depends on how profit will be distributed in future firms. The same is true for an owner's incentive to provide wages or bonuses. Thus, it is necessary to solve for a self-enforcing equilibrium at the level of the market as a whole, and the efficiency of resource allocation cannot be separated cleanly from issues of income distribution.

At a still higher level of generality, I emphasized in Chapters 2–5 that there is an isomorphism between KMFs and LMFs when markets are complete and competitive. I then argued in Chapters 6–8 that any theory capable of explaining observed asymmetries between KMFs and LMFs would require two elements: a source of market imperfection and an underlying asymmetry between capital and labor. The market imperfection in this chapter is simple and deep: there are no legally binding contracts, so *all* relevant markets are missing. Even so, outside ownership and joint ownership support the same resource allocations. The lesson to be drawn is that while market imperfections are *necessary* to explain the differences between KMFs and LMFs, they are not *sufficient*. One must also identify an asymmetry between capital and labor. I return to this point in Chapters 17–19.

The idea that markets are missing due to a lack of legally binding contracts is not a new one. Transaction cost economics argues that incomplete contracts are fundamental to the very existence of firms (see Chapter 14). In particular, theorists of the firm often assume that investments in firm-specific physical or human capital cannot be subjected to legally binding contracts (see Chapter 15). Theorists also routinely accept the view that worker effort is noncontractible due to problems of observation or verification.

Nevertheless, it is often assumed that wages can be conditioned on individual or team output, an idea that underpins principal-agent theory (Mas-Colell, Whinston, and Green, 1995, ch. 14). But when external enforcers cannot verify the quantity or quality of output, such contracts are also ruled out. Even a contract requiring an unconditional transfer at a particular point in time (like the wages or rental fees from Chapter 15) may be infeasible if outsiders cannot verify the occurrence or size of such side payments.

In fact, external contract enforcement in a firm may be impossible or prohibitively costly for a number of reasons (Dow, 2004):

   (a) Third parties cannot verify compliance with contract terms.
   (b) Third parties lack incentives to carry out costly enforcement tasks.
   (c) Third parties cannot impose large penalties on violators, because the latter are hard to find or have limited wealth.
   (d) Third parties are unwilling to punish violators for legal or moral reasons.
   (e) The agents directly involved cannot anticipate all future events, cannot write them down, or cannot spell out detailed state-contingent obligations.

The study of firms based on self-enforcement thus holds more than hypothetical interest.

There is a close kinship between the theory developed here and earlier repeated game models of effort supply (Cremer, 1986; Bull, 1987; Putterman and Skillman, 1992; Dong and Dow, 1993a). My focus on dismissal threats as a source of effort incentives is also in the spirit of efficiency wage models (Shapiro and Stiglitz, 1984; Bowles, 1985). The closest previous research is by MacLeod and Malcomson (1989, 1993, 1998) on self-enforcing labor market equilibria. These authors adopt a repeated game framework and derive market-wide incentive constraints like those in Section 16.3. However, MacLeod and Malcomson treat outside ownership as a given and focus on bonuses and efficiency wages rather than the nature of property rights within firms.

Section 16.2 outlines the general modeling framework. Incentive constraints for economies with outside and joint asset ownership are derived in Sections 16.3 and 16.4. Section 16.5 establishes the main isomorphism result and discusses some welfare issues. Section 16.6 provides some concluding remarks, 16.7 is a postscript, and 16.8 is an appendix containing further information on the formal propositions.

16.2 The Model

Consider a labor market with many identical firms and many identical workers. Production requires an indestructible asset and a team of $n \geq 2$ workers. The production function is $q(e_1, e_2, .. e_n)$ where $e_i \geq 0$ is the effort supplied by worker i. This function is symmetric, concave, increasing when all inputs are positive, and twice continuously differentiable. Inputs are essential ($e_i = 0$ for any i gives $q = 0$) and complementary (all cross partials are nonnegative). The physical asset is also essential and assumed to be alienable among the agents.

Workers have utility functions $u_i = y_i - c(e_i)$ where y_i is current income and $c(e_i)$ is the cost of effort. This cost function is identical for all workers with $c(0) = c'(0) = 0$, $c(e_i) > 0$ and $c'(e_i) > 0$ for $e_i > 0$, and $c''(e_i) > 0$ for $e_i \geq 0$. An asset owner's utility is simply her current-period income. It does not matter how physical assets are created, and their cost is ignored. Output is sold at a competitive price $p > 0$. The surplus $\pi = pq(e_1 .. e_n) - \Sigma_i\, c(e_i)$ has a finite maximum for any $p > 0$. All agents are risk neutral and infinitely lived, with a per-period discount factor $\delta \in (0,1)$. Workers can get a zero payoff in any period from home production, while owners of physical assets can get a zero payoff by shutting down.

For outside ownership, events in each period unfold as follows. The first three steps apply only to firms where one or more jobs are vacant at the start of a period. The remaining steps apply to all firms.

(a) *Search:* Unmatched agents search for partners. A firm having one or more job vacancies either fills all of its vacancies or fills none. The probability of filling vacancies is $\beta_K \in (0,1]$. The probability that an unemployed worker gets a job is $\beta_L \in (0,1]$.

(b) *Investment:* The owners of assets may need to alter them prior to use by new workers, and new workers may need to acquire firm-specific skills before producing. The costs of these specialized investments per new worker are denoted by $g_K \geq 0$ and $g_L \geq 0$.

(c) *Fees:* After investment, there are simultaneous transfers from the asset owner to each new worker, $m_K \geq 0$, and from newly hired workers to the asset owner, $m_L \geq 0$.

(d) *Wages:* In all firms, side payments can be made prior to production. A wage payment from the asset owner to a worker is denoted by $w_K \geq 0$. A simultaneous rental payment from a worker to the owner for use of the physical asset is denoted by $w_L \geq 0$.

(e) *Effort:* Workers in each firm choose effort levels simultaneously, and output is produced according to the function $q(e_1 .. e_n)$.

(f) *Appropriation:* After output has been produced, the resulting firm revenue pq is divided. Each worker receives the fraction $s \in [0, 1/n]$ of pq, with the remaining share $1 - ns$ going to the asset owner.

(g) *Bonuses:* After output has been produced and appropriated, simultaneous side payments are again possible. A post-production side payment from an owner to a worker is denoted by $b_K \geq 0$. A transfer from a worker to an owner is denoted by $b_L \geq 0$.

(h) *Renewal:* At the end of the period, the owner decides whether to fire some or all workers, and workers simultaneously decide whether to stay or quit. With probability $1-\alpha \in (0,1)$, nature dissolves the team even if the owner and all workers want to continue.

Because no output can be produced unless all jobs are occupied, I assume that firms either fill all of their vacancies or none of them. Workers who do not find jobs get zero payoffs for the current period and can search again in the next period. Likewise, if a job is not filled, the asset owner can return to the market in the next period.

When firm-specific investments (g_K, g_L) are positive, they are borne by the owner and worker, respectively. In this case, either party can refrain from investment, which is equivalent to a vacancy remaining unfilled: no output is produced, and the owner and worker search again next period. If the required expenditure for an agent is zero, that agent is automatically productive and her investment decision can be ignored.

Fees at the start of a new match determine how present values will be distributed. Wage or rental payments can be used to reassign the profit flow from an ongoing match, while bonuses enable owners to condition current-period worker compensation on effort. Further opportunities for side payments would not alter any conclusions. Indeed, there is some redundancy in the use of both fees and wages, but this is helpful in two ways. First, it makes the point that, when suppliers of nonscarce inputs receive rents, it is not merely because fees have been omitted from the arsenal of tools used to clear the labor market—a criticism sometimes advanced against efficiency wage theory. Second, the nature of the equilibrium incentive scheme differs across ownership systems. I will show at the end of Section 16.3 that when capital is fully utilized and inputs are generic, outside ownership implies nonpositive fees, so workers do not pay up front for jobs. I will also show at the end of Section 16.4 that under the same conditions, joint ownership implies nonnegative fees, so firms may charge a positive price for membership.

Production revenues are divided at the appropriation stage. For simplicity, I treat the share parameter as an exogenous element in the ownership system of the firm. While this conflicts with the self-enforcement assumption used elsewhere, the share parameter could be endogenized without changing any conclusions. If the owner and workers play a zero-sum game to divide revenue after it has been generated and the equilibrium shares in this appropriation game do not depend on the amount of revenue to be distributed, the payoffs supportable in the larger game are identical to those in the present model. In any case, it should not simply be assumed that the natural sharing scheme is one in which the asset owner appropriates all revenue and redistributes it through side payments. As noted in the remarks after Proposition 1 in Section 16.3, this actually maximizes the temptations for cheating. Such firms are at a disadvantage relative to outside ownership firms where workers share revenues among themselves and pay rental fees to the asset owner.

The renewal stage reflects the fact that continuation of employment relationships is voluntary. Nature may also dissolve a production team exogenously. I abstract from sources of labor turnover that are idiosyncratic to individual workers, which complicates the analysis without adding further insight.

Throughout the chapter, I assume that agents observe all events occurring in their own firms but nothing occurring in any other firm. In particular, asset owners and incumbent workers observe all new matches, investments, fees, wages, effort, bonuses, and renewal decisions. Unemployed workers do not see any of these actions. At the investment stage, newly matched workers are uninformed about the total number of vacancies filled in the current period; at the fee stage, they know only whether investments were made for their own job. After the fee stage, they learn how many jobs were filled in the current period, discover what investments were made for the other jobs, and observe all further actions within the firm. In an equilibrium with no quitting or firing, Bayesian reasoning requires newcomers to believe that vacancies either arose by exogenous dissolution in an earlier period or reflect a lack of success in filling jobs since the firm was founded. New workers do not infer from the existence of a vacancy that some earlier deviation triggered dismissal or quitting; thus they continue along the equilibrium path when hired. I discuss some alternative assumptions about effort monitoring in Section 16.6.

When firms have outside asset owners, the strategies of owners and workers are denoted by σ_K and σ_L. For each possible sequence of past moves, σ_K determines for the owner whether to search if vacancies exist, whether to invest ($g_K \geq 0$) if a vacancy is filled, what fee ($m_K \geq 0$) to pay each new worker, what wage ($w_K \geq 0$) to pay each worker before production, what bonus ($b_K \geq 0$) to pay each worker after production, and whether to fire each worker at the renewal stage. For each possible sequence of past moves, σ_L determines for the worker whether to search for a job if unemployed, whether to invest ($g_L \geq 0$) if matched, what fee ($m_L \geq 0$) to pay the owner, what rental ($w_L \geq 0$) to pay the owner before production, what effort level ($e \geq 0$) to choose, what bonus ($b_L \geq 0$) to pay the owner after production, and whether to quit at the renewal stage.

Identical agents are assumed to adopt identical strategies in equilibrium, and asset owners treat all workers identically. I refer to such equilibria as symmetric equilibria. I limit attention to stationary equilibria in which actions are identical in every period along the equilibrium path. All equilibria are required to be subgame perfect.

16.3 Equilibrium with Outside Ownership

When firms have outside owners, a stationary and symmetric market equilibrium can be summarized by (m_K, m_L; w_K, w_L; e; b_K, b_L) where e is effort and the other variables are nonnegative side payments. In a nontrivial equilibrium, unattached agents must be willing to search and invest. All equilibria discussed here have this property. There are two kinds of stationary equilibria: those where matches end by quitting and/or firing after one period and those where matches are renewed until dissolved by nature. Quitting or firing is the harshest possible response to any deviation, because worse punishments can always be avoided by quitting (for workers) or firing (for owners). One-period equilibria can be used to punish deviations from equilibria with renewal, but they only support one-shot Nash effort levels. The same effort levels can be supported when matches are renewed, so I focus here on equilibria with renewal.

Suppose that (σ_K, σ_L) is a stationary, symmetric, subgame perfect strategy pair where search, investment, and renewal occur. Let V_K be the owner's equilibrium present value per job after the fee stage when all jobs are filled, with V_L as the corresponding present value for a worker. Let U_K be the equilibrium present value per job the owner obtains by search in a period where all jobs are vacant, with U_L as the present value an unemployed worker obtains by search. Define $m \equiv m_L - m_K$ to be the net fee paid by each new worker, $w \equiv w_K - w_L$ to be the net wage paid by the asset owner to each worker, and $b \equiv b_K - b_L$ to be the net bonus paid by the owner to each worker on the equilibrium path. Let $q(e)$ be output when all workers choose the same effort level e. Stationarity implies

$$V_K = -w + (1/n - s)pq(e) - b + \delta[\alpha V_K + (1 - \alpha)U_K] \qquad (1a)$$

$$V_L = w + spq(e) - c(e) + b + \delta[\alpha V_L + (1 - \alpha)U_L] \qquad (1b)$$

The present value per job derived from search by an owner who has n vacancies is $U_K = \beta_K(V_K + m - g_K)[1 + \delta(1-\beta_K) + \delta^2(1-\beta_K)^2 + ..]$, and U_L is specified in a similar way. This gives

$$U_K = \beta_K(V_K + m - g_K)/[1 - \delta(1 - \beta_K)] \qquad (2a)$$

$$U_L = \beta_L(V_L - m - g_L)/[1 - \delta(1 - \beta_L)] \qquad (2b)$$

It will often be convenient to use the following change of variables. Define

$$z_K \equiv -w + (1/n - s)pq(e) - b + (1 - \alpha\delta)(m - g_K) \qquad (3a)$$

$$z_L \equiv w + spq(e) - c(e) + b - (1 - \alpha\delta)(m + g_L) \qquad (3b)$$

These are the per-job profit flows for the owner and a worker, adjusted to express fees and investments as per-period averages over the life of the relationship. The total profit stream available for distribution between an owner and worker is

$$z(e) = z_K + z_L = pq(e)/n - c(e) - (1 - \alpha\delta)G \qquad (4)$$

where $G = g_K + g_L$ is the total expenditure on match-specific investments.

Solving the earlier equations for V_K, V_L, U_K, U_L and substituting z_K and z_L yields

$$U_K = \beta_K z_K/(1 - \delta)[1 - \alpha\delta(1 - \beta_K)] \geq 0 \qquad (5a)$$

$$U_L = \beta_L z_L/(1 - \delta)[1 - \alpha\delta(1 - \beta_L)] \geq 0 \qquad (5b)$$

where the inequalities follow from the fact that owners and workers are willing to search. Thus the profit distribution (z_K, z_L) uniquely determines the present values (U_K, U_L) from participation in the labor market. It can also be shown that

$$V_K - U_K = (1 - \beta_K)z_K/[1 - \alpha\delta(1 - \beta_K)] - m + g_K \geq 0 \qquad (6a)$$

$$V_L - U_L = (1 - \beta_L)z_L/[1 - \alpha\delta(1 - \beta_L)] + m + g_L \geq 0 \qquad (6b)$$

where the inequalities follow from the fact that on the equilibrium path, input suppliers are willing to renew their relationships at the end of each period.

Let $Q(e', e)$ be output when one worker chooses e' while all other workers choose e, and define $T(e|s) \equiv \max_{e'} [spQ(e', e) - c(e')] - [spQ(e, e) - c(e)] \geq 0$. A best reply exists by the assumptions of Section 16.2. $T(e|s)$ is the largest net benefit a worker can gain by deviating from e when everyone else is supplying e. Holding side payments fixed, this is the temptation for an individual worker to cheat. Now let $\theta_K \equiv \alpha\delta(1 - \beta_K)/[1 - \alpha\delta(1 - \beta_K)]$ and $\theta_L \equiv \alpha\delta(1 - \beta_L)/[1 - \alpha\delta(1 - \beta_L)]$. I also write $V = V_K + V_L$ and $U = U_K + U_L$.

Proposition 1
Outside ownership economy: The effort $e \geq 0$ and profit division $(z_K, z_L) \geq 0$ with $z_K + z_L = z(e)$ can be supported by a stationary, symmetric, and subgame perfect strategy pair (σ_K, σ_L) with search, investment, and renewal in equilibrium, starting from a history in which every firm has either n vacancies or no vacancies at the search stage, if and only if $\theta_K z_K + \theta_L z_L \geq T(e|s) - \alpha\delta G$. This is equivalent to $\alpha\delta(V-U) \geq T(e|s)$.

The full proof is lengthy and can be found at www.cambridge.org/ 9781107132979. A description of the equilibrium strategies is provided in Section 16.8.

Remark

Let $e^N > 0$ be the unique nontrivial Nash equilibrium effort level for the one-shot effort supply game in which each worker has the residual claim $s = 1/n$. If $e \in [0, e^N]$, there is a share $s \in [0, 1/n]$ such that $T(e|s) = 0$. If $e > e^N$, $T(e|s)$ is minimized at $s = 1/n$ for the given e, which yields $T(e|1/n) > 0$.

If effort e does not exceed the level e^N, there is some value of the share parameter s that removes any temptation for workers to cheat. By Proposition 1, at this value of s, any distribution $(z_K, z_L) \geq 0$ of the profit $z_K + z_L = z(e)$ can be supported because $T(e|s) = 0$ and $G \geq 0$. In cases for which e exceeds e^N, the temptation to cheat is minimized by giving workers the largest possible residual claim $s = 1/n$, implying that the asset owner has no direct claim on revenues. However, some temptation remains, and Proposition 1 may impose restrictions on the distribution of $z(e)$ as discussed later. Because this is the interesting case, I assume that $e > e^N$ and $s = 1/n$ unless otherwise stated and abbreviate $T(e) \equiv T(e|1/n)$.

The investment expenditure (G) plays two roles in the model. First, it appears in Proposition 1, where the incentive constraint is relaxed for higher G because preservation of existing employment relationships becomes more valuable, giving quitting and firing threats additional force. However, higher up-front costs also reduce the joint profit from any match according to (4). In both cases, only total firm-specific investment matters; the sunk costs (g_K, g_L) do not matter separately.

Figure 16.1 depicts supportable effort levels and profit distributions when capital is scarce relative to labor ($\beta_K > \beta_L$). Each line with slope -1 in Figure 16.1 corresponds to a fixed effort level and therefore a constant total profit $z(e)$. The first best effort e^* that maximizes $z(e)$ can be supported if and only if the present value of production surpluses per worker, adjusted for search and match-specific setup costs, is large enough relative to the maximum one-period payoff a worker can obtain by deviating to some other effort level. The figure is drawn under the assumption that the first best effort is not feasible.

The inequality $\beta_K > \beta_L$ implies $\theta_K < \theta_L$ in Proposition 1. Using the fact that $z(e)$ is constant along an isoprofit line and substituting $z_K + z_L = z(e)$

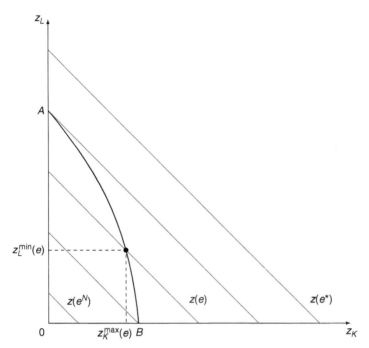

Figure 16.1 Second-Best Frontier for Outside Ownership Economy (Capital Scarce
Relative to Labor: $\beta_K > \beta_L$)

into the incentive constraint, Proposition 1 imposes a lower bound $z_L^{\min}(e)$
on the profit stream paid to labor for a given effort e, or equivalently an
upper bound $z_K^{\max}(e)$ on the profit paid to capital. The curve AB is the
second-best payoff frontier for an outside ownership economy. Along AB,
the market incentive constraint holds with equality, while all (z_K, z_L) pairs
below this curve satisfy the incentive constraint with inequality.
Distributions of profit must also satisfy $(z_K, z_L) \geq 0$ due to the participation
constraints $(U_K, U_L) \geq 0$ from (5). The intercept A is obtained by setting
$z_K = 0$ in Proposition 1 so that $z_L = z(e) = [T(e|s) - \alpha\delta G]/\theta_L$ and finding the
largest value of e for which this equality holds. The intercept B is found in a
similar way.

According to the remark after Proposition 1, all points along the isoprofit line for $z(e^N)$ are feasible when $s = 1/n$ and all points below this line
are feasible for some $s < 1/n$. The vertical intercept A exceeds the horizontal
intercept B, and the frontier cannot go above the isoprofit line passing
through A or below the isoprofit line passing through B. The frontier cuts

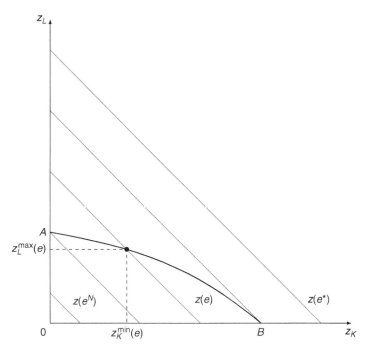

Figure 16.2 Second-Best Frontier for Outside Ownership Economy (Labor Scarce Relative to Capital: $\beta_K < \beta_L$)

across each intermediate isoprofit line just once. Backward-bending segments are not excluded as long as no isoprofit line is crossed more than once.

Figure 16.2 shows the situation in which labor is scarce relative to capital ($\beta_K < \beta_L$). As in Figure 16.1, the first best effort e^* is assumed to be infeasible. Again one can substitute $z_K + z_L = z(e)$ into the incentive constraint in Proposition 1. This now yields an upper bound $z_L^{max}(e)$ on the profit to workers for a given effort level or, equivalently, a lower bound $z_K^{min}(e)$ on profit to capital. In this case, the horizontal intercept B exceeds the vertical intercept A, and the frontier cuts each isoprofit line once from below. Again backward-bending segments cannot be ruled out.

The last case arises if capital and labor are equally abundant ($\beta_K = \beta_L$). In this case, Proposition 1 imposes no restriction on profit distribution because only the sum $z_K + z_L = z(e)$ appears in the incentive constraint. Effort e is supportable if and only if $\theta z(e) \geq T(e) - \alpha \delta G$. The second-best frontier is a straight line with slope -1 corresponding to the maximum feasible $z(e)$, which may coincide with the first-best frontier or lie below it.

Figure 16.1 indicates that newly matched workers may receive a rent if capital is scarce and labor is abundant, because $z_L > 0$ implies $U_L > 0$ by (5b). This conflicts with the Walrasian idea that wages should fall when labor is in excess supply. Notice that in Figure 16.2 asset owners may have to receive a rent even though it is only workers who might shirk. Thus, it is the market environment summarized by the search parameters β_K and β_L, not the identity of potential shirkers, that places restrictions on profit distribution.

It is worth emphasizing that workers may need to receive an ex ante rent in Figure 16.1 where labor is abundant relative to capital, even though asset owners are explicitly allowed to charge up-front hiring fees at the start of each new employment relationship. It is not any lack of flexibility in side payments that accounts for the possible existence of non–market-clearing equilibria. The underlying problem is that moral hazard is bilateral: workers can shirk and quit, but conversely owners can cheat on bonuses and fire innocent workers. Any market-wide change in the level of hiring fees mitigates one moral hazard problem while aggravating the other. It can also be shown that nonnegative bonuses are always paid by asset owners to workers along the frontier, and if $s = 1/n$ so temptations for cheating are minimized, workers lease assets from owners.

Stronger results are obtained when capital scarcity leads to $\beta_K = 1$ (vacancies are filled immediately). If it is also true that $G = 0$ so both inputs are generic, the inequality in Proposition 1 becomes $\theta_L z_L \geq T(e|s)$. The temptation $T(e|s)$ is strictly positive if effort exceeds the one-shot level. Thus, the incentive constraint implies that labor must receive a rent, and the renewal constraint $V_K \geq U_K$ from (6a) implies that the net fee satisfies $m \leq 0$. Despite the rent to newly matched workers, owners cannot collect hiring fees in such a market. This is consistent with the fact that capitalist firms almost never demand up-front fees in exchange for employment, even when employees enjoy large wage premiums and applicants queue for jobs.

16.4 Equilibrium with Joint Ownership

Joint ownership of an asset implies that team members cannot be deprived of their ownership stakes as a punishment for shirking, because they have property rights in their jobs. Of course, incumbent team members are free to quit and can sell their ownership claims if they do so. In this section, I assume that all firms have joint asset ownership and compare this system with the outside ownership economy from Section 16.3.

Capital and labor supply are bundled under joint ownership, so no one can buy a claim on a firm without also becoming a labor supplier. When an unemployed worker is matched to a vacant job, she must first decide whether to invest $G = g_K + g_L$. By contrast with Section 16.3, it is the new worker who invests g_K, because there is no outside owner and the previous incumbent has departed. At the fee stage, the newcomer can make a voluntary transfer of $(m - g_K) \geq 0$ to her predecessor. A newly matched worker does not obtain property rights in a firm until after this fee has been paid. I assume that the worker's predecessor can block access to the firm but is indifferent toward doing so and makes the job available as long as the equilibrium side payment is forthcoming. The effort and renewal stages are as before, except that team members cannot be fired. After a worker leaves by quitting or exogenous dissolution, the resulting vacancy is filled in the next period with probability β_K. Along the equilibrium path, this leads to a payment $(m - g_K)$ from the worker's successor. All informational assumptions are identical to those used in Sections 16.2 and 16.3. I ignore any wealth constraints or credit market imperfections that might prevent workers from financing claims on a joint ownership firm.

Because joint owners are symmetric, there is no need to consider side payments at the wage or bonus stages. Such transfers create unnecessary temptations for cheating and cancel out ex ante from a distributional standpoint. Accordingly, in what follows only the search, investment, fee, effort, and renewal stages are relevant. At the appropriation stage, $s = 1/n$ because no outsider has a claim on revenue. For each possible sequence of past moves, the worker strategy σ specifies whether to search, whether to invest, what to pay the previous incumbent, what effort to supply, and whether to continue or quit.

Equilibria in which everyone quits after one period are uninteresting except as punishments for deviations from an equilibrium path involving renewal. Therefore, I investigate stationary, symmetric equilibria where unemployed workers search, firm-specific investments occur, and workers renew their membership positions in firms along the equilibrium path. Let V be the equilibrium present value of membership after the fee stage but prior to production, and let U be the equilibrium present value prior to search for a worker who resigned from a firm at the end of the preceding period and has an unsold claim on that firm. Writing $U = U_K + U_L$, stationarity implies

$$V = pq(e)/n - c(e) + \delta[\alpha V + (1 - \alpha)U] \tag{7}$$

$$U_K = \beta_K(m - g_K)/[1 - \delta(1 - \beta_K)] \tag{8a}$$

$$U_L = \beta_L(V - m - g_L)/[1 - \delta(1 - \beta_L)] \tag{8b}$$

U_K is the present value obtained by a departing member from the sale of her membership rights in a firm, and U_L is the present value obtained by searching for a new position.

It is often more illuminating to split the present value U in a slightly different way. Define

$$\underline{U}_K = U_K + \beta_L\delta(1 - \alpha)U_K/(1 - \delta)[1 - \alpha\delta(1 - \beta_L)] \tag{9a}$$

$$\underline{U}_L = U_L - \beta_L\delta(1 - \alpha)U_K/(1 - \delta)[1 - \alpha\delta(1 - \beta_L)] \tag{9b}$$

Thus $\underline{U}_K + \underline{U}_L = U_K + U_L = U$. The underscored present values are pure returns to capital and labor from the search process, netting out the income associated with future sales of membership rights from U_L and treating this instead as a return to capital.

Profit flows are defined as in (3) and (4):

$$z_K \equiv (1 - \alpha\delta)(m - g_K) \tag{10a}$$

$$z_L \equiv pq(e)/n - c(e) - (1 - \alpha\delta)(m + g_L) \tag{10b}$$

$$z(e) = z_K + z_L = pq(e)/n - c(e) - (1 - \alpha\delta)G \tag{11}$$

Let $\eta \equiv [1-\delta(1-\beta_L)]/[1-\delta(1-\beta_K)]$. Solving for V, U_K, and U_L from (7) and (8), switching to $\underline{U}_K$ and $\underline{U}_L$, and substituting for (z_K, z_L) from (10) gives

$$\underline{U}_K = \eta\beta_K z_K/(1 - \delta)[1 - \alpha\delta(1 - \beta_L)] \tag{12a}$$

$$\underline{U}_L = \beta_L z_L/(1 - \delta)[1 - \alpha\delta(1 - \beta_L)] \tag{12b}$$

The solution for $\underline{U}_L$ in (12b) is identical to U_L in (5b). The expression for $\underline{U}_K$ in (12a) differs from U_K in (5a) in two ways: first, by the multiplicative constant η, which exceeds unity when $\beta_L > \beta_K$ and is less than unity in the reverse case; and second, because the denominator of $\underline{U}_K$ in (12a) involves the labor search parameter β_L rather than the capital search parameter β_K as in (5a). For compactness of notation, I define $\Delta \equiv \{\beta_K/(1-\alpha\delta)[1-\delta(1-\beta_K)]\}\cdot\{[1-\delta(1-\beta_K)]/[1-\alpha\delta(1-\beta_K)] - [1-\delta(1-\beta_L)]/[1-\alpha\delta(1-\beta_L)]\}$. Equations parallel to (6a) and (6b) can now be derived.

$$\underline{V}_K - \underline{U}_K = (1 - \beta_K)z_K/[1 - \alpha\delta(1 - \beta_K)] - m + g_K + \Delta z_K \qquad (13a)$$

$$\underline{V}_L - \underline{U}_L = (1 - \beta_L)z_L/[1 - \alpha\delta(1 - \beta_L)] + m + g_L \qquad (13b)$$

These are the pure continuation surpluses to capital and labor, where by construction $\underline{V}_K + \underline{V}_L = V$ and $\underline{U}_K + \underline{U}_L = U$. The labor surplus in (13b) is identical to (6b), but the capital surplus in (13a) differs from (6a) by the term Δz_K. The coefficient Δ is positive if capital is scarce ($\beta_K > \beta_L$) and negative if labor is scarce ($\beta_K < \beta_L$).

Proposition 2

Joint ownership economy: The effort $e \geq 0$ and profit division (z_K, z_L) with $z_K + z_L = z(e)$, $z_K \geq 0$, and $z_L \geq -z_K\delta(1-\alpha)\beta_K/(1-\alpha\delta)[1-\delta(1-\beta_K)]$ can be supported by a stationary, symmetric, and subgame perfect strategy σ with search, investment, and renewal in equilibrium, starting from a history in which every firm has either n vacancies or no vacancies at the search stage, if and only if $(\theta_K + \alpha\delta\Delta)z_K + \theta_L z_L \geq T(e) - \alpha\delta G$. This is equivalent to $\alpha\delta(V-U) \geq T(e)$.

The full proof is lengthy and can be found at www.cambridge.org/ 9781107132979. Section 16.8 describes the nature of the equilibrium strategies.

Assuming that $s = 1/n$ applies in both cases, the only difference between the incentive constraints in Propositions 1 and 2 is the term $\alpha\delta\Delta z_K$ in Proposition 2. The participation constraint $z_K \geq 0$ is identical because this is equivalent to $U_K \geq 0$ in both cases. However, the labor participation constraint $z_L \geq 0$ from Proposition 1 is replaced in Proposition 2 by the weaker inequality $z_L \geq -z_K\delta(1-\alpha)\beta_K/(1-\alpha\delta)[1-\delta(1-\beta_K)]$, corresponding to $U_L \geq 0$ under joint ownership. This occurs because the returns to labor and capital are now bundled so that the participation constraint $U_L \geq 0$ is compatible with a negative profit flow to labor ($z_L < 0$), as long as the profit flow to capital ($z_K > 0$) is large enough to compensate for it.

Figure 16.3 compares supportable distributions of profit for the outside and joint ownership economies when capital is scarce relative to labor ($\beta_K > \beta_L$). As in previous graphs, the first-best effort level is assumed to be infeasible. Capital scarcity implies that $\Delta > 0$, so the second-best frontier AC for joint ownership lies to the right of the

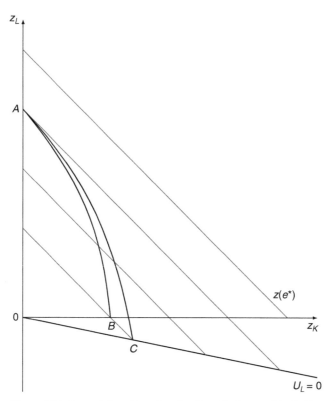

Figure 16.3 Second-Best Frontiers for Outside Ownership (AB) and Joint Ownership (AC) (Capital Scarce Relative to Labor: $\beta_K > \beta_L$)

frontier AB for outside ownership whenever capital receives positive profit ($z_K > 0$). As in Figure 16.1, substituting $z_K + z_L = z(e)$ into the incentive constraint yields a lower bound $z_L^{min}(e)$ for the profit to labor on a given isoprofit line, or an upper bound $z_K^{max}(e)$ on the profit to capital. This distributional constraint is less restrictive under joint ownership. When $z_K = 0$ so $U_K = 0$, the frontiers meet at the point A and profit is the same in the two ownership systems. The two points B and C where $U_L = 0$ holds under outside and joint ownership, respectively, are also on a common isoprofit line.

Figure 16.4 compares the two systems when labor is scarce relative to capital ($\beta_K < \beta_L$). In this case $\Delta < 0$, so the joint ownership frontier AC lies to the left of the outside ownership frontier AB. For a given isoprofit line, there is an upper bound $z_L^{max}(e)$ on the profit to labor, or a lower

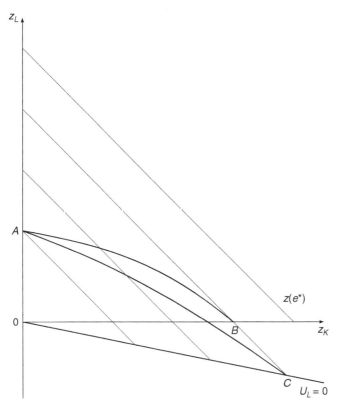

Figure 16.4 Second-Best Frontiers for Outside Ownership (AB) and Joint Ownership (AC) (Labor Scarce Relative to Capital: $\beta_K < \beta_L$)

bound on the profit to capital. This distributional constraint is less restrictive under outside ownership. Again, the frontiers coincide at point A where $U_K = 0$ and the points B and C where $U_L = 0$ are located on the same isoprofit line.

As mentioned at the end of Section 16.3, when capital is scarce and vacancies are filled immediately, $\beta_K = 1$ occurs. If the inputs are also generic ($G = 0$), the participation constraints $U_K \geq 0$ and $U_L \geq 0$ reduce to $V \geq m \geq 0$ in (8). By contrast with the system of outside ownership where only nonpositive fees ($m \leq 0$) were possible for $\beta_K = 1$ and $G = 0$, only nonnegative fees can arise under joint ownership. This is consistent with the fact that labor-managed firms often charge substantial membership fees (Estrin, Jones, and Svejnar, 1987; Craig and Pencavel, 1992), although capitalist firms almost never do.

16.5 The Equivalence Theorem

Sections 16.3 and 16.4 show that outside and joint ownership economies differ in the restrictions they impose upon profit distribution. The fact that one second-best payoff frontier is uniformly further out than the other in Figures 16.3 and 16.4 may suggest that it is possible to achieve a Pareto improvement through a transition from one ownership regime to the other. This impression is misleading. In this section, I show that the two ownership systems are equivalent. For each point on one frontier, there is a unique point on the other frontier that gives every agent the same present value. This isomorphism emerges because the bundling or unbundling of capital and labor supply cancels out the distributional effects resulting from shifts in the incentive constraint.

Proposition 3

Equivalence: Assume that $\beta_K \neq \beta_L$ so the second-best frontiers AB and AC in Figures 16.3 and 16.4 are distinct. For each point (z_K, z_L) on one frontier, there is a unique point (z_K', z_L') on the other frontier, along the same isoprofit line, such that these points have $V' = V$, $U_K' = U_K$, and $U_L' = U_L$.

Proof

The outside ownership frontier intersects each isoprofit line between points A and B once, and does not intersect any other isoprofit line. The joint ownership frontier from A to C has the same feature. Because B and C are located on the same isoprofit line, for any (z_K, z_L) on one frontier, there is a unique (z_K', z_L') on the other with identical profit.

Choose two points along the same isoprofit line such that (z_K, z_L) is on the outside ownership frontier and (z_K', z_L') is on the joint ownership frontier. Let $e \equiv e'$ be the effort level yielding profit $z = z_K + z_L = z_K' + z_L'$. This effort is unique in $[0, e^*]$, because $z(e)$ is increasing on this interval. The constraints from Propositions 1 and 2 can be written as $\alpha\delta(V-U) \geq T(e)$ and $\alpha\delta(V'-U') \geq T(e')$. Because both points are on their respective frontiers, $\alpha\delta(V'-U') = T(e') = T(e) = \alpha\delta(V-U)$, which implies that $V'-V = U'-U$. Summing (1a) and (1b) gives $V = pq/n - c + \delta[\alpha V + (1-\alpha)U]$, while (7) gives $V' = pq'/n - c' + \delta[\alpha V' + (1-\alpha)U']$. The equality $e' = e$ gives $pq'/n - c' = pq/n - c$. Subtracting the first equation from the second gives $V'-V = \delta(1-\alpha)(U'-U)/(1-\alpha\delta)$. This is possible only if $V' = V$ and $U' = U$. Using $U' = U$ and manipulating (5), (9), and (12), it can be shown that $U_K' = U_K$. This implies that $U_L' = U_L$ also holds.

Proposition 3 shows the equivalence of ownership systems from the perspective of present values. The rest of this section develops welfare implications. I show that an allocation that is efficient subject to the incentive constraint for outside ownership cannot be destabilized by Pareto-improving shifts of individual firms to joint ownership, or vice versa. However, firms with differing property rights structures can coexist.

Let (z_K, z_L) be a profit distribution with $z_K + z_L = z(e)$ satisfying the incentive and participation constraints derived in Sections 16.3 and 16.4, and let (z_K', z_L') be a deviation from this distribution with $z_K' + z_L' = z(e')$. This deviation may or may not involve a shift in ownership structure. I call (z_K', z_L') a *destabilizing deviation* (DD) if $\alpha\delta(V'-U') \geq T(e')$, $U_K' \geq U_K$, and $U_L' \geq U_L$, where at least one of the latter two inequalities is strict. If the deviation involves outside asset ownership, V', U_K', U_L' are computed as in (5) and (6). If it involves joint ownership, these values are computed as in (9), (12), and (13).

The equilibria discussed in Sections 16.3 and 16.4 were noncooperative and so were not tested against coordinated deviations by groups of agents. Here I impose the refinement that in order for an equilibrium to qualify as stable, it must be impossible to devise a joint deviation that makes both newly matched workers and owners with newly filled vacancies at least as well off and one of these parties better off. Both are at least as well off if $U_K' \geq U_K$ and $U_L' \geq U_L$, because these are the present values from a new match discounted to reflect search time. It can be shown that $V' > V$ holds whenever at least one of these inequalities is strict, so the aggregate present value of a new match is larger under such deviations. If there are mutual gains from a deviation in one match, the same is true in all subsequent matches by stationarity, so the parties can reasonably expect the same deviation to be implemented in future matches as well. This justifies the idea that V', U_K', U_L' are computed as in (5) and (6), or alternatively as in (9), (12), and (13). Finally, (z_K', z_L') must be supportable when repeated in all future matches. This is true if and only if $\alpha\delta(V'-U') \geq T(e')$, as in Propositions 1 and 2.

Corollary 1

Consider any market equilibrium (z_K, z_L) with outside ownership. There is a destabilizing deviation involving outside ownership if and only if there is some feasible (z_K', z_L') that Pareto dominates (z_K, z_L). If there is no DD with outside ownership, there is no DD with joint ownership. The terms "joint" and "outside" can be interchanged here.

Proof

Suppose that (z_K, z_L) is an equilibrium with outside ownership, and consider deviations (z_K', z_L') also involving outside ownership. If (z_K', z_L') dominates (z_K, z_L), then (U_K', U_L') dominates (U_K, U_L) by (5). If (z_K', z_L') is also feasible, $\alpha\delta(V'-U') \geq T(e')$, and (z_K', z_L') is a DD. Conversely, suppose that there is no (z_K', z_L') that is both feasible and dominates (z_K, z_L), but there is a DD. The DD pair (z_K', z_L') satisfies $\alpha\delta(V'-U') \geq T(e')$ and thus is feasible, and its present values (U_K', U_L') dominate (U_K, U_L). From (5), (z_K', z_L') thus dominates (z_K, z_L), which is false. Hence there is no DD involving outside ownership.

Suppose that there is no DD involving outside ownership but that there is a DD with joint ownership. This implies that there is a (z_K', z_L') satisfying $\alpha\delta(V'-U') \geq T(e')$ with (U_K', U_L') dominating (U_K, U_L), where the present values are computed as in (9), (12), and (13). It can be assumed that $\alpha\delta(V'-U') = T(e')$ holds, because otherwise z_K' or z_L' or both can be increased until equality holds without decreasing U_K' or U_L'. By Proposition 3, there is a third distribution (z_K'', z_L'') that is on the outside ownership frontier and yields $U_K'' = U_K'$ and $U_L'' = U_L'$. Because (z_K'', z_L'') is on the outside ownership frontier, it is feasible and (U_K'', U_L'') dominates (U_K, U_L). This implies that there is a DD with outside ownership, which is false. Hence there is no DD involving joint ownership.

The proof starting from joint ownership is identical.

The corollary shows two things. First, to be stable, an economy in which all firms have the same property rights structure must be operating at an undominated point on its second-best frontier. This is reassuring because there are many equilibria in Figures 16.3 and 16.4 with inefficiently low effort. Propositions 1 and 2 establish that these inefficient outcomes can be supported. However, if one adds the refinement that an equilibrium not be vulnerable to destabilizing deviations, all Pareto-dominated points are ruled out. This provides a first welfare theorem for an economy with self-enforcement.

Corollary 1 also shows that if an economy is stable with respect to deviations that leave firm ownership unchanged, it must likewise be immune to voluntary transformations in the property rights structures of firms. However, this stability property is weak because it only rules out Pareto-improving deviations. Individual firms can change property rights in ways that leave everyone indifferent, so mixed asset ownership systems can arise.

Corollary 2

Consider an outside ownership economy in which the profit division (z_K, z_L) is immune to destabilizing deviations. Any subset of firms can be converted to joint asset ownership with an alternative profit division (z_K', z_L') in such a way that all agents are left indifferent. The reverse is true starting from a joint ownership economy.

Proof

Because (z_K, z_L) is not vulnerable to any DD, by Corollary 1 it is on the frontier for an outside ownership economy. By Proposition 3, there is a profit division (z_K', z_L') on the frontier of the joint ownership economy with identical effort and profit that has $V'= V$, $U_K' = U_K$, and $U_L' = U_L$. Let some subset of firms switch to joint ownership and operate at (z_K', z_L'). From Propositions 1 and 2, the incentive constraints are satisfied in each type of firm if $\alpha\delta(V'-U') = T(e') = T(e) = \alpha\delta(V-U)$. Because $V'= V$ and $U' = U$, effort incentives are unaffected by the change in ownership. Unemployed workers are indifferent toward the type of firm they join owing to $U_L' = U_L$, and asset owners with job vacancies are indifferent toward ownership structures owing to $U_K' = U_K$. Combining $V'= V$, $U_K' = U_K$, and $U_L' = U_L$ with (2) and (8) yields $m' - m = V_K$. Workers employed in an outside ownership firm can buy the productive asset at this price. The previous owner is indifferent, while the workers exchange the present value V_L for an equal present value $V' - (m' - m)$. The same argument is reversed starting from a joint ownership economy.

By Corollary 2, any combination of ownership structures can coexist. The fact that stability is weak means that, in the absence of other causal forces tending to favor one organizational form over the other, the mix of ownership structures in a particular economy is a matter of social convention or historical accident.

Finally, some normative conclusions can be reached. I have shown that Pareto improvements cannot be achieved through changes in asset ownership if an economy is operating at an undominated point on its second-best frontier. A stronger requirement is aggregate welfare maximization, which amounts to maximizing total profit $z(e)$ subject to incentive and participation constraints.

Corollary 3

When capital is scarce $(\beta_K > \beta_L)$, welfare is maximized at point A in Figure 16.3, where $U_K = 0$. When labor is scarce $(\beta_K < \beta_L)$, welfare is maximized at point B or C in Figure 16.4, where $U_L = 0$. In each case, maximum welfare can be achieved through outside ownership, joint ownership, or any combination of the two.

Proof

If $\beta_K > \beta_L$, maximization of $z(e)$ occurs at point A in Figure 16.3 regardless of the ownership structure. $U_K = 0$ follows from $z_K = 0$. If $\beta_K < \beta_L$, maximization of $z(e)$ can be achieved at either point B or C, because both are on the highest feasible isoprofit line. $U_L = 0$ follows from $z_L = 0$ at B and holds by construction at C. The neutrality of ownership for welfare maximization follows as in Corollary 2.

The main point of Corollary 3 is that, while ownership is neutral with respect to aggregate welfare maximization, the distribution of profit is not. If capital is scarce, all profit should go to labor; if labor is scarce, all profit should go to capital. Although this may seem counterintuitive, it follows naturally from the discussion in Sections 16.3 and 16.4. Giving a larger present value to the abundant input relaxes incentive constraints by reducing the temptation for suppliers of the scarce input to cheat.

Another point involves membership fees. When labor is scarce, maximization of aggregate welfare requires a binding labor participation constraint—that is, $U_L = 0$. In an outside ownership economy, workers must have low-enough wages or pay high-enough fees to ensure that they get no rent. Similarly, in a joint ownership economy, newly matched workers must pay a market-clearing membership fee so that they derive no net benefit from joining a firm. This would be inefficient in an economy with scarce capital, because then welfare maximization requires $U_K = 0$. In the latter situation, membership fees for joint ownership firms should only cover the cost of match-specific capital ($m = g_K$).

16.6 Conclusion

While it may seem obvious that reshuffling property rights to a fixed profit stream cannot alter effort incentives, this point has been overlooked in the modern theory of the firm. Contrary claims range from the idea that outside ownership is flawed because asset owners will cheat employees to the notion that joint ownership is flawed because workers who cannot be fired will shirk. The equivalence of the two structures only becomes clear when they are compared within a unified analytic framework involving self-enforcement.

From another perspective, however, the neutrality of ownership is less surprising. There is a long literature on equivalence or isomorphism relationships between capitalist and labor-managed firms. Chapters 3–5 reviewed this literature and derived equivalence results using competitive membership markets. Along similar lines, Roemer (1988) used a general equilibrium approach to show that an economy with worker-owned firms would simply replace profits to shareholders by interest payments to lenders. The results in this chapter add self-enforcement to the list of economic environments in which ownership by investors is equivalent to ownership by workers.

One purpose of an equivalence theorem is to refute claims that organizations of type X cannot work well by showing that organizations of type X work as well as those of type Y, where everyone agrees on the viability of type Y. Another purpose is to cast doubt on certain theoretical explanations for empirical facts. For example, the results in this chapter cast doubt on the notion that work incentives or asset specificity explain the dominance of KMFs with outside ownership. The results instead steer attention toward other explanations, such as capital constraints for LMFs with collective asset ownership.

It could be argued that something essential has been lost by having input suppliers observe one another's actions perfectly. Perhaps costly or imperfect monitoring along the lines discussed by Alchian and Demsetz (1972), Shapiro and Stiglitz (1984), and Bowles (1985) would drive a wedge between outside and joint ownership. However, if there are imperfect but publicly observed signals about effort supply, the noisiness of the signal simply increases the continuation surplus needed to keep agents on the equilibrium path (MacLeod and Malcomson, 1993). To explain outside asset ownership by monitoring, one must assume that the outsiders are better at observing effort than workers are when they monitor each other (Putterman, 1984). This seems implausible.

Another extension involves assets whose value can be diminished by inadequate maintenance or overuse, in place of the indestructible assets examined here. Holmstrom and Milgrom (1991, 1994) show that misuse of assets can be curbed by combining high-powered effort incentives with asset ownership by workers, or alternatively low-powered incentives with ownership by outsiders. Their approach generates predictions about asset ownership if the existence of an external revenue claimant (the principal) is assumed. In the Holmstrom and Milgrom model, the only reason why it is desirable to contract with a principal at all, rather than having workers receive revenue directly, is that principals are needed to provide insurance to risk-averse workers.

Under risk neutrality, the fact that workers face two margins in supplying effort (producing output and maintaining assets) does not alter the thrust of the argument in this chapter. In a world of self-enforcement, the incentive constraint still involves a trade-off between gains from deviation and loss of a continuation surplus if the current match ends. As long as there is conservation of surplus across systems, outside and joint ownership should remain equivalent. In Chapter 17, however, I develop a model where assets can be depreciated too rapidly, and where the difference in alienability between capital and labor leads to a difference in continuation surplus for KMFs and LMFs. In this framework, the equivalence result does break down.

16.7 Postscript

This chapter is a lightly edited version of my article "On the Neutrality of Asset Ownership for Work Incentives" published in the *Journal of Comparative Economics* (Dow, 2000). I thank Bentley MacLeod, Gil Skillman, Vincent Crawford, Louis Putterman, Samuel Bowles, and Herbert Gintis for comments on the original paper. Versions of this paper were presented at the Universities of Montreal, Western Ontario, California-Riverside, California-San Diego, Southern California, Alberta, British Columbia, and Victoria, as well as at Simon Fraser University and a Brookings conference on Human Capital and the Theory of the Firm in May 1997. The Swedish Collegium for Advanced Study in the Social Sciences, the Social Sciences and Humanities Research Council of Canada, and the Brookings Institution supplied financial assistance. I would especially like to thank Margaret Blair (then at Brookings) for her encouragement. All opinions are my own.

I became interested in repeated game models of effort supply in connection with my work with Xiao-yuan Dong on Chinese collective farms (Dong and Dow, 1993a,b). I sent off an initial version of the material in this chapter to the *Journal of Comparative Economics* in 1997. At the time, I did not understand the isomorphism between outside and joint ownership, and the first draft made a misguided attempt to show that property rights affected effort incentives. Even so, the editor generously asked for a revision.

While working on the revision, I became increasingly frustrated that I could not seem to pin down the exact ways in which asset ownership affected work incentives. On a Saturday night in a hotel room in Prince George, British Columbia, it finally dawned on me: *asset ownership did not make any difference*, because aggregate surplus would be the same in the two ownership systems; and in a repeated game environment, only aggregate surplus affected effort incentives. I have not had many eureka moments, but this was one. I completely refocused the paper, and the *Journal of Comparative Economics* accepted the massively revised manuscript. The resulting paper is one of my favorites, and I am happy to include it here.

16.8 Appendix

The core of the proof of Proposition 1 is to show that the following inequalities are necessary and sufficient for the net transfers (m, w, b) and effort e to be supportable.

renewal: $V_K \geq U_K$ and $V_L \geq U_L$

bonus: $-\alpha\delta(V_L - U_L) \leq b \leq \alpha\delta(V_K - U_K)$

effort: $b + \alpha\delta(V_L - U_L) \geq T(e|s)$

wage: $-(spq - c) - b - \alpha\delta(V_L - U_L) \leq w \leq (1/n - s)pq - b$
$+ \alpha\delta(V_K - U_K)$

fee: $w - (1/n - s)pq + b - \alpha\delta(V_K - U_K) \leq m \leq w + spq - c + b$
$+ \alpha\delta(V_L - U_L)$

investment: $g_K + w - (1/n - s)pq + b - \alpha\delta(V_K - U_K) \leq m$
$m \leq -g_L + w + spq - c + b + \alpha\delta(V_L - U_L)$

search: $U_K \geq 0$ and $U_L \geq 0$

To construct equilibrium strategies, use the side payments $m_K = \max\{-m, 0\}$, $m_L = \max\{m, 0\}$; $w_K = \max\{w, 0\}$, $w_L = \max\{-w, 0\}$; $b_K = \max\{b, 0\}$, $b_L = \max\{-b, 0\}$.

On the equilibrium path, σ_K searches, invests g_K in every job, pays m_K to every worker, pays w_K to every worker, pays b_K to every worker, and renews every worker. Off the equilibrium path, σ_K searches, sets $g_K' = 0$ for every newly filled job if $m_L < g_K$ but invests g_K if $m_L \geq g_K$, pays $m_K' = 0$ to every new worker, pays $w_K' = 0$ to every worker, pays $b_K' = 0$ to every worker, and fires every worker.

On the equilibrium path, σ_L searches, invests g_L, pays m_L to the owner, pays w_L to the owner, supplies effort e, pays b_L to the owner, and renews. Off the equilibrium path, σ_L pays $m_L' = 0$, pays $w_L' = 0$, supplies $e' = 0$, pays $b_L' = 0$, and quits.

The core of the proof of Proposition 2 is to show that the following inequalities are necessary and sufficient for the fee $m \geq g_K$ and effort $e \geq 0$ to be supportable:

renewal: $V \geq U$

effort: $\alpha\delta(V - U) \geq T(e)$

fee: $pq/n - c + \alpha\delta(V - U) + \delta U_K \geq m - g_K$

investment: $pq/n - c + \alpha\delta(V - U) + \delta U_K \geq m + g_L$

search: $U_L \geq 0$ and $U_K \geq 0$

On the equilibrium path, σ searches, invests, pays m-g_K, supplies e, and renews. Off the equilibrium path, σ pays $m' - g_K' = 0$, supplies $e' = 0$, and quits.

Capital Stocks and Labor Flows

17.1 Introduction

One popular hypothesis about the rarity of labor-managed firms is that workers tend to be poor and that LMFs cannot gain access to credit on the same terms as KMFs (see Chapter 8). Worker poverty implies that LMFs cannot be financed directly by insiders, and biases in the credit market imply that LMFs financed by outsiders cannot compete effectively against KMFs. I will refer to this as the "capital constraint" hypothesis.

This story is not wrong, but it is incomplete in several ways. First, while worker poverty may explain why workers do not create LMFs using their own savings, it does not explain why wealthy investors create KMFs rather than LMFs (see Chapter 10 for a possible explanation). Second, one needs to spell out why a wealthy outsider such as a bank would be biased against borrowers seeking to create LMFs as compared with those seeking to create KMFs, because parallel adverse selection or moral hazard problems can arise in each case (see Gintis, 1989, for a hypothesis of this kind). Third, even if LMFs cannot be financed through debt for some reason, the leasing of productive assets or the sale of nonvoting equity shares might still enable LMFs to compete effectively.

This chapter develops a model where workers may be unable to attract capital to an LMF even though investors can attract labor to a KMF. I do not rely on informational asymmetries. Instead, the market imperfection involves the absence of any commitment mechanism with respect to input contributions or transfers among agents. This source of imperfection has received much less attention in the LMF literature than have the conventional information arguments, but it offers a powerful strategy for theoretical unification with respect to the asymmetries between KMFs and LMFs.

The key idea is that the agents who control firms (workers in the LMF, investors in the KMF) must make credible promises to the noncontrolling agents (investors in the LMF, workers in the KMF). Specifically, controllers have to persuade noncontrollers that costs associated with input supply today will be adequately compensated tomorrow. I carry out the analysis using a repeated game framework and interpret credibility in the sense of subgame perfection.

To gain some initial intuition, recall from Chapter 16 that when side payments are self-enforced, it is necessary to have a sufficiently large surplus from continuation of the relationship in order to deter cheating. The larger the temptation to cheat, the larger this continuation surplus must be. When capital stocks are lumpy, LMFs may be tempted to cheat investors by withholding large leasing or debt service payments after capital has been supplied to the firm. This temptation may exceed the surplus from preservation of the relationship between the LMF and its investors, especially if the LMF need not return to the capital market once retained earnings have begun to flow. However, the KMF can only cheat workers by withholding current wages, because after it cheats, the workers will quit. Under certain conditions this is less tempting, so the employment relationship in the KMF need not involve as large a surplus as the financial relationship in the LMF does.

The simplest comparison between KMFs and LMFs is one involving an apparent symmetry. Suppose that KMFs own physical assets and lease human assets, while LMFs own human assets (or more precisely, their members do) and lease physical assets. One might think that in this situation any difficulties LMFs would have in making credible promises to capital suppliers would be symmetric to the difficulties KMFs would have in making parallel promises to labor suppliers. But the alienability distinction between capital and labor can drive a wedge between the two cases. Physical assets are separate from their owners and are not under their continual control. It may therefore be possible for LMFs to rapidly depreciate leased physical assets and stop paying the asset owners. Depending on the circumstances, this temptation could be large. By contrast, human assets are under continual control by their owners, and an outside party is normally unable to depreciate a worker's endowment of time, skill, or knowledge in an opportunistic way. Accordingly, the temptation for the KMF is simply to stop paying wages. This may well be smaller than the temptation for the LMF to cheat outside asset owners.

Another comparison is to assume that neither the KMF nor the LMF can lease physical assets because this is prohibitively costly for all firms. For example, assets of this kind might be highly specialized, and the transacting parties might engage in costly bargaining over quasi-rent or might fail to make ex ante investments because the latter are noncontractible (see Chapter 15). Alternatively, physical assets might be vulnerable to rapid depreciation as described earlier, regardless of whether they are leased by KMFs or LMFs. Suppose that for any of these reasons the firms using physical assets must also own them. This does not pose a problem for a KMF controlled by wealthy investors, but it poses a major problem for an LMF controlled by poor workers, who must now transact with outside investors to finance the purchase of these assets.

I will show that in a repeated game setting where side payments are self-enforced, the commitment problem facing an LMF that borrows to finance the purchase of physical assets is strategically identical to the problem facing an LMF that leases the same assets. There is an identical temptation to depreciate the assets rapidly and default on the firm's financial obligations, whether these involve leasing payments or debt service payments. Hence the situation reduces to the previous problem, where again the temptation for the LMF to cheat investors may exceed the temptation for the KMF to cheat workers.

Another solution to the LMF financing problem has occasionally been proposed in the literature: have labor-managed firms issue nonvoting equity shares (for a review, see Jossa, 2014, 57–59). In principle, this would enable LMFs to finance collective assets and share risk without ceding any control to investors. Unfortunately, it also creates large temptations for LMFs to cheat on dividend payments. I will show that an LMF with nonvoting equity is less viable than one relying on leasing or borrowing, which may account for the empirical rarity of nonvoting equity shares.

The ideas in this chapter have deep roots. Discussions of commitment problems in the context of LMF financing date back at least to Schlict and von Weizsäcker (1977), who argued that LMFs would have difficulty attracting capital because workers can walk away from a failing firm. Jensen and Meckling (1979) maintained that outside financiers would hesitate to supply funds to a firm in which workers held control rights. Gui (1985) showed that LMFs could face an upper bound on debt financing if workers were able to liquidate projects in order to avoid repayment. Williamson (1985, 304–306) asserted that boards of directors are normally elected by shareholders in order to prevent employees from expropriating equity capital.

Other origins trace to the insight in the efficiency wage literature that shirking by workers can be punished through termination of the employment relationship (Shapiro and Stiglitz, 1984; Bowles, 1985). This led to two further developments. First, a number of authors used repeated game models to study the problem of effort supply in firms (see the references from Chapter 16, especially MacLeod and Malcomson, 1989, 1993, 1998). Second, Bowles and Gintis (1990, 1993a) generalized the efficiency wage framework to address termination threats in both capital and labor markets, under the umbrella term of "contested exchange." They combined this approach with a deep interest in the financing problems facing LMFs (Bowles and Gintis, 1993b, 1993c, 1993d, 1994, 1996a, 1996b).

Section 17.2 presents the modeling framework and derives first-best results for the case where a single agent supplies both capital and labor to the firm. Beginning in Section 17.3, I assume that distinct agents supply capital and labor, and I consider a KMF in which output goes to the capital supplier. In the KMF model, incentive constraints limit the wages the firm can credibly promise to the worker, and thus the level of effort that can be extracted from the worker in each period. Section 17.4 considers an LMF in which output goes to the labor supplier. In the LMF, the incentive constraints limit the repayment the firm can credibly promise to the investor in exchange for provision of the firm's capital stock.

Section 17.5 compares the viability of the KMF and LMF. The KMF distorts the sequence of output levels to satisfy incentive constraints, while the LMF does not, so the LMF has superior productivity with respect to the present value it achieves from a given capital stock. But if agents place enough weight on the future, under plausible conditions the KMF has a smaller temptation to cheat on the wage as compared with the temptation for the LMF to cheat on debt service or leasing payments. When capital is too costly, the LMF cannot credibly promise to repay its investors, and the KMF prevails.

Section 17.6 discusses some interpretive issues, and Section 17.7 summarizes the conclusions of the chapter. Proofs of formal propositions not given in the main text are supplied in Section 17.8.

17.2   The Model

Production requires capital and labor, and occurs in two periods indexed by $t \in \{0, 1\}$. I think of capital as a machine having the maximum potential output $Q > 0$ over its lifespan, which starts in period $t = 0$ and ends in period $t = 1$. Following $t = 1$, the machine fails with certainty and can no longer be used. I refer to the parameter Q as the capacity of the machine, where Q can be converted into any sequence of actual outputs $(q_0, q_1) \geq 0$ such that $q_0 + q_1 \leq Q$. I refer to the latter inequality as the capacity constraint. Capital does not depreciate during its two-period lifespan, and all agents discount payoffs received at $t = 1$ using the common factor $\delta \in (0,1)$.

Labor effort is measured in the same units as output and indicates the amount of potential output converted into actual output in a given period. Thus $q_t \geq 0$ is also effort in period t, which has a cost to the worker of $c(q_t)$.

A1   The cost function satisfies $c(0) = c'(0) = 0$, $c'(q) > 0$ for $q > 0$ with $c'(\infty) = \infty$, and $c''(q) > 0$ for all $q \geq 0$. Output is sold at a parametric price $p > 0$. The profit $\pi(q) = pq - c(q)$ has $\pi(0) = 0$, $\pi'(0) > 0$, and $\pi''(q) < 0$ for all $q \geq 0$. It also has a unique maximizer $q^* > 0$ such that $\pi'(q^*) = 0$.

This section characterizes the output decisions of a single agent who supplies both capital and labor. The results define the first-best allocation and are used as a benchmark in later sections. The present value of a new machine is obtained by solving

$$\max\{\pi(q_0) + \delta\pi(q_1) \text{ subject to } q_0 \geq 0, \ q_1 \geq 0, \text{ and } q_0 + q_1 \leq Q\} \quad (1)$$

Proposition 1
First-best solution: Problem (1) has a unique solution such that

(a) If $2q^* \leq Q$, then $q_0 = q_1 = q^*$
(b) If $2q^* > Q$ and $\pi'(Q) \geq \delta\pi'(0)$, then $q_0 = Q$ and $q_1 = 0$
(c) If $2q^* > Q$ and $\pi'(Q) < \delta\pi'(0)$, then $q_0 > 0$, $q_1 > 0$, $q_0 + q_1 = Q$, and $\pi'(q_0) = \delta\pi'(q_1)$

The maximum present value in (1) is strictly positive in all cases.

Proof
This is a straightforward exercise involving Kuhn-Tucker multipliers.

The nature of the solution is easy to grasp. The unconstrained output q^* is produced in both periods, as in (a), if this is possible. Otherwise, the machine is used at full capacity. If the discount factor δ is low, the entire capacity of the machine is used immediately, as in (b). But if δ is high enough, positive output is produced in the second period, as in (c), and marginal profit is equalized across periods in present value terms. The maximum present value is strictly positive, because small positive outputs yield positive profit.

The discount factor δ plays no role if the solution in Proposition 1 is of type (a). The interesting cases are those in (b) and (c), so I introduce the following restriction.

A2   The capacity constraint binds at the solution in (1); that is, $2q^* > Q$.

Remark
Due to the finite time horizon and the strict concavity of profit, the solution in (1) is well defined for $\delta = 1$. In this case, A2 gives $q_0 = q_1 = Q/2$ from Proposition 1(c). Also, because the maximum present value in (1) is positive, A2 implies $\pi(Q/2) > 0$.

Let the up-front cost of a machine be $F \geq 0$. This cost is sunk once the machine is installed. Machines are profitable if the present value in (1) is at least F, where the output sequence is as described in Proposition 1. Machines are indivisible, so one cannot buy a fraction of a machine for a fraction of the fixed cost F. But after the first machine fails at the end of period $t = 1$, one can acquire a second machine at the beginning of period 2 by paying a new fee F. For simplicity, I assume that even if the solution in (1) is of type (b) so the full capacity of the machine is used up in period $t = 0$, it is necessary to wait until the start of period $t = 2$ before installing a new machine. If the investment in period $t = 0$ is profitable, then it is also profitable to repeat the investment with the same output plan starting in period 2, in period 4, and so on.

17.3 Incentives in the Capital-Managed Firm

In the rest of the chapter, I assume that some agents are endowed with labor but no capital, while others are endowed with capital but no labor. Investors who want to create KMFs must therefore attract employees, while workers who want to create LMFs must attract financiers. A firm requires two agents, named (unsurprisingly) K and L.

I use a repeated game framework in which there are no binding agreements about effort or side payments. The controlling input supplier appropriates the output generated by production. When creating a firm, the controlling agent announces a subgame perfect equilibrium in the game to be played with the noncontrolling agent. Upon agreeing to participate, the noncontroller accepts the SPE proposed by the controller.

In the KMF, events proceed as follows. K decides in period $t = 0$ whether to invest F. If this occurs, L chooses effort and thus output (q_t) in each period t. After observing output in period t, K chooses a wage (w_t). K's payoff in period t is $pq_t - w_t$, while L's payoff is $w_t - c(q_t)$.

At the end of each period, K and L simultaneously decide whether to continue the relationship or terminate it. If either party quits at the end of a period $t \in \{0, 1\}$, both get a present value of zero at the start of period $t + 1$ and the game ends. If F was invested at $t = 0$ and the relationship was not terminated in period 0 or 1, K and L receive the present values $(V^K, V^L) \geq 0$ at the start of period 2.

When K invests F and the relationship is not dissolved along the equilibrium path, the initial present values of K and L at the start of $t = 0$ are

$$V_0{}^K = pq_0 - w_0 + \delta(pq_1 - w_1) + \delta^2 V^K - F \qquad (2a)$$

$$V_0{}^L = w_0 - c(q_0) + \delta[w_1 - c(q_1)] + \delta^2 V^L \qquad (2b)$$

Proposition 2
SPE for KMF: The output pair $q = (q_0, q_1) \geq 0$ with $q_0 + q_1 \leq Q$, the wage pair $w = (w_0, w_1)$, and investment F can be supported by a subgame perfect equilibrium (SPE) if and only if the following conditions hold.

$IC_0{}^K$ $w_0 \leq \delta(pq_1 - w_1) + \delta^2 V^K$
$IC_1{}^K$ $w_1 \leq \delta V^K$
$IC_0{}^L$ $c(q_0) \leq w_0 + \delta[w_1 - c(q_1)] + \delta^2 V^L$
$IC_1{}^L$ $c(q_1) \leq w_1 + \delta V^L$
PC^K $F \leq pq_0 - w_0 + \delta(pq_1 - w_1) + \delta^2 V^K$

where IC indicates an incentive constraint and PC indicates a participation constraint.

Corollary 1
Let $V \equiv V^K + V^L$ be the aggregate continuation surplus. For a fixed $V \geq 0$, K's present value $V_0{}^K$ in (2a) is maximized subject to $V_0{}^L \geq 0$ in (2b) by choosing $q = (q_0, q_1)$ to solve

$$\begin{aligned} \max \quad & \pi(q_0) + \delta\pi(q_1) + \delta^2 V - F \\ \text{subject to} \quad & CC \quad q_0 \geq 0, \ q_1 \geq 0, \ q_0 + q_1 \leq Q \\ & IC_0 \quad c(q_0) \leq \delta\pi(q_1) + \delta^2 V \\ & IC_1 \quad c(q_1) \leq \delta V \end{aligned} \qquad (3)$$

and choosing $w = (w_0, w_1)$ so that $w_0 = c(q_0)$ and $w_1 = c(q_1) - \delta V^L$. This wage pair gives $V_0^L = 0$. The maximization problem for q has a unique solution.

K adopts an SPE that maximizes the present value of the controller while leaving zero for the noncontroller. In each period, L is indifferent toward providing the required effort, because the wage w_t is just sufficient to motivate the effort q_t. L is also indifferent toward continuation of the relationship. The key incentive issue is why K pays the wage after output has been produced in each period. K will not cheat if the total surplus from continuing the relationship is large enough, and L's ability to destroy this surplus by quitting provides the deterrence needed to keep K on the equilibrium path.

The next step is to study the optimal q in (3). For this purpose I use Figure 17.1. It is easy to show that when $V = 0$, the only output pair consistent with both IC_0 and IC_1 is $q_0 = q_1 = 0$. When V is positive, IC_1 yields a horizontal line, as in the graph, and places an upper bound on q_1 that is independent of q_0. IC_0 yields a maximum value of q_0 for any given q_1. The IC_0 boundary has a positive horizontal intercept, and initially the maximum q_0 rises as a function of q_1. However, the IC_0 boundary may eventually bend backward if $q_1 \geq q^*$ can occur. At sufficiently low values of V, both IC_0 and IC_1 bind, and the capacity constraint is irrelevant. In this case, the feasible set is the shaded area shown in Figure 17.1, and the solution for output lies at the intersection of IC_0 and IC_1.

The locus generated by increasing V while both IC_0 and IC_1 hold with equality is indicated in Figure 17.1 by the heavy curve. I call this curve the expansion path (EP). It is described by

$$q_1 = c(q_0)/\delta p \qquad (4)$$

Under the conditions in A1, the expansion path is strictly convex, with a zero slope at the origin. It begins below the 45° line but eventually rises above this line and intersects the capacity boundary $q_0 + q_1 = Q$, as in Figure 17.1. I indicate the latter intersection by point A in the graph.

A central issue is whether the expansion path intersects CC to the left or right of the first-best solution $q(\delta)$ from Proposition 1.

Lemma 1
Let $q(\delta) \equiv [q_0(\delta), q_1(\delta)]$ be the first-best solution from Proposition 1, which is located on CC by A2. There is a discount factor $\underline{\delta} \in (0, 1)$ with the following properties.

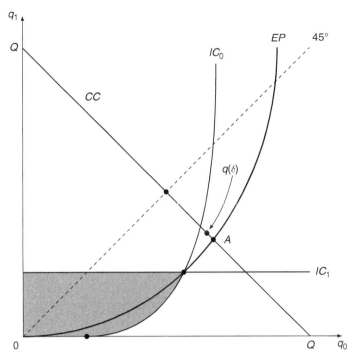

Figure 17.1 Capacity Constraint, Incentive Constraints, and Expansion Path for KMF
(Case (c) in Lemma 1)

(a) If $\delta < \underline{\delta}$, then the expansion path intersects CC to the left of $q(\delta)$.
(b) If $\delta = \underline{\delta}$, then the expansion path intersects CC at $q(\delta)$.
(c) If $\delta > \underline{\delta}$, then the expansion path intersects CC to the right of $q(\delta)$.

Figure 17.1 is drawn to illustrate the case in Lemma 1(c).

Lemma 2
Let $V^A > 0$ be the unique value of V associated with the point A at which the expansion path from (4) intersects the CC boundary $q_0 + q_1 = Q$ from (3). Thus $q_1^A = Q - q_0^A = c(q_0^A)/\delta p$ with $V^A = c(q_1^A)/\delta$ using IC_1 from (3).

(a) Suppose that $\delta < \underline{\delta}$ so Lemma 1(a) applies. If $V \geq V^A$ but the first-best solution $q(\delta)$ is not feasible in problem (3), then IC_0 binds and IC_1 is irrelevant.
(b) Suppose that $\delta = \underline{\delta}$ so Lemma 1(b) applies. If $V \geq V^A$, then the first-best solution $q(\delta)$ is feasible in problem (3).

(c) Suppose that $\delta > \underline{\delta}$ so Lemma 1(c) applies. If $V \geq V^A$ but the first-best solution $q(\delta)$ is not feasible in problem (3), then IC_1 binds and IC_0 is irrelevant.

Proof
These results can be obtained using the graphical approach in Figure 17.1. For all cases, whenever $V \geq V^A$ there is an interval along CC on which both IC_0 and IC_1 hold. In cases (a) and (c), if $q(\delta)$ is not in this interval then it is optimal to move as far as possible in the direction of $q(\delta)$. In case (b), $q(\delta)$ is in the relevant interval for all $V \geq V^A$.

We can now characterize the minimum present value V^B required for a first-best solution.

Lemma 3
Again write the first-best solution from (1) as $q(\delta)$. Let $V^B \geq V^A$ be the lowest V at which $q(\delta)$ is feasible.

(a) If Lemma 2(a) applies, then $V^B = [c(q_0(\delta)) - \delta\pi(q_1(\delta))]/\delta^2 > V^A$
(b) If Lemma 2(b) applies, then $V^B = V^A$
(c) If Lemma 2(c) applies, then $V^B = c(q_1(\delta))/\delta > V^A$

Proof
$V^B \geq V^A$ holds, because if instead $V^B < V^A$, then CC cannot hold with equality for any $V \leq V^B$, and $q(\delta)$ cannot be achieved, which contradicts the definition of V^B. The rest of the proof follows from Lemma 2, along with IC_0 and IC_1 from (3).

I will sometimes write $V^A(\delta)$ and $V^B(\delta)$ when the dependence of these thresholds on the discount factor is important.

A3   Case (c) holds in Lemmas 1, 2, and 3, so $\delta \in (\underline{\delta}, 1)$.

I adopt A3 throughout the rest of this chapter for two reasons. First, in this case all of the relevant solutions have $q_1 \leq Q/2 < q^*$ where the second inequality follows from A2. This makes it unnecessary to consider situations with a backward-bending IC_0 curve. Second, I will compare the viability of KMFs and LMFs for values of δ near unity in Section 17.5, so case (c) will be relevant at that stage in the discussion.

Now suppose that the investment F is repeated in period 2, period 4, and so on. If K uses the output and wage policy from Corollary 1, K will capture the entire present value from this series of investments, yielding $V^L = 0$ and $V^K = V$. Stationarity gives

$$V = \max\{-F + \pi(q_0) + \delta\pi(q_1) + \delta^2 V\} \tag{5}$$

where the maximization is subject to CC, IC_0, and IC_1, as in (3).

The properties of the solution for V in (5) can be studied by defining the functions

$$Y(V, \delta) = \max \pi(q_0) + \delta\pi(q_1) \text{ subject to CC, } IC_0,$$
$$\text{and } IC_1 \text{as in (3) and} \tag{6a}$$

$$Z(V, \delta) = Y(V, \delta) + \delta^2 V \tag{6b}$$

Lemma 4
Assume that A3 applies. The maximum value $Y(V, \delta)$ has the following features, where primes indicate differentiation with respect to V.

(a) $Y(0, \delta) = 0$
(b) $Y'(0, \delta) = +\infty$
(c) $Y'(V, \delta) > 0$ and $Y''(V, \delta) < 0$ for $V \in (0, V^A)$
(d) $Y'(V, \delta) > 0$ and $Y''(V, \delta) < 0$ for $V \in (V^A, V^B)$
(e) $Y'(V, \delta)$ is undefined at V^A. The left derivative exceeds the right derivative at this point.
(f) $Y'(V, \delta) \to 0$ as $V \to V^B$
(g) $Y'(V, \delta) = 0$ for $V \geq V^B$

The form of the function Y is shown in Figure 17.2, where V is on the horizontal axis with Y and Z on the vertical axis. To begin, suppose that fixed cost F is zero. When the terminal present value is $V = 0$ in (3), the only feasible output pair is $q = 0$, which yields $Y(0, \delta) = 0$. Because $Y'(V, \delta) \to \infty$ as $V \to 0$, the function $Y(V, \delta)$ is initially above the 45° line. For $V \in (0, V^A)$, positive outputs become feasible. Both IC_0 and IC_1 hold with equality, with CC slack. On this interval, $Y(V, \delta)$ is strictly concave. The kink at V^A in Lemma 4(e) reflects the fact that at this continuation value, IC_0 drops out as a constraint and is replaced by CC. This kink does not alter the overall strict concavity of Y for $V \in [0, V^B]$. For $V \in (V^A, V^B)$, IC_1 binds due to A3, with CC holding with equality and IC_0 irrelevant, and again $Y(V, \delta)$ is strictly concave. For $V \geq V^B$, the first-best solution from (1) is adopted and $Y(V, \delta)$ becomes a constant. The properties of the function Z, also shown in Figure 17.2, are similar. This function inherits the strict concavity of

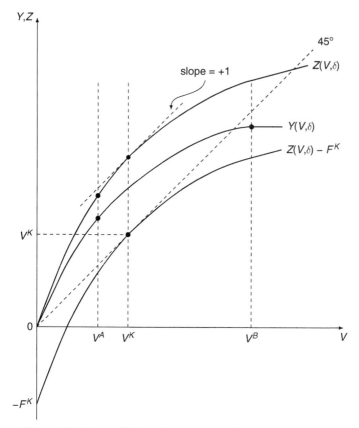

Figure 17.2 Present Values, Stationarity, and Maximum Fixed Cost for the KMF

Y on $(0, V^B)$ along with the kink at V^A, and it becomes linear with slope δ^2 for $V \geq V^B$.

Ignoring the trivial solution $V = 0$, the curve $Z(V, \delta)$ crosses the 45° line only once, as shown in Figure 17.2. When $F = 0$, this point satisfies the stationarity condition in (5). As F increases, the curve $Z(V, \delta) - F$ shifts down parallel to $Z(V, \delta)$ in the graph. For small $F > 0$, the curve $Z(V, \delta) - F$ crosses the 45° line twice, where the intersection having the higher V is of economic interest. The latter value falls as F increases.

The maximum F consistent with (5) is found by maximizing the vertical distance between $Z(V, \delta)$ and the 45° line in Figure 17.2. With some notational abuse involving (2), let V^K be the unique maximizer of the expression $Z(V, \delta) - V$. Then define $F^K \equiv Z(V^K, \delta) - V^K$. When the fixed cost is F^K, the curve $Z(V, \delta) - F^K$ is tangent to the 45° line at the present value V^K, as in Figure 17.2. The graph depicts the case $V^A < V^K < V^B$, but the possibility $0 < V^K < V^A$ is not excluded. If $V^K = V^A$, the tangency is replaced by a similar condition involving the kink described in Lemma 4(e). At the cost F^K, the present value V^K satisfies the stationarity requirement in (5), and it would be impossible to satisfy this requirement at any higher cost $F > F^K$.

The maximization of $Z(V, \delta) - V$ has one immediate implication. When $\delta < 1$, we cannot have $V^B \leq V^K$, because this implies $Y'(V^K, \delta) = 0$ and $Z'(V^K, \delta) = \delta^2$. Thus $Z(V, \delta) - V$ would be decreasing at V^K, contradicting the definition of V^K as a maximizer. Due to $V^K < V^B$, it is impossible to have the first-best outputs at V^K. Instead the KMF distorts its outputs away from the first-best solution in order to satisfy an incentive constraint.

Proposition 3

Viability of KMF: Assume that $\delta \in (\underline{\delta}, 1)$, where $\underline{\delta}$ is defined as in Lemma 1. Let $V^K(\delta)$ be the unique maximizer of $Y(V, \delta) - (1 - \delta^2)V$, where $V^K(\delta) < V^B(\delta)$ and the outputs (q_0, q_1) are distorted away from the first-best $q(\delta)$. The maximum fixed cost for which the KMF can satisfy all capacity, incentive, and stationarity constraints is

$$F^K(\delta) = Y[V^K(\delta), \delta] - (1 - \delta^2)V^K(\delta) > 0. \tag{7}$$

Conversely, when the KMF's fixed cost is $F^K(\delta)$, the only present value consistent with all capacity, incentive, and stationarity constraints is $V^K(\delta)$.

Proof

As described above

17.4 Incentives in the Labor-Managed Firm

Suppose now that L wants to organize an LMF in which L appropriates all output. L must make a credible commitment to K that the capital supply transaction will result in a nonnegative present value for K. In such a transaction, K pays the fixed cost $F > 0$ in exchange for a flow of payments $r = (r_0, r_1)$ over the investment cycle.

K begins the process by choosing whether to invest F. Assuming that K invests, L chooses both q_t and r_t and obtains the payoff $pq_t - c(q_t) - r_t$ in period $t \in \{0, 1\}$. The sequence of these actions within a period is unimportant, but one can imagine that L sells output and then uses the resulting revenue to pay K. I do not include period-by-period liquidity constraints in the model, but they will be discussed later. At the end of each period, K and L simultaneously decide whether to quit. If either player quits, then both receive zero present values and the game ends. If no one quits in periods 0 or 1, K and L receive present values $(V^K, V^L) \geq 0$ in period 2. In this case, the players have the initial present values

$$V_0{}^K = r_0 + \delta r_1 + \delta^2 V^K - F \tag{8a}$$

$$V_0{}^L = \pi(q_0) - r_0 + \delta[\pi(q_1) - r_1] + \delta^2 V^L \tag{8b}$$

The simplest interpretation of the model involves leasing, where K supplies a machine with capacity Q at the start of t = 0. K is entitled to remove the machine from the firm at the end of each period through termination of the lease, which precludes any further relationship between the parties. As with the wage payments w = (w_0, w_1) in the KMF, there is no legal commitment for L to make the rental payments r = (r_0, r_1), so these payments must be self-enforced. At the end of this section, I will discuss an alternative interpretation involving debt, along with a variant involving nonvoting equity shares.

Proposition 4
SPE for LMF: The output pair q = $(q_0, q_1) \geq 0$ with $q_0 + q_1 \leq Q$, the rental pair r = (r_0, r_1), and the investment F can be supported by a subgame perfect equilibrium (SPE) if and only if the following conditions hold.

$IC_0{}^L$ $\pi^d(Q) \leq \pi(q_0) - r_0 + \delta[\pi(q_1) - r_1]$
          $+ \delta^2 V^L$
$IC_1{}^L$ $\pi^d(Q - q_0) \leq \pi(q_1) - r_1 + \delta V^L$
PC^K $F \leq r_0 + \delta r_1 + \delta^2 V^K$ where $\pi^d(q) \equiv \pi[\min \{q^*, q\}]$

The expression $\pi^d(Q)$ is the maximum profit L can get from a new machine by using it in one period. When $q^* < Q$, this is accomplished by choosing the unconstrained maximizer q^*, even though this leaves some capacity unexploited. When $q^* \geq Q$, it involves the full use of the machine's capacity. As I explain in detail later, this function can be interpreted as the size of the temptation for L to cheat on the financing arrangements with K.

From now through Equation (9), I employ the more compact notation q^f in place of q(δ) to indicate the first-best outputs from Section 17.2.

Corollary 2

If some (q, r) satisfies the constraints in Proposition 4, these constraints are also satisfied by the first-best outputs q^f in Proposition 1 and the rental payments $r_0^f = F - \delta^2 V^K$ and $r_1^f = 0$. Whenever the feasible set is nonempty, (q^f, r^f) maximizes V_0^L in (8b) subject to $V_0^K \geq 0$ in (8a).

Assuming that L chooses an SPE to maximize the present value V_0^L of an LMF subject to $V_0^K \geq 0$ and the feasible set is nonempty, (q^f, r^f) is both feasible and optimal. As in Corollary 1, the noncontrolling input gets a zero present value.

Proposition 4 and Corollary 2 ignored period-by-period liquidity constraints. It can be objected that if L cannot afford the investment F, there is surely some doubt about whether L can pay K the lump sum r_0^f at the end of period t = 0. One may therefore want to impose an additional constraint that r_0 cannot exceed the revenue obtained in period 0. If anything, this makes it harder for the LMF to achieve viability. By ignoring liquidity constraints of this kind, I am biasing the analysis in favor of the LMF, which strengthens later conclusions about conditions under which the KMF is viable but the LMF is not.

In any event, the LMF's problem is starkly exhibited by the repayment plan in Corollary 2. The problem is that K must place the present value F in the custody of L, but L can choose not to return an equivalent present value to K later. Whether L cheats by failing to make payments to K in period 0, period 1, or a combination of the two is a secondary consideration.

An optimizing L selects an SPE, as in Corollary 2, that maximizes the discounted value of firm profit while forcing K down to zero present value. Repeating this plan in period 2, period 4, and so on, writing $V^K = 0$ and $V = V^L$, and exploiting the stationarity of V gives

$$V = -F + \pi(q_0^f) + \delta\pi(q_1^f) + \delta^2 V \quad \text{subject to} \quad \pi^d(Q) \leq V \quad (9)$$

The capacity constraint in Proposition 4 is satisfied for q^f by construction, PC^K is satisfied for r^f by construction, and IC_1^L is always satisfied by (q^f, r^f). The only constraint relevant for (9) is IC_0^L, which imposes the inequality involving $\pi^d(Q)$.

I now switch back to the notation q(δ) for the first-best outputs from Proposition 1 in order to facilitate comparisons with the KMF results in Section 17.3. In parallel to (6), define the functions

$$Y^f(\delta) \equiv \pi[q_0(\delta)] + \delta\pi[q_1(\delta)] \tag{10a}$$

$$Z^f(V, \delta) \equiv Y^f(\delta) + \delta^2 V \tag{10b}$$

This differs from (6), because the functions in (10) involve first-best outputs rather than the distorted outputs used in the KMF.

The solution for V in (9) is illustrated in Figure 17.3. $Y^f(\delta)$ is independent of V in the LMF case, so the function $Z^f(V, \delta)$ is simply a line with the vertical intercept $Y^f(\delta)$ and the slope $\delta^2 < 1$. This line crosses the 45° line at $V^C > 0$, which is the only present value consistent with the stationarity requirement in (9) when F = 0. The maximum one-period profit $\pi^d(Q)$ is a constrained version of the first-best present value $\pi[q_0(\delta)] + \delta\pi[q_1(\delta)]$. When Proposition 1(b) applies, we have $\pi^d(Q) = Y^f(\delta)$. When Proposition 1(c) applies, we have $\pi^d(Q) < Y^f(\delta)$. In either case, $\pi^d(Q) < V^C$, so the constraint in (9) is irrelevant.

When F > 0, the right-hand side in (9) is $Z^f(V, \delta) - F$, so the line for Z^f in Figure 17.3 is shifted down in a parallel way. As this occurs, the stationary present value V^C moves to the left. At a sufficiently large value of F, the intersection point between the locus $Z^f(V, \delta) - F$ and the 45° line occurs at the horizontal line determined by $\pi^d(Q)$. I write F^L for the fixed cost at which this occurs and V^L for the resulting present value as shown in Figure 17.3. No higher value of F is compatible with the constraint in (9).

Proposition 5

Viability of LMF: The largest fixed cost $F^L(\delta)$ for which the LMF can satisfy $IC_L{}^\circ$ and the stationarity requirement in (9) is

$$F^L(\delta) = Y^f(\delta) - (1 - \delta^2)\pi^d(Q) \tag{11}$$

Conversely, when the LMF's fixed cost is $F^L(\delta)$, the only present value consistent with IC_0 and stationarity is $V^L(\delta) = \pi^d(Q)$.

Proof

As described above

So far I have been treating the LMF model as a leasing arrangement in which the firm rents the capital stock from K. In this case, K has an obvious response if L cheats on the rental fee r, which is to withdraw the asset and

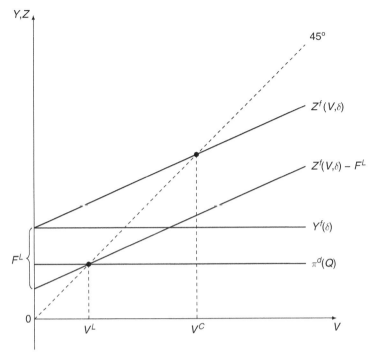

Figure 17.3 Present Values, Stationarity, and Maximum Fixed Cost for the LMF

terminate the relationship at the end of the current period. Whether L wants to cheat depends on the maximum profit $\pi^d(Q)$ that L can capture from a one-time deviation before K has time to respond.

An alternative interpretation involves borrowing. Suppose that K provides F in the form of a loan and L uses this amount to acquire a machine, which the firm then owns. The pair $r = (r_0, r_1)$ is interpreted as a sequence of debt service payments. If L deviates from a promised payment, K can repossess the machine, which functions as collateral. But K can no longer deny access to the machine if L merely deviates on output without deviating on debt payments, because the firm owns the machine and decides how to use it. However, if L deviates on debt payments, K can take away any remaining production capacity through bankruptcy proceedings at the end of the period in which the deviation occurred. This ends the relationship with L.

In this framework, K has exactly the same recourse when there is a deviation from r as would be available under a leasing arrangement.

The only difference is that K cannot punish L for deviations from q. But if L is considering a deviation from r, then L should pursue the best one-shot output deviation in the same period, because defaulting on a debt service obligation triggers removal of the capital stock in any case. Once deviations for q and r are considered simultaneously, the incentive constraints IC_0^L and IC_1^L are the same as before, and there is no economic difference between leasing and debt.

The collateral value of the asset plays no role in the model, because in equilibrium L does not deviate. L is not kept on the equilibrium path by the value the asset may have to K as collateral, but rather by a comparison of L's equilibrium present value with what L could get by depreciating the entire capital stock in one period and refraining from any further payments. It is unimportant what K could obtain by withdrawing the asset in response to disequilibrium behavior by L, as long as this payoff does not exceed the present value of the remaining payments from L along the equilibrium path. The latter issue could arise when $r_1^f = 0$. Here it is necessary that K not be able to obtain a positive present value by retrieving the asset opportunistically at the end of period 0.

As mentioned in Section 17.1, writers in the LMF literature sometimes suggest the use of nonvoting equity shares. To see what this entails, treat r as a stream of dividend payments on shares of nonvoting equity that are sold to finance the fixed cost F. By the definition of an LMF, these shares do not give K any voice in the determination of either q or r. Moreover, in this interpretation K has no right to remove the capital stock during the current investment cycle. If L deviates in any way, K's only recourse is a refusal to renew the relationship in period 2, after the current capital stock has been exhausted.

This reformulation does matter, because now if L deviates from r, L can do better than exploiting the entire capital stock in one period. Because L cannot be deprived of remaining potential output in the current cycle, L can continue with the first-best outputs as before, but without paying further dividends to K. The only penalty for stopping the dividend flow is the loss of the present value V from renewing the relationship at period 2. Because this is lost anyway when K uses punishment strategies in the leasing or debt case and L need not distort outputs when deviating on dividends, the temptation for L to cheat is greater with nonvoting equity. If leasing or debt arrangements cannot provide a viable financing strategy for the LMF, then equity cannot do so either. It is probably not coincidental that real LMFs sometimes rent physical assets or borrow money from banks but very rarely sell nonvoting equity shares.

17.5 Viability Comparisons

We are now ready to compare KMF and LMF viability for identical values of the output price (p) and capacity limit (Q) when the discount factor δ is near one. The key issue is the size of the fixed cost F that each type of firm can accommodate. This cost is a measure of "capital requirements" or "capital intensity." The KMF is viable for $F \in [0, F^K(\delta)]$ where $F^K(\delta)$ is defined by (7) in Proposition 3. Similarly, the LMF is viable for $F \in [0, F^L(\delta)]$ where $F^L(\delta)$ is defined by (11) in Proposition 5.

At "high" values of δ, the first-best outputs are approximately $q_0 = q_1 = Q/2$. One point to notice is that $F^K(\delta)$ and $F^L(\delta)$ are both well defined at $\delta = 1$ and take on the same value: $F^K(1) = F^L(1) = 2\pi(Q/2)$. Given the equivalence of the KMF and LMF at $\delta - 1$, I compare $F^K(\delta)$ and $F^L(\delta)$ when δ is near unity but below it. I leave the details to Section 17.8 and focus here on the interpretation.

Proposition 6
Comparison of KMF and LMF viability:

(a) KMF advantage: if $\pi^d(Q) > c(Q/2)$, then there is some $\varepsilon > 0$ such that $\delta \in (1-\varepsilon, 1)$ implies $F^K(\delta) > F^L(\delta)$.
(b) LMF advantage: if $\pi^d(Q) < c(Q/2)$, then there is some $\varepsilon > 0$ such that $\delta \in (1-\varepsilon, 1)$ implies $F^K(\delta) < F^L(\delta)$.

Recall that $\pi^d(Q) \equiv \pi(\min \{q^*, Q\})$ is the maximum one-period profit an LMF can achieve using a new machine. This is the size of the temptation for an LMF to cheat its investors, when the investors can respond by depriving the LMF of any remaining capital after cheating occurs. This temptation is compared with $c(Q/2)$, which is the effort cost in a single period when agents do not discount the future so the first-best output in each period is Q/2. Because the KMF pays a wage at the end of each period equal to the cost of effort in that period, the temptation for the KMF to cheat is the gain from withholding a wage of the size $c(Q/2)$. If this is less than the LMF temptation as in Proposition 6(a), there is an interval of fixed cost $(F^L(\delta), F^K(\delta)]$ for which the KMF is viable but the LMF is not. The conclusion is reversed in Proposition 6(b). In general, the firm in which the controller has less temptation to cheat can operate with a lower continuation surplus and therefore can accommodate a higher capital cost.

The expression $c(Q/2)$ is independent of the output price p, because machine capacity Q is a technological parameter. The inequalities in Proposition 6 are most naturally studied by varying the price p, which determines the profit $\pi^d(Q)$. I think of p as being determined exogenously, perhaps on a world market. At high enough prices, Proposition 6(a) applies and the KMF has an incentive advantage, while at low enough prices Proposition 6(b) applies and the opposite is true. One implication is that KMFs tend to thrive when the product market is "generous" in the sense that large rents or quasi-rents are on the table. LMFs tend to do better when the product market is less generous, because then there is less to be gained from a large surge in output and the temptation to cheat investors is correspondingly smaller.

An example. Useful intuition can be gained from the case where effort costs are quadratic: $c(q) = aq^2$ where $a > 0$. This gives $c(Q/2) = aQ^2/4$. The unconstrained output q^* from Section 17.2 is $q^*(p) = p/2a$. Let $p^* = aQ$, which gives $q^* = Q/2$. At the price p^* we have $\pi^d(Q) = \pi(q^*) = c(Q/2) = aQ^2/4$. For $p \le p^*$ we have $q^* \le Q/2$, and condition A2 in Section 17.2 is violated. For $p > p^*$, A2 is satisfied. In the expression $\pi^d(Q) = \pi(\min \{q^*, Q\})$, the output q^* is initially smaller than Q for $p > p^*$ and increases with price. As price rises, so does $\pi^d(Q) = \pi[q^*(p)]$, and this gives $\pi^d(Q) > c(Q/2)$. The price $p^{**} = 2aQ$ yields $q^* = Q$. Further increases in p beyond p^{**} do not increase $\min \{q^*, Q\}$ because Q becomes the minimum, but $\pi^d(Q)$ continues to rise while output remains fixed at Q.

The central features of the quadratic case are as follows:

(i) $p \le aQ$ implies that A2 is violated.

(ii) $p \in (aQ, 2aQ]$ implies that A2 is satisfied with

$$Q/2 \; < \; q^*(p) \le Q \quad \text{and} \quad \pi^d(Q) = \pi[q * (p)] \; > \; c(Q/2)$$

(iii) $p > 2aQ$ implies that A2 is satisfied with

$$Q < q^*(p) \quad \text{and} \quad \pi^d(Q) = \pi(Q) > c(Q/2)$$

At any price high enough to satisfy the requirement A2, Proposition 6(a) applies, and the KMF can accommodate higher capital costs than the LMF when agents are patient. Thus for the quadratic case, one can regard a KMF advantage as the "normal" situation.

A conjecture. This chapter studies an investment cycle of two periods. Suppose instead that we have any finite cycle $t \in \{0, 1, .. T\}$ with the capacity constraint $\Sigma_{t=0}^{T} q_t \le Q$. My conjecture is that the corresponding condition for a KMF advantage in Proposition 6 will be $\pi^d(Q) > c[Q/(T+1)]$, which holds for any fixed (p, Q) when T is large enough.

I have two reasons for this expectation. The first is that in the general model, the KMF has an incentive constraint in every period: IC_0, IC_1 .. IC_T. We saw in the case $T = 1$ that as $\delta \to 1$, only IC_1 mattered. It seems reasonable to think that in the more general model, for δ near unity only IC_T will matter, so only the temptation to cheat on the last wage payment will matter. When δ is near unity, the last output will be near $Q/(T+1)$ and the last wage will be near $c[Q/(T+1)]$.

The second consideration is that the LMF's maximum temptation to cheat comes at $t = 0$. At this point, the LMF can exploit the entire machine capacity, pay nothing to the outside financier, and quit the relationship. There is no benefit from waiting longer before cheating. Accordingly, I expect that the temptation for the LMF to cheat will still be $\pi^d(Q)$, which does not depend on T. If $c(Q/2)$ is replaced by $c[Q/(T+1)]$ in Proposition 6, the fact that the latter is near zero for large T means that KMFs have an advantage over LMFs whenever investment cycles are sufficiently long.

17.6 Some Caveats

A few cautionary points should now be mentioned. First, as discussed in Section 17.4, I ignored period-by-period liquidity constraints for the LMF. If such constraints are important, the LMF may have to postpone debt service until its cash flow can cover these costs. It could also shift its output forward in time to accelerate payments to financiers, although this distorts the output sequence. Either way, if the KMF has an advantage in Proposition 6, it should retain this advantage when the LMF faces additional constraints.

I argued in Section 17.4 that leasing and debt are equivalent in the present model. This leaves the question of why LMFs sometimes prefer one over the other. Difficulties with leasing could include inefficient bargaining over the quasi-rents generated by firm-specific investments (see Chapter 15) and moral hazard issues involving the maintenance of leased assets. On the other hand, leasing could be chosen when an asset can be rented on a competitive market, there is little danger of opportunistic depreciation by users, and there is a large temptation for opportunistic default on a loan to purchase the asset.

In this chapter I have ignored entry by new firms, which may be attracted by the existence of a continuation surplus. One possible effect might be to bid up the price of machines F. Another effect might be to depress the output price p. In general, there is a duality relationship between p and F: if the KMF can operate at a higher value of F when both firms face the same output price p, then the KMF can also operate at a lower value of p when both firms face the same fixed cost F. A key issue involving entry is that there is a tension between the rents needed for incentive purposes and the zero-profit condition familiar from textbook microeconomic theory. In long run equilibrium, potential entrants must stay out of the market because they know that further entry would lead to a violation of incentive constraints. Potential entrants of this sort would not be price takers.

Another caveat is that I have not solved for a market-wide equilibrium. In this chapter, I simply assumed that if the relationship between K and L ends, each agent gets an exogenous present value of zero. These reservation payoffs could be endogenized by having unemployed agents return to the market and seek new partners (as was the case in Chapter 16 and will be the case in Chapter 18). I would expect the main insights from this chapter to survive in a more complex model along these lines.

Finally, the model of this chapter does not resolve distributional issues. Both firm types require a continuation surplus for incentive reasons. In KMFs this rent goes to the capital supplier, while in LMFs it goes to the labor supplier. If only one organizational form is viable, that settles the distributional issue, but if both are viable, the model says that whoever controls the firm gets the surplus. Indeterminacies of this sort are a central feature of repeated game models and will be discussed further in Chapter 18.

17.7 Conclusion

The controllers of firms generally internalize costs associated with the inputs they supply (e.g., depreciation costs in the KMF or effort costs in the LMF). But opportunism by controllers may lead to frictions in markets for the inputs supplied by noncontrollers. Other things equal, the organizational form with the smaller temptation for controllers to cheat noncontrollers will have a competitive advantage. The alienability of capital can allow LMFs to rapidly depreciate physical assets, while the inalienability of labor means that KMFs cannot depreciate human assets in the same way. With quadratic effort costs, this asymmetry enables the KMF to support larger capital investments than the LMF can.

I also showed, using a more general cost function, that leasing and borrowing are strategically equivalent for the LMF in a repeated game setting. Thus, if there is a danger of opportunistic depreciation when the LMF leases physical assets, the LMF cannot solve this problem by financing collective asset ownership through debt, because the temptation for cheating is identical in the two cases. Of course, this equivalence was established in a model where payments among input suppliers are self-enforced. It would not necessarily hold when lenders and lessors enjoy different degrees of contractual or legal protection.

By contrast with most arguments about capital constraints and LMFs, I have not appealed to asymmetric information in the present chapter. While market imperfections of this kind are certainly prominent in the real world, the model shows that they are not logically necessary to the hypothesis that LMFs are capital constrained. A different type of market imperfection, the lack of commitment devices, will suffice.

Another feature of the model is that it incorporates both financing issues and work incentives. These topics have received much attention in theories about LMF rarity (see Chapter 8), but they are usually discussed separately. The idea of imperfect commitment unifies them. Together with alienability factors, imperfect commitment can explain why LMFs have more trouble attracting capital than KMFs have attracting labor. I build on these ideas in Chapter 18, which addresses both adverse selection and moral hazard, and considers the market shares of KMFs and LMFs for the economy as a whole.

17.8 Appendix

Proof of Proposition 2

Necessity. Suppose that the incentive constraint IC_0^K does not hold. By continuing along the equilibrium path, K gets the payoff $-w_0 + \delta(pq_1 - w_1) + \delta^2 V^K < 0$. By paying a zero wage in period $t = 0$ and quitting, K gets a zero payoff. This shows that IC_0^K is necessary for a SPE supporting (q, w, F). The arguments for IC_1^K, IC_0^L, and IC_1^L are similar. PC^K is necessary because if it does not hold, K will not invest the fixed cost F. We do not need participation constraints for L, because IC_1^L ensures that L gets a nonnegative present value starting at $t = 1$ and IC_0^L ensures that L gets a nonnegative present value starting at $t = 0$. We do not need any participation constraint for K at $t = 1$ or after F is paid at $t = 0$.

Sufficiency. Suppose that K pays the wage w_t in period $t = 0, 1$ if there has never been a deviation but pays zero otherwise, and continues if there has never been a deviation but quits otherwise. Suppose that L supplies the effort q_t in period $t = 0, 1$ if there has never been a deviation but supplies zero otherwise, and continues if there has never been a deviation but quits otherwise. When the conditions in Proposition 2 hold, these strategies yield a Nash equilibrium after every history where the investment F has been made, and it is optimal for K to make the initial investment.

Proof of Corollary 1

Summing (2a) and (2b) gives the aggregate present value $V_0 \equiv V_0^K + V_0^L = \pi(q_0) + \delta\pi(q_1) + \delta^2 V - F$, which is the objective function in (3). The capacity constraint CC must hold. Summing IC_0^K and IC_0^L from Proposition 2 gives the aggregate incentive constraint IC_0 in (3), and summing IC_1^K and IC_1^L from Proposition 2 gives the aggregate incentive constraint IC_1 in (3). Because the inequalities in Proposition 2 are necessary conditions for an SPE, the aggregate constraints IC_0 and IC_1 in (3) are also necessary for an SPE. Therefore, no SPE can support a total present value V_0 larger than the value associated with the solution of (3) subject to CC, IC_0, and IC_1. Furthermore, K cannot have $V_0^K > V_0$ where V_0 is the maximum present value from (3), because $V_0^K + V_0^L = V_0$ and $V_0^L \geq 0$ must hold. The q that solves (3) subject to CC, IC_0, and IC_1 achieves the maximum V_0, and the w in Corollary 1 gives $V_0^L = 0$ from (2b), so V_0^K is maximized. It may be necessary to have $w_1 < 0$, depending on the values of q_1 and V^L. However, $V^L = 0$ will be relevant later, and in that case $w_1 \geq 0$. Existence and uniqueness for the solution for q in (3) are established later in Section 17.3. The (q, w) pair in Corollary 1 satisfies all conditions in Proposition 2, so there is an SPE that supports this pair.

Proof of Lemma 1

First I show that for $\delta = 1$, the expansion path intersects CC below the 45° line. When $\delta = 1$, EP is described by $q_1 = c(q_0)/p$ from (4), or $pq_1 = c(q_0)$. From the remark after A2 in Section 17.2, we have $\pi(Q/2) > 0$ or equivalently $pQ/2 > c(Q/2)$. This implies that at the point (q_0, q_1) on EP where $q_0 = Q/2$, we must have $q_1 < Q/2$. If instead $q_1 \geq Q/2$, then $pq_1 \geq pQ/2 > c(Q/2) = pq_1$, which is a contradiction. Therefore EP is below the 45° line at $q_0 = Q/2$ and also intersects CC below this line. To complete the proof, we make the following observations. When δ is small, EP from (4) intersects CC above the 45° line, while $q(\delta)$ is on CC and below the 45° line. When $\delta = 1$, EP from (4) intersects CC below the 45° line, while $q(1)$ is on CC and on the 45° line. Continuity and monotonicity imply that there is a unique intermediate $\underline{\delta}$ as described in Lemma 1.

Proof of Lemma 4

(a) From the constraints in (3), when $V = 0$ the only feasible output pair is $q = 0$.

(b) On the interval $(0, V^A)$, both IC_0 and IC_1 bind, while the capacity constraint is slack. From the envelope theorem, $Y'(V, \delta) = \mu_0\delta^2 + \mu_1\delta$ where μ_0 and μ_1 are the Kuhn-Tucker multipliers for IC_0 and IC_1. Manipulation of first order conditions gives $\mu_0 = \pi'(q_0)/c'(q_0)$ and $\mu_1 = \delta\pi'(q_1)[1 + \pi'(q_0)/c'(q_0)]/c'(q_1)$. Because $V \rightarrow 0$ implies $q_0 \rightarrow 0$ and $q_1 \rightarrow 0$, both multipliers go to infinity and so does $Y'(V, \delta)$.

(c) $Y'(V, \delta) > 0$ holds because the multipliers are positive in (b). $Y''(V, \delta) < 0$ can be obtained as follows. Use the equations IC_0 and IC_1 as a system of identities that implicitly define $q_0(V)$ and $q_1(V)$. Substituting into the objective function gives $Y(V, \delta) = pq_0(V)$. Differentiating this twice and using the convexity of the cost function gives the desired result.

(d) On the interval (V^A, V^B), CC and IC_1 bind, while IC_0 is slack (recall that we are using A3). The multipliers of the binding constraints are both positive, so the derivative $Y'(V, \delta)$ is positive by the envelope theorem. To obtain the result $Y''(V, \delta) < 0$, use the equations for CC and IC_1 as a system of identities that implicitly define $q_0(V)$ and $q_1(V)$ as in (c). Differentiating twice, using the convexity of the cost function, using $q_0(V) > q_0(\delta)$, and using $q_1(V) < q_1(\delta)$ gives the desired result.

(e) Compute the derivative $Y'(V, \delta)$ on the intervals $(0, V^A)$ and (V^A, V^B) using the relevant constraints in each case. The output pair q^A associated with point A in Figure 17.1 is determined by $q_0^A + q_1^A = Q$ and $q_1^A = c(q_0^A)/\delta p$ using CC and EP. Evaluate the derivative obtained from each interval at q^A. The envelope theorem and manipulation of first order conditions show that when A3 applies, the left derivative is larger than the right derivative.

(f) This follows from the fact that $q(V) \rightarrow q(\delta)$ as $V \rightarrow V^B$.

(g) This follows from the fact that $q(\delta)$ is feasible whenever $V \geq V^B$.

Proof of Proposition 4

Necessity. Consider IC_0^L and suppose that $\pi^d(Q) > \pi(q_0) - r_0 + \delta[\pi(q_1) - r_1] + \delta^2 V^L$. By deviating to the output level min $\{q^*, Q\}$ in period $t = 0$, L gets the profit $\pi^d(Q)$, which is the maximum one-period profit from a new machine. If L also pays nothing to K at t = 0 and quits, L gets π^d (Q), which exceeds what L can get by continuing with q and r. This shows that $IC_0{}^L$ is necessary for SPE. The argument for $IC_1{}^L$ is similar, except now the profit $\pi^d(Q)$ is replaced by $\pi^d(Q - q_0)$ at the start of t = 1. PC^K is necessary in order for K to invest F.

Sufficiency. Suppose that K makes Q available at the start of t = 0 and makes the remaining capacity available at the start of period t = 1 if there has never been a deviation but quits at the end of t = 0 or t = 1 if a deviation has occurred. Suppose that L implements (q, r) if there has never been a deviation but deviates according to $\pi^d(Q_t)$, sets $r_t = 0$, and quits in period t if a deviation has occurred. When the conditions in Proposition 4 are satisfied, these strategies yield a Nash equilibrium after every history where an initial investment F has been made. Due to PC^K, it is optimal for K to invest F.

Proof of Corollary 2
For (q^f, r^f), $IC_1{}^L$ reduces to $\pi^d(q_1{}^f) \leq \pi(q_1{}^f) + \delta V^L$. Proposition 1 and A2 imply that $q_1{}^f < q^*$ and thus $\pi^d(q_1{}^f) = \pi(q_1{}^f)$. Therefore $IC_1{}^L$ holds for (q^f, r^f) whenever $V^L \geq 0$. Now suppose that (q, r) satisfies the constraints in Proposition 4. Because (q, r) satisfies $IC_0{}^L$, we have $\pi^d(Q) \leq \pi(q_0) - r_0 + \delta[\pi(q_1) - r_1] + \delta^2 V^L$. But $\pi(q_0) + \delta\pi(q_1) \leq \pi(q_0{}^f) + \delta\pi(q_1{}^f)$ for all feasible output plans from the definition of q^f. Also, because (q, r) satisfies PC^K, we have $r_0 + \delta r_1 \geq F - \delta^2 V^K = r_0{}^f + \delta r_1{}^f$. Combining these gives $\pi^d(Q) \leq \pi(q_0{}^f) + \delta\pi(q_1{}^f) + \delta^2 V^L - r_0{}^f - \delta r_1{}^f$ so (q^f, r^f) satisfies $IC_0{}^L$. The present value $V_0{}^L$ obtained from (q^f, r^f) is at least as large as the present value from any other feasible (q, r), because $\pi(q_0) + \delta\pi(q_1)$ in (8b) is maximized by q^f and the expression $r_0 + \delta r_1$ in (8b) is minimized by r^f subject to $V_0{}^K \geq 0$ in (8a).

Proof of Proposition 6
I first show that for all sufficiently large values of δ, the derivative of the function $Y(V, \delta) - (1-\delta^2)V$ is strictly positive when evaluated on the right-hand side of the kink V^A from Lemma 4(e). This will establish that for all sufficiently large δ, the solution $V^K(\delta)$ is in the interval $(V^A(\delta), V^B(\delta))$. It suffices to show that $Y'[V^A(\delta), \delta] \rightarrow Y'[V^A(1), 1] > 0$. The output pair $q^A(\delta)$ associated with point A in Figure 17.1 is determined by $q_0{}^A(\delta) + q_1{}^A(\delta) = Q$ and $q_1{}^A(\delta) = c[q_0{}^A(\delta)]/\delta p$ using CC and EP. The resulting solution $q^A(\delta)$ is a differentiable function of δ and well defined at $\delta = 1$. We have $V^A(\delta) = \delta c[q_1{}^A(\delta)]$ from the constraint IC_1 in (3). This is also differentiable and well defined at

$\delta = 1$. The derivative of $Y(V, \delta)$ on the interval (V^A, V^B) where CC and IC_1 bind and IC_0 is irrelevant is computed from $Y(V, \delta) = \pi[q_0(V)] + \delta\pi[q_1(V)]$ where $q_0(V) + q_1(V) = Q$ and $V = \delta c[q_1(V)]$. Carrying out the differentiation and evaluating the result at $V^A(\delta)$ gives $Y'[V^A(\delta), \delta] = \{\delta\pi'[q_1{}^A(\delta)] - \pi'[q_0{}^A(\delta)]\}/\delta c'[q_1{}^A(\delta)]$. For $\delta = 1$, this is $Y'[V^A(1), 1] = \{\pi'[q_1{}^A(1)] - \pi'[q_0{}^A(1)]\}/\delta c'[q_1{}^A(1)] > 0$. The positive sign follows from $q_0{}^A(1) > q_1{}^A(1)$ because at $\delta = 1$ the expansion path intersects the capacity constraint below the 45° line (see the proof of Lemma 1). This justifies the assumption for the remainder of the proof that $V^K(\delta)$ is in the interval $(V^A(\delta), V^B(\delta))$.

The optimal present value $V^K(\delta)$ satisfies $Y'[V^K(\delta), \delta] \equiv (1-\delta^2)$. Consider $F^K(\delta) = Y[V^K(\delta), \delta] - (1-\delta^2)V^K(\delta)$. At $\delta = 1$, this is $F^K(1) = Y[V^K(1), 1] = 2\pi(Q/2)$. Computing the derivative of $F^K(\delta)$ gives $F^{K\prime}(\delta) = \partial Y[V^K(\delta), \delta]/\partial\delta + 2\delta V^K(\delta)$, because terms involving the optimization with respect to V^K drop out by the envelope theorem. Setting up the Kuhn-Tucker expression for $Y[V^K(\delta), \delta]$, differentiating with respect to δ, and ignoring indirect effects through V^K by the envelope theorem results in $\partial Y[V^K(\delta), \delta]/\partial\delta = \pi[q_1(V^K(\delta))]$. Therefore $F^{K\prime}(\delta) = \pi[q_1(V^K(\delta))] + 2\delta V^K(\delta)$.

Next consider $F^L(\delta) \equiv Y^f(\delta) - (1-\delta^2)\pi^d(Q)$. At $\delta = 1$, we have $F^L(1) \equiv Y^f(1) = 2\pi(Q/2)$. The derivative is $F^{L\prime}(\delta) \equiv \pi[q_1(\delta)] + 2\delta\pi^d(Q)$ where $q_1(\delta)$ is the first-best output in period 1, and again we have used the envelope theorem.

Because $F^K(1) = F^L(1) = 2\pi(Q/2)$, we compare the derivatives $F^{K\prime}(\delta)$ and $F^{L\prime}(\delta)$ at $\delta = 1$. Both derivatives are continuous and strictly positive, so if $F^{K\prime}(1) < F^{L\prime}(1)$, then $F^K(\delta) > F^L(\delta)$ for a neighborhood of $\delta = 1$ and Proposition 6(a) applies. If the first inequality is reversed, then $F^K(\delta) < F^L(\delta)$ for a neighborhood of $\delta = 1$ and Proposition 6(b) applies. We have $F^{K\prime}(1) = \pi[q_1(V^K(1))] + 2V^K(1)$ and $F^{L\prime}(1) \equiv \pi[q_1(1)] + 2\pi^d(Q)$. The period-1 output is first best in both cases because $V^K(1) = V^B(1)$, so the first terms are identical. The issue therefore reduces to a comparison of $V^K(1)$ against $\pi^d(Q)$. However, $V^K(1) = c[q_1{}^f(1)] = c(Q/2)$. This gives the desired result.

18

Honest and Dishonest Controllers

18.1 Introduction

Those who argue that labor-managed firms are rare because they face difficulties in the capital market often point to problems of moral hazard and adverse selection. It is well known that borrowers may face high interest rates or credit rationing if they can take actions contrary to the interests of lenders after a contract has been signed, or if lenders cannot distinguish between borrowers with good projects and those with bad ones before a contract is signed. It is plausible that imperfections of this sort might be related to the rarity of LMFs, because poor workers who cannot finance LMFs must convince investors to supply capital. By contrast, wealthy investors can avoid these capital market problems by creating KMFs using their own financial endowments.

However, a few questions require attention. If moral hazard and adverse selection cause trouble for LMFs in the capital market, do they also cause trouble for KMFs in the labor market? Could workers avoid these labor market problems by creating LMFs using their own time endowments? Is there any reason to believe that the problems confronting workers in the capital market are more severe than the problems confronting investors in the labor market? A satisfactory theory should offer answers to these questions.

This chapter develops a unified model of capital and labor markets with elements of both moral hazard and adverse selection. There are no legally binding contracts about payments from the controllers of firms to the noncontrollers, so in KMFs investors can cheat on wages and in LMFs workers can cheat on rental fees or loan repayment. Such cheating is prevented, or at least restrained, by self-enforcement in a repeated game. The moral hazard concept is absorbed into the broader concept of "opportunism," defined to be strategic behavior not subject to contractual restraint where agent interests are in conflict.

The adverse selection component arises because individual workers or investors have entrepreneurial projects that differ in quality. These productivity differences are not observable in advance by noncontrolling agents. An agent's productivity only matters when that agent manages the firm, and it is irrelevant when the agent is a noncontroller. The adverse selection problem interacts with the moral hazard problem because, other things equal, low productivity agents who become controllers of firms are more tempted to cheat the noncontrollers. I assume that the distribution of productivities is identical for capital and labor suppliers, so asymmetries in the prevalence of KMFs and LMFs are not attributable to differences in the quality of the projects pursued by investors and workers.

To make the analysis manageable, I have stripped away several elements that are commonly found in models of moral hazard or adverse selection. For example, I do not include any effort costs, and there are no issues surrounding the possibility that workers might shirk (in either type of firm). I also assume risk neutrality so there is no trade-off between incentives and insurance, as one typically finds in principal-agent models of moral hazard. Nor are there contracts where the pay of a noncontroller (e.g., the wage in a KMF) can be tied to the output of the firm. I also ignore complexities associated with the durability of capital. Here, nonhuman assets only last for one period, and after that workers in an LMF have to repeat the process of acquiring them. This contrasts with the assumptions of Chapter 16 (where physical assets lasted forever) and Chapter 17 (where they were used up gradually over time). All of these simplifications have the same goal: to highlight the incentives for controllers to cheat noncontrollers with regard to transfer payments. The point of the model is to make as much headway as possible in explaining the formation of KMFs and LMFs without introducing additional factors beyond this.

The model in this chapter starts from symmetry between capital and labor, and I spend a considerable amount of time developing the implications of this symmetry. Near the end, I introduce an important asymmetry: investors may be wealthy enough that they are not only able to supply physical assets such as machines, but can also pay wages in advance of production. On the other hand, workers are not endowed with either physical or financial capital and thus cannot pay investors before production takes place. Almost by definition, investors have resources now, while workers need resources now in order to obtain income later. This asymmetry in the intertemporal structure of transactions in KMFs and LMFs influences the incentives for controllers to cheat noncontrollers, with a variety of important consequences relative to the symmetric baseline.

Section 18.2 begins by describing the model. I only consider steady states where individual agents use stationary strategies and all aggregate market variables (the number of firms, the number of unemployed agents, and so on) remain constant over time. The problem is simplified to the point that only three strategies are relevant: seek a control position and make the customary transfer to noncontrollers, seek a control position and cheat noncontrollers, or be a noncontroller. Each agent chooses optimally among these strategies in light of his or her privately known productivity as a controller. I use steady state requirements to impose structure on the beliefs of noncontrollers about the honesty of controllers. An equilibrium is defined to be a combination of prices, beliefs, and firm market shares where (a) all agents choose strategies optimally; (b) all beliefs are correct; and (c) markets clear, in the sense that the total demand for labor by KMFs is equal to the total supply of labor to KMFs, and likewise for capital in LMFs.

Section 18.3 considers equilibria without adverse selection, where all controllers of firms are honest. Such equilibria exist if and only if agents place enough weight on future payoffs and there is enough market friction that cheaters cannot find new (naive) partners too quickly. In all such equilibria, KMFs and LMFs exist in equal numbers.

Section 18.4 extends the analysis to equilibria with adverse selection, where some controllers of firms are dishonest. Equilibria of this kind exist under essentially the same conditions as the equilibria where all controllers are honest. There are multiple equilibria that differ with respect to income distribution and the market shares of KMFs and LMFs.

Section 18.5 examines whether there can be equilibria where only KMFs exist. I answer this question in the affirmative. Such equilibria can exist for parameter values similar to those that led to existence in Sections 18.3 and 18.4, although with additional restrictions on the distribution of productivities. In equilibria where all firms are KMFs, the controllers of KMFs are expected to pay the customary wage, while the controllers of LMFs are expected to cheat on rental fees or loan repayments. The fact that the model can generate equilibria in which all firms are KMFs is reassuring, because this resembles the world in which we live. However, there is still an abstract symmetry between capital and labor, so it would also be theoretically possible to have an equilibrium in which all firms are LMFs.

Section 18.6 introduces the asymmetry with respect to liquidity discussed earlier. The general effect is to remove temptations for investors to cheat, because investors can pay the wage up front and workers can block production when the wage is not paid. This alters the strategic foundations of the model and modifies the results from preceding sections. In particular, equilibria where all firms are KMFs exist for a wider range of parameter values. Section 18.7 offers concluding thoughts.

18.2 The Model

I consider two types of agents, labeled K and L. Those of type K are endowed with capital but not labor, while those of type L are endowed with labor but not capital. There are equally many agents of each type. A firm is a match between one K supplier and one L supplier. I denote the total number of such matches by N. The remaining agents, numbering M of each type, are unattached and seek matches with agents of the complementary type. Both N and M are assumed to be large. The reservation payoff of an agent when not matched is normalized at zero. All agents are risk neutral.

In each firm, one agent is the controller and the other is the noncontroller. The firms controlled by agents of type K are called KMFs and those by agents of type L, LMFs. In a given time period, events in a firm unfold as follows. First, the agents cooperate to produce an output $q \geq 0$. This output is determined by the productivity of the agent who controls the firm and is appropriated by that agent. I assume that control rights give enough power to the controller that it is impossible for the noncontroller to capture any output directly.

Second, after output has been produced and appropriated, the controlling agent can make a transfer to the noncontrolling agent. I denote these transfers by $w \geq 0$ in a KMF and $r \geq 0$ in an LMF, where w is a wage and r is a rental fee for the use of a nonhuman asset. As in Chapters 16 and 17, there are no legally enforceable contracts that compel controllers to provide the payments (w, r).

Thirdly and finally, the two agents simultaneously choose whether to continue the match or quit. If both want to continue, the match proceeds to the next period with the probability $\alpha \in (0, 1)$ and ends for exogenous reasons with the probability $1-\alpha$. If either agent quits, the match ends with certainty. When a firm dissolves, both parties enter the pool of unattached agents and search for a new partner at the start of the next period.

In place of the interpretation of r as a rental fee, one might instead interpret it as the net payment on a loan used to acquire a productive asset with a one-period lifespan. For this context, it should be noted that the model only deals with the possibility that an LMF might cheat on the net proceeds to the lender rather than the entire principal used to purchase the asset. This is reasonable if the asset has perfect collateral value and can be reclaimed by the lender in case of default. But if the principal of the loan is vulnerable, the model understates the temptation for the LMF to cheat.

Time is discrete, and all agents have a one-period discount factor $\delta \in (0, 1)$. I will be concerned with steady states where the number of firms (N) and the number of match-seekers of each type (M) remain constant over time. In each period, the probability that an unmatched agent finds a new partner and this results in the creation of a new firm is $\beta \in (0, 1)$. By contrast with Chapter 16, here this probability is identical for agents of types K and L. One can imagine that unattached agents of each type announce whether they want a role as a controller or noncontroller and are placed in the appropriate queue for the formation of KMFs or LMFs.

The productivity of an agent is the output (q) produced in a firm controlled by that agent. Differences in productivity across agents may be related to entrepreneurial ability, access to information about technology or market conditions, or other factors. An agent's productivity is uniformly distributed on $[q_0, q_1]$ where $0 \leq q_0 < q_1$. This distribution is identical for agents of types K and L, so asymmetries in the numbers of KMFs and LMFs are not driven by differences in productivity for capital and labor suppliers. Unattached agents do not observe the productivities of potential partners when matches are formed.

Strategies. I limit attention to stationary strategies where an agent takes the same actions along the equilibrium path in every period during which he or she is matched. All agents ignore events from earlier periods, whether they occurred in the current match or a previous one. This yields three feasible strategies, labeled X, Y, and Z.

(X) *Honest controller:* Along the equilibrium path, seek a controlling position when unmatched; pay w or r after output has been appropriated in a match; and continue if w or r has been paid, but quit otherwise.

(Y) *Dishonest controller:* Along the equilibrium path, seek a controlling position when unmatched; do not pay w or r after output has been appropriated in a match; and continue if w or r has been paid, but quit otherwise.

(Z) *Noncontroller:* Along the equilibrium path, seek a noncontrolling position when unmatched; and continue if w or r has been paid, but quit otherwise.

The terms "honest" and "dishonest" provide a convenient verbal shorthand, but they do not reflect virtue or vice with respect to character traits. Rather, each agent uses the strategy that maximizes her present value. As long as there is a continuation surplus for each agent as in Chapters 16 and 17, "continue" is a best reply to "continue" and "quit" is a best reply to "quit," so strategies X, Y, and Z yield a Nash equilibrium on every subgame.

The continuation surplus is generated here by the assumption $\beta < 1$. This search friction forces dishonest controllers to pay a price for cheating, because matches dissolve immediately after cheating occurs and a dishonest agent may have to wait several periods before being matched again. It may seem peculiar that a dishonest controller would want to preserve the match on a subgame where w or r has been paid, as in strategy Y. But if cheating is profitable, then in such a (disequilibrium) situation it is better to preserve the match and cheat immediately in the next period rather than quit and endure a spell of unemployment before having another opportunity to cheat.

The present value from each strategy depends on the agent's productivity q, the market prices (w, r), and the agent's beliefs. First, consider honest controllers. Let V_K^X be the present value of an honest controller in a KMF in a period where a match exists, and let U_K^X be the present value of an honest K who is unmatched and seeking a control position in a new firm. Stationarity gives

$$V_K^X = q - w + \delta[\alpha V_K^X + (1 - \alpha)U_K^X] \tag{1}$$

because K appropriates the output q and pays the wage w on the equilibrium path, both K and the noncontrolling L choose to continue, and nature continues the match in the next period with probability α.

From the fact that an unattached agent has the probability β of being matched in each period, we also have

$$U_K{}^X = \beta V_K{}^X + \delta(1 - \beta)\beta V_K{}^X + \delta^2(1 - \beta)^2 \beta V_K{}^X + .. \text{ or}$$

$$U_K{}^X = \beta V_K{}^X / [1 - \delta(1 - \beta)] \tag{2}$$

Substituting (2) into (1) yields

$$V_K{}^X = (q- w)[1 - \delta(1 - \beta)]/(1 - \delta)[1 - \alpha\delta(1 - \beta)] \tag{3a}$$

Similar reasoning for agents of type K using strategy Y gives $V_K{}^Y = q + \delta U_K{}^Y$ and $U_K{}^Y = \beta V_K{}^Y / [1-\delta(1-\beta)]$. Such agents appropriate the output q when matched but do not pay the wage w. This terminates the match immediately. The resulting present value is

$$V_K{}^Y = q[1 - \delta(1 - \beta)]/(1 - \delta) \tag{3b}$$

The present value for an agent of type K using the noncontroller strategy Z is a bit more complex, because such agents may be uncertain about whether the controlling agent in an LMF will be honest. The probability that an unattached agent of type L who wants to set up an LMF will turn out to be honest is θ_L. Let $V_K{}^{ZX}$ be the present value to K if the controller is honest, and let $V_K{}^{ZY}$ be the present value if the controller is dishonest. At the beginning of a new match, $V_K{}^Z = \theta_L V_K{}^{ZX} + (1-\theta_L)V_K{}^{ZY}$. When a controller is found to be honest, $V_K{}^{ZX} = r + \delta[\alpha V_K{}^{ZX} + (1-\alpha)U_K{}^Z]$, because the payment r occurs each period and the firm continues until exogenous separation occurs. When the controller is found to be dishonest, $V_K{}^{ZY} = \delta U_K{}^Z$, because r is not paid and K quits immediately. Combining these equations with $U_K{}^Z = \beta V_K{}^Z / [1-\delta(1-\beta)]$ as in (2), we obtain

$$V_K{}^Z = \theta_L r[1 - \delta(1 - \beta)]/(1 - \delta)[1 - \alpha\delta(1 - \beta\theta_L)] \tag{3c}$$

The noncontrolling present value $V_K{}^Z$ does not involve the agent's own productivity q, which only matters when K is a controller. It also does not involve w but does involve the rental fee r paid to capital suppliers by honest LMFs, along with the beliefs θ_L.

Next we need to examine which of the roles X, Y, or Z an agent of type K prefers to adopt. Ignoring the common factor $[1-\delta(1-\beta)]/(1-\delta)$ appearing in (3a), (3b), and (3c), which has no effect on comparisons among the three strategies, these present values are shown in Figure 18.1 as functions of the agent's productivity q. This graph is drawn under the

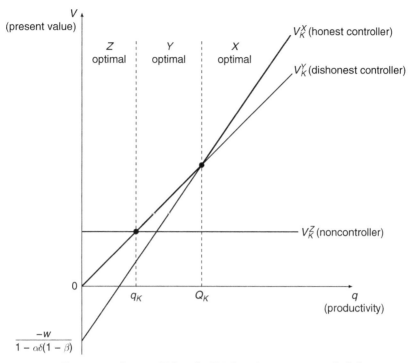

Figure 18.1 Present Values for K When Strategy Y Is Included

assumption that strategy Y is profitable for some values of q. The alternative case where Y is never profitable will be discussed later.

The present value $V_K{}^X$ of an honest controller is indicated by the line with the vertical intercept $-w/[1-\alpha\delta(1-\beta)]$ and slope $1/[1-\alpha\delta(1-\beta)]$. The present value $V_K{}^Y$ of a dishonest controller is given by the 45° line. These lines intersect at the productivity level

$$Q_K = w/\alpha\delta(1-\beta) \qquad (4)$$

Conditional on being the controller of a KMF, agents with $q \geq Q_K$ find honesty (X) to be optimal, and those with $q \leq Q_K$ find dishonesty (Y) to be optimal. The maximum present value as a function of productivity is indicated by the heavy locus with a kink at Q_K.

Agents of type K who are noncontrollers in LMFs receive the present value $V_K{}^Z$ in (3c), which is independent of q and therefore is a horizontal line in Figure 18.1. The productivity level at which $V_K{}^Z = \max\{V_K{}^X, V_K{}^Y\}$ is denoted by q_K. In Figure 18.1, the line for $V_K{}^Z$ intersects the heavy locus below the kink at Q_K so that $q_K < Q_K$. This gives

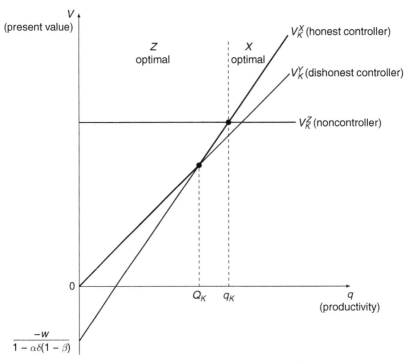

Figure 18.2 Present Values for K When Strategy Y Is Excluded

$$q_K = r\theta_L/[1 - \alpha\delta(1 - \beta\theta_L)] \qquad (\text{Y included for K}; \ q_K < Q_K) \qquad (5)$$

Type K agents with productivity below q_K want to be noncontrollers in LMFs (strategy Z). Those with productivity between q_K and Q_K want to control KMFs but cheat workers (strategy Y). Those with productivity above Q_K want to be honest controllers of KMFs (strategy X).

In the alternative case shown in Figure 18.2, $V_K{}^Z$ intersects the heavy locus at or above the kink at Q_K so that $q_K \geq Q_K$. This gives

$$q_K = w + r\theta_L[1 - \alpha\delta(1 - \beta)]/[1 - \alpha\delta(1 - \beta\theta_L)]$$
$$(\text{Y excluded for K}; \ q_K \geq Q_K) \qquad (6)$$

When Figure 18.2 applies, the dishonest strategy Y is never used by any agent of type K. Those with productivities below q_K want to be noncontrollers in LMFs, while those with productivities above q_K want to be honest controllers in KMFs.

The analysis for agents of type L is entirely symmetric. The results from (3) go through with a reversal of subscripts and an interchange of w and r.

$$V_L{}^X = (q-r)[1 - \delta(1-\beta)]/(1-\delta)[1 - \alpha\delta(1-\beta)] \qquad (7a)$$

$$V_L{}^Y = q[1 - \delta(1-\beta)]/(1-\delta) \qquad (7b)$$

$$V_L{}^Z = \theta_K w[1 - \delta(1-\beta)]/(1-\delta)[1 - \alpha\delta(1-\beta\theta_K)] \qquad (7c)$$

Symmetry also yields

$$Q_L = r/\alpha\delta(1-\beta) \qquad (8)$$

$$q_L = w\theta_K/[1 - \alpha\delta(1-\beta\theta_K)] \qquad \text{(Y included for L; } q_L < Q_L) \qquad (9)$$

$$q_L = r + w\theta_K[1 - \alpha\delta(1-\beta)]/[1 - \alpha\delta(1-\beta\theta_K)]$$
$$\text{(Y excluded for L; } q_L \geq Q_L) \qquad (10)$$

Figure 18.1 describes the situation in (9), and Figure 18.2 describes the situation in (10), with appropriate reversals of notation between K and L (and w and r) in each case.

Beliefs. I will require that the beliefs (θ_K, θ_L) be correct in the sense that they accurately reflect the relative frequencies of honest K and L among unmatched agents of each type who want control positions. First it is necessary to introduce further notation and derive preliminary results. I assume throughout that a steady state prevails.

I denote the stock of KMFs by λN and the stock of LMFs by $(1-\lambda)N$. I also use λ for the fraction of unattached K who seek control rights in the matching market. This has the following rationale. In equilibrium, market clearing will require that the fraction of unattached type K agents seeking control rights be equal to the fraction of unattached type L agents seeking noncontrolling positions. If both fractions are equal to λ, this is the share of newly created firms that will be KMFs. In a steady state, the share of KMFs in the flow of new firms must equal the share in the stock of existing firms. Thus I use λ to indicate the fraction of KMFs in both the stock and flow contexts.

The stock of KMFs with honest controllers will be denoted by $\mu_K \lambda N$, and the stock of LMFs with honest controllers will be denoted by $\mu_L(1-\lambda)N$. Among unattached K who want control rights, θ_K is the fraction who are honest, and among unattached L who want control rights, θ_L is the fraction who are honest. In general we expect $\mu_K \neq \theta_K$ and $\mu_L \neq \theta_L$, because firms with dishonest controllers dissolve with certainty, while firms with honest controllers do not, so dishonest agents are disproportionately common among unattached agents relative to their representation among controllers of existing matches.

The relationships among μ_K, μ_L, θ_K, and θ_L can be formalized as follows. Let π_K be the economy-wide fraction of type K agents who use strategy X. The total number of type K agents using this strategy is $\pi_K(N + M)$. Within this group, $\mu_K \lambda N$ are controllers of existing KMFs and $\theta_K \lambda M$ are unattached agents seeking control in future KMFs. Hence, $\pi_K(N + M) = \lambda(\mu_K N + \theta_K M)$. This and the parallel equation for L give

$$\pi_K = \lambda[\mu_K/(1 + \eta) + \theta_K \eta/(1 + \eta)] \tag{11a}$$

$$\pi_L = (1 - \lambda)[\mu_L/(1 + \eta) + \theta_L \eta/(1 + \eta)] \qquad \text{where } \eta \equiv M/N \tag{11b}$$

Now consider the controlling agents of type K who are honest. The number of such agents who become unattached in each period is $N\lambda\mu_K(1-\alpha)$ because there are N firms, λ is the fraction of firms that are KMFs, μ_K is the fraction of KMFs with honest controllers, and $(1-\alpha)$ is the fraction of KMFs with honest controllers that dissolve in each period. The number of unattached honest K who become controllers of new KMFs in each period is $M\lambda\theta_K\beta$ where M is the total number of agents of type K seeking new matches, λ is the fraction of the unattached K searching for positions as controllers, θ_K is the fraction of these K who are honest, and β is the fraction of these unattached agents who are successfully matched in a given period. In a steady state, the flow of honest K into the matching pool $N\lambda\mu_K(1-\alpha)$ and the corresponding flow of honest K out of the pool $M\lambda\theta_K\beta$ must be equal.

When $\lambda > 0$, this steady state condition and the parallel one for dishonest K give

$$\beta\eta\theta_K = (1 - \alpha)\mu_K \qquad \text{(honest K seeking to form KMFs)} \tag{12a}$$

$$\beta\eta(1 - \theta_K) = 1 - \mu_K \qquad \text{(dishonest K seeking to form KMFs)} \tag{12b}$$

$$\beta\eta = 1 - \alpha\mu_K \qquad \text{(all K seeking to form KMFs)} \tag{12c}$$

where the third equation is obtained by summing the first two. When $\lambda < 1$, we have

$$\beta\eta\theta_L = (1 - \alpha)\mu_L \qquad \text{(honest L seeking to form LMFs)} \tag{13a}$$

$$\beta\eta(1 - \theta_L) = 1 - \mu_L \qquad \text{(dishonest L seeking to form LMFs)} \tag{13b}$$

$$\beta\eta = 1 - \alpha\mu_L \qquad \text{(all L seeking to form LMFs)} \tag{13c}$$

where again the third equation is obtained by summing the first two.

When $\lambda > 0$, Equations (12a) and (12c) can be substituted in (11a) to derive the relationship between π_K and θ_K. This yields

$$\pi_K = \lambda g(\theta_K) \text{ where } g(\theta) \equiv \theta(\beta + 1 - \alpha)/[1 - \alpha + \beta(1 - \alpha + \alpha\theta)] \quad (14a)$$

When $\lambda < 1$, the same can be done for L using (11b), (13a), and (13c), yielding

$$\pi_L = (1 - \lambda)g(\theta_L) \quad (14b)$$

The function $g(\theta)$ in (14) is strictly increasing with $g(0) = 0$ and $g(1) = 1$.

Finally, if $0 < \lambda < 1$ so that both KMFs and LMFs exist, (12) and (13) imply

$$\mu_K = \mu_L = \mu \quad \text{and} \quad \theta_K = \theta_L = \theta \quad (15)$$

In this case, steady state conditions imply that the fraction of KMFs controlled by honest agents must equal the fraction of LMFs controlled by honest agents. This extends to the composition of the matching pool: the fraction of unattached K seeking control rights who are honest must equal the fraction of unattached L seeking control rights who are honest. The boundary cases $\lambda = 0$ and $\lambda = 1$ will be discussed in Section 18.5.

Equilibrium. I define an equilibrium to be a combination $(w, r, \theta_K, \theta_L, \lambda)$ with three features. First, there is an optimality requirement: at $(w, r, \theta_K, \theta_L)$ the agents must choose strategies that maximize their present values in light of their private productivity q. Next, there is a restriction on beliefs: θ_K must be the true proportion of honest agents within the set of unattached agents who are seeking to become controllers of KMFs, and likewise for θ_L. Finally, there is a market-clearing condition: λ must simultaneously be the fraction of unattached type K agents who want to control KMFs and the fraction of unattached type L agents who want to be noncontrollers in KMFs. In short, the demand for labor by KMFs must equal the supply of labor to KMFs. When this is so, the demand for capital by LMFs automatically equals the supply of capital to LMFs. Thus there is no aggregate imbalance among candidates for the various organizational roles.

Here I express these requirements somewhat more formally:

An *equilibrium* is a combination $(w, r, \theta_K, \theta_L, \lambda)$ with $w \geq 0$, $r \geq 0$, $\theta_K \in [0, 1]$, $\theta_L \in [0, 1]$, and $\lambda \in [0, 1]$ satisfying the following conditions.

(a) *Optimality:* Each agent adopts a strategy from the set {X, Y, Z} that maximizes his or her present value, given (w, r, θ_K, θ_L) and the agent's own productivity q.

(b) *Beliefs:* Among the set of unattached agents of type K who use X or Y, θ_K is the fraction using X. Among the set of unattached agents of type L who use X or Y, θ_L is the fraction using X.

(c) *Market clearing:* λ is the fraction of all agents of type K who use X or Y, and it is also the fraction of all agents of type L who use Z.

When there is no equilibrium of this kind, the temptations for controllers to cheat noncontrollers are too strong to be overcome by repeated game effects, and the agents must be content with their reservation payoffs. In later sections, I explore the usual questions of existence and uniqueness for this equilibrium concept. I also examine the equilibrium values of (w, r) and implications for the market shares of KMFs and LMFs.

Sections 18.3 and 18.4 consider equilibria where both firm types exist $(0 < \lambda < 1)$. Section 18.3 studies equilibria without any adverse selection where the dishonest strategy Y is never used, while Section 18.4 studies equilibria where adverse selection does occur. Section 18.5 explores the boundary cases where all firms are KMFs ($\lambda = 1$) or all firms are LMFs ($\lambda = 0$). Section 18.6 introduces an asymmetry where investors are endowed not only with productive assets but also liquid wealth and describes the effects on the equilibria from preceding sections.

18.3 Equilibrium without Adverse Selection

This section considers equilibria in which both KMFs and LMFs exist ($0 < \lambda < 1$). From (15) this implies $\theta_K = \theta_L = \theta$. I further narrow the focus to equilibria where all of the controlling agents are honest ($\theta = 1$), so only strategies X and Z from Section 18.2 are used in equilibrium. There is no adverse selection problem, because the noncontrollers never meet unmatched controllers of the opposite type who will cheat them. Among the agents of type K, those with productivity below q_K become noncontrollers in LMFs, and those with productivity above q_K become honest controllers in KMFs. The same holds for agents of type L and the productivity threshold q_L.

An equilibrium with $0 < \lambda < 1$ and $\theta = 1$ requires a situation like the one shown in Figure 18.2, where strategy Y is excluded for K. This is true because some agents of type K must use strategy X, while others must use strategy Z. In the case shown in Figure 18.1 where Y is included for a nondegenerate productivity interval, this implies the existence of K who use Y, which violates $\theta_K = 1$. When Figure 18.2 applies, no K uses strategy Y, so this problem does not arise. Strategy Y must be excluded for L for the same reasons.

The relevant algebraic expressions for the breakpoints q_K and q_L are given by (6) and (10). Substituting $\theta = 1$ in q_K and q_L gives $q_K = q_L = w + r$. To have noncontrollers we require $0 \le q_0 < q_K = q_L = w + r$, so both prices cannot be zero. In fact, both must be positive. Suppose that $w = 0$ and $r > 0$. From (8) and (10) this implies $Q_L = r/\alpha\delta(1-\beta) \le q_L = r$, which is false when $r > 0$. A similar argument rules out $w > 0$ and $r = 0$.

To reduce clutter, I adopt the notation

$$\rho \equiv \alpha\delta(1 - \beta)\in (0, 1) \qquad (16)$$

Combining (4) and (6) with $q_K \ge Q_K$ and $\theta_L - 1$ yields the upper bound

$$w/r \le \rho/(1 - \rho) \qquad (17a)$$

Similarly, combining (8) and (10) with $q_L \ge Q_L$ and $\theta_K = 1$ yields the lower bound

$$(1 - \rho)/\rho \le w/r \qquad (17b)$$

Putting these results together, a necessary condition for the existence of an equilibrium with $0 < \lambda < 1$ and $\theta_K = \theta_L = 1$ is

$$\rho \equiv \alpha\delta(1 - \beta) \ge 1/2 \qquad (17c)$$

The interpretation of (17c) is intuitive. To deter cheating, it is necessary to have enough weight on future payoffs that cheaters care about being punished (large $\alpha\delta$) and enough market friction that cheaters cannot find new partners quickly (low β).

Assuming that $\rho \ge 1/2$, choose any price ratio w/r satisfying (17a) and (17b). Along with $\theta_K = \theta_L = 1$, this guarantees that (i) for type K agents it is optimal to use Z when $q \le q_K$ and X when $q \ge q_K$, and (ii) for type L agents it is optimal to use Z when $q \le q_L$ and X when $q \ge q_L$. Because the dishonest strategy Y is never used, the beliefs $\theta_K = \theta_L = 1$ are correct. This satisfies parts (a) and (b) in the definition of equilibrium.

Now consider part (c). Because the productivities are distributed uniformly on $[q_0, q_1]$ for agents of each type and $q_K = q_L = w + r$, the fraction of K using X is $(q_1 - q_K) / (q_1 - q_0) = (q_1 - w - r) / (q_1 - q_0)$ and the fraction of L using Z is $(q_L - q_0) / (q_1 - q_0) = (w + r - q_0) / (q_1 - q_0)$. Equating these gives

$$\lambda = 1/2 \qquad \text{with } w + r = (q_0 + q_1)/2 \qquad (18)$$

Thus half of the firms must be KMFs and the other half must be LMFs. We also find that the sum of the prices paid to noncontrollers must equal the mean productivity.

For future reference, I summarize these results as follows.

Proposition 1
Equilibrium without adverse selection: An equilibrium with $0 < \lambda < 1$ and $\theta_K = \theta_L = 1$ exists if and only if $\rho \equiv \alpha\delta(1-\beta) \geq 1/2$. Any price ratio w/r satisfying $(1-\rho)/\rho \leq w/r \leq \rho/(1-\rho)$ can occur in equilibrium. In all such equilibria, the prices satisfy $w + r = (q_0 + q_1)/2$ and there are equal numbers of KMFs and LMFs.

Proof
As above

18.4 Equilibrium with Adverse Selection

This section extends the analysis to equilibria where some of the agents seeking to be controllers of firms are dishonest. As in the last section, I assume that both kinds of firms exist in equilibrium ($0 < \lambda < 1$), so from (15) the beliefs can be written $\theta_K = \theta_L = \theta < 1$.

Before going to the main results, I first rule out an equilibrium with $\theta = 0$. In this situation, everyone who wants to control a firm is dishonest and cheats the noncontroller. From (3c) and (7c), this implies $V_K^Z = V_L^Z = 0$. The horizontal line corresponding to V_K^Z in Figures 18.1 and 18.2 is therefore identical to the horizontal axis, and no agent adopts strategy Z. This makes it impossible to satisfy the market-clearing condition.

I therefore consider equilibria with $0 < \theta < 1$. Because some agents of types K and L use strategy Y in equilibrium, we need $q_K < Q_K$ and $q_L < Q_L$, where the relevant algebraic expressions are obtained from (4), (5), (8), and (9) and the relevant graph is Figure 18.1. From (4) and (8) we have $Q_K = w/\rho$ and $Q_L = r/\rho$. Both prices must be strictly positive in order to satisfy $q_K < Q_K$ and $q_L < Q_L$.

From (5) and (9) we have

$$q_K = rh(\theta) \quad \text{and} \quad q_L = wh(\theta) \quad \text{where } h(\theta) \equiv \theta/[1 - \alpha\delta(1 - \beta\theta)]$$

$$(19)$$

The function $h(\theta)$ is strictly increasing with $h(0) = 0$ and $h(1) = 1/(1\text{-}\rho)$. Optimality implies that for agents of type K, those with $q \leq q_K$ are noncontrollers using Z, those with $q_K < q < Q_K$ are dishonest controllers using Y, and those with $Q_K \leq q$ are honest controllers using X. Parallel statements apply to agents of type L.

The inequalities $q_K < Q_K$ and $q_L < Q_L$ place bounds on the price ratio

$$\rho h(\theta) < w/r \ < \ 1/\rho h(\theta) \tag{20}$$

Thus a necessary condition for equilibrium is $\rho h(\theta) < 1$.

Market clearing requires that the fraction λ of firms that are KMFs must be both the fraction of type K agents who want to be controllers (honest and dishonest alike) and the fraction of type L agents who want to be noncontrollers. This gives

$$\lambda = (q_1 - q_K)/(q_1 - q_0) = (q_L - q_0)/(q_1 - q_0) \tag{21}$$

Substituting in (21) for q_K and q_L from (19) gives

$$w + r = (q_0 + q_1)/h(\theta) \tag{22}$$

This determines the equilibrium sum of the prices as a function of the beliefs θ. Because we assumed that $0 < \lambda < 1$, we must have $q_0 < q_K < q_1$ and $q_0 < q_L < q_1$. These inequalities hold automatically when (20) and (22) hold.

In an equilibrium with $0 < \lambda < 1$ and beliefs $\theta_K = \theta_L = \theta$, the aggregate shares of honest controllers for each type must satisfy the following conditions from (14).

$$\begin{aligned} \pi_K = \lambda g(\theta) = (q_1 - Q_K)/(q_1 - q_0) \qquad &\text{where } Q_K = w/\rho \\ \pi_L = (1 - \lambda)g(\theta) = (q_1 - Q_L)/(q_1 - q_0) \qquad &\text{where } Q_L = r/\rho \end{aligned} \tag{23}$$

In each case, the second equality follows from optimality conditions. Substituting the values of Q_K and Q_L and summing the expressions in (23) gives

$$w + r = \rho[2q_1 - g(\theta)(q_1 - q_0)] \tag{24}$$

Combining (22) and (24) gives another necessary condition for equilibrium:

$$q_0 + q_1 = \rho h(\theta)[2q_1 - g(\theta)(q_1 - q_0)] \tag{25}$$

This imposes a restriction on equilibrium beliefs involving only exogenous parameters. Any solution $\theta^* \in (0, 1)$ in (25) has $\rho h(\theta^*) < 1$ and accordingly satisfies the necessary condition associated with (20).

For $\theta = 0$, the right-hand expression in (25) is zero. For $\theta = 1$, the right-hand side is $[\rho/(1-\rho)](q_0 + q_1)$. By continuity, if $\rho > 1/2$ there is at least one interior solution $\theta^* \in (0, 1)$ in (25). This is only a sufficient condition for an interior solution in (25), and I will not attempt to rule out the existence of such a solution when $\rho \leq 1/2$.

Next, I show how to construct an equilibrium. Suppose that a solution $\theta^* \in (0, 1)$ exists in Equation (25). Choose any prices $(w, r) > 0$ such that the sum satisfies $w + r = (q_0 + q_1)/h(\theta^*)$ and the ratio satisfies $\rho h(\theta^*) < w/r < 1/\rho h(\theta^*)$. As mentioned earlier, the interval for w/r is automatically nonempty. Use these prices to determine $q_K = r/h(\theta^*)$, $q_L = w/h(\theta^*)$, $Q_K = w/\rho$, and $Q_L = r/\rho$.

At these prices and beliefs, it is optimal for agents of type K to use Z when $q \in [q_0, q_K]$; Y when $q \in (q_K, Q_K)$; and X when $q \in [Q_K, q_1]$. The same is true for agents of type L upon changing subscripts. Market clearing holds because $\lambda = [q_1 - rh(\theta^*)]/(q_1 - q_0) = [wh(\theta^*) - q_0]/(q_1 - q_0) \in (0, 1)$. The beliefs are correct because θ^* satisfies (25).

I summarize the results of this section for future reference.

Proposition 2
Equilibrium with adverse selection:

(a) Consider an equilibrium $(w, r, \theta_K, \theta_L, \lambda)$ with $0 < \lambda < 1$, so that both types of firms exist. Any such equilibrium has $\theta_K = \theta_L = \theta > 0$.

(b) A necessary and sufficient condition for the existence of such an equilibrium with $\theta < 1$, so there are some dishonest controllers, is that Equation (25) have a solution $\theta^* \in (0, 1)$. A sufficient condition for this to occur is $\rho > 1/2$.

(c) Any equilibrium with $0 < \lambda < 1$ and $0 < \theta^* < 1$ has the following features:

   (i) The prices (w, r) are both positive.
   (ii) The sum of the prices is $w + r = (q_0 + q_1)/h(\theta^*)$.
   (iii) The ratio of the prices satisfies $\rho h(\theta^*) < w/r < 1/\rho h(\theta^*)$.
   (iv) Agents of type K use Z when $q \in [q_0, q_K]$; Y when $q \in (q_K, Q_K)$; and X when $q \in [Q_K, q_1]$, where $q_K = rh(\theta^*)$ and $Q_K = w/\rho$. Parallel statements apply to agents of type L with $q_L = wh(\theta^*)$ and $Q_L = r/\rho$.
   (v) The fraction of firms that are KMFs is $\lambda = [q_1 - rh(\theta^*)]/(q_1 - q_0) \in (0, 1)$ or equivalently $\lambda = [wh(\theta^*) - q_0]/(q_1 - q_0) \in (0, 1)$.

Proof
As above

Some comparisons with Proposition 1 may be illuminating. In each proposition, we are only concerned with equilibria where both types of firms occur. From Proposition 1, the parameter restriction $\rho \geq 1/2$ guarantees the existence of equilibria without adverse selection ($\theta = 1$). When this is strengthened to $\rho > 1/2$, Proposition 2 indicates that there are additional equilibria with adverse selection ($\theta < 1$).

Proposition 1 establishes that if $\rho < 1/2$, there are no equilibria without adverse selection. However, I have not ruled out the possibility that $\rho < 1/2$ could occur while at the same time an interior solution exists in (25). This would imply that equilibria with adverse selection exist even though equilibria without adverse selection do not. I will leave it for interested readers to determine whether situations of this sort can arise.

When there is an equilibrium with adverse selection, its properties are described by Proposition 2(c). Part (c)(ii) determines the sum of the equilibrium prices $w + r$, and (c)(iii) places limits on the ratio w/r. Because $\rho h(\theta^*) < 1$, the prices can always be equal, but (within bounds) they can also deviate from equality.

In Proposition 1 where all controllers were honest ($\theta = 1$), the market share of KMFs was uniquely determined to be $1/2$. An interesting feature of Proposition 2 is that when some controllers are dishonest ($\theta < 1$), this is no longer true. It is possible to have equal numbers of KMFs and LMFs, which occurs if the prices (w, r) are equal. But the nondegenerate interval of price ratios from (c)(iii) corresponds to an interval on which the market shares of the firms can vary.

Given a fixed θ^* from (25), the share of KMFs is an increasing function of the wage or equivalently a decreasing function of the rental fee r, as indicated in Proposition 2(c)(v). One might have expected KMFs to be more common with a low wage, but this intuition is incorrect. Because the sum $w + r$ is fixed, a higher wage must be associated with a lower rental fee. The lower fee paid to capital in the LMF reduces the opportunity cost of the KMF for agents of type K, and this effect dominates, raising the KMF market share. The lower bound on the KMF share is $\lambda_{min} = [q_1 \rho h(\theta^*) - q_0]/[1 + \rho h(\theta^*)](q_1 - q_0)$, and the upper bound is $\lambda_{max} = [q_1 - q_0 \rho h(\theta^*)]/[1 + \rho h(\theta^*)](q_1 - q_0)$.

This multiplicity of equilibria supports a view of capital and labor markets in which firm organization, the prices paid to noncontrollers, and the extent of dishonesty among controllers are matters of social convention, within limits imposed by optimal behavior, correct beliefs, and market clearing. Multiplicity of this sort exists even when

Equation (25) has a unique interior solution. If (25) has more than one interior solution, this introduces another source of multiplicity. I return to these issues in Section 18.7.

18.5 Capitalist Equilibrium

The equilibria in Propositions 1 and 2 involved both KMFs and LMFs, either in precisely equal numbers (the former) or subject to bounds on market shares (the latter). Here I explore the case where all firms are KMFs ($\lambda = 1$). I maintain the earlier abstract symmetry between capital and labor in this section, and one can obtain equilibria where all firms are LMFs ($\lambda = 0$) by reversing the notation in a straightforward way.

When all firms are KMFs, the market-clearing condition (c) from the definition of equilibrium holds if and only if all agents of type K use strategy X or Y and all agents of type L use strategy Z. From the optimality condition (a), this is true if and only if

$$q_K \leq q_0 \quad \text{and} \quad q_1 \leq q_L \tag{26}$$

The remaining restrictions involve condition (b) for beliefs.

Equilibrium beliefs about the honesty of K can be determined as follows. Recall that $Q_K = w/\rho$ always holds. Given that all agents of type K are using X or Y from (26), the aggregate fraction of all agents of type K using the honest controller strategy X is

$$
\begin{aligned}
\pi_K &= 1 & &\text{if } w/\rho \leq q_0 \\
\pi_K &= (q_1 - w/\rho)/(q_1 - q_0) & &\text{if } q_0 < w/\rho < q_1 \\
\pi_K &= 0 & &\text{if } q_1 \leq w/\rho
\end{aligned} \tag{27a}
$$

When $\lambda = 1$, we have $\pi_K = g(\theta_K)$ from (14). Because g is strictly increasing, this can be inverted to give a relationship between the beliefs θ_K and the fraction π_K. It follows that

$$
\begin{aligned}
\theta_K &= 1 & &\text{if and only if } w/\rho \leq q_0 \\
\theta_K &= 0 & &\text{if and only if } q_1 \leq w/\rho
\end{aligned} \tag{28a}
$$

The main novelty for the boundary case where $\lambda = 1$ is that the restriction $\theta_K = \theta_L$ in (15) need not hold, because in equilibrium there are no agents of type L seeking control over firms. Thus the fraction of such agents who are honest is undefined. If an agent of type K does meet an agent of type L who wants control, this is a disequilibrium event, and it is unclear how K should form beliefs about L.

I approach this problem as follows. Suppose that when an unattached K meets an unattached L seeking control, K does not infer anything about L's productivity and retains the prior belief that L's productivity is distributed uniformly on $[q_0, q_1]$. However, K also believes that once L is in a controlling position and the strategy Z is no longer relevant, L will choose between X and Y based on the threshold $Q_L = r/\rho$ from (8). This implies that

$$
\begin{aligned}
\theta_L &= 1 && \text{if } r/\rho \leq q_0 \\
\theta_L &= (q_1 - r/\rho)/(q_1 - q_0) && \text{if } q_0 < r/\rho < q_1 \\
\theta_L &= 0 && \text{if } q_1 \leq r/\rho && \text{and therefore}
\end{aligned}
$$

(27b)

$$
\begin{aligned}
\theta_L &= 1 && \text{if and only if } r/\rho \leq q_0 \\
\theta_L &= 0 && \text{if and only if } q_1 \leq r/\rho
\end{aligned}
$$

(28b)

The only subtle point is that K must assume that L will pursue the same deviant strategy in all future matches, that these will all be LMFs, and that L therefore calculates present values as in (7). However, it is not obvious what else to assume, and the symmetry of (28a) and (28b) is appealing because we are not introducing asymmetries between KMFs and LMFs through arbitrary claims about disequilibrium beliefs.

The next point is that we may have equilibria where the agents of type K could use the dishonest strategy Y at some productivity levels, as in Figure 18.1, or equilibria where agents of type K would never use Y at any productivity level, as in Figure 18.2. The same is true for type L. In what follows, I use more-compact notation by writing

$$
\begin{aligned}
h_K &\equiv \theta_K/[1 - \alpha\delta(1 - \beta\theta_K)] \in [0, 1/(1 - \rho)] \\
h_L &\equiv \theta_L/[1 - \alpha\delta(1 - \beta\theta_L)] \in [0, 1/(1 - \rho)]
\end{aligned}
$$

(29)

Algebraically, the following cases arise:

Y included for K : $q_K = rh_L < w/\rho = Q_K$ (30a)

Y excluded for K : $q_K = w + rh_L(1 - \rho) \geq w/\rho = Q_K$ (30b)

Y included for L : $q_L = wh_K < r/\rho = Q_L$ (31a)

Y excluded for L : $q_L = r + wh_K(1 - \rho) \geq r/\rho = Q_L$ (31b)

The derivations of (30) and (31) are the same as in Section 18.2. Together these provide four situations that need to be considered.

The central question is whether for each situation there can be an equilibrium with $\lambda = 1$. The interior cases $0 < \theta_K < 1$ and $0 < \theta_L < 1$ lead to an algebraic swamp, so I focus on beliefs involving certainty.

Proposition 3
Capitalist equilibrium: Confine attention to equilibria where all firms are KMFs ($\lambda = 1$) and beliefs have the form $(\theta_K, \theta_L) \in \{0, 1\}^2$.

(a) A necessary condition for the existence of such an equilibrium is $\rho > 1/2$.
(b) In all such equilibria, the beliefs are $\theta_K = 1$ and $\theta_L = 0$, the prices satisfy $w < r$, and the strategy Y is included for K.
(c) Such an equilibrium exists if and only if $[q_0, q_1] \subseteq [w/\rho,$ min $\{w/(1-\rho), r/\rho\}]$.
(d) If the (strict) minimum in (c) is $w/(1-\rho)$, Y is included for L and $w/r < (1-\rho)/\rho < 1$. If the (weak) minimum in (c) is r/ρ, Y is excluded for L and $(1-\rho)/\rho \leq w/r < 1$.

Proof
The procedure is to check all sixteen combinations generated by (28), (30), and (31), with four possible patterns for beliefs and four possible patterns for inclusion or exclusion of strategy Y for types K and L. The algebra is tedious but not hard.

It should be emphasized that the beliefs in part (b) are the only ones involving certainty that are compatible with all firms being KMFs. There are no such equilibria with $\theta_K = \theta_L = 0$, $\theta_K = 0$ and $\theta_L = 1$, or $\theta_K = \theta_L = 1$.

The upshot of Proposition 3 is that subject to the restriction that beliefs take the form $\theta_K \in \{0, 1\}$ and $\theta_L \in \{0, 1\}$, there is only one way to have an equilibrium where all firms are capitalist. All investors with control rights are believed to be honest (they will pay the wage w), and all workers seeking control rights are believed to be dishonest (they will not pay the fee r). Even with these rather extreme beliefs, parameter restrictions are needed. By now the necessary condition $\rho > 1/2$ in part (a) is familiar from Sections 18.3 and 18.4. A new feature is the need to restrict the support of the productivity distribution by having $[q_0, q_1]$ satisfy the requirement in part (c).

The dishonest strategy Y must be included for K in the sense that there are some imaginable values of the productivity q where this strategy would be used by an agent of type K. However, in equilibrium K never uses Y because, for the relevant interval $q \in [q_0, q_1]$, all agents of type K prefer strategy X. The only relevance of the strategy Y for type L involves the price ratio w/r, which determines whether this strategy is included or excluded for L in part (c). In either case, w < r is required in order to justify optimistic beliefs about K's promises to pay the wage while at the same time justifying pessimistic beliefs about L's promises to pay the rental fee. Proposition 3 puts no upper bound on r.

Because there are no LMFs in equilibrium, no agent of type L ever confronts a decision about whether or not to pay the fee r. Nevertheless, this fee does help support the equilibria in Proposition 3. The fee must be large enough that K does not believe that it would actually be paid in an LMF, and this belief must be justified in the sense that if an LMF ever arose, no L would pay it.

Symmetric arguments can be used to construct an equilibrium in which all firms are LMFs. All that is needed is a reversal of the notation in Proposition 3.

Proposition 4

Laborist equilibrium: Confine attention to equilibria where all firms are LMFs ($\lambda = 0$) and beliefs have the form $(\theta_K, \theta_L) \in \{0, 1\}^2$.

(a) A necessary condition for the existence of such an equilibrium is $\rho > 1/2$.
(b) In all such equilibria, the beliefs are $\theta_K = 0$ and $\theta_L = 1$, the prices satisfy r < w, and the strategy Y is included for L.
(c) Such an equilibrium exists if and only if $[q_0, q_1] \subseteq [r/\rho, \min \{r/(1-\rho), w/\rho\}]$.
(d) If the (strict) minimum in (c) is $r/(1-\rho)$, Y is included for K and $r/w < (1-\rho)/\rho < 1$. If the (weak) minimum in (c) is w/ρ, Y is excluded for K and $(1-\rho)/\rho \leq r/w < 1$.

The implications of Propositions 3 and 4 together are shown in Figure 18.3. The existence requirement $\rho > 1/2$ is assumed to be satisfied. Above the 45° line, there are equilibria where all firms are KMFs as long as the productivity interval $[q_0, q_1]$ satisfies the restrictions indicated in the graph. It is impossible to have an equilibrium where all firms are LMFs. Below the 45° line, there are equilibria where all firms are LMFs, again subject to restrictions on the productivity interval, but there are no equilibria where all firms are KMFs.

18.6 Liquidity Issues

So far I have assumed that agents of type K are endowed with productive assets like machines, but I have said nothing about endowments of

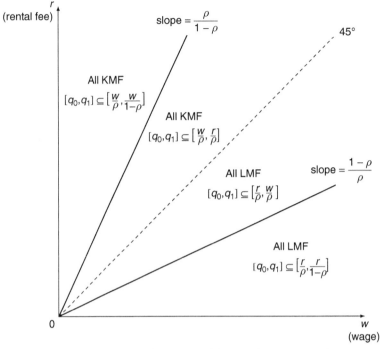

Figure 18.3 All-KMF and All-LMF Equilibria with Symmetry ($\rho > 1/2$ Needed for Existence)

financial wealth. For both KMFs and LMFs, I have taken it for granted that payments to noncontrollers occur after output has been obtained, so these payments can be financed out of revenues resulting from production. Here I depart from this framework by assuming that in addition to their endowments of physical assets, investors also have endowments of financial wealth. This allows them to pay wages before output arrives. Workers lack such endowments and can only pay rental fees (or repay loans) using the revenue from production. In a nutshell, the agents of type K have working capital while those of type L do not.

This asymmetry leads to a crucial change in the timing of events, and therefore a change in the strategic situation. If a KMF cheats by withholding wages at the start of a period, workers can punish the investor immediately by blocking production. There is no symmetric solution to the opportunism problem in an LMF if workers lack the financial wealth necessary to pay investors up front for the use of productive assets. I will rule out the accumulation of wealth among workers over time by assuming that output evaporates if it is not consumed in the current period. Investors, on the other hand, have continuing liquidity because they enjoy a flow of new income in each period. These assumptions are stark, but they are useful in thinking through the consequences of asymmetric liquidity.

For the KMF, events now unfold as follows. K first decides whether or not to pay the wage w. L then decides whether or not to block production. L is indifferent between cooperating with K to produce output or accepting the reservation payoff of zero. After L decides whether to produce, both agents decide simultaneously whether to quit. All other events unfold as in earlier sections. In particular, the sequence in the LMF is exactly the same as before: L chooses whether or not to pay the fee r after output arrives.

An honest KMF controller pays the wage, continues if the wage has been paid and production has occurred, and quits otherwise. A dishonest KMF controller does not pay the wage, continues if the wage has been paid and production has occurred, and quits otherwise. A noncontrolling L produces and continues if the wage has been paid and blocks production and quits otherwise. Along the equilibrium path, this yields payoffs (q-w, w) when the controller is honest and (0, 0) when the controller is dishonest.

After any history where the wage has not been paid or output has not been produced (or both), there is mutual quitting at the end of the period—a Nash equilibrium. After a history where the wage has not been paid, L is indifferent between producing or not at the production stage and cannot affect match continuation because K will quit, so it is a best reply for L to block production and then quit. At the start of the period, K pays the wage when $q \geq w$ and does not pay when $q < w$. As long as there is a nonnegative continuation surplus, a wage payment ensures that L is willing to produce and both parties are willing to continue the match.

For convenience, I continue to use the notation X, Y, and Z for the strategies, but with the understanding throughout this section that these are modified as described above for agents in a KMF. Present values for the KMF are computed as in Section 18.2, where, as before, an honest controlling K receives V_K^X and a noncontrolling K receives V_K^Z. But now it is impossible for a dishonest controller K to capture any present value above zero, whatever his or her productivity q. Given the strategy used by noncontrollers in KMFs, from K's standpoint the strategy Z is always at least as good as Y, and accordingly all of the type K agents choose between X and Z. The strategies and present values for agents of type L are the same as in Section 18.2, except for the modifications in L's strategy described earlier when L is working in a KMF.

Because agents of type K never choose Y when Z is available, the productivity threshold Q_K no longer plays any role when these agents compare a controlling position in a KMF against a noncontrolling position in an LMF. The cutoff in the productivity distribution for this decision is always q_K, which is the point of indifference between X and Z. The threshold Q_L remains relevant for L because there may be circumstances in which it is profitable for L to be dishonest.

Now consider beliefs. Agents of type L who consider working in a KMF believe that the controller of the firm will be honest (X), because any agent of type K with a low enough productivity to be dishonest (preferring Y to X due to $q < w$) would have been better off as a noncontroller (preferring Z to Y). Whenever KMFs exist in equilibrium, I therefore set $\theta_K = 1$ and substitute this belief into L's present values as well as the level of productivity q_L. Beliefs when KMFs do not exist in equilibrium will be discussed later.

For the existing stock of KMFs, the fraction of controllers who are honest is now $\mu_K = 1$, and therefore the market share of KMFs is $\lambda = \pi_K$ from (11a). This is simply the economy-wide fraction of type K agents who want to be controllers. From (12) we have $M/N \equiv \eta = (1-\alpha)/\beta$, so the unemployment rate is determined by exogenous parameters governing the search process. When $0 < \lambda < 1$ so both types of firms exist, (13) gives $\theta_L = \mu_L = 1$. In equilibrium it is not only true that all controllers of KMFs must be honest, but also that all controllers of LMFs must be honest.

In the rest of this section, I discuss various implications of investor liquidity for the results in Propositions 1–4. For the sake of brevity, I do not provide proofs, but they can be constructed without much difficulty.

First consider Proposition 1 in Section 18.3, where there were firms of both types ($0 < \lambda < 1$) and all controllers were honest ($\theta_K = \theta_L = 1$). One might think that liquidity would have no effect on the conclusions in Proposition 1, because in equilibrium no one is using strategy Y anyway, so ruling it out for K would not matter. Indeed, a number of earlier results do go through. Strategy Y must still be excluded for L, the price ratio must still satisfy $w/r \geq (1-\rho)/\rho$ if $r > 0$, the sum of the prices is still $w + r = (q_0 + q_1)/2$, and we still have equal numbers of KMFs and LMFs.

One difference from Proposition 1 is that the requirement $\rho > 1/2$ for existence of equilibrium is dropped, and now any $\rho > 0$ is compatible with existence. Another is that now the only restriction on the price ratio is $w \geq r(1-\rho)/\rho$, which is the condition under which strategy Y is excluded for L. This leaves open the possibility $r = 0$. By contrast with Proposition 1, there is no upper bound on w/r, because there is no need to exclude strategy Y for K in order to keep agents of type K from cheating. The deletion of this incentive constraint makes it possible to overcome adverse selection for all $\rho > 0$. This establishes that the bilateral character of the moral hazard problem in Section 18.3 was a crucial feature of the economic environment.

Readers familiar with repeated game models may find it strange that one can deter cheating even when future payoffs have negligible weight (ρ close to zero). It may seem reasonable that the KMF can be deterred from cheating on the wage because workers are indifferent toward blocking production. However, we also need to deter cheating on the rental fee r by the LMF. The trick is to recognize that when ρ becomes small, the rental fee can also be made small, so the LMF has little temptation to cheat. Indeed, when r is sufficiently small relative to w, the issue is not that agents of type L might be tempted to switch from X to Y; it is that they might be tempted to switch from X to Z and work for KMFs in order to obtain a high wage. The latter temptation can be regulated through the wage level even when the rental fee r is negligible. Because there is no longer any need to restrain the wage in order to limit cheating by KMFs, the wage can be used to achieve the balance between strategies X and Z required for markets to clear.

Now consider Proposition 2 in Section 18.4, where again there were firms of both types ($0 < \lambda < 1$) and adverse selection was a problem because some controllers of each type would cheat ($\theta_K = \theta_L = \theta < 1$). Under the assumptions of this section, there is no counterpart to this proposition. For the reasons discussed earlier, it must be true that all controllers in all firms are honest. Again, the removal of the incentive constraint for K has implications not just for the relative frequency of firm types, but for the existence of an entire class of equilibria. The adverse selection problem effectively vanishes, at least whenever both firm types exist, because honesty by one class of controllers imposes the same kind of honesty on the other class of controllers.

Next, consider Proposition 3 in Section 18.5, where we had only KMFs ($\lambda = 1$) and focused on beliefs with certainty—$(\theta_K, \theta_L) \in \{0, 1\}^2$. Under the new assumptions of this section, we still impose the beliefs $\theta_K = 1$ and $\theta_L = 0$, and the same rules apply as in Proposition 3 regarding the inclusion or exclusion of strategy Y for type L agents.

The contrast is that under the assumptions of this section, an all-KMF equilibrium exists if and only if $[q_0, q_1] \subseteq [w, \min \{w/(1-\rho), r/\rho\}]$. This differs from Proposition 3(c) in that the old lower bound w/ρ is replaced by the new lower bound w. This allows the requirement $\rho > 1/2$ to be removed, so now any $\rho > 0$ is consistent with existence of such an equilibrium. Also, for any given ρ and prices (w, r), the constraints on the productivity interval $[q_0, q_1]$ are relaxed. This occurs because it is no longer necessary to have a wage low enough to prevent controllers of KMFs from cheating. The lower bound on the wage now comes from a market-clearing condition, which is less restrictive.

Previously, the symmetry of K and L enabled us to derive symmetric conditions for an all-KMF equilibrium and an all-LMF equilibrium, as indicated in Propositions 3 and 4, and as shown in Figure 18.3. This is no longer the case. Consider an equilibrium where all firms are LMFs $(\lambda = 0)$ and the beliefs are $(\theta_K = 0, \theta_L = 1)$, as in Proposition 4. The new condition for the existence of an all-LMF equilibrium is $[q_0, q_1] \subseteq [r/\rho, w]$. As for the KMF case, the previous existence condition $\rho > 1/2$ is dropped and instead any $\rho > 0$ is compatible with existence.

The implications for all-KMF and all-LMF equilibria are shown in Figure 18.4. As in Figure 18.3, when an all-KMF equilibrium exists, then an all-LMF equilibrium does not, and vice versa. Furthermore, as in Figure 18.3, existence of equilibrium requires that the productivity interval $[q_0, q_1]$ satisfy the restrictions shown in each region of the graph.

In the situation where investors have liquid wealth, the all-KMF case is no longer confined to the region above the 45° line as it was in Figure 18.3. Rather, when $\rho < 1/2$, there are all-KMF equilibria at some points below the 45° line in Figure 18.4 (recall that in Section 18.5, the inequality $\rho < 1/2$ was incompatible with existence of an equilibrium in which all firms are of the same type). The all-LMF case is limited to the region below the ray with slope ρ in Figure 18.4.

Reducing the parameter $\rho \equiv \alpha\delta(1-\beta)$ expands the region in Figure 18.4 in which an all-KMF equilibrium can arise. This occurs when good matches are less likely to be maintained (lower α), the agents put less weight on future payoffs (lower δ), or search frictions are smaller (higher β). All of these factors enhance the incentive benefit from having controllers make payments to noncontrollers up front and thus favor the KMF when investors have liquid wealth but workers do not. The prospects for an all-LMF equilibrium improve when these parameters move in the opposite direction (i.e., more-persistent matches, more-patient agents, and long

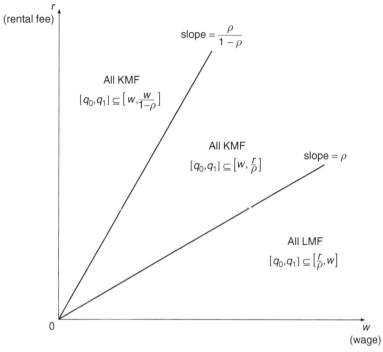

Figure 18.4 All-KMF and All-LMF Equilibria with Investor Liquidity ($\rho > 0$ Needed for Existence)

search durations), because liquidity then becomes less vital as a way of solving incentive problems.

Holding ρ constant and thinking of (w, r) as determined by custom or convention so the prices can be treated as exogenous, Figure 18.4 shows that an all-KMF equilibrium occurs when the wage w is relatively low for a given rental fee r. This is consistent with the usual intuition that KMFs are favored when labor is cheap. Conversely, an all-LMF equilibrium occurs when the rental fee r is relatively low for a given wage w, consistent with the intuition that LMFs are favored when capital is cheap.

18.7 Conclusion

Several lessons can be taken away from this chapter. First and foremost, moral hazard and adverse selection problems do help determine the market shares of KMFs and LMFs. The idea that such barriers obstruct LMF formation thus deserves attention.

However, the asymmetry principle from Chapter 8 also deserves attention. If one wants to explain why KMFs and LMFs do not have equal market shares in the real world, one must specify a source of asymmetry between capital and labor. Just having a market imperfection is not enough. This is highlighted by the results in Section 18.3, where the two firm types had precisely equal shares in equilibrium. The results were less strong in Section 18.4 because there was a continuum of equilibrium market shares, but again an equal number of KMFs and LMFs was a possibility.

Section 18.5 showed that even with symmetry of capital and labor, the model could generate equilibria where all firms are KMFs, subject to suitable restrictions on parameter values and prices. Section 18.6 broke the symmetry between capital and labor by introducing liquidity issues. This change in the strategic foundations of the model eliminated a major parameter restriction needed for existence in Section 18.3. However, equality of market shares for KMFs and LMFs was preserved. A more dramatic result was the elimination of all of the equilibria in Section 18.4. Changing moral hazard from a two-sided problem to a one-sided problem in effect made it possible to dispose of adverse selection entirely. Finally, removing the incentive constraint for KMFs altered the results from Section 18.5 by allowing existence of all-KMF equilibria for a wider range of wages and rental fees, under conditions in which matches often break down exogenously, agents strongly discount future payoffs, and unattached agents find new partners quickly.

Repeated game models are well known for having a multiplicity of equilibria, and this chapter is no exception. In particular, the wage (w) and rental fee (r) are not uniquely determined, and these prices play a crucial role in determining whether KMFs or LMFs prevail. This leaves considerable room for history, politics, convention, chance, or other factors that may be responsible for equilibrium selection. If one wants to argue that the dominance of KMFs is just an accident of history and that LMFs would be dominant if we were living in a parallel universe with a different history, the analysis of this chapter offers a degree of support. But the requirements of optimal choice, rational beliefs, and market clearing do impose some intellectual discipline, and the model does have some predictive content. My view is that while history and chance no doubt play a role, more-systematic economic explanations for the prevalence of KMFs should be sought. I take up this challenge in Chapter 19.

PART VIII

SYNTHESIS AND AGENDA

19

Breaking the Symmetry

19.1 Introduction

Here I synthesize the theoretical ideas developed in earlier chapters. The goal is to construct a unified causal framework for the labor-managed firm and show how it can be used to explain many of the empirical patterns in Chapters 6–8. The foundation of my theory is the proposition that capital is alienable while labor is not. This distinction acts in concert with market imperfections to determine organizational form.

Although the causal framework in this chapter is complicated, the main message is simple. The short version is that in many industries where LMFs do not currently exist, such firms would probably have productivity advantages over KMFs and could probably survive successfully in competition with them. However, LMFs do not usually arise spontaneously, partly for reasons involving market failures that could be remedied through public policy (see Chapter 20).

The causal structure is summarized in Figure 19.1, which begins at the top with the asymmetry between capital and labor with respect to alienability. The four columns correspond to implications of alienability for (a) control transactions, (b) control group composition, (c) stocks and flows, and (d) the roles of capital and labor suppliers in the production process. In each column, the relevant alienability effect is modulated by one or more market imperfections, such as adverse selection, collective choice, or a lack of commitment devices. Each alienability effect, together with the market imperfections, leads to a distinctive cluster of organizational problems: appropriation problems, public good problems, and so on.

At the bottom of the diagram, I list observable consequences of each problem. The four causal pathways corresponding to the four columns of Figure 19.1 influence the formation of firms, the conversion of LMFs into

355

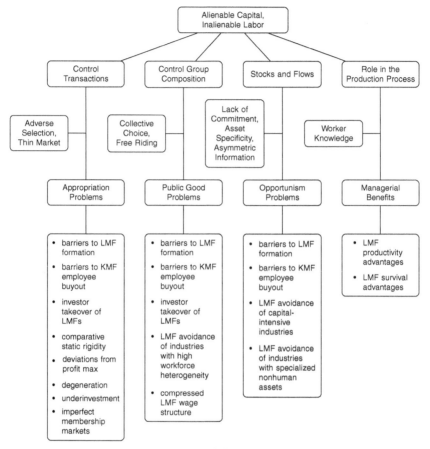

Figure 19.1 Causal Framework for the Labor-Managed Firm

KMFs or vice versa, and the survival of firms, all of which shape prevailing populations of KMFs and LMFs. The four pathways also affect LMF behavior, the distribution of LMFs across industries, and some design features that successful LMFs tend to have.

The columns of Figure 19.1, read from left to right, are roughly in the order in which ideas were presented in Chapters 9–18. Appropriation took center stage in Chapters 9–11, public goods in Chapters 12–13, and opportunism in Chapters 14–15, with elaboration in Chapters 16–18. One exception is the rightmost column, dealing with the roles of capital and labor in production and the implications for firm management. This causal channel did not received sustained attention in earlier chapters, but

I believe it often gives LMFs productivity advantages relative to KMFs, for reasons to be discussed later.

Sections 19.2, 19.3, and 19.4 discuss appropriation, public good, and opportunism problems, respectively. Section 19.5 considers potential managerial benefits that LMFs may derive from the role of workers in the production process, along with some caveats about the causal effects in the first three columns of Figure 19.1, which may not always favor KMFs. The implications for the rarity of LMFs are summarized in Section 19.6. I suggest an agenda for theoretical work in Section 19.7 and an agenda for empirical work in Section 19.8. Finally, I offer a few closing thoughts in Section 19.9.

19.2 Appropriation Problems

The first implication of alienability, developed in the leftmost column of Figure 19.1, is that ownership of physical capital (or less-tangible nonhuman assets) can readily be transferred from one person or group to another. Thus, in a KMF, old controllers can exit and new controllers can enter without any change in the physical inputs of the firm, through paper or electronic transactions that shift ownership of the firm's capital stock from one party to another. In an LMF, however, any turnover within the control group implies turnover in the identities of the individuals supplying labor, and therefore in the nature of the firm's labor inputs.

One reason why this matters is that workers are heterogeneous with respect to skills and preferences. If individual workers know their own characteristics while firms or other workers do not, adverse selection problems arise. In an LMF, these problems have consequences in the market for control. If outsiders are uncertain about the true characteristics of insiders, they are less willing to pay a membership fee to join the firm (see Chapter 10). If insiders are uncertain about the true characteristics of outsiders, they are less willing to allow open trading in control positions (see Chapter 11).

Another implication of inalienable labor is that LMF membership markets are thin, becoming active only when a worker changes firms. Unlike stock markets, where claims on firms are highly divisible and can be traded instantaneously, LMF membership markets involve lumpy claims with infrequent transactions. This can lead to high search costs and the replacement of competitive markets with bilateral bargaining. Workers are also likely to suffer from a lack of liquidity, because it could take a long time to recruit a suitable replacement worker willing to pay for membership rights.

The LMF may try to solve this problem by repurchasing the membership rights of departing members and then selling them to new members. KMFs have less need for such procedures. The liquidity of control positions may occasionally be an issue, especially in privately held KMFs, but rarely to the same degree as for LMFs. Often it is easy to turn an equity share into cash.

Adverse selection and market thinness interact. KMF insiders may know more about the firm's true profitability than outsiders do, and a wise investor is aware that such informational asymmetries exist. But when the market for a firm's equity shares is large, there is a large demand for research about the firm, and highly paid specialists offer such information to outside investors. The market price of a firm's equity shares is no doubt a noisy signal, but considerable information about the firm's true profitability is often built into these prices. There is nothing comparable in the LMF membership market.

Appropriation problems for an LMF are particularly acute at the formation stage, when firms do not have long track records and it can be very difficult to distinguish good projects from bad ones. An entrepreneur cannot organize a new LMF without engaging in control transactions with workers. But adverse selection in the market for control will predictably limit what workers are willing to pay for membership in LMFs and lower the profitability of LMF creation, as explained in Chapter 10. The geographic agglomeration of LMFs (see Section 7.6) may in part reflect "track record" effects (see Section 10.6).

A wealthy entrepreneur with a good project who wants to create a KMF faces no similar adverse selection problem, because in this case the entrepreneur does not have to persuade workers (or anyone else) about the merits of the project. Even if LMFs would sometimes be more productive than KMFs, entrepreneurs may forego these productivity benefits for the sake of superior rent appropriation in the KMF. I regard this as a major barrier to LMF formation, as indicated in Figure 19.1.

A different but related problem arises for employee buyouts of established firms. Such firms may have long track records as KMFs, so there is no uncertainty about the firm's current profitability. However, there may still be a question about how profitable the firm would be if it were reorganized as an LMF. If the KMF investors or managers know the answer but workers do not, an adverse selection problem arises. Furthermore, if a few workers gather information about this subject, obtain promising results, acquire control rights, and then attempt to create an LMF by selling membership rights to other workers, again there is an adverse selection problem, now between the informed and the uninformed workers.

Chapter 13 focused on free rider issues associated with employee buyout, but appropriation problems raise related barriers to the conversion of KMFs into LMFs, as indicated in Figure 19.1.

Due to adverse selection and thin markets, LMF insiders are likely to have trouble appropriating the full value of the membership rights sold to outsiders. The relevance of this point in the real world is suggested by the underpricing of membership rights in U.S. plywood cooperatives (see Section 7.3). In Section 9.5, I showed in a dynamic framework that imperfect appropriation may create incentives for LMF insiders to convert a firm into a KMF by selling it to investors, even if the firm has higher productivity as an LMF. For this reason, I list investor takeover of LMFs as a possible consequence of appropriation problems in Figure 19.1.

Controllers who cannot capture the full value of membership rights to outsiders will make decisions systematically different from those of controllers who can. Chapter 9 showed that imperfect appropriation leads to comparative static rigidities. It is well documented empirically that LMFs have less-elastic output supply and input demand functions than KMFs (see Section 6.4). In a related vein, Chapter 9 showed that appropriation problems can account for findings that LMFs deviate from profit maximization (see Section 6.5).

Chapter 9 also indicated that imperfect appropriation may lead to a "degeneration" problem where LMFs replace retiring members with hired hands and an underinvestment problem where LMFs grow more slowly than similar KMFs over time. The existence of these phenomena is controversial, with some researchers finding evidence for them while others do not (see Sections 7.4 and 7.5). I believe the underlying temptations are real but that LMFs can often overcome such temptations through suitable institutional rules. One solution is to commit the firm by a charter, constitution, or other founding document to a maximum fraction of nonmember workers (to avoid degeneration) and a minimum level of retained earnings (to avoid underinvestment). The widespread view that such rules are necessary suggests that the theory is correct. Although rules of this sort may be helpful or even vital, they impose constraints on LMFs that have no counterpart for KMFs.

Chapter 11 investigated the implications of adverse selection for professional partnerships. Adverse selection creates a temptation for a departing worker to sell out to the highest bidder, even if that person's productivity is low. To get around this problem, in a partnership departing workers are required to sell their positions to the firm, which recruits a successor.

Similar rules are used in other LMFs where membership positions are treated as transferable assets.

19.3 Public Good Problems

The inalienability of labor has implications for control group composition, which are developed in the second column of Figure 19.1. There are two issues: the size of the control group and the heterogeneity of its membership. First, consider control group size. In all firms except the smallest, labor must be provided by multiple individuals, because there are natural limits on any individual's endowment of time and skill. The number of workers required is roughly proportional to the scale of the firm's operations. But there is no limit on the accumulation of capital, so in principle one person or a small group could finance even a relatively large firm. For this reason, LMFs frequently have larger control groups than do KMFs of similar size operating in the same industry.

Now consider heterogeneity. If firms were numerous enough relative to worker types, workers could sort themselves across firms in such a way that the membership of each firm had unanimous preferences toward firm policies. But in a world where scale economies are important, this is unlikely to be possible. Alternatively, if workers were mobile enough, for a large economy one could rely on theoretical arguments that workers would be unanimous within each firm (see Chapter 12). But the inalienability of labor limits the mobility of workers, so these arguments may not apply to LMFs.

If production requires a worker team of significant size and the heterogeneity of worker preferences and beliefs cannot be handled through sorting or mobility, there is an immediate barrier to LMF formation: it becomes necessary to recruit a group of workers who are sufficiently homogeneous to agree on the merits of a joint project. The search costs involved in assembling such a team may be substantial, and it is unclear who will incur these costs. No individual worker can easily capture the collective gains from such a project. Public good problems therefore create additional barriers to LMF formation, as indicated in the second column of Figure 19.1.

Chapter 13 argued that free rider problems among employees may create barriers to employee buyouts of existing KMFs. The problem arises because the productivity of the firm as an LMF is uncertain. Investments of time, effort, and money can reduce this uncertainty, but the benefits are spread broadly across the workforce and it is difficult for any individual or small group to capture the full social gain from conversion to an LMF. As a result, too few KMFs are converted. The parallel KMF problem is not symmetric, because one or a few investors can often finance the takeover of an LMF, so free rider problems in this case may be negligible.

Chapter 12 showed that preference heterogeneity among workers often makes LMFs vulnerable to takeover by profit-maximizing investors. The instability of LMFs can be avoided by abolishing individual membership rights that can be sold to outsiders, but this solution may lead to other rigidities, as in Chapters 9–11. Chapter 12 also argued that KMFs are typically sustainable against employee buyout. Notice that the source of the obstacle to employee buyout differs in Chapters 12 and 13. In the former, it involves the difficulty of assembling a worker coalition that is sufficiently homogeneous to make a coherent buyout proposal to investors, while in the latter it involves a free rider problem.

Writers who believe that LMFs are rare for collective choice reasons often stress transaction costs and argue that LMFs tend to avoid those industries where workers have heterogeneous skills or preferences (see Chapter 8). The models in Chapters 12 and 13 do not rely on transaction costs, but Chapter 12 has similar implications for the incidence of LMFs across industries. Chapter 13 is concerned with firm size and uncertainties about productivity rather than workforce heterogeneity and predicts that an employee buyout is less likely when a firm is large and its profitability as an LMF is difficult to ascertain.

Another public good problem involves wage compression in LMFs. Theorists have argued that the median voter in an LMF will usually want to shift wages away from members with higher productivity toward those with lower productivity. Tendencies of this kind are well documented (see Section 6.7). The parallel phenomenon for KMFs is a temptation for majority shareholders to exploit minority shareholders. While such issues do arise, they seem easier to resolve, perhaps because KMFs can readily commit to rules under which all shareholders receive identical dividends per share.

19.4 Opportunism Problems

The third column of Figure 19.1 traces the implications of another fact derived from alienability: firms can acquire capital as a stock, but they can only acquire labor as a flow. In some situations there can be technological or economic advantages from having a firm own a stock of capital rather than renting nonhuman assets from an outsider. For example, leasing can lead to underinvestment in firm-specific assets due to bargaining over quasi-rents (see Chapters 14 and 15) or to poor incentives for asset maintenance. If KMF investors are wealthy enough, they can readily finance the collective ownership of nonhuman assets. But if the workers in an LMF have little personal wealth, they need to secure access to these assets through leasing, debt, or other arrangements with outsiders.

At this point, a crucial market imperfection enters the story: the incomplete nature of legal contracts. Transaction cost economics asserts that comprehensive contracting is often infeasible for production activities, so firms rely on authority relationships instead. However, I argued in Chapter 14 that one generic problem with authority relationships is that they can be abused opportunistically. In the language of this book, the controllers of firms can abuse noncontrollers. Chapter 15 developed a model in which the controllers appropriate output, while the noncontrollers either bargain over a wage (in the KMF) or a rental payment (in the LMF). I showed that in market equilibrium, control rights were assigned to suppliers of specialized physical or human capital.

It might seem that the opportunism problem is symmetric: KMFs can cheat workers and LMFs can cheat investors. Indeed, Chapter 16 showed that in a model where effort and side payments were self-enforced, it did not matter whether productive assets were owned jointly by the workforce or by an outsider. This symmetry was broken, however, in Chapters 17 and 18. I established in Chapter 17 that the difference between stocks and flows is critical, because the temptation for an LMF to cheat investors by withholding rental or debt service payments can exceed the temptation for a KMF to cheat workers by withholding wages. This gives KMFs an advantage in industries with high capital costs. I argued in Chapter 18 that liquidity constraints affect KMFs and LMFs in asymmetric ways, because KMF investors can pay their employees prior to production, while LMF members cannot pay outside investors until after production. This expands the range of conditions under which there is an equilibrium having only KMFs.

These conclusions are consistent with the cross-industry distribution of LMFs (see Section 6.3). Professional partnerships are widespread, and worker cooperatives tend to emerge in construction, transport, and services, along with light manufacturing. These activities have a common feature: they are all relatively labor intensive. Indeed, we have direct econometric evidence that LMFs are more likely to enter labor-intensive industries (see Section 7.1).

The present theory provides two explanations for this pattern. First, Chapter 15 showed that when nonhuman assets are specialized, KMFs tend to be favored because they induce investment in such assets. A related factor is that highly specialized assets are unlikely to function well as loan collateral, so LMFs will have difficulty financing them. Second, Chapter 17 showed that when capital requirements are large, KMFs are favored because LMFs have difficulty making credible commitments to investors. This problem is compounded by the fact that human capital cannot be used as collateral due to the inalienability of labor (see Hart and Moore, 1994). These points are consistent with the view that LMFs may have capital-to-labor ratios similar to those of KMFs in industries they choose to enter, while they avoid industries where limited access to capital would be a serious competitive liability (see Section 7.7).

19.5 Managerial Benefits

The rightmost column of Figure 19.1 identifies a source of LMF advantage. Due to the inalienability of labor, suppliers of this input are physically present at the point of production. By engaging in production activities, workers often gain detailed knowledge about technology, organization, market conditions, and so on. This information can be used both for direct decision-making and monitoring the performance of managers. In addition, workers routinely obtain information about the skills and performance of fellow workers, which may lead to better task assignments and diminish the need for monitoring by supervisors.

Because LMFs put ultimate control in the hands of informed workers, one might expect them to enjoy higher productivity than KMFs in the same industry. While KMFs can certainly try to elicit information held by employees, this requires more roundabout organizational procedures and could run into incentive difficulties as discussed later. Empirically, it does appear that productivity comparisons favor LMFs more often than not (see Section 6.6). LMFs also appear to have better survival rates than similar KMFs (see Section 7.2), which may result from higher productivity, greater wage flexibility, a stronger commitment to job security, or other factors.

I have not developed a full-blown model of the productivity differences between KMFs and LMFs. Section 9.5 and Chapter 10 assumed higher productivity for LMFs in order to generate interesting trade-offs with appropriation problems. Chapter 13 allowed productivity either to rise or fall when a firm was converted from a KMF into an LMF. In Chapter 17,

LMFs had a productivity advantage because KMFs tended to distort the time path of output to satisfy incentive constraints. In Chapter 18, agents had differing productivities as controllers of firms, but the productivity distribution was the same for workers and investors. I will return to productivity issues in Section 19.7.

The causal pathways in the first three columns of Figure 19.1 do not invariably favor KMFs, and several countervailing effects deserve mention. In the appropriation column, it should be noted that KMF controllers may not appropriate all of the social costs and benefits of the firm, because employees often capture rents or quasi-rents. Due to asymmetric information or a lack of commitment devices, KMFs may maintain rigid wages and lay off workers in response to negative shocks, while LMFs vary wages or hours. With imperfect markets, it cannot be assumed that KMFs always act as simple Walrasian profit maximizers or that LMF employment rigidity is always a bad thing.

In the public goods column, one could argue that LMFs tend to provide an array of local public goods better suited to worker preferences. Furthermore, in large publicly traded firms with many individual shareholders, there may in fact be more investors than workers. Accordingly, the free rider problem facing investors in monitoring managerial performance for a KMF may be greater than the parallel problem for workers in an LMF.

In the opportunism column, LMFs are almost surely better able to make credible commitments to workers, with the foremost example being a commitment to job security. This may induce LMF members to invest in firm-specific human capital. Another gain from credible commitment in the LMF is that workers are more inclined to share private information with managers (e.g., about the productivities of their own jobs), because they have less reason to believe that such information will be used against their interests in the future (e.g., by increasing production quotas or lowering piece rates; see Carmichael and MacLeod, 2000). Such commitment possibilities reinforce the productivity and survival advantages of LMFs from the fourth column of Figure 19.1 and help explain why KMFs find it difficult to replicate LMF performance by eliciting private employee information.

19.6 The Rarity of Labor-Managed Firms

How does the theory explain the rarity of labor-managed firms documented in Section 6.2? One point is that vastly more KMFs than LMFs are created from scratch. Because wealthy entrepreneurs could create LMFs if they found it profitable to do so, and LMFs would probably enjoy a productivity advantage in some circumstances, a plausible inference is that entrepreneurs have trouble appropriating the productivity benefits from an LMF. The causal channel from the first column of Figure 19.1 is therefore a prime suspect. A related factor is that LMFs tend to spread their productivity benefits across control groups of significant size, as in the second column of Figure 19.1, leading to diffuse incentives for individual workers to create such firms. Heterogeneity of worker preferences and beliefs reinforces this problem by creating significant search costs for anyone organizing an LMF. Even if these problems could somehow be overcome, poor workers might be unable to attract capital from outside investors, as in the third column of Figure 19.1. All three of these factors probably erect barriers to LMF entry.

Another explanation for the rarity of LMFs involves transformation of LMFs into KMFs and vice versa. Despite an enormous population of KMFs that could be converted into LMFs and the likelihood that some conversions would raise productivity, the LMF sector displays little tendency toward expansion by this route. It is interesting that even though KMFs are created from scratch much more often than LMFs, it also seems true that of the LMFs we do have, a large majority were created from scratch rather than by conversion of existing KMFs (see Sections 7.1 and 7.2).

I think the most likely reason for the rarity of LMFs derived from the conversion of KMFs is that the collective choice and free rider problems associated with the second column of Figure 19.1 tend to obstruct employee buyouts of KMFs, even if productivity gains would ensue. Capital constraints associated with the third column of Figure 19.1 probably also make it difficult to finance employee buyouts, especially for profitable firms in capital-intensive industries. The paucity of employee buyouts is reinforced by occasional transformations of LMFs into KMFs, either through "degeneration" as in the first column of Figure 19.1 or investor takeover as in the second column of Figure 19.1.

LMFs do seem to have one advantage with respect to organizational demography—namely, a higher survival rate. My guess is that this is largely associated with the positive productivity effects arising in the fourth column of Figure 19.1, along with the ability of LMFs to overcome opportunism directed against workers. But whatever its source, this survival advantage alone is not enough to support a large population of LMFs.

19.7 Theoretical Agenda

Although I have attempted to provide a reasonably comprehensive synthesis, alert readers will have noticed that a number of theoretical issues were either ignored or placed on the back burner during the course of the book. Here I sketch a few of these omissions, moving from left to right across the columns in Figure 19.1.

In the first column, on appropriation problems, one key gap involves the idea that control markets for LMFs are likely to be thin, that as a result LMF members will suffer from liquidity problems, and that this exacerbates appropriation problems at the level of the firm as a whole. I have not provided a formal model of this idea, and it is unclear to what extent an LMF can solve the problem by promising individual members that when they leave, it will buy back their membership shares at their current fair market value. An interesting way to smooth out the resulting financial liabilities for the firm is to give departing members a bond that can be sold on an external financial market (Tortia, 2007).

In the second column of Figure 19.1, on public good problems, Chapter 12 could be extended in various ways. For example, one could impose a constraint on the ability of workers to diversify their labor supply across firms and study sorting processes where individual workers self-select into firms based on their preferences about the local public goods supplied by each firm. One could also consider situations where individual agents are endowed with both capital and labor. Finally, it would be desirable to determine the equilibrium policies of firms rather than studying small deviations from existing policies.

I consider risk aversion in the context of the third column of Figure 19.1 because it is usually discussed in conjunction with LMF capital constraints. Almost all models in this book have assumed risk neutrality. One reason I have not devoted more attention to risk aversion is that there is mixed empirical evidence about its importance for LMFs, as discussed in Chapter 8. But another reason is that it is not obvious how best to model it.

The standard story is that diversification goals make LMF members less willing to finance their own firms out of whatever personal wealth they possess, which increases the need for capital from outside sources. This is a reasonable starting point, but it should be observed that LMF members can use control rights as an insurance device. For example, LMFs usually respond to market shocks by maintaining employment and varying wages, while KMFs frequently respond by maintaining wages and varying employment. A good model should explain why control rights are used differently in these two cases, and what the implications are for the overall risks borne by workers, rather than just treating these risks as exogenous or assuming that workers bear no risk in KMFs.

A good model should also address the point frequently made in the literature that workers cannot diversify their human capital across firms (because labor is inalienable), which may limit their willingness to invest financial capital in the firms where they work. A further layer of complexity arises because workers may differ in their risk tolerances and may choose between KMFs and LMFs based upon these preferences. I do not see an easy way to construct a model that includes all of these factors, and I am unsure about the value of a model that omits any of them. I leave these matters for readers to ponder.

Another topic relevant for the third column of Figure 19.1 is the issue of liquidity constraints in relation to the capital market (as opposed to the liquidity issues connected with control transactions in the first column). KMFs financed by wealthy investors do not face any important liquidity constraints with respect to working capital or investments in collectively owned assets. But LMFs seeking outside financing do face constraints of this kind, at least until retained earnings become available. I touched lightly on this point in Chapters 17 and 18, but much more can be done.

Chapter 18 emphasized adverse selection involving entrepreneurial projects, but I did not consider the potential role of signaling. Agents with substantial wealth can make large up-front investments in their own firms, something that would not be profitable unless they knew their projects were good. If investors with bad projects are more tempted to cheat workers by not paying wages or doing so in other ways, signaling would help good KMFs attract labor. The founders of an LMF might be less able to send positive signals to investors and therefore might have trouble attracting capital even when they have a good project and would not be tempted to cheat investors.

Another omission, already mentioned in Section 19.5, is that I have not tried to develop a serious model to explain why LMFs often have productivity advantages. As a result, the fourth column in Figure 19.1 is fuzzier than the first three. Several factors are likely to be important: (a) the information acquired by workers from direct participation in the production process, including mutual monitoring of effort; (b) the credibility of commitments by LMF controllers not to use information supplied by workers against them; (c) the credibility of commitments by LMF controllers to protect employment, encouraging investments in firm-specific human capital; and (d) the fact that workers with more job security put more weight on the future when they play repeated games with managers or other workers.

A related point about productivity is that LMFs with collective capital ownership may mitigate or eliminate distributional conflicts between capital and labor suppliers. In KMFs, such conflicts can result in high bargaining costs (including strikes and lockouts), rigid wages, resistance to innovation, and so on. Due to the inalienability of labor, these problems cannot be solved by having KMFs own the human capital of their employees, but they can potentially be solved by having LMFs own productive nonhuman assets. Of course, if LMF asset ownership is financed by outside investors, the conflict between capital and labor does not disappear; it simply shifts to the capital market. But LMFs can at least avoid day-to-day workplace conflicts with investors or their representatives.

The direct role of workers in the production process can also lead to less-tangible advantages for the LMF. These include a sense of control over one's own work life and a sense of community in the workplace. These psychological and social benefits may enter into worker utility functions, may affect worker willingness to pay for control rights, and may be difficult or impossible for a KMF to replicate. We need further research on the conditions under which these effects tend to emerge and on their importance relative to pecuniary factors. Experimental work on the intrinsic value of control rights (Fehr et al., 2013; Bartling et al., 2014) offers intriguing insights and should be accommodated in a more comprehensive theory of the labor-managed firm.

19.8 Empirical Agenda

In my view, the question of why LMFs are rare is fundamentally a question about organizational demography. To answer it in a convincing way, we need to obtain detailed information on the birth rates of KMFs and LMFs, the death rates of KMFs and LMFs, and the rates at which each type of firm is converted into the other. The net result from these processes is an equilibrium population of KMFs and LMFs.

I would like to see data sets of this kind spanning diverse countries, years, and industries, using standardized definitions to classify organizational forms. These data sets could be used for aggregate work on LMF entry and exit over the business cycle, like that done by Pérotin (2006), but it would be highly desirable to disaggregate to the industry level. If we knew more about the ways in which LMF entry and exit are affected by industry characteristics like capital intensity, risk, average firm size, workforce heterogeneity, and so on, this would be quite illuminating for theorists. For example, it would be helpful to know whether the findings by Podivinsky and Stewart (2007, 2009) about the effects of capital intensity and risk on LMF entry can be replicated for other countries besides the U.K. and for other decades besides the 1980s.

I would also like to know whether there are differences between LMFs and KMFs operating in the same industry with respect to (a) their characteristics at the time of entry, (b) their growth rates over time, and (c) the conditions under which they exit. Interesting comparisons of firm sizes and capital-labor ratios have been carried out by Fakhfakh et al. (2012), and comparisons of firm sizes and wages at the startup stage have been done by Burdín (2014). It would be useful to have further research at the industry level along these lines, including replications for additional countries.

In all of this, it is vital to distinguish between LMFs formed from scratch versus those formed through employee buyouts of KMFs and to distinguish between LMFs lost through financial failure versus those lost through investor takeover. Simply knowing the aggregate size of the conversion flows relative to birth and death rates would be valuable, because it would tell theorists whether organizational conversion is an important part of the overall story about LMF rarity. There may be too few conversions to allow confident inferences at the industry level, but I would also be interested to know whether transitions from one organizational form to the other are triggered by any identifiable events or have firm-level correlates. For example, I would like to know whether LMFs created through employee buyout emerge disproportionately from financially distressed KMFs. Is this a robust fact across countries and time periods?

A good deal of empirical research has been done on worker cooperatives, and this has been indispensable. But what about professional partnerships? Are there patterns in the formation of worker-controlled and investor-controlled firms in professional services, such as law firms, or in the disappearance of firms of each type? What about conversions of LMFs into KMFs or vice versa in the professional services sector?

A particularly interesting line of research that would benefit from extensions and replications involves productivity and survival comparisons between KMFs and LMFs in the same industry. The most convincing productivity results so far are those by Fakhfakh et al. (2012) for France, but it would be highly desirable to go beyond one country. For example, do the French results extend to Italy or Spain? Similarly, the most convincing survival results to date are for France and Uruguay. The French survival results are at an aggregate level, so for industry-level survival comparisons we are essentially relying on a single country. Do the Uruguayan results obtained by Burdín (2014) generalize? Can we say anything about the sources of the LMF survival advantage?

I will close with a suggestion that the causal framework in this chapter be treated as a source of hypotheses. Can we test ideas about imperfect appropriation, beyond the existing research on LMF comparative static behavior and objective functions? Can we test the idea that LMFs are less likely to form or persist in industries with high workforce heterogeneity or the idea that employee buyouts are less likely in larger firms? Can we show that specialized physical capital makes LMFs less likely while specialized human capital makes LMFs more likely? Can we learn how existing LMFs have been financed or discover the specific capital market imperfections that limit the expansion of the LMF sector? Can we identify the circumstances under which LMFs tend to have productivity advantages and explain how these advantages arise? The topics are endless, and I will leave judgments about the feasibility of particular projects to empirical researchers.

19.9 Conclusion

In Chapter 1 and again in Chapter 8, I argued that a good theory of the LMF should adhere to some general principles. First, we had the imperfection principle: to explain the empirical differences between KMFs and LMFs, one should identify relevant departures from an environment of complete and competitive markets. Next, we had the asymmetry principle: one should identify differences in the characteristics of capital and labor, and show why it matters which group of input suppliers has control. And finally, we had the replication principle: one should not attribute empirical asymmetries between KMFs and LMFs to features of one organizational form that are easily replicated by the other.

Does the theoretical synthesis in this chapter satisfy these requirements? I claim that it does. In my view, the difference between alienable capital and inalienable labor is sufficiently fundamental to explain a wide range of stylized facts about KMFs and LMFs. I also considered an extensive list of market imperfections, including adverse selection, public goods, asset specificity, and a lack of commitment devices. Each of these factors modulates one or more aspects of the alienability distinction.

The resulting causal structure is complex. First, the alienability distinction has multiple implications, as indicated by the four columns in Figure 19.1. Second, the key is the interaction between alienability factors and market imperfections: neither alone offers a sufficient explanatory framework. Third, more than one source of market imperfection can operate simultaneously. Fourth, there can be interactions across columns in Figure 19.1. Finally, even when the causal pathways do not interact directly, in some cases they reinforce one another, while in other cases they push in opposite directions. For example, the overall rarity of LMFs is the net result of effects derived from the first three columns, which are largely negative, and those from the fourth column, which are largely positive.

With regard to the replication principle, I have tried to tie my theory as closely as possible to the intrinsic differences between capital and labor, and to the implications of these differences for firm behavior and performance. My goal was to construct a theory that would be immune to the objection that LMFs can solve their problems by imitating what KMFs do or vice versa. I hope that by and large, readers will be satisfied that the replication principle has been respected.

An important criterion in evaluating any theory is the test of unification: can the theory account for a broad range of facts in a coherent way? I have argued that the theory developed here not only explains the general rarity of LMFs, but also accounts for a large number of empirical patterns surveyed in Chapters 6–7. I sought unification by absorbing what seemed most valuable in the prevailing theories of the LMF discussed in Chapter 8, while discarding notions that appeared less useful in explaining the facts as we presently understand them.

The resulting synthesis reflects personal idiosyncrasies with regard to research interests, modeling techniques, views about the relative importance of various market imperfections, and so forth. I also recognize that it neglects a number of causal factors, including history, politics, institutions, and culture. But I hope that the theory includes many of the factors an economist would care about and proves useful for the next generation of LMF researchers.

20

Policy Directions

20.1 Introduction

A reader who has absorbed the arguments of earlier chapters might respond by saying, "I agree that the alienability difference between capital and labor is significant and that it probably helps to account for the rarity of LMFs. However, I fail to see how policy interventions could promote the spread of LMFs, because this difference between capital and labor is immutable and cannot be remedied through public policy." What this statement overlooks is the fact that alienability does not act in isolation; it acts in concert with market imperfections to shape firm organization. These market imperfections may be remediable through policy.

Governments routinely correct for market power, externalities, public goods, adverse selection, moral hazard, and a lack of commitment devices, using an assortment of legislative and regulatory instruments. It is not farfetched to think that some of what has been holding LMFs back could be fixed in a similar way. One should also remember that LMFs sometimes have advantages with respect to productivity and survival. Perhaps all that is needed for LMFs to grow and thrive is a modest cultivation effort.

This chapter largely ignores the role of political pressures in determining policy outcomes, because I have little to say about the political strategies LMF advocates may wish to pursue. Instead, I use the causal framework from Chapter 19 to devise economic strategies for alleviating the market failures that currently restrain LMFs. I do this with trepidation. Policy analysis is hard, because policies are implemented in the real world, which is much more complicated than any theoretical model. At best, theories can offer guidance for policy. They do not provide guarantees. But the pragmatic test of whether one believes in a theory is whether one is willing to act on it, so I will try to spell out the implications of my theory for action in the real world.

Granting that LMFs do not face a systematic survival problem once they exist, a perspective based on organizational demography directs attention to two key processes: (a) how LMFs can be created from scratch, and (b) how KMFs can be transformed into LMFs. In what follows, I call these the formation and conversion problems, respectively. I will also consider (c) how to avoid unwanted transformations of LMFs into KMFs.

The LMF formation problem has three facets, corresponding to the appropriation, public good, and opportunism problems from Chapter 19. The LMF birth rate is tiny in relation to the KMF birth rate. Raising it is a challenge, because the formation problem has multiple sources, but I will offer a proposal about how this might be done.

I suspect that barriers to the conversion of KMFs into LMFs are largely due to appropriation and public good problems that discourage employee buyouts. However, the need to attract capital probably also matters, especially for employees who want to buy out capital-intensive and/or financially successful KMFs. The number of KMFs is huge, so even a small percentage increase in the rate of employee buyout would expand the LMF population substantially. Effective policies in this area might go a long way toward compensating for the low LMF birth rate.

In addition to employee buyouts of KMFs, there is a flow of firms in the opposite direction due to occasional investor buyouts of LMFs. I believe this flow largely results from appropriation and public good difficulties in LMFs. The LMF population is small, so any losses from investor buyouts seriously undermine the viability of the LMF sector as a whole. Therefore, this kind of conversion also requires attention.

Market failures and feasibility constraints on governments are discussed in Section 20.2. Economic criteria for evaluating policy interventions are discussed in Section 20.3. Then in Section 20.4 I suggest ways of avoiding investor takeovers of LMFs and make related points about LMF design. Section 20.5 describes a policy to promote employee buyouts of KMFs. In Section 20.6, I expand this framework to include LMF federations, which in my opinion offer the best hope for solving the formation problem. Section 20.7 provides concluding thoughts.

20.2 Market Failures

The first theorem of welfare economics shows that complete and competitive markets yield a Pareto efficient allocation of resources.

A benevolent, omniscient, and omnipotent social planner could achieve the same resource allocation. Such allocations are called "first best." In reality, market imperfections make it impossible to achieve first-best allocations. Allocations that are Pareto efficient subject to constraints on information, commitment opportunities, and the like are called "second best."

Consider a situation in which the market does not achieve a first-best allocation due to informational asymmetries (e.g., employers cannot distinguish workers with high productivity from those with low productivity). In such cases, it is common practice to assume that a social planner or a government faces the same informational constraints as uninformed private agents. This sometimes implies that governments cannot improve on the efficiency of the allocations generated by the market. But even when a government is uninformed in this sense (e.g., it cannot determine whether an individual worker has high or low productivity), the government can still improve on market outcomes in some circumstances. For example, the labor market may have multiple equilibria that can be Pareto ranked, and the government may be able to replace a bad equilibrium with a good one by regulating wages (Mas-Colell et al., 1995, ch. 13).

Governments and private agents could confront different information constraints. "Uninformed" private agents may have better information about the statistical distribution of preferences or abilities among the population than would a politician or civil servant. But the government may enjoy scale economies in knowledge production and dissemination, and may be better able to solve free rider problems in these areas. It may also be efficient for governments to regulate private behavior directly rather than disseminate information and expect individuals to respond appropriately (consider food and drug regulation, where most consumers lack the technical expertise to assess complex knowledge claims).

Similarly, governments and private agents may confront different constraints on their ability to make binding commitments. Governments have greater coercive power, which can be useful in solving public good or externality problems. But politicians in democratic countries are elected for finite terms, and a legislature today cannot tie the hands of a legislature tomorrow. This limits a government's capacity to make binding commitments about its own future actions. On the other hand, later governments may find it costly to reverse decisions made by earlier governments, creating inertia in the political system.

I tend to be skeptical of sweeping claims about the informational or commitment constraints facing governments as compared with private agents. Much depends on the details of the issue, so a case-by-case assessment of such matters is generally required.

20.3 Evaluation Criteria

Assuming that we understand the constraints on government action, we are left with questions of desirability: how do we determine whether a policy intervention provides economic gains? The criterion of Pareto improvement or Pareto efficiency is usually too strict to be useful for policy decisions. Almost every policy change involves winners and losers, both because preferences and beliefs differ across individuals and because changes in policy almost always redistribute income to some degree.

Even so, we might try to salvage the Pareto criterion by applying it to "typical" or "representative" members of groups, rather than to every individual agent. For example, converting a KMF into an LMF might make a typical employee better off while making a typical shareholder no worse off. I call such policy evaluations "partially aggregative." A still more aggregative approach would merely investigate the costs and benefits for the economy as a whole (e.g., whether total social surplus increases when a KMF is converted into an LMF), without considering the distribution of costs and benefits across individual agents or groups within the economy. This is the Kaldor-Hicks test.

Total surplus maximization is generally too coarse to serve as a policy criterion, because the distribution of gains and losses across individuals or subgroups is normally not a matter of indifference. Pursuing every potential Pareto improvement in the Kaldor-Hicks sense, regardless of whether the losers are actually compensated, is unappealing for two reasons. First, I am not ready to assume that distributional effects somehow average out over a large number of different policy interventions. Second, I am not confident that the political authorities will maintain a just distribution of income or wealth through tax and spending policies at the level of the economy as a whole.

Having said this, there are some arguments for an aggregate surplus criterion in the context of LMFs. If one believes that policy interventions favoring LMFs typically lead to progressive or neutral effects on income distribution, then it makes sense to use simple models based upon aggregate surplus. In those (presumably rare) cases where a policy favoring LMFs has regressive distributional effects, there may be some easy way to modify the policy to compensate (most of) the losers, so the search for ways to raise aggregate surplus is a useful starting point. More generally, if one believes that for the foreseeable future developed economies will likely have slow growth, rising inequality, and increasing hereditary wealth (Piketty, 2014), then policies to promote LMFs that are financed by levies on wealth or capital income seem very unlikely to have any negative distributional effect and might help redress the inequities of the market.

20.4 Discouraging Investor Takeovers

If one wants to expand the LMF sector, it is important first to maintain the LMFs that already exist and ensure that newly created LMFs do not slip back into the KMF column. I suggested in Chapter 19 that appropriation and public good problems can lead to investor takeover of LMFs. Historically this phenomenon has been more prominent in the U.S. than in Europe, and we can learn a good deal from the European experience about how to design LMFs in ways that avoid this danger.

First, I review some theory. We saw from Chapter 9 that LMFs with undervalued membership shares may not only grow more slowly than similar KMFs, but may also sell out to outside investors. This can occur even if LMFs have higher static productivity and even if transformation into a KMF reduces aggregate surplus in the present value sense. We also saw in Chapter 9 that when membership markets are imperfect, LMF insiders are tempted to replace departing members with hired employees rather than new members. I classified both of these hazards as appropriation problems in Chapter 19.

Chapter 12 showed that LMFs are unsustainable against investor takeover in cases where profit-maximizing investors can make binding commitments about the policies to be adopted after they gain control. Even if investors cannot make such commitments in advance, LMFs remain vulnerable to takeovers if 51% of the membership wants the firm to modify its policies in a profit-maximizing direction. I classified this hazard as a public good problem in Chapter 19.

With respect to the appropriation problem, I do not believe that it would be useful to attempt a solution by "perfecting" the membership market. It is true at a theoretical level that the problems I mentioned would disappear with a perfect membership market, and this was a central message in Chapters 3–5. However, in the real world there are simply too many reasons why LMF membership markets are likely to be imperfect. The public good problem is similar in the sense that we have no magic wand with which to abolish preference heterogeneity in LMFs. As long as individual members are free to sell their control rights to outside investors, there is a danger that investors will accumulate shares through a series of bilateral transactions with individual workers or that a coalition of members (perhaps those close to retirement) will sell out as a group.

For these reasons, LMFs should adopt constitutional rules against the sale of membership rights to anyone who does not plan to work in the firm and impose ceilings on the allowable share of workers who are nonmembers. These are standard policies in European worker cooperatives. U.S. experience with "degeneration" in some (but not all) plywood cooperatives indicates that in the absence of such policies, conversion of LMFs into KMFs is a serious possibility. Indeed, I would go further and entrench provisions of this kind in legislation governing the LMF sector. This seems necessary because insider majorities may be tempted to revise firm-level rules against selling out to investors or to relax rules limiting the use of hired employees.

One could argue that members should be free to abandon the LMF organizational structure if they find it attractive to do so. I have some sympathy for this view, but there are three counterarguments. First, the decision by a (possibly temporary) majority to sell out to investors can be contrary to the interests of a minority that does not want the firm to move in a profit-maximizing direction. Much as corporate law provides protection to minority shareholders in a KMF, cooperative law should provide protection to minority members of an LMF. Second, Chapter 9 showed that conversion of an LMF into a KMF can come at the expense of future LMF members, through the loss of the rents the latter would receive upon joining the firm. Third, I will argue in later sections for the use of public funds to expand the LMF sector. Allowing LMF insiders to sell out to investors for personal gain would subvert this program.

Assuming that LMF membership rights cannot be sold to outside investors, should we allow departing members to sell their positions to new members? This is a more difficult question. Given the heterogeneity of worker skills and preferences, and the likelihood of adverse selection problems, it is best to prohibit direct transactions of this kind. Instead, departing members should sell their positions back to the firm so that the continuing members can choose their replacements. As discussed in Chapter 11, partnership law in developed countries follows this rule. The U.S. plywood coops, the best-known example of worker cooperatives with membership markets, typically required majority approval by insiders before a transaction with an outsider could proceed.

An alternative solution is to abolish the membership market entirely. I do not want to go this far, because membership markets can be useful in allocating resources and pose no particular threat to the LMF sector as a whole. Such markets can assist with short run problems of labor allocation across firms (see Chapter 3) and can help solve the long run "horizon problem" (see Chapter 4). By capitalizing income streams to be received by future workers, membership markets encourage insiders to base investment decisions on present value calculations that extend beyond their own expected tenure in the firm.

European worker cooperatives typically have no such market, although they often require workers to pay a membership fee, which is usually refunded with interest when a member departs. Although this may be a useful way of screening applicants, and loans from members may be a useful source of capital for the firm, this arrangement does not capitalize future income in a way that affects the present value calculations of members. Therefore, it does not correct for possible underinvestment due to the horizon problem.

The empirical evidence for underinvestment is weak (see Section 7.5). European worker cooperatives generally address this problem through rules specifying a minimum share of profit that must be reinvested. Some authors are so concerned about the horizon problem that they want rules requiring LMFs to finance investment by debt rather than retained earnings (see Chapter 4). Debt may certainly be useful, but I would be loath to impose constraints on the financing methods used by LMFs, given the difficulties they already face in attracting capital on external markets. When LMFs can finance growth from internal resources, they should be encouraged to do so.

Partly for investment reasons, partly to improve the functioning of labor markets, and partly to provide financial liquidity to individual LMF members, my preference is to have LMFs buy the membership rights of departing workers using valuation procedures like those used in professional partnerships and sell membership rights to new workers at market-clearing prices. This strategy is best suited to firms where workers have uniform skills and might be impractical with diverse occupational mixes. It also presupposes that the LMF has the financial resources to make good on guarantees to buy back membership rights. But a blanket prohibition on membership markets serves no useful purpose, and it almost certainly hampers the LMF sector more than it helps.

20.5 Encouraging Employee Buyouts

One straightforward way to encourage conversions of KMFs into LMFs is to tax KMFs and use the proceeds to subsidize LMFs. I suggested at the end of Chapter 13 that this might be a sensible way to correct for the free rider problems that obstruct employee buyouts. KMFs are already taxed, and in numerous countries employee stock ownership plans are already subsidized, so no novel issues arise in extending such policies to cover LMFs. The principal concern would be to ensure that such transformations involve real workers' control, not just cosmetic reorganizations to obtain tax breaks. However, it may be desirable to target firms that are especially good candidates for conversion or to focus on capital market imperfections, so I consider some alternative approaches in what follows.

In *Governing the Firm* (Dow, 2003, ch. 12), I suggested a policy framework to convert some KMFs into LMFs. There is no need to repeat all of the details here, but I will sketch the general idea and then make some comments based on Chapter 19. The proposal is to give the employees of certain firms (e.g., publicly traded corporations) the right to trigger a referendum on whether their firm will be bought out and converted into an LMF. If the referendum succeeds, a payroll deduction is levied on employees, with the proceeds going to a labor trust whose goal is to buy up the equity shares of the firm. During the transition process, any dividends paid by the firm on shares held by the trust are reinvested in the trust. As employees accumulate shares, they gain seats on the board of directors in proportion to their share of total equity, but with voting rights distributed among employees based on the rule of one person, one vote. Once the labor trust owns 100% of the firm's equity, workers elect all representatives on the board of directors and collectively own the firm's capital stock. Workers who leave the firm sell their control rights to the labor trust, which resells them to new members.

This procedure has a number of attractive features. First, it buys out existing shareholders at a market price, so firm valuation is straightforward, and in principle no shareholders are made worse off in the conversion process. Second, it guarantees that a conversion occurs only if a majority of employees want to proceed, so in this sense it is voluntary for workers. If employees prefer to consume rather than save, or want more diversified portfolios, they can vote against a buyout. Third, although worker voting rights are proportional to worker equity ownership at the level of the firm as a whole, individual workers have equal voting rights during the transition and afterward, so the end result is a genuine labor-managed firm. Fourth, the LMF retains collective asset ownership if this is useful. And fifth, the referendum serves as a screening device where those firms with higher potential productivity as LMFs are more likely to be converted.

A natural question is whether any policy intervention is really needed to obtain these benefits. Why can't employees simply agree among themselves to buy out a firm? What market failure is corrected under this proposal? The answer is that the conversion of a KMF into an LMF involves the supply of public goods from the standpoint of the individual employees. For the reasons discussed in Chapter 13, it is very difficult for any small group of workers to capture the social benefits from conversion, which are spread diffusely across the workforce. The goal of the proposal is to enable employees to "tax" themselves to acquire the public goods from a buyout and to standardize procedures for triggering a referendum in a way that does not impose an excessive cost on the subset of employees attempting to organize a buyout. Although there is no guarantee that this will result in a Pareto improvement (a minority of the workforce may be made worse off), the proposal probably passes the "partially aggregative" test because the productivity benefits from an LMF are likely to be widely shared and the typical shareholder is no worse off.

Nevertheless, problems remain. One is that achieving majority equity ownership (let alone 100% ownership) can take a long time. The necessary time varies with the size of the payroll deduction, the capital intensity of the firm, the extent to which the firm can be financed by debt, and the rate of return on capital. The best candidates for buyout are KMFs with a high labor intensity and a high debt-to-equity ratio. However, except under unusually favorable conditions, achieving a full-fledged LMF may take a decade or more (see Dow, 2003, ch. 12, for sample calculations). One might question whether a majority of employees would be willing to accept such a long wait. Acceleration of the transition process would require either transactions with outside financiers (e.g., banks), raising all of the usual issues about LMF capital constraints, or alternatively public subsidies to the payroll deduction process.

Another problem is achieving credible commitment toward shareholders. There is no reason for shareholders to fear employee accumulation of equity shares in the range from 0% to 49% as long as shareholders unanimously favor maximization of profit or present value. But once workers have 51% or more of the firm's equity shares and therefore 51% or more of the seats on the board of directors, shareholders might quite reasonably fear that wages will rise at the expense of dividends, or more generally that costs will rise at the expense of profit. This is a version of the LMF temptation to cheat investors modeled in Chapter 17 and falls under the heading "Opportunism Problems" in Chapter 19. For a variety of economic and political reasons, I want to avoid the systematic expropriation of investors at late stages in a transition process. One strategy to circumvent this problem is for employees to buy up the last 51% of the firm's shares in a single transaction financed by debt, which changes the problem into one of making binding commitments to lenders.

Difficulties involving long transition times and the need for credible commitment to existing shareholders could both be resolved if the problem of capital constraints could be. Although I continue to believe that the referendum process described previously makes sense, I now think that this must be coupled with some financing mechanism that goes beyond employee savings. The question then becomes this one: can public funds be used to help finance employee buyouts in a way that avoids any temptation for LMF members to behave opportunistically toward government? Or, if one thinks capital constraints mainly arise from information asymmetry, can we finance employee buyouts using public funds in a way that improves on what private markets can do?

With respect to credible commitment, governments do have instruments that are unavailable to private lenders, including the power to tax. The temptation for members of LMFs to cheat investors, as in Chapter 17, arises because the members can walk away from financial liabilities after depreciating collectively owned assets. This need not be a problem for government loans backed up by the capacity to collect taxes from individual workers in case of default. Whether one wants to go in this direction is certainly open to debate, but an analogy may be useful.

Consider educational loans, where the relevant collateral is the present value of higher labor income in the future. No one can force students to work at lucrative jobs after graduation, and students who default cannot have their human capital taken away. Accordingly, private banks are more reluctant to finance a university education than they would be to finance home ownership or the purchase of machinery by a firm. A standard solution is to have government agencies bear default risks either directly (through public educational loans) or indirectly (by guaranteeing the loans made by private banks). I see no reason why similar methods could not be used to lend money to labor-managed firms, where each member would retain individual liability for a share of collective debts after leaving the firm and governments would handle default risks using procedures similar to those used for educational loans.

One might object to my analogy on the grounds that individual students decide whether to take on educational debts, while LMF debts would be imposed on workers by majority voting. But professional partnerships impose responsibility for collective debts on individual partners, so it is unclear why the same rule would be unacceptable in other LMFs. Furthermore, individuals share responsibility for collective debts in many settings that do not involve production activities, such as housing cooperatives or condominiums. Workers who prefer to avoid exposure to liabilities of this kind need not join LMFs.

Professional partnerships historically have had unlimited individual liability for firm debts, where in principle each partner is responsible for all of the debts incurred by the firm as a whole. However, it may not be necessary to go this far (and at least in the U.S., partnerships with limited liability have become increasingly common). It might be enough for each LMF member to be liable for a pro rata fraction of the incremental debt incurred by the LMF during that member's tenure with the firm, as long as the individual member cannot shed this liability by quitting the firm.

If one believes that the main source of capital market constraints is informational asymmetry rather than lack of commitment, the labor market model from Mas-Colell et al. (1995, ch. 13) cited in Section 20.2 may be illuminating. In their framework where employers cannot observe the productivities of individual workers, the government can achieve a Pareto improvement by establishing a minimum wage if there are multiple equilibria. This is true even though the government faces informational constraints identical to those of private agents. The key insight is that no workers are made worse off by an equilibrium with a higher wage, and under competitive conditions employers have zero expected profit in the long run regardless of which equilibrium occurs.

In principle the same logic carries over to adverse selection in the capital market. Suppose that private lenders cannot distinguish LMFs with high productivity from those with low productivity, and there are multiple equilibria with different interest rates. Moving from an equilibrium with a high interest rate to an equilibrium with a lower interest rate does not make any borrower worse off, and if the financial services sector is competitive, then lenders will have zero expected profit in the long run either way. This goal can be achieved either by a maximum interest rate, subject to the constraint that private lenders break even, or by having governments directly extend loans to LMFs at low rates.

Even if it is not possible to achieve a strict Pareto improvement, a policy of this kind might well raise aggregate surplus by financing the conversion of KMFs into higher-productivity LMFs. For readers who question the political viability of such strategies, I observe that employee stock ownership plans (ESOPs) in the U.S. enjoy large tax breaks (roughly in the 30% range), with similar subsidies for employee share ownership in other developed countries (Dow, 2003). Given that we are already offering subsidies to hybrid firms of this kind, which usually do not have worker representation on boards of directors and probably yield productivity gains lower than what LMFs could achieve, we should be able to subsidize full-fledged LMFs at least to the same degree.

My conclusion is that the proposal to facilitate employee buyouts presented by Dow (2003, ch. 12) should be augmented by a publicly financed bank that extends loans for the conversion of KMFs into LMFs. I remain cautious about some details, however. First, it is important to ask employees to contribute a substantial part of the financing for such conversions in order to screen out firms with little chance of achieving productivity gains through reorganization as an LMF. Second, it is important to arrange financing so that minority shareholders are not put at serious risk during a transition. This probably means a large debt transaction to buy out the last half of the firm's equity. Firms that are labor intensive or have collectively owned assets with strong collateral value to support a debt transaction are the best candidates for conversion. Third, the goal is to establish an LMF, not a KMF where the employees own capital shares. Firms should only qualify for subsidies when workers enjoy equal voting rights regardless of their capital contributions (aside from probationary members, some maximum number of contract workers, and so on) and when the board of directors is elected entirely by the firm's workforce.

20.6 Creating Federations

I am reasonably confident that policies like those in Section 20.5 could increase the LMF population while passing muster on the aggregate surplus test, and probably also a "partially aggregative" test along the lines described in Section 20.3. But raising the rate at which KMFs are converted into LMFs is the low-hanging fruit. The problem of LMF formation is more challenging because it is difficult to see how public policy can induce entrepreneurs to create more LMFs from scratch. Easier access to capital might help, but this would not eliminate the appropriation and public good problems from Chapter 19.

One clue to solving this puzzle is the fact that LMFs benefit from the existence of other LMFs. Anecdotally, LMFs often appear to cluster by industry, geography, and time period. I review historical cases of this phenomenon for the U.S. in Dow (2003, ch. 10).

Section 7.6 discussed econometric research on LMF agglomeration in Spain (see Arando et al., 2012). This indicated that the presence of existing

LMFs in a local geographic area raised the probability that more LMFs would enter. No agglomeration benefits flowed from KMFs to LMFs. These observations are not surprising. Given the rarity of LMFs and the low level of information about this organizational form, a few successful firms can inspire attempts at replication. New LMFs probably also find it useful to operate in regions or industries where other relevant parties (suppliers of capital or raw materials, customers, lawyers, accountants, and so forth) have experience with similar firms.

I have come to believe that the best solution to the LMF formation problem is to exploit agglomeration effects through LMF federations. The models I have in mind are the Mondragon system in the Basque country of Spain and the Lega federation in Italy. These are not the only extant LMF federations (there are others in Italy, France, the U.K., and elsewhere), but they are among the largest and most durable, and are widely viewed as economic success stories. Each of these federations includes many individual LMFs and has an array of central institutions like banks, insurance companies, and managerial consulting agencies. They also have long track records of collective entrepreneurship in the formation of new LMFs from scratch, as well as conversions of KMFs into LMFs. Space limitations prevent a detailed account here, but interested readers should see the descriptions in Dow (2003, chs. 3–4). A theoretical model of LMF federations inspired by the Mondragon and Lega cases is provided by Joshi and Smith (2008).

The Mondragon and Lega groups offer startup financing for workers who want to establish new LMFs, along with technical consulting and risk management services. Due to rules requiring investment in collective reserves and a desire to limit firm size in order to maintain democratic control in each firm, capital tends to flow from individual firms to worker-controlled financial institutions and then into the creation of new LMFs. Central bodies responsible to LMF members allocate capital across firms, facilitate the mobility of labor across firms, and supply insurance both to individual workers and to their firms.

It is instructive to consider how such federations solve the appropriation, public good, and opportunism problems from Chapter 19. First take the appropriation problem. Federations shift entrepreneurial activities to a collective level and do not rely on profit incentives for individual entrepreneurs. They also have specialists who are experienced in the creation of new LMFs. Given the track record of the federation as a whole, and the fact that LMF members hire and fire federation managers, workers interested in creating a new LMF need not fear that an individual entrepreneur with a bad project will exploit an informational advantage. If necessary, any financial claim a worker may have on the firm at the time of departure can be met from the resources of the federation as a whole.

With respect to the public good problem, Mondragon and the Lega have no issue with potential investor takeover, because there is no way for outside investors to acquire a controlling share in an individual member firm. Workers may well have heterogeneous preferences—though there is often screening for ideological and social compatibility, and the use of membership fees probably excludes less-committed applicants. But collective choice problems like those in Chapter 12 are handled through representative democracy, involving elections to boards of directors, combined with the delegation of operational decisions to managers. Mondragon has had a history of wage compression, as one might expect from Section 6.7, but nevertheless has been able to attract and retain managers of sufficiently high caliber. The free rider problem from Chapter 13 involving conversion of KMFs is reduced, because the entire burden of organizing such conversions is not placed on individual workers or small groups in the firms to be converted. These workers also have access to substantial expertise on transition planning, organizational and financial challenges, and the likely profitability of a newly converted LMF.

Finally, federations are very useful in solving opportunism problems. By virtue of having central financial institutions, federations can overcome the capital constraints facing individual LMFs. The danger that LMFs will cheat investors is handled in various ways: rules about the allocation of firm income, a requirement that firms deposit funds in federation-controlled banks, close monitoring of firms by these banks, and a tight grip on access to the capital that individual firms may require. In extreme cases, members of a firm may forfeit their control rights. Although this gives considerable power to central agencies of the federation, these agencies are themselves accountable to democratically chosen representatives of the individual firms. Distributional conflict between investors and workers is muted in a system where labor representatives at the center allocate capital to other labor representatives in individual firms. This replaces high-powered incentives to cheat other parties with low-powered incentives that can be managed through repeated game and reputation effects, with support from social norms and culture.

For all of these reasons, federations are an attractive way to stimulate the creation of new LMFs and to help solve other chronic problems facing LMFs. But at this point a skeptic can pose a new version of the question first raised in Chapter 1. Instead of asking, "If LMFs are so great, why are they so rare?" the skeptic can ask "If LMF federations are so great, why are they so rare?" The answer is that, again, there are appropriation, public good, and opportunism problems, but now they arise for the creation of a federation as a whole. How can any individual or small group capture the social benefit from an LMF federation? How can a federation gain access to financial resources?

Mondragon and the Lega overcame these problems in idiosyncratic ways that would be difficult for individual workers or LMFs to replicate. Mondragon exploited a quirk of Spanish banking law that allowed cooperative banks to pay higher interest rates to depositors than other banks, giving it an advantage in raising capital (Dow, 2003, 66). The Lega had extensive political support from local, regional, and national governments in the form of public contracts, tax breaks, and other subsidies (at the same time, these governments often constrained LMFs through numerous arbitrary regulations; see Dow, 2003, ch. 4). This sustained political support is undoubtedly a major reason why Italy has the largest worker cooperative sector among developed countries today.

A policy of promoting LMFs could combine the ideas about organizational design in Section 20.4 with the proposal from Section 20.5 for a publicly funded bank to finance conversion of KMFs into LMFs and embed both of these in a federation that would have a mandate to create LMFs from scratch. The main danger I see with such a system is that of a soft budget constraint. One does not want to encourage the belief, either at the level of individual firms or the federation as a whole, that public funds are in limitless supply.

Ideally, one would like to endow a federation with enough seed money to have a substantial long run impact on the LMF sector, but with a credible commitment that the system must become self-financing over time. This may argue for endowing a series of independent federations, not just one, with the understanding that no single federation is indispensable. But it is important to recognize that moral hazard issues of this kind are not limited to LMF federations. They arise routinely between governments and private banks in a capitalist economy. I see no convincing reason why LMF federations would lead to greater moral hazard problems than those for conventional financial institutions, and I don't regard this concern as a reason for avoiding institutional experimentation.

20.7 Conclusion

In her classic book *Governing the Commons*, Elinor Ostrom (1990) discusses two free rider problems that arise for common pool resources.

The first order problem is that individuals may overuse the resource or fail to maintain it. The second order problem is that individuals may free ride on attempts by others to create a collective institution that solves the first order problem.

Labor-managed firms confront three nested free rider problems. The first order problem is that individual workers may shirk in their contributions to production or the maintenance of collectively owned assets. Once they have been created, LMFs seem to be good at solving such problems through mutual monitoring and repeated game effects.

The second order problem is to create a labor-managed firm. As we have seen, this is difficult for various reasons. Even if an LMF would have substantial productivity advantages, it may not be in the interest of a single individual or small group to incur the cost of creating one, because other agents will appropriate most of the resulting benefits. This is true both for creation of new firms and the conversion of conventional firms into LMFs. There are thousands of successful LMFs around the world, so it is not impossible to solve the second order problem, but thousands more might arise if this problem were addressed in a conscious and sustained way through public policy.

The third order problem is the creation of federations of labor-managed firms. Such federations can alleviate many of the difficulties surrounding formation of LMFs. They can also mobilize capital, manage risk, and exploit scale economies. No individual LMF can capture the full social benefit from a federation, because most of these benefits go to other LMFs, now or in the future. Experience shows that LMF federations can be very successful once they exist, but they seldom evolve spontaneously. Due to the third order free rider problem, government action is required.

One starting point is to link together the firms that are converted from KMFs into LMFs through employee buyout, as in Section 20.5. Other supportive institutions such as unions, foundations, and local or regional governments could be encouraged to engage in collective entrepreneurship within a uniform institutional framework established at the national level. Because high unemployment is a stimulus to LMF entry (see Section 7.1), it may be particularly useful to make such efforts when macroeconomic conditions are poor and conventional firms are failing. But the goal is to sow the seeds for federations that persist and grow over many business cycles, and LMFs should be designed in ways that prevent a return to conventional forms of organization when conditions improve. If one wants continuing expansion of the LMF sector, one needs a ratchet effect.

Federations should be designed in ways that exploit agglomeration economies. They should not simply be loosely affiliated groups of like-minded firms. For example, Arando et al. (2012, 199) point out that strategies to encourage labor-managed firms are more likely to be effective when resources are concentrated geographically. As discussed in Section 20.6, it is also essential to have strong central agencies like banks and technical consulting services that can regulate access to capital and intervene in the management of individual firms when necessary, while at the same time ensuring that central institutions are democratically accountable to individual firms and their members.

We do not yet live in the best of all possible worlds. Institutional innovation is continuing in many arenas of economic, political, and social life. One century ago, the publicly traded corporation was a recent invention. Hybrid firms that assign ultimate control rights to investors but welcome employee involvement in financing and decision-making are a still more recent development. Further organizational innovation may push these hybrids toward greater worker control.

Earlier modes of economic organization may well have succeeded at least in part because they solved appropriation problems, not just because they had high productivity or generated a large aggregate surplus. High productivity is good for economic viability, but enterprises are more likely to be created when a single person or a small coalition can capture a large fraction of the resulting social benefit. In particular, capitalist firms may dominate modern economies in part because they concentrate economic surplus on small groups of investors or managers, while labor-managed firms spread a larger surplus across many present and future workers. Further institutional progress is likely to require better alignment of firm formation with aggregate surplus.

This has been a book about economics, so I have not discussed moral arguments for labor-managed firms, such as democracy, equality, dignity, and community (for my views on these matters, see Dow, 2003, ch. 2). But partly for these moral reasons, many people want an alternative to capitalism. For these people, the labor-managed firm is still out there. The available evidence shows that the labor-managed firm is a viable mode of economic organization despite its current marginal status. Furthermore, economic theory suggests that capitalist firms need not be superior from an efficiency standpoint, despite their current market dominance. Policy experiments to expand the labor-managed sector, if well designed and patiently implemented, might yield impressive results at reasonable cost. We should find out.

References

Abramitzky, Ran, 2008, The limits of equality: Insights from the Israeli kibbutz, *Quarterly Journal of Economics* 123(3), August, 1111–1159.

2009, The effect of redistribution on migration: Evidence from the Israeli kibbutz, *Journal of Public Economics* 93(3–4), April, 498–511.

2011, Lessons from the kibbutz on the equality-incentives trade-off, *Journal of Economic Perspectives* 25(1), Winter, 185–208.

Akerlof, George, 1970, The market for "lemons": Quality uncertainty and the market mechanism, *Quarterly Journal of Economics* 84(3), August, 488–500.

Alchian, Armen A., 1950, Uncertainty, evolution and economic theory, *Journal of Political Economy* 58(3), June, 211–222.

Alchian, Armen A. and Harold Demsetz, 1972, Production, information costs, and economic organization, *American Economic Review* 62(5), December, 777–795.

Allen, Marcus T., 1995, Capital structure determinants in real estate limited partnerships, *The Financial Review* 30(3), August, 399–426.

Alves, Guillermo, Gabriel Burdín, and Andrés Dean, 2016, Workplace democracy and job flows, *Journal of Comparative Economics* 44(2), May, 258–271.

Andolfatto, David and Ed Nosal, 1997, Optimal team contracts, *Canadian Journal of Economics* 30(2), May, 385–396.

Arando, Saioa, Monica Gago, Jan M. Podivinsky, and Geoff Stewart, 2012, Do labour-managed firms benefit from agglomeration? *Journal of Economic Behavior and Organization* 84(1), September, 193–200.

Arrow, Kenneth J., 1974, *The Limits of Organization*, New York, Norton.

Arrow, Kenneth J. and F. H. Hahn, 1971, *General Competitive Analysis*, San Francisco, Holden-Day Inc.

Banks, R. C. I'Anson, 1990, *Lindley and Banks on Partnership*, 16th ed., London, Sweet and Maxwell.

Barber, Brad M., 1996, Forecasting the discounts of market prices from appraised values for real estate limited partnerships, *Real Estate Economics* 24(4), Winter, 471–491.

Bartlett, Will, 1994, Employment in small firms: Are cooperatives different? Evidence from southern Europe, in J. Atkinson and D. Storey, eds., *Employment, the Small Firm and the Labour Market*, New York, Routledge, 256–287.

Bartlett, Will, John Cable, Saul Estrin, Derek C. Jones, and Stephen C. Smith, 1992, Labor-managed cooperatives and private firms in North Central Italy: An empirical comparison, *Industrial and Labor Relations Review* 46(1), October, 103–118.

Bartling, Björn, Ernst Fehr, and Holger Herz, 2014, The intrinsic value of decision rights, *Econometrica* 82(6), November, 2005–2039.

Benham, Lee and Philip Keefer, 1991, Voting in firms: The role of agenda control, size and voter homogeneity, *Economic Inquiry* 29(4), October, 706–719.

Ben-Ner, Avner, 1984, On the stability of the cooperative form of organization, *Journal of Comparative Economics* 8(3), September, 247–260.

   1988, The life cycle of worker-owned firms in market economies: A theoretical analysis, *Journal of Economic Behavior and Organization* 10(3), October, 287–313.

Ben-Ner, Avner and Byoung Jun, 1996, Employee buyout in a bargaining game with asymmetric information, *American Economic Review* 86(3), June, 502–523.

Berman, Katrina V., 1967, *Worker-Owned Plywood Companies: An Economic Analysis*, Pullman, WA, Bureau of Economic and Business Research, Washington State University Press.

Berman, Katrina V. and Matthew D. Berman, 1989, An empirical test of the theory of the labor-managed firm, *Journal of Comparative Economics* 13(2), June, 281–300.

Binmore, Ken, Ariel Rubinstein, and Asher Wolinsky, 1986, The Nash bargaining solution in economic modelling, *RAND Journal of Economics* 17(2), Summer, 176–188.

Bonin, John P., Derek C. Jones, and Louis Putterman, 1993, Theoretical and empirical studies of producer cooperatives: Will ever the twain meet? *Journal of Economic Literature* 31(3), September, 1290–1320.

Bonin, John P. and Louis Putterman, 1987, *Economics of Cooperation and the Labor-Managed Economy*, Fundamentals of Pure and Applied Economics No. 14, New York, Harwood Academic Publishers.

Bowles, Samuel, 1985, The production process in a competitive economy: Walrasian, neo-Hobbesian, and Marxian models, *American Economic Review* 75(1), March, 16–36.

Bowles, Samuel and Herbert Gintis, 1990, Contested exchange: New microfoundations of the political economy of capitalism, *Politics and Society* 18(2), June, 165–222.

   1993a, The revenge of Homo economicus: Post-Walrasian economics and the revival of political economy, *Journal of Economic Perspectives* 7(1), Winter, 83–102.

   1993b, A political and economic case for the democratic enterprise, *Economics and Philosophy* 9(1), April, 75–100.

   1993c, The democratic firm: An agency-theoretic evaluation, ch. 2 in Samuel Bowles, Herbert Gintis, and Bo Gustafsson, eds., *Markets and Democracy: Participation, Accountability and Efficiency*, New York, Cambridge University Press, 13–39.

   1993d, A political and economic case for the democratic enterprise, ch. 9 in David Copp, Jean Hampton, and John E. Roemer, eds., *The Idea of Democracy*, New York, Cambridge University Press, 375–399.

   1994, Credit market imperfections and the incidence of worker-owned firms, *Metroeconomica* 45(3), October, 209–223.

1996a, The distribution of wealth and the viability of the democratic firm, ch. 5 in Ugo Pagano and Robert Rowthorn, eds., *Democracy and Efficiency in the Economic Enterprise*, New York, Routledge, 82–97.

1996b, Is the demand for workplace democracy redundant in a liberal economy? ch. 4 in Ugo Pagano and Robert Rowthorn, eds., *Democracy and Efficiency in the Economic Enterprise*, New York, Routledge, 64–81.

Bowles, Samuel, Herbert Gintis, and Bo Gustafsson, eds., 1993, *Markets and Democracy: Participation, Accountability and Efficiency*, New York, Cambridge University Press.

Brewer, A. A. and Martin Browning, 1982, On the "employment decision" of a labour-managed firm, *Economica* 49(194), May, 141–146.

Bull, Clive, 1987, The existence of self-enforcing implicit contracts, *Quarterly Journal of Economics* 102(1), February, 147–159.

Burdín, Gabriel, 2014, Are worker-managed firms more likely to fail than conventional enterprises? Evidence from Uruguay, *Industrial and Labor Relations Review* 67(1), January, 202–238.

2016, Equality under threat by the talented: Evidence from worker-managed firms, *Economic Journal* 126(594), August, 1372–1403.

Burdín, Gabriel and Andrés Dean, 2009, New evidence on wages and employment in worker cooperatives compared with capitalist firms, *Journal of Comparative Economics* 37(4), December, 517–533.

2012, Revisiting the objectives of worker-managed firms: An empirical assessment, *Economic Systems* 36(1), March, 158–171.

Carberry, Edward J., ed., 2011, *Employee Ownership and Shared Capitalism: New Directions in Research*, Ithaca, NY, Cornell University Press.

Carmichael, H. Lorne and W. Bentley MacLeod, 2000, Worker cooperation and the ratchet effect, *Journal of Labor Economics* 18(1), January, 1–19.

Carr, Jack and Frank Mathewson, 1990, The economics of law firms: A study in the legal organization of the firm, *Journal of Law and Economics* 33(2), October, 307–330.

Coase, Ronald H., 1937, The nature of the firm, *Economica* 4(16), November, 386–405.

1960, The problem of social cost, *Journal of Law and Economics* 3, October, 1–44.

Craig, Ben and John Pencavel, 1992, The behavior of worker cooperatives: The plywood companies of the Pacific Northwest, *American Economic Review* 82(5), December, 1083–1105.

1993, The objectives of worker cooperatives, *Journal of Comparative Economics* 17(2), June, 288–308.

1995, Participation and productivity: A comparison of worker cooperatives and conventional firms in the plywood industry, in Martin Neil Baily, Peter C. Reiss, and Clifford Winston, eds., *Brookings Papers on Economic Activity: Microeconomics*, Washington, DC, Brookings Institution Press, 121–174.

Cremer, Jacques, 1986, Cooperation in ongoing organizations, *Quarterly Journal of Economics* 101(1), February, 33–49.

DeAngelo, Harry, 1981, Competition and unanimity, *American Economic Review* 71(1), March, 18–27.

Debreu, Gerard, 1959, *Theory of Value: An Axiomatic Analysis of Economic Equilibrium*, New Haven, CT, Yale University Press.

deMarzo, Peter, 1993, Majority voting and corporate control: The rule of the dominant shareholder, *Review of Economic Studies* 60(3), July, 713–734.

Denning, Karen C. and Kuldeep Shastri, 1993, Changes in organizational structure and shareholder wealth: The case of limited partnerships, *Journal of Financial and Quantitative Analysis* 28(4), December, 553–564.

Diamond, Peter, 1967, The role of the stock market in a general equilibrium model with technological uncertainty, *American Economic Review* 57(4), September, 759–776.

Domar, Evsey, 1966, The Soviet collective farm as a producer cooperative, *American Economic Review* 56(4), Part I, September, 743–757.

Dong, Xiao-yuan and Gregory K. Dow, 1993a, Does free exit reduce shirking in production teams? *Journal of Comparative Economics* 17(2), June, 472–484.

1993b, Monitoring costs in Chinese agricultural teams, *Journal of Political Economy* 101(3), June, 539–553.

Dow, Gregory K., 1983, Labor management in a competitive society, Working Paper No. 1008, August, Institution for Social and Policy Studies, Yale University, New Haven, CT.

1984, Myopia, amnesia, and consistent intertemporal choice, *Mathematical Social Sciences* 8(2), October, 95–109.

1985, Internal bargaining and strategic innovation in the theory of the firm, *Journal of Economic Behavior and Organization* 6(3), September, 301–320.

1986, Control rights, competitive markets, and the labor management debate, *Journal of Comparative Economics* 10(1), March, 48–61.

1987, The function of authority in transaction cost economics, *Journal of Economic Behavior and Organization* 8(1), March, 13–38.

1988, Information, production decisions, and intra-firm bargaining, *International Economic Review* 29(1), February, 57–79.

1989, Knowledge is power: Informational precommitment in the capitalist firm, *European Journal of Political Economy* 5(2/3), 161–176.

1993a, Democracy versus appropriability: Can labor-managed firms flourish in a capitalist world? ch. 11 in Samuel Bowles, Herbert Gintis, and Bo Gustafsson, eds., *Markets and Democracy: Participation, Accountability and Efficiency*, New York, Cambridge University Press, 176–195.

1993b, The appropriability critique of transaction cost economics, ch. 6 in Christos Pitelis, ed., *Transaction Costs, Markets and Hierarchies*, Oxford, Basil Blackwell, 101–132.

1993c, Why capital hires labor: A bargaining perspective, *American Economic Review* 83(1), March, 118–134.

1996a, Replicating Walrasian equilibria using markets for membership in labor-managed firms, *Economic Design* 2(2), November, 147–162.

1996b, Authority relations in the firm: Review and agenda for research, ch. 9 in John Groenewegen, ed., *Transaction Cost Economics and Beyond*, Boston, MA, Kluwer, 171–188.

1997, The new institutional economics and employment regulation, ch. 2 in Bruce E. Kaufman, ed., *Government Regulation of the Employment Relationship*, Madison, WI, Industrial Relations Research Association, 57–90.

1998, Review of B. Jossa and G. Cuomo, The economics of socialism and the labour-managed firm, *Journal of Economic Literature* 36(2), June, 992–994.

2000, On the neutrality of asset ownership for work incentives, *Journal of Comparative Economics* 28(3), September, 581–605.

2001, Allocating control over firms: Stock markets versus membership markets, *Review of Industrial Organization* 18(2), March, 201–218.

2002, The ultimate control group, *Journal of Economic Behavior and Organization* 49(1), September, 39–49.

2003, *Governing the Firm: Workers' Control in Theory and Practice*, New York, Cambridge University Press.

2004, The firm as a nexus of strategies, *International Game Theory Review* 6(4), December, 525–554.

2010, Worker participation and adverse selection, ch. 10 in Gregory K. Dow, Andrew Eckert, and Douglas West, eds., *Industrial Organization, Trade, and Social Interaction. Essays in Honour of B. Curtis Eaton*, Toronto, University of Toronto Press, 203–222.

2014, Partnership markets with adverse selection, *Review of Economic Design* 18(2), June, 105–126.

2018, The theory of the labor-managed firm: Past, present, and future, *Annals of Public and Cooperative Economics* 89(1).

Dow, Gregory K. and Louis Putterman, 1999, Why capital (usually) hires labor: An assessment of proposed explanations, ch. 1 in Margaret M. Blair and Mark J. Roe, eds., *Employees and Corporate Governance*, Washington, DC, Brookings Institution Press, 17–57.

2000, Why capital suppliers (usually) hire workers: What we know and what we need to know, *Journal of Economic Behavior and Organization* 43(3), November, 319–336.

Dow, Gregory K. and Gilbert L. Skillman, 2007, Collective choice and control rights in firms, *Journal of Public Economic Theory* 9(1), February, 107–125.

Drèze, Jacques H., 1976, Some theory of labor management and participation, *Econometrica* 44(6), November, 1125–1139.

1989, *Labour Management, Contracts and Capital Markets: A General Equilibrium Approach*, Oxford, Basil Blackwell.

Drèze, Jacques H. and Kare P. Hagen, 1978, Choice of product quality: Equilibrium and efficiency, *Econometrica* 46(3), May, 493–513.

Edwards, Richard, 1979, *Contested Terrain*, New York, Basic Books.

Elster, Jon, 1983, *Explaining Technical Change*, New York, Cambridge University Press.

Estrin, Saul, 1991, Some reflections on self-management, social choice, and reform in Eastern Europe, *Journal of Comparative Economics* 15(2), June, 349–366.

Estrin, Saul and Derek C. Jones, 1992, The viability of employee-owned firms: Evidence from France, *Industrial and Labor Relations Review* 45(2), January, 323–338.

1998, The determinants of investment in employee-owned firms: Evidence from France, *Economic Analysis* 1(1), February, 17–28.

Estrin, Saul, Derek C. Jones, and Jan Svejnar, 1987, The productivity effects of worker participation: Producer cooperatives in western economies, *Journal of Comparative Economics* 11(1), March, 40–61.

Estrin, Saul and Virginie Pérotin, 1987, Producer cooperatives: The British experience, *International Review of Applied Economics* 1(2), 152–175.

Eswaran, Mukesh and Ashok Kotwal, 1984, The moral hazard of budget-breaking, *RAND Journal of Economics* 15(4), Winter, 578–581.

1989, Why are capitalists the bosses? *Economic Journal* 99(394), March, 162–176.

Fakhfakh, Fathi, Virginie Pérotin, and Monica Gago, 2012, Productivity, capital, and labor in labor-managed and conventional firms: An investigation on French data, *Industrial and Labor Relations Review* 65(4), October, 847–879.

Fehr, Ernst, 1993, The simple analytics of a membership market in a labor-managed economy, ch. 16 in Samuel Bowles, Herbert Gintis, and Bo Gustafsson, eds., *Markets and Democracy: Participation, Accountability and Efficiency*, New York, Cambridge University Press, 260–276.

Fehr, Ernst, Holger Herz, and Tom Wilkening, 2013, The lure of authority: Motivation and incentive effects of power, *American Economic Review* 103(4), June, 1325–1359.

Friedman, Milton, 1953, The methodology of positive economics, in *Essays in Positive Economics*, Chicago, University of Chicago Press.

Furubotn, Eirek G., 1971, Toward a dynamic model of the Yugoslav firm, *Canadian Journal of Economics* 4(2), May, 182–197.

1976, The long-run analysis of the labor-managed firm: An alternative interpretation, *American Economic Review* 66(1), March, 104–124.

Furubotn, Eirek G. and Svetozar Pejovich, 1970, Property rights and the behavior of the firm in a socialist state: The example of Yugoslavia, *Zeitschrift für Nationalökonomie* 30(3–4), September, 431–454.

Gintis, Herbert, 1976, The nature of labor exchange and the theory of capitalist production, *Review of Radical Political Economics* 8(2), July, 36–54.

1989, Financial markets and the political structure of the enterprise, *Journal of Economic Behavior and Organization* 11(3), May, 311–322.

Goldberg, Victor P., 1976, Regulation and administered contracts, *Bell Journal of Economics* 7(2), Autumn, 426–448.

1980, Bridges over contested terrain: Exploring the radical account of the employment relationship, *Journal of Economic Behavior and Organization* 1(3), September, 249–274.

Gordon, Jeffrey N., 1999, Employee stock ownership in economic transitions: The case of United and the airline industry, ch. 10 in Margaret M. Blair and Mark J. Roe, eds., *Employees and Corporate Governance*, Washington, DC, Brookings Institution Press, 317–354.

Graw, Stephen, 1996, *An Outline of the Law of Partnership*, rev. ed., Sydney, The Law Book Company Limited.

Grossman, Sanford and Oliver Hart, 1986, The costs and benefits of ownership: A theory of vertical and lateral integration, *Journal of Political Economy* 94(4), August, 691–719.

Gui, Benedetto, 1985, Limits to external financing: A model and an application to labor-managed firms, in Derek C. Jones and Jan Svejnar, eds., *Advances in the Economic Analysis of Participatory and Labor-Managed Firms: A Research Annual 1*, Greenwich, CT, JAI Press, 107–120.

Hansmann, Henry, 1988, Ownership of the firm, *Journal of Law, Economics, and Organization* 4(2), Fall, 267–305.

1990a, When does worker ownership work? ESOPs, law firms, codetermination, and economic democracy, *Yale Law Journal* 99(8), June, 1749–1816.

1990b, The viability of worker ownership: An economic perspective on the political structure of the firm, ch. 8 in Masahiko Aoki, Bo Gustafsson, and Oliver Williamson, eds., *The Firm as a Nexus of Treaties*, London, Sage Publications, 162–184.

1996, *The Ownership of Enterprise*, Cambridge, MA, Belknap Press of Harvard University Press.

Hart, Oliver, 1977, Takeover bids and stock market equilibria, *Journal of Economic Theory* 16(1), October, 53–83.

1979a, On shareholder unanimity in large stock market economies, *Econometrica* 47(5), September, 1057–1083.

1979b, Monopolistic competition in a large economy with differentiated commodities, *Review of Economic Studies* 46(1), January, 1–30.

Hart, Oliver and John Moore, 1990, Property rights and the nature of the firm, *Journal of Political Economy* 98(6), December, 1119–1158.

1994, A theory of debt based on the inalienability of human capital, *Quarterly Journal of Economics* 109(4), November, 841–879.

Hashimoto, Masanori, 1981, Firm-specific human capital as a shared investment, *American Economic Review* 71(3), June, 475–482.

Hillman, Robert W., 1995, RUPA and former partners: Cutting the Gordian knot with continuing partnership entities, *Law and Contemporary Problems* 58(2), Spring, 7–28.

Holmstrom, Bengt, 1982, Moral hazard in teams, *Bell Journal of Economics* 13(2), Autumn, 324–340.

Holmstrom, Bengt and Paul Milgrom, 1991, Multitask principal-agent analyses: Incentive contracts, asset ownership, and job design, *Journal of Law, Economics, and Organization* 7, special issue, 24–52.

1994, The firm as an incentive system, *American Economic Review* 84(4), September, 972–991.

Hynes, J. Dennis, 1995, Foreword, *Law and Contemporary Problems* 58(2), Spring, 1–5.

Jensen, Michael C. and William Meckling, 1979, Rights and production functions: An application to labor-managed firms and codetermination, *Journal of Business* 52(4), October, 469–506.

Jones, Derek C., 2007, The productive efficiency of Italian producer cooperatives: Evidence from conventional and cooperative firms, in Sonja Novkovic and Vania Sena, eds., *Advances in the Economic Analysis of Participatory and Labor-Managed Firms, Cooperative Firms in Global Markets: Incidence, Viability and Economic Performance*, vol. 9, Amsterdam, Elsevier, 3–28.

Jones, S. R. H., 1982, The organization of work: A historical dimension, *Journal of Economic Behavior and Organization* 3(2–3), June–September, 117–137.

Joshi, Sumit and Stephen C. Smith, 2008, Endogenous formation of coops and cooperative leagues, *Journal of Economic Behavior and Organization* 68(1), October, 217–233.

Jossa, Bruno, 2014, *Producer Cooperatives as a New Mode of Production*, New York, Routledge.

Jossa, Bruno and Gaetano Cuomo, 1997, *The Economic Theory of Socialism and the Labour-Managed Firm: Markets, Socialism, and Labour Management*, Cheltenham, U.K., Edward Elgar Publishing Ltd.

Kihlstrom, Richard E. and Jean-Jacques Laffont, 1979, A general equilibrium entrepreneurial theory of firm formation based on risk aversion, *Journal of Political Economy* 87(4), August, 719–748.

Klein, Benjamin, Robert Crawford, and Armen Alchian, 1978, Vertical integration, appropriable rents, and the competitive contracting process, *Journal of Law and Economics* 21(2), October, 297–326.

Kramer, Gerald H., 1973, On a class of equilibrium conditions for majority rule, *Econometrica* 41(2), March, 285–297.

Kremer, Michael, 1997, Why are worker cooperatives so rare? NBER Working Paper No. 6118, July.

Kruse, Douglas L., Richard B. Freeman, and Joseph R. Blasi, eds., 2010, *Shared Capitalism at Work: Employee Ownership, Profit and Gain Sharing, and Broad-Based Stock Options*, Chicago, University of Chicago Press.

Landers, Renee M., James B. Rebitzer, and Lowell J. Taylor, 1996, Rat race redux: Adverse selection in the determination of work hours in law firms, *American Economic Review* 86(3), June, 329–348.

Langlois, Richard, 1984, Internal organization in a dynamic context: Some theoretical considerations, in M. Jussawalla and H. Ebenfield, eds., *Communication and Information Economics: New Perspectives*, Amsterdam, North-Holland, 23–49.

Leland, Hayne E., 1979, Quacks, lemons, and licensing: A theory of minimum quality standards, *Journal of Political Economy* 87(6), December, 1328–1346.

Levin, Jonathan and Steven Tadelis, 2005, Profit sharing and the role of professional partnerships, *Quarterly Journal of Economics* 120(1), February, 131–171.

MacLeod, W. Bentley, 1984, A theory of cooperative teams, CORE Discussion Paper No. 8441, Université Catholique de Louvain.

MacLeod, W. Bentley and James M. Malcomson, 1989, Implicit contracts, incentive compatibility, and involuntary unemployment, *Econometrica* 57(2), March, 447–480.

1993, Wage premiums and profit maximization in efficiency wage models, *European Economic Review* 37(6), August, 1223–1249.

1998, Motivation and markets, *American Economic Review* 88(3), June, 388–411.

Magill, Michael and Martine Quinzii, 1996, *Theory of Incomplete Markets* (vol. 1), Cambridge, MA, MIT Press.

Makowski, Louis, 1983a, Competition and unanimity revisited, *American Economic Review* 73(3), June, 329–339.

1983b, Competitive stock markets, *Review of Economic Studies* 50(2), April, 305–330.

Makowski, Louis and Lynne Pepall, 1985, Easy proofs of unanimity and optimality without spanning: A pedagogical note, *Journal of Finance* 40(4), September, 1245–1250.

Marglin, Stephen A., 1974, What do bosses do? The origins and functions of hierarchy in capitalist production, *Review of Radical Political Economics* 6(2), Summer, 60–112.

1982, Knowledge and power, ch. 9 in Frank H. Stephen, ed., *Firms, Organization and Labour: Approaches to the Economics of Work Organization*, London, Macmillan, 146–164.

Mas-Colell, Andreu, Michael D. Whinston, and Jerry R. Green, 1995, *Microeconomic Theory*, New York, Oxford University Press.

McKelvey, Richard D., 1979, General conditions for global intransitivities in formal voting models, *Econometrica* 47(5), September, 1085–1125.

Meade, James, 1972, The theory of labour-managed firms and profit-sharing, *Economic Journal* 82(325), supplement, March, 402–428.

Mikami, Kazuhiko, 2003, Market power and the form of enterprise: Capitalist firms, worker-owned firms and consumer cooperatives, *Journal of Economic Behavior and Organization* 52(4), December, 533–552.

2011, *Enterprise Forms and Economic Efficiency: Capitalist, Cooperative and Government Firms*, New York, Routledge.

2013, Raising capital by issuing transferable membership in a worker cooperative, *Annals of Public and Cooperative Economics* 84(3), September, 253–266.

2016, Cooperatives, transferable shares, and a unified business law, *Annals of Public and Cooperative Economics* 87(3), September, 365–390.

Miyazaki, Hajime, 1984, On success and dissolution of the labor-managed firm in the capitalist economy, *Journal of Political Economy*, 92(5), October, 909–931.

Miyazaki, Hajime and Hugh M. Neary, 1983, The Illyrian firm revisited, *Bell Journal of Economics* 14(1), Spring, 259–270.

Nelson, Richard R. and Sidney G. Winter, 1982, *An Evolutionary Theory of Economic Change*, Cambridge, MA, Belknap Press of Harvard University Press.

O'Flaherty, Brendan and Aloysius Siow, 1995, Up-or-out rules in the market for lawyers, *Journal of Labor Economics* 13(4), October, 709–735.

Osborne, Martin and Ariel Rubinstein, 1990, *Bargaining and Markets*, New York, Academic Press.

Ostrom, Elinor, 1990, *Governing the Commons: The Evolution of Institutions for Collective Action*, New York, Cambridge University Press.

Pejovich, Svetozar, 1969, The firm, monetary policy, and property rights in a planned economy, *Western Economic Journal* 7(3), September, 193–200.

Pencavel, John, 2001, *Worker Participation: Lessons from the Worker Co-ops of the Pacific Northwest*, New York, Russell Sage Foundation.

2013a, ed., *The Economics of Worker Cooperatives*, Cheltenham, U.K., Edward Elgar Publishing Ltd.

2013b, Worker cooperatives and democratic governance, ch. 24 in Anna Gandori, ed., *The Handbook of Economic Organization: Integrating Economic and Organization Theory*, Cheltenham, U.K., Edward Elgar Publishing Ltd., 462–480.

2015, The labor supply of self-employed workers: The choice of working hours in worker co-ops, *Journal of Comparative Economics* 43(3), August, 677–689.

Pencavel, John and Ben Craig, 1994, The empirical performance of orthodox models of the firm: Conventional firms and worker cooperatives, *Journal of Political Economy* 102(4), August, 718–744.

Pencavel, John, Luigi Pistaferri, and Fabinao Schivardi, 2006, Wages, employment, and capital in capitalist and worker-owned firms, *Industrial and Labor Relations Review* 60(1), October, 23–44.

Pérotin, Virginie, 2006, Entry, exit, and the business cycle: Are cooperatives different? *Journal of Comparative Economics* 34(2), June, 295–316.

2016, What do we really know about worker co-operatives? Manchester, UK, Co-operatives UK, February, available at www.uk.coop/resources/what-do-we -really-know-about-worker-co-operatives

Perrow, Charles, 1981, Markets, hierarchies and hegemony, in Andrew H. Van de Ven and William F. Joyce, eds., *Perspectives on Organization Design and Behavior*, New York, Wiley, 371–386.

1986, *Complex Organizations: A Critical Essay*, 3rd ed., New York, Random House.

Piketty, Thomas, 2014, *Capital in the Twenty-First Century*, translated by Arthur Goldhammer, Cambridge, MA, Belknap Press of Harvard University Press.

Plott, Charles, 1967, A notion of equilibrium and its possibility under majority rule, *American Economic Review* 57(4), September, 787–806.

Podivinsky, Jan M. and Geoff Stewart, 2007, Why is labour-managed firm entry so rare? An analysis of UK manufacturing data, *Journal of Economic Behavior and Organization* 63(1), May, 177–192.

Podivinsky, Jan M. and Geoff Stewart, 2009, Modeling proportions: Random effects models of UK firm entry, *Singapore Economic Review* 54(3), August, 367–377.

Prime, Terence and Gary Scanlan, 1995, *The Law of Partnership*, London, Butterworth.

Prychitko, David L. and Jaroslav Vanek, eds., 1996, *Producer Cooperatives and Labor-Managed Systems* (2 vols.), Cheltenham, U.K., Edward Elgar Publishing Ltd.

Putterman, Louis, 1981, The organization of work: Comment, *Journal of Economic Behavior and Organization* 2(3), September, 273–279.

1984, On some recent explanations of why capital hires labor, *Economic Inquiry* 22(2), April, 171–187.

1988a, The firm as association versus the firm as commodity: Efficiency, rights, and ownership, *Economics and Philosophy* 4(2), October, 243–266.

1988b, Asset specificity, governance, and the employment relation, in G. Dlugos, W. Dorow, and K. Weiermair, eds., *Management under Differing Labour Market and Employment Systems*, Berlin, Walter de Gruyter.

1993, Ownership and the nature of the firm, *Journal of Comparative Economics* 17(2), June, 243–263.

Putterman, Louis and Gilbert Skillman, 1992, The role of exit costs in the theory of cooperative teams, *Journal of Comparative Economics* 16(4), December, 596–618.

Robinson, Joan, 1967, The Soviet collective farm as a producer cooperative: Comment, *American Economic Review* 57(1), March, 222–223.

Roemer, John, 1988, *Free to Lose: An Introduction to Marxist Economic Philosophy*, Cambridge, MA, Harvard University Press.

Rothschild, Joyce and J. Allen Whitt, 1986, *The Cooperative Workplace*, Cambridge, U.K., Cambridge University Press.

Rothschild, Michael and Joseph E. Stiglitz, 1976, Equilibrium in competitive insurance markets: An essay on the economics of imperfect information, *Quarterly Journal of Economics* 90(4), November, 630–649.

Rubinstein, Ariel, 1982, Perfect equilibrium in a bargaining model, *Econometrica* 50(1), January, 97–109.

Russell, Raymond, 1985a, *Sharing Ownership in the Workplace*, Albany, NY, State University of New York Press.

    1985b, Employee ownership and internal governance: An "organizational failures" analysis of three populations of employee-owned firms, *Journal of Economic Behavior and Organization* 6(3), September, 217–241.

Ryoo, Jaewoo, 1996, Lemons models of professional labor markets reconsidered, *Eastern Economic Journal* 22(3), Summer, 355–363.

Sadanand, Asha and John Williamson, 1991, Equilibrium in a stock market economy with shareholder voting, *International Economic Review* 32(1), February, 1–35.

Schlicht, Ekkehart and Carl Christian von Weizsäcker, 1977, Risk financing in labour managed economies: The commitment problem, *Zeitschrift für die gesamte Staatswissenschaft* 133, special issue, 53–66.

Sertel, Murat R., 1982, A rehabilitation of the labor-managed firm, ch. 2 in *Workers and Incentives*, Amsterdam, North-Holland.

    1987, Workers' enterprises are not perverse, *European Economic Review* 31(8), December, 1619–1625.

    1991, Workers' enterprises in imperfect competition, *Journal of Comparative Economics* 15(4), December, 698–710.

Shapiro, Carl and Joseph E. Stiglitz, 1984, Equilibrium unemployment as a worker discipline device, *American Economic Review* 74(4), September, 433–444.

Sherstyuk, Katerina, 1998, Efficiency in partnership structures, *Journal of Economic Behavior and Organization* 36(3), August, 331–346.

Simon, Herbert, 1976, *Administrative Behavior*, 3rd ed., New York, Free Press.

Skillman, Gilbert L. and Harl E. Ryder, 1993, Wage bargaining and the choice of production technique in capitalist firms, ch. 13 in Samuel Bowles, Herbert Gintis, and Bo Gustafsson, eds., *Markets and Democracy: Participation, Accountability and Efficiency*, New York, Cambridge University Press, 217–227.

Smith, Adam, [1776] 1994, *The Wealth of Nations*, New York, Random House.

Spence, A. Michael, 1973, Job market signaling, *Quarterly Journal of Economics* 87(3), August, 355–374.

Spurr, Stephen J., 1987, How the market solves an assignment problem: The matching of lawyers with legal claims, *Journal of Labor Economics* 5(4), Part 1, October, 502–532.

Steinherr, Alfred and J.-F. Thisse, 1979, Are labor managers really perverse? *Economics Letters* 2(2), 137–142.

Stephen, Frank H., 1984, *The Economic Analysis of Producers' Cooperatives*, London, Macmillan Press.

Stiglitz, Joseph E. and Andrew Weiss, 1981, Credit rationing in markets with imperfect information, *American Economic Review* 71(3), June, 393–410.

Teece, David J., 1980, Economies of scope and the scope of the enterprise, *Journal of Economic Behavior and Organization* 1(3), September, 223–247.

Teece, David J., 1982, Towards an economic theory of the multiproduct firm, *Journal of Economic Behavior and Organization* 3(1), March, 39–63.

Tortia, Ermanno C., 2007, Self-financing in labor-managed firms (LMFs): Individual capital accounts and bonds, in Sonja Novkovic and Vania Sena, eds., *Advances in the Economic Analysis of Participatory and Labor-Managed Firms*, vol. 10, Amsterdam, Elsevier, JAI Press, 233–261.

VanDuzer, J. Anthony, 1997, *The Law of Partnerships and Corporations*, Concord, Ontario, Canada, Irwin Law.

Vanek, Jaroslav, 1970, *The General Theory of Labor-Managed Market Economies*, Ithaca, NY, Cornell University Press.

1971a, Some fundamental considerations on financing and the form of ownership under labor management, Cornell Department of Economics Working Paper No. 16, June, reprinted as ch. 8 in 1977, *The Labor-Managed Economy: Essays by Jaroslav Vanek*, Ithaca, NY, Cornell University Press, 171–185.

1971b, The basic theory of financing of participatory firms, Cornell Department of Economics Working Paper No. 27, July, reprinted as ch. 9 in 1977, *The Labor-Managed Economy: Essays by Jaroslav Vanek*, Ithaca, NY, Cornell University Press, 186–198.

Varian, Hal R., 1993, *Microeconomic Analysis*, 3rd ed., New York, Norton.

Ward, Benjamin, 1958, The firm in Illyria: Market syndicalism, *American Economic Review* 48(4), September, 566–589.

Williamson, Oliver E., 1975, *Markets and Hierarchies*, New York, Free Press.

1976, Franchise bidding for natural monopolies—in general and with respect to CATV, *Bell Journal of Economics* 7(1), Spring, 73–104.

1979, Transaction-cost economics: The governance of contractual relations, *Journal of Law and Economics* 22(2), October, 233–261.

1980, The organization of work, *Journal of Economic Behavior and Organization* 1(1), March, 5–38.

1981a, The modern corporation: Origins, evolution, attributes, *Journal of Economic Literature* 19(4), December, 1537–1568.

1981b, The organization of work: Reply, *Journal of Economic Behavior and Organization* 2(3), September, 281–283.

1985, *The Economic Institutions of Capitalism*, New York, Free Press.

1987, Transaction cost economics: The comparative contracting perspective, *Journal of Economic Behavior and Organization* 8(4), December, 617–625.

1988, Corporate finance and corporate governance, *Journal of Finance* 43(3), July, 567–591.

Williamson, Oliver E. and William G. Ouchi, 1981, The markets and hierarchies program of research: Origins, implications, prospects, in Andrew H. Van de Ven and William F. Joyce, eds., *Perspectives on Organization Design and Behavior*, New York, Wiley Interscience.

Willman, Paul, 1982, Opportunism in labour contracting: An application of the organisational failures framework, *Journal of Economic Behavior and Organization* 2(1), March, 83–98.

Wollack, Richard and Brent R. Donaldson, 1992, *Limited Partnerships: How to Profit in the Secondary Market*, Chicago, Dearborn Financial Publishing Inc.

Index

401

total factor productivity, 95, 96
total surplus, 40, 134, 148, 179, 181, 185, 247, 248, 249, 250, 251, 252–256, 257, 263, 264, 270, 304, 375
tradeable membership rights, 211
transaction
  bilateral transactions, 377
  control transactions, 8, 355, 358, 367
  discrete transactions, 236
  insider transactions, 30–33, 36
  outsider transactions, 30–33, 36
transaction cost economics (TCE)
  asset ownership, 272
  authority, use and abuse, 237–239
  characteristics of, 236, 241
  competition, 243
  conceptual framework, 234–237
  efficiency and causality, 242–246
  governance structures, 235–237, 243–244
  intentionality, 242–243
  introduction to, 25, 233–234
  opportunism, 234, 238, 239–240
  transactions, 235
  work organization, 239–242
transaction costs, 237, 243, 246
two-period stock market model, 195, 196–201
two-person partnership, 209

U.K. industries, 86, 88, 89, 103–104, 110
unanimity, 10, 12, 44, 45, 57, 65, 66–67, 71, 193–194, 209
unanimity theorems, 194
unattached workers, 178, 181, 188, 336
underinvestment, 109–110, 133, 134, 148–152, 378
unemployment rates, 104
unification, of theory, 297, 371
Uniform Partnership Act (UPA), 175
uninformed private agents, 374
Uruguay, 86, 88, 89–90, 91–92, 94, 98, 104, 105–106, 108, 213, 369–370
U.S. plywood cooperatives
  capital/labor ratios, 109
  degeneration, 108
  firm formation, 166–167
  membership markets, 106
  overview of, 85, 90, 94, 98
  policy directions, 377
  risk aversion, 123
utility functions of workers, 273

value maximization, 54, 57–59, 72, 73, 209
verification, 264, 272
viability
  economic viability, 388
  of KMFs, 205, 249, 300, 306, 309, 315–317
  of LMFs, 115, 128, 147, 205, 206, 208, 249, 300, 306, 311, 312, 315–317
  of organizational forms, 259
voluntary quits, 99
voting power, 56, 68
voting rights, 30–31, 68, 72

wage
  from asset owners, 274
  distribution of, 113–114
  growth in, 105
  inequality of, 99
  labor excess and, 282
  structure of, 97–101
  variations, 90, 92
wage bargaining, 254–257
wage flexibility, 105, 363
wage gaps, 97
Walrasian economy, 37, 38, 41, 46–47, 64, 65, 75, 77
Walrasian firm, 25–26, 35, 51, 57, 59, 61–62
Walrasian general equilibrium theory
  comparisons to, 73–75
  control groups and, 25–26
  institutional setting of, 23–25
  labor-managed firm, 46–47
  overview of, 11, 21–22
  wages and labor excess, 282
Walrasian model, 21–22, 26, 68, 76
Ward-Domar-Vanek (WDV) firm
  comparative statics, 134–142
  dividend maximization, 93
  ex post capital shares, 48–49
  introduction to, 35–38, 51–53, 133
  maximization of income per worker, 93
  profit maximizing and, 50, 51, 94
  Sertel-Dow (SD) firm *vs.*, 38–41
  summary of, 50, 61–62, 79–80
wealth constraints, 119–120, 122, 123, 128, 154, 283
wealth effect, 194, 202–203, 209
The Wealth of Nations (Smith), 175
welfare analysis, 183–186
welfare maximization, 216–218, 217f, 219f, 221–224
Williamson, Oliver, 233, 237, 239–242, 244